CHARACTERS

Date Technical High School

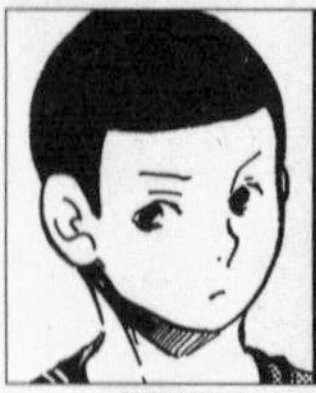
YUTAKA OBARA
2ND YEAR
WING SPIKER

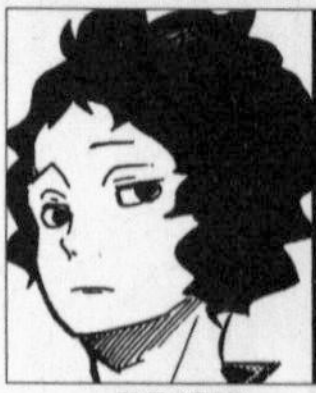
TARO ONAGAWA
2ND YEAR
WING SPIKER

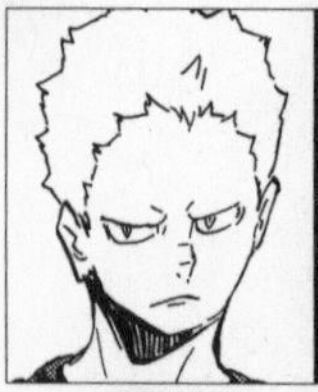
TAKANOBU AONE
2ND YEAR
MIDDLE BLOCKER

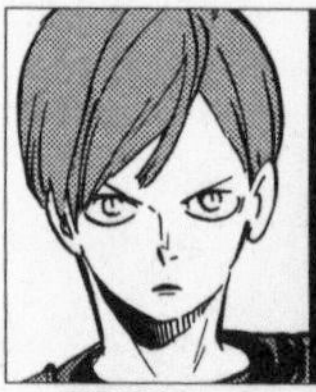
KENJI FUTAKUCHI
2ND YEAR (CAPTAIN)
WING SPIKER

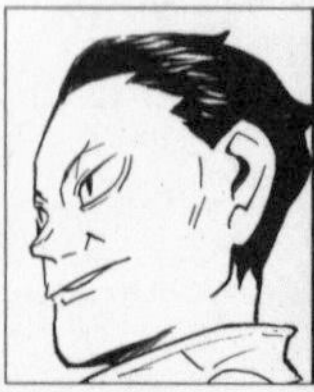
TAKURO OIWAKE
HEAD COACH

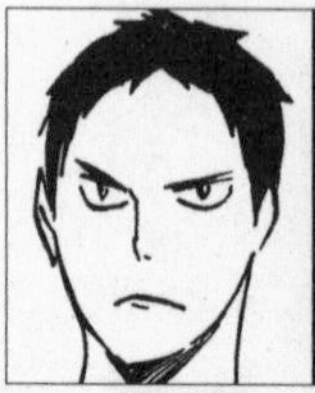
JINGO FUKIAGE
1ST YEAR
MIDDLE BLOCKER

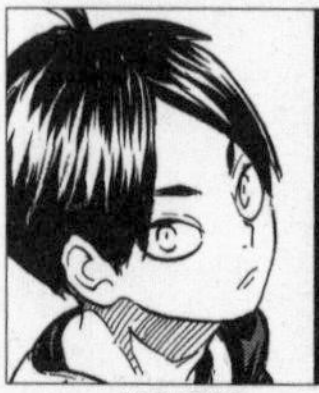
KOSUKE SAKUNAMI
1ST YEAR
LIBERO

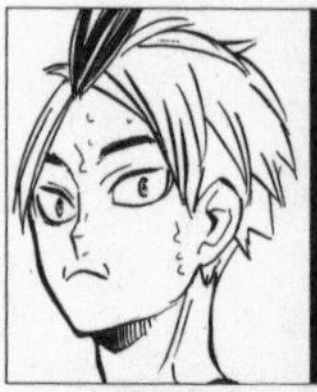
KANJI KOGANEGAWA
1ST YEAR
SETTER

Fukurodani Academy

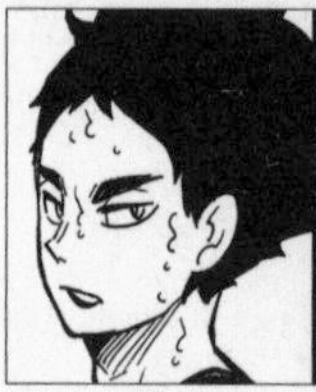
KEIJI AKAASHI
2ND YEAR
SETTER

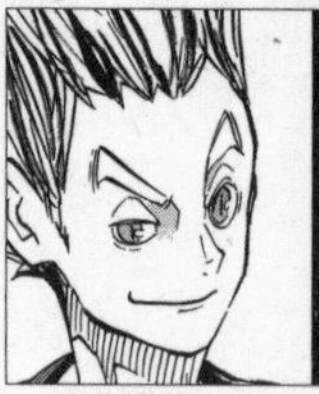
KOTARO BOKUTO
3RD YEAR (CAPTAIN)
WING SPIKER

Nekoma High School

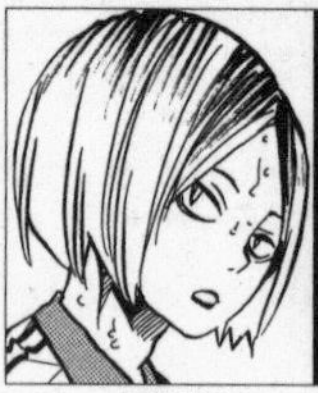
KENMA KOZUME
2ND YEAR
SETTER

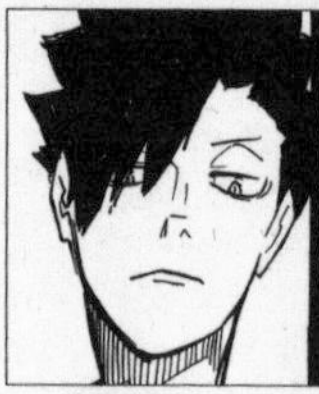
TETSURO KUROO
3RD YEAR (CAPTAIN)
MIDDLE BLOCKER

Ever since he saw the legendary player known as "the Little Giant" compete at the national volleyball finals, Shoyo Hinata has been aiming to be the best volleyball player ever! He decides to join the volleyball club at his middle school and gets to play in an official tournament during his third year. His team is crushed by a team led by volleyball prodigy Tobio Kageyama, also known as "the King of the Court." Swearing revenge on Kageyama, Hinata graduates middle school and enters Karasuno High School, the school where the Little Giant played. However, upon joining the club, he finds out that Kageyama is there too! The two of them bicker constantly, but they bring out the best in each other's talents and become a powerful combo. After a long and bitterly fought game, Karasuno finally defeats Shiratorizawa and wins the Miyagi Prefecture Qualifiers! With the Spring Tournament only a month away, Kageyama and Hinata return from their respective training camps ready to show off what they've learned in a practice game against Date Tech! But the first set goes so poorly that Kageyama loses his cool! Realizing that his old "kingly" ways are coming back, Kageyama apologizes, but the team tells him that they accept his attitude—and a new King of the Court is born!

HAIKYU!!

26 BATTLE LINES

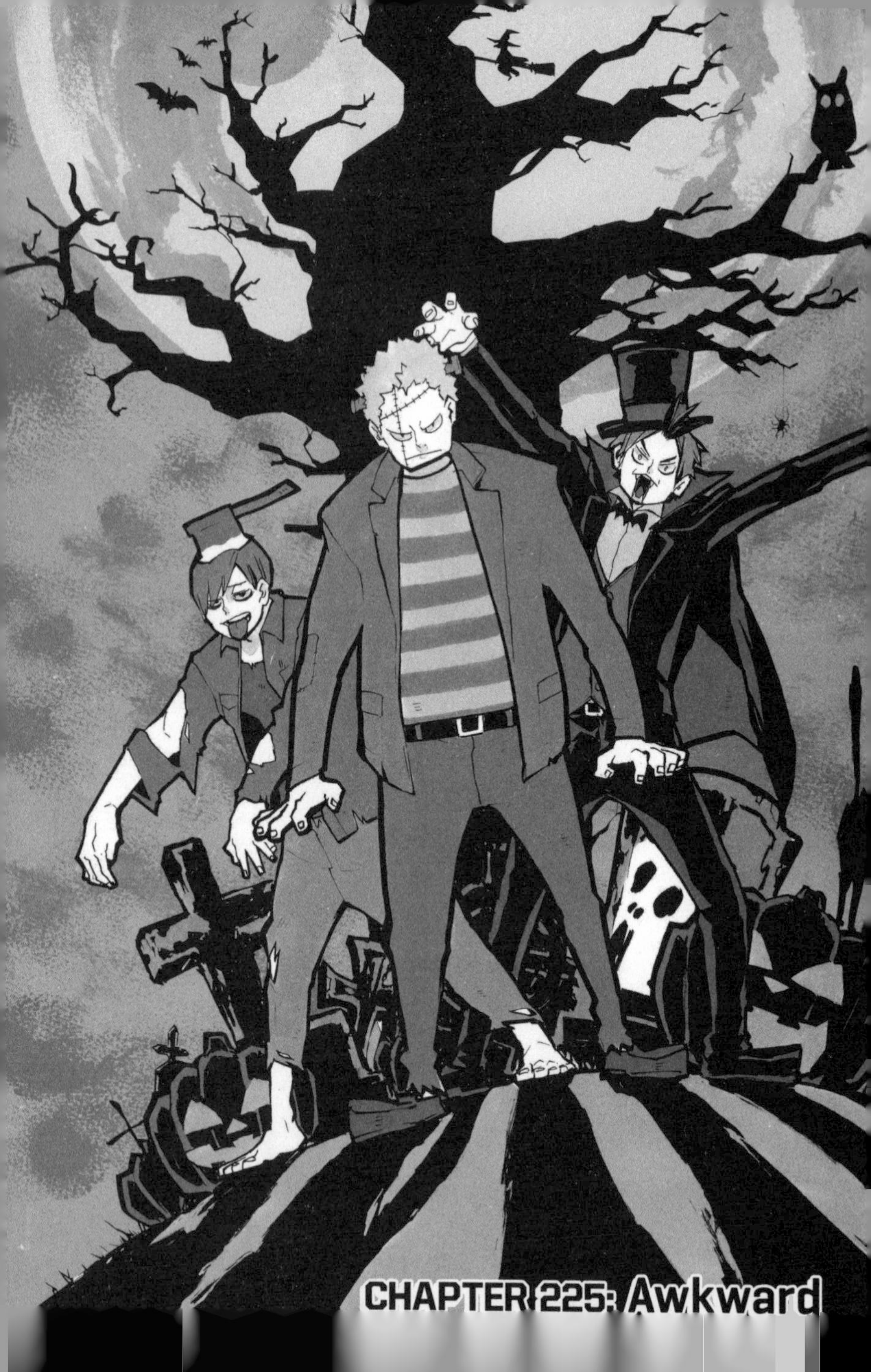

CHAPTER 225: Awkward

HAIKYU!!

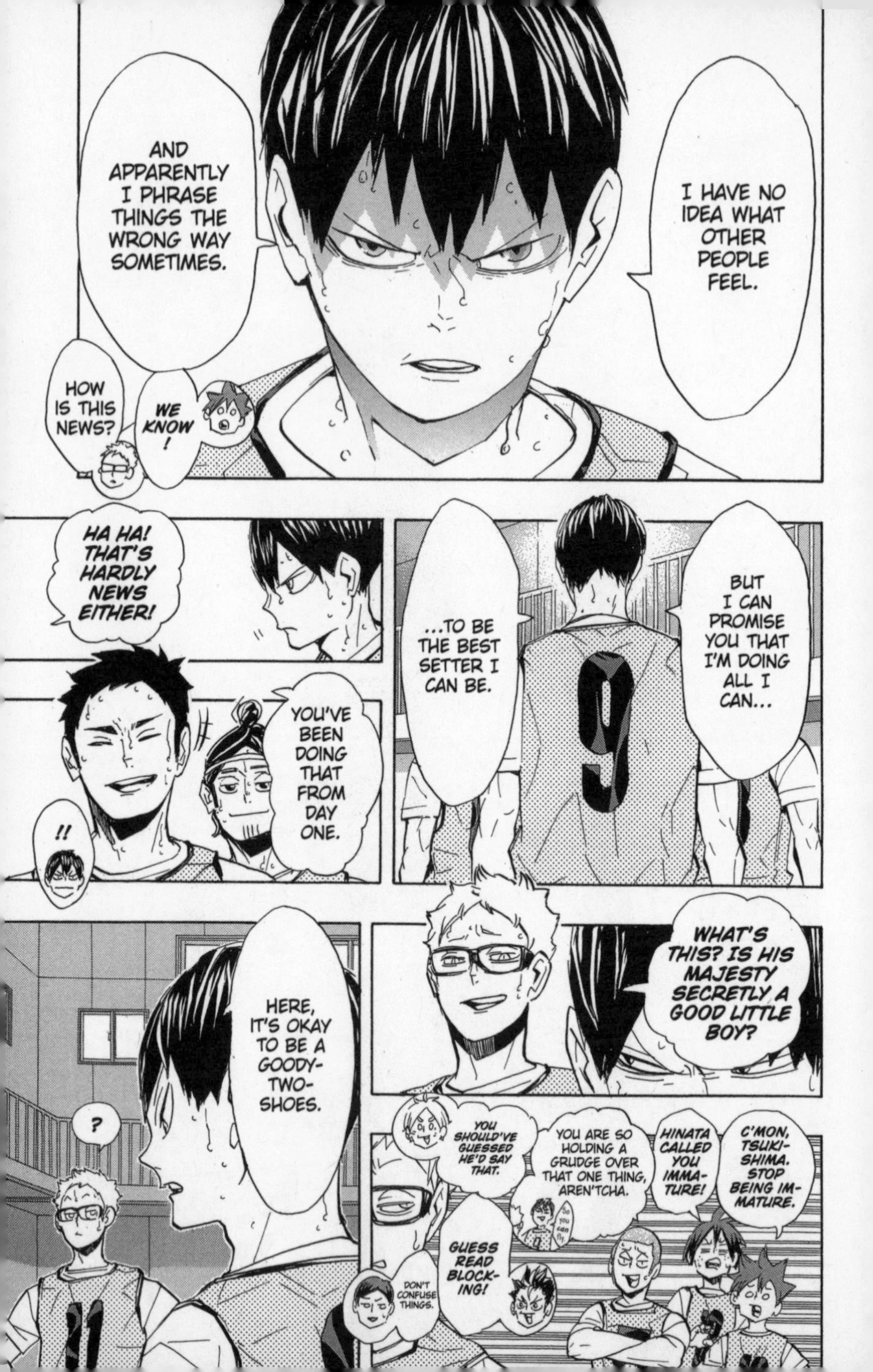

I HAVE NO IDEA WHAT OTHER PEOPLE FEEL.
AND APPARENTLY I PHRASE THINGS THE WRONG WAY SOMETIMES.
WE KNOW!
HOW IS THIS NEWS?
BUT I CAN PROMISE YOU THAT I'M DOING ALL I CAN...
...TO BE THE BEST SETTER I CAN BE.
HA HA! THAT'S HARDLY NEWS EITHER!
YOU'VE BEEN DOING THAT FROM DAY ONE.
!!
WHAT'S THIS? IS HIS MAJESTY SECRETLY A GOOD LITTLE BOY?
C'MON, TSUKISHIMA. STOP BEING IMMATURE.
HINATA CALLED YOU IMMATURE!
YOU ARE SO HOLDING A GRUDGE OVER THAT ONE THING, AREN'TCHA.
YOU SHOULD'VE GUESSED HE'D SAY THAT.
GUESS READ BLOCKING!
DON'T CONFUSE THINGS.
HERE, IT'S OKAY TO BE A GOODY-TWO-SHOES.
?

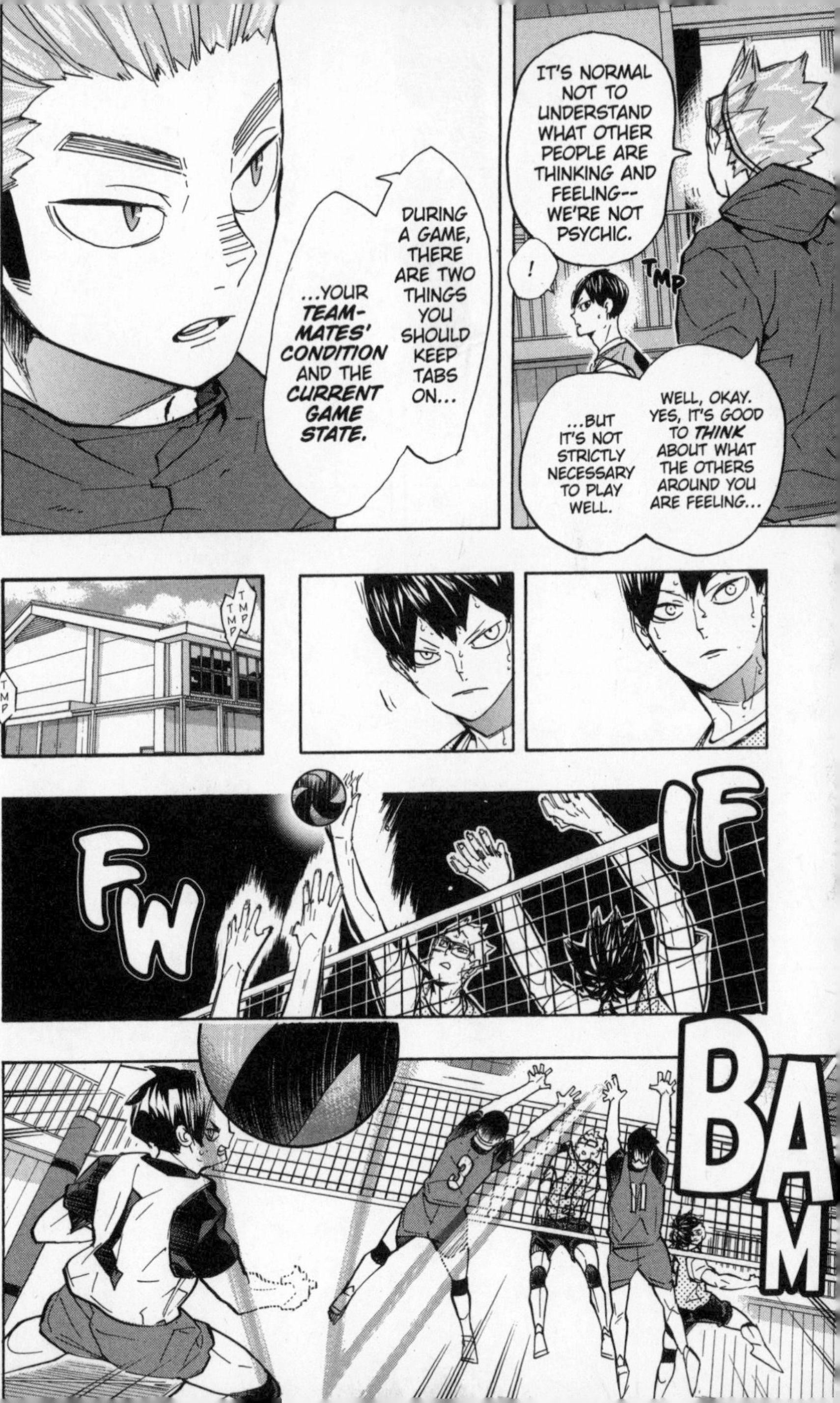
IT'S NORMAL NOT TO UNDERSTAND WHAT OTHER PEOPLE ARE THINKING AND FEELING-- WE'RE NOT PSYCHIC.
!
TMP
WELL, OKAY. YES, IT'S GOOD TO *THINK* ABOUT WHAT THE OTHERS AROUND YOU ARE FEELING...
...BUT IT'S NOT STRICTLY NECESSARY TO PLAY WELL.
DURING A GAME, THERE ARE TWO THINGS YOU SHOULD KEEP TABS ON...
...YOUR *TEAMMATES' CONDITION* AND THE *CURRENT GAME STATE.*
TMP TMP
TMP
FWIF
BAM

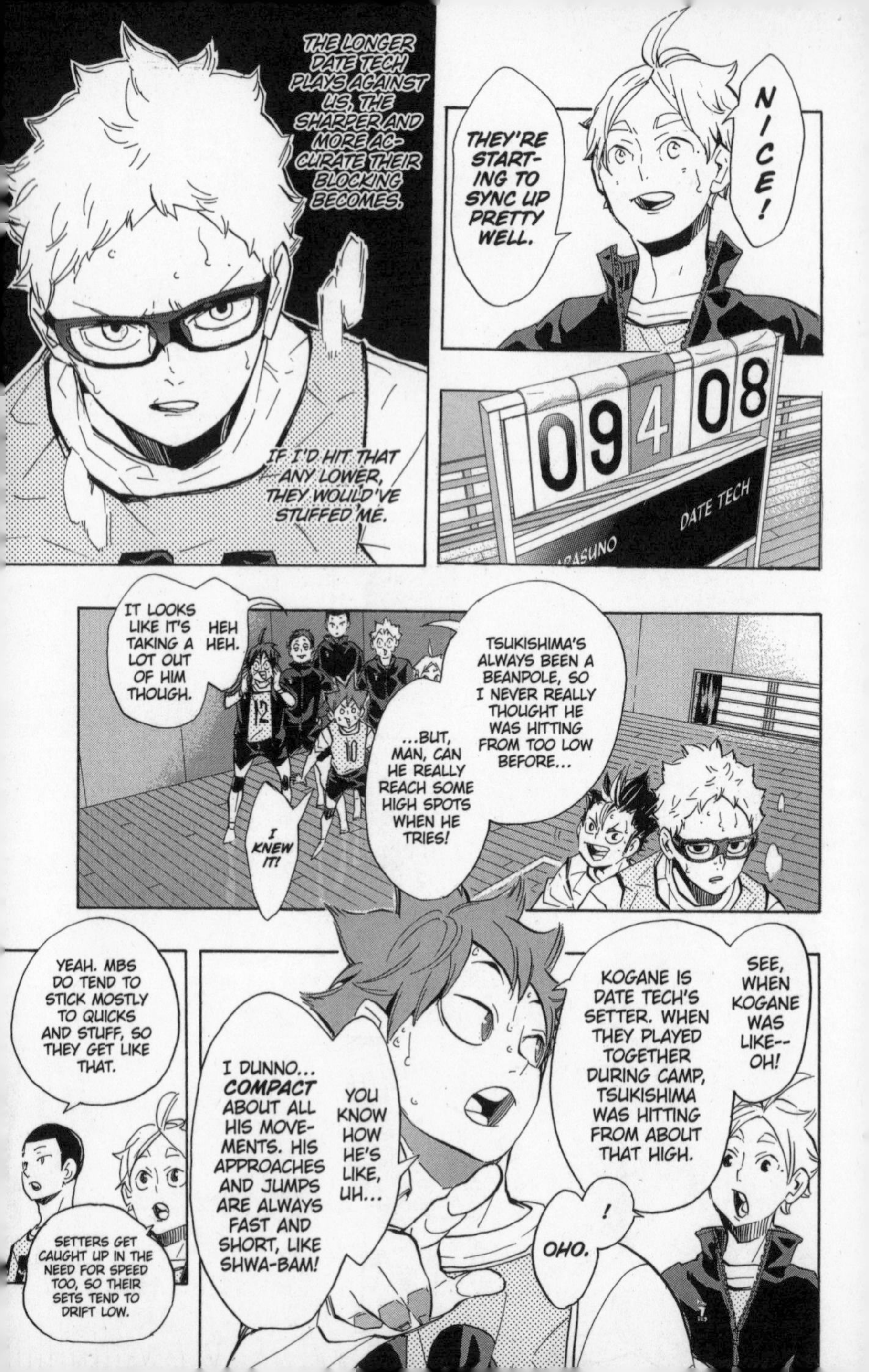

NICE!
THEY'RE STARTING TO SYNC UP PRETTY WELL.
09 4 08
DATE TECH
THE LONGER DATE TECH PLAYS AGAINST US, THE SHARPER AND MORE ACCURATE THEIR BLOCKING BECOMES.
IF I'D HIT THAT ANY LOWER, THEY WOULD'VE STUFFED ME.
TSUKISHIMA'S ALWAYS BEEN A BEANPOLE, SO I NEVER REALLY THOUGHT HE WAS HITTING FROM TOO LOW BEFORE...
...BUT, MAN, CAN HE REALLY REACH SOME HIGH SPOTS WHEN HE TRIES!
HEH HEH.
IT LOOKS LIKE IT'S TAKING A LOT OUT OF HIM THOUGH.
I KNEW IT!
SEE, WHEN KOGANE WAS LIKE-- OH!
KOGANE IS DATE TECH'S SETTER. WHEN THEY PLAYED TOGETHER DURING CAMP, TSUKISHIMA WAS HITTING FROM ABOUT THAT HIGH.
!
OHO.
YOU KNOW HOW HE'S LIKE, UH...
I DUNNO... **COMPACT** ABOUT ALL HIS MOVEMENTS. HIS APPROACHES AND JUMPS ARE ALWAYS FAST AND SHORT, LIKE SHWA-BAM!
YEAH. MBS DO TEND TO STICK MOSTLY TO QUICKS AND STUFF, SO THEY GET LIKE THAT.
SETTERS GET CAUGHT UP IN THE NEED FOR SPEED TOO, SO THEIR SETS TEND TO DRIFT LOW.

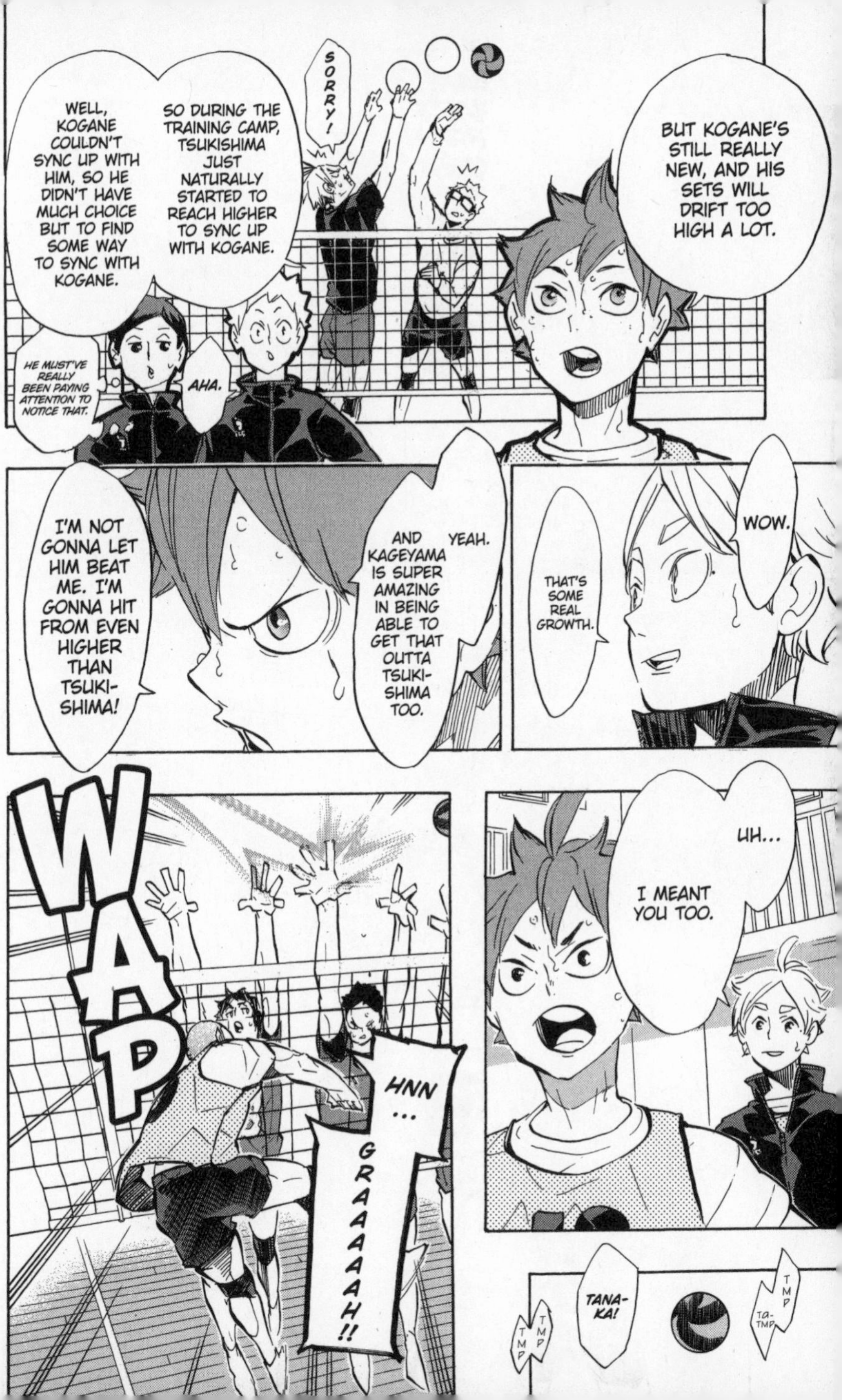
BUT KOGANE'S STILL REALLY NEW, AND HIS SETS WILL DRIFT TOO HIGH A LOT.
SORRY!
SO DURING THE TRAINING CAMP, TSUKISHIMA JUST NATURALLY STARTED TO REACH HIGHER TO SYNC UP WITH KOGANE.
WELL, KOGANE COULDN'T SYNC UP WITH HIM, SO HE DIDN'T HAVE MUCH CHOICE BUT TO FIND SOME WAY TO SYNC WITH KOGANE.
AHA.
HE MUST'VE REALLY BEEN PAYING ATTENTION TO NOTICE THAT.
WOW.
THAT'S SOME REAL GROWTH.
YEAH.
AND KAGEYAMA IS SUPER AMAZING IN BEING ABLE TO GET THAT OUTTA TSUKISHIMA TOO.
I'M NOT GONNA LET HIM BEAT ME. I'M GONNA HIT FROM EVEN HIGHER THAN TSUKISHIMA!
UH...
I MEANT YOU TOO.
TMP TA-TMP
TANAKA!
TMP TMP TMP
WAP
HNN...
GRAAAAAAH!!

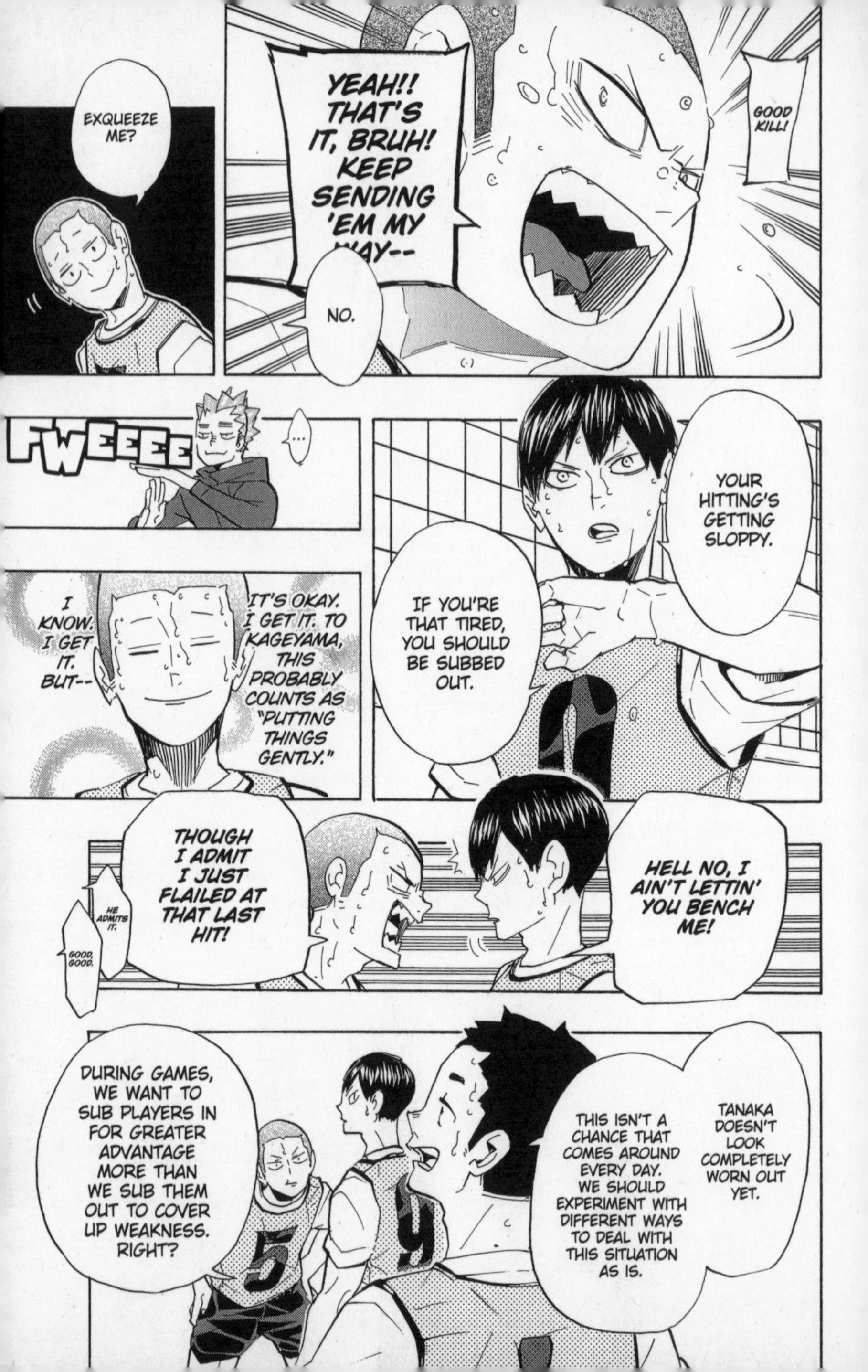
GOOD KILL!
YEAH!! THAT'S IT, BRUH! KEEP SENDING 'EM MY WAY--
NO.
EXQUEEZE ME?
YOUR HITTING'S GETTING SLOPPY.
IF YOU'RE THAT TIRED, YOU SHOULD BE SUBBED OUT.
...
FWEEEE
IT'S OKAY. I GET IT. TO KAGEYAMA, THIS PROBABLY COUNTS AS "PUTTING THINGS GENTLY."
I KNOW. I GET IT. BUT--
HELL NO, I AIN'T LETTIN' YOU BENCH ME!
THOUGH I ADMIT I JUST FLAILED AT THAT LAST HIT!
HE ADMITS IT.
GOOD, GOOD.
TANAKA DOESN'T LOOK COMPLETELY WORN OUT YET.
THIS ISN'T A CHANCE THAT COMES AROUND EVERY DAY. WE SHOULD EXPERIMENT WITH DIFFERENT WAYS TO DEAL WITH THIS SITUATION AS IS.
DURING GAMES, WE WANT TO SUB PLAYERS IN FOR GREATER ADVANTAGE MORE THAN WE SUB THEM OUT TO COVER UP WEAKNESS. RIGHT?

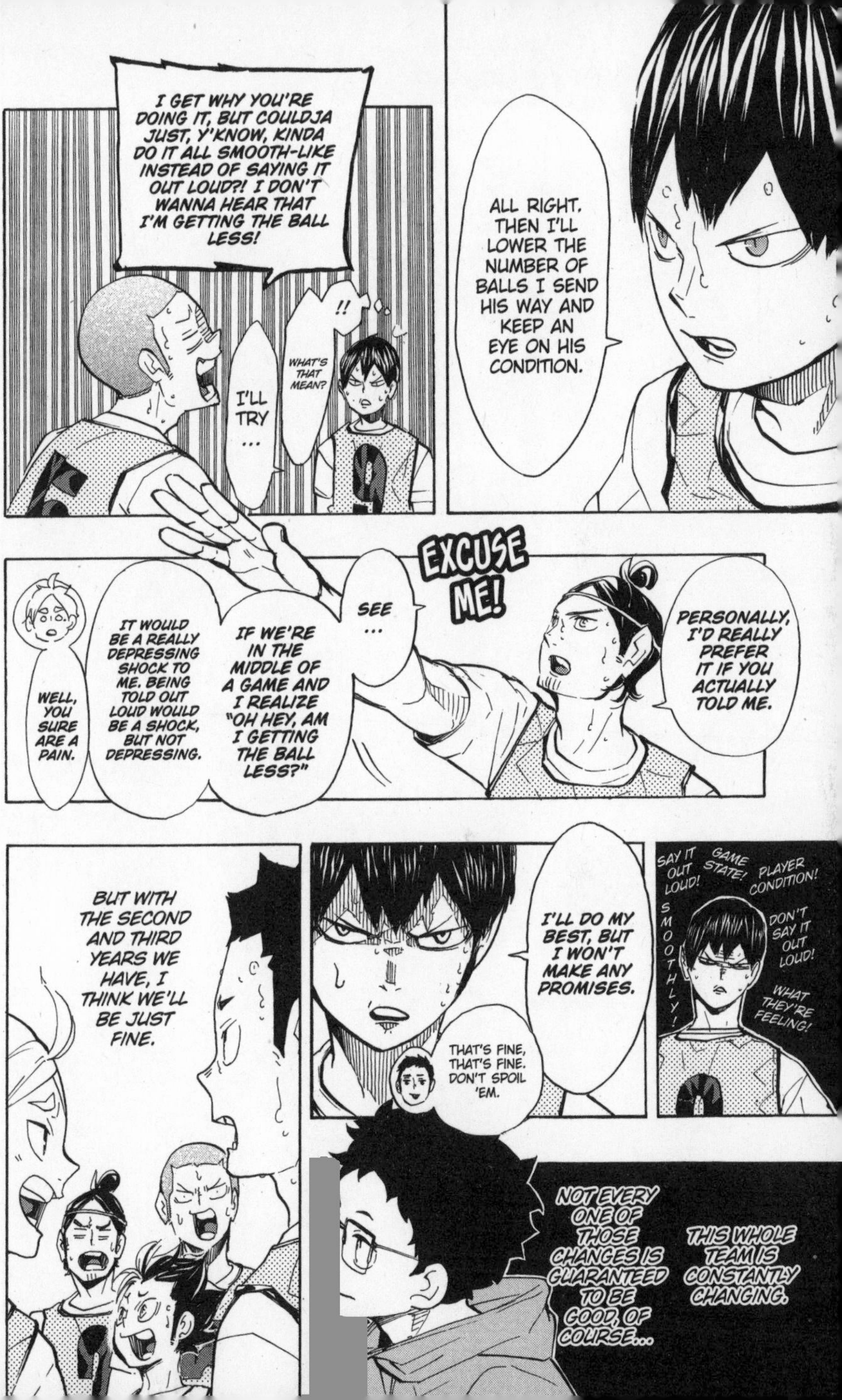
ALL RIGHT. THEN I'LL LOWER THE NUMBER OF BALLS I SEND HIS WAY AND KEEP AN EYE ON HIS CONDITION.
I GET WHY YOU'RE DOING IT, BUT COULDJA JUST, Y'KNOW, KINDA DO IT ALL SMOOTH-LIKE INSTEAD OF SAYING IT OUT LOUD?! I DON'T WANNA HEAR THAT I'M GETTING THE BALL LESS!
!!
WHAT'S THAT MEAN?
I'LL TRY ...
EXCUSE ME!
PERSONALLY, I'D REALLY PREFER IT IF YOU ACTUALLY TOLD ME.
SEE ...
IF WE'RE IN THE MIDDLE OF A GAME AND I REALIZE "OH HEY, AM I GETTING THE BALL LESS?"
IT WOULD BE A REALLY DEPRESSING SHOCK TO ME. BEING TOLD OUT LOUD WOULD BE A SHOCK, BUT NOT DEPRESSING.
WELL, YOU SURE ARE A PAIN.
SAY IT OUT LOUD!
GAME STATE!
PLAYER CONDITION!
SMOOTHLY!
DON'T SAY IT OUT LOUD!
WHAT THEY'RE FEELING!
I'LL DO MY BEST, BUT I WON'T MAKE ANY PROMISES.
THAT'S FINE, THAT'S FINE. DON'T SPOIL 'EM.
THIS WHOLE TEAM IS CONSTANTLY CHANGING.
NOT EVERY ONE OF THOSE CHANGES IS GUARANTEED TO BE GOOD, OF COURSE...
BUT WITH THE SECOND AND THIRD YEARS WE HAVE, I THINK WE'LL BE JUST FINE.

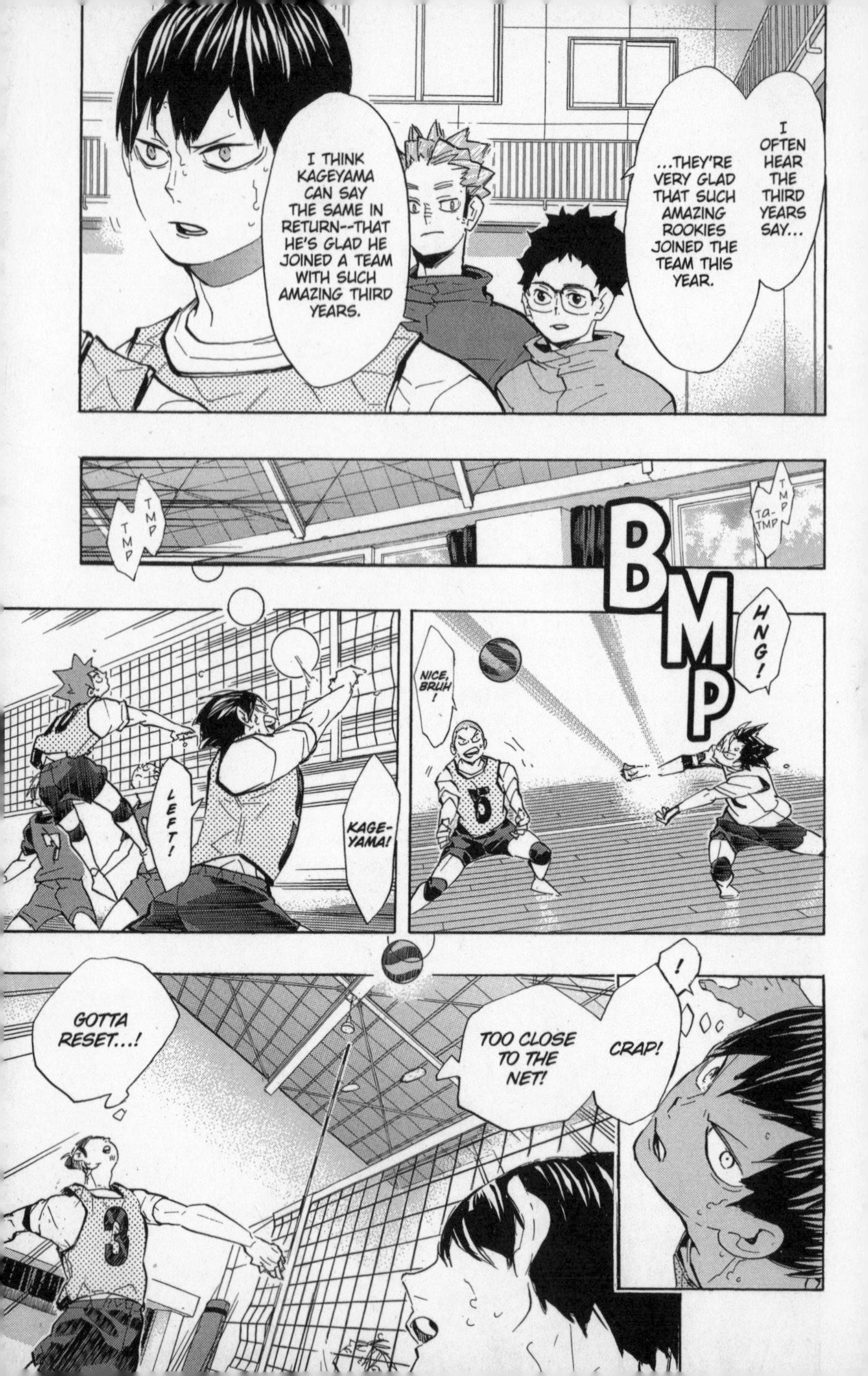
I OFTEN HEAR THE THIRD YEARS SAY...
...THEY'RE VERY GLAD THAT SUCH AMAZING ROOKIES JOINED THE TEAM THIS YEAR.
I THINK KAGEYAMA CAN SAY THE SAME IN RETURN--THAT HE'S GLAD HE JOINED A TEAM WITH SUCH AMAZING THIRD YEARS.
TMP TA-TMP
BMP
TMP TMP
HNG!
NICE, BRUH!
KAGE-YAMA!
LEFT!
!
CRAP!
TOO CLOSE TO THE NET!
GOTTA RESET...!

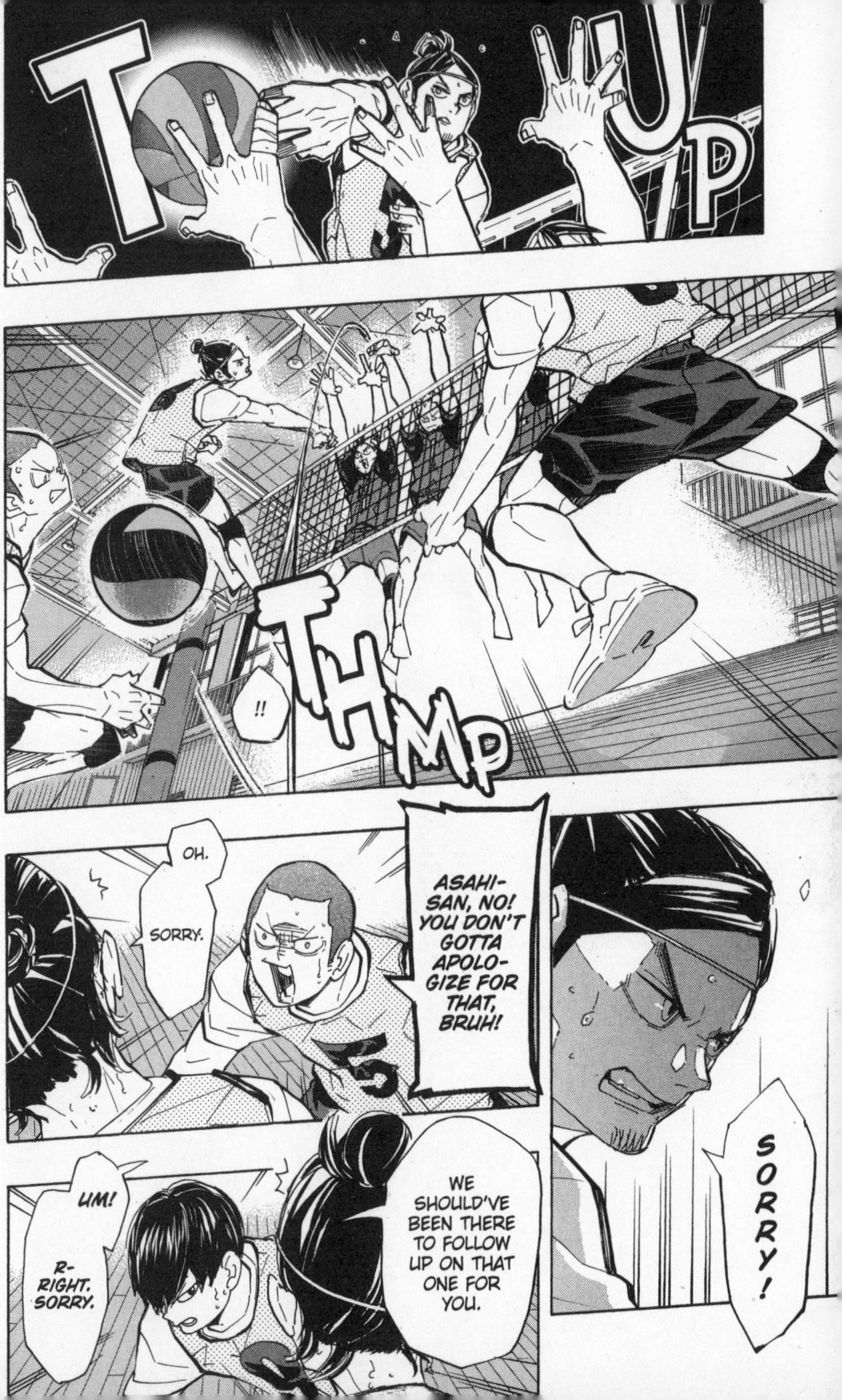
TUP
!!
THMP
SORRY!
ASAHI-SAN, NO! YOU DON'T GOTTA APOLOGIZE FOR THAT, BRUH!
OH.
SORRY.
WE SHOULD'VE BEEN THERE TO FOLLOW UP ON THAT ONE FOR YOU.
UM!
R-RIGHT. SORRY.

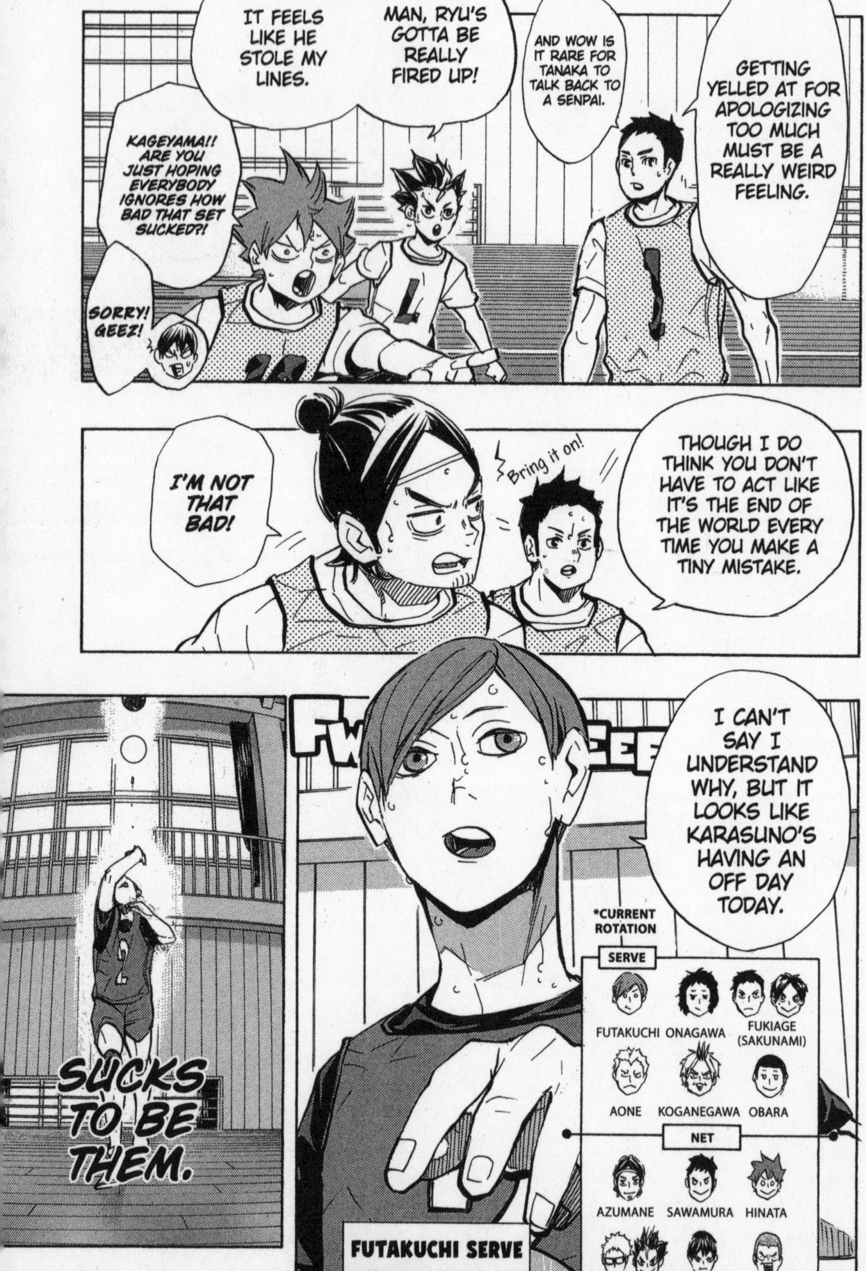
GETTING YELLED AT FOR APOLOGIZING TOO MUCH MUST BE A REALLY WEIRD FEELING.
AND WOW IS IT RARE FOR TANAKA TO TALK BACK TO A SENPAI.
MAN, RYU'S GOTTA BE REALLY FIRED UP!
IT FEELS LIKE HE STOLE MY LINES.
KAGEYAMA!! ARE YOU JUST HOPING EVERYBODY IGNORES HOW BAD THAT SET SUCKED?!
SORRY! GEEZ!
THOUGH I DO THINK YOU DON'T HAVE TO ACT LIKE IT'S THE END OF THE WORLD EVERY TIME YOU MAKE A TINY MISTAKE.
Bring it on!
I'M NOT THAT BAD!
I CAN'T SAY I UNDERSTAND WHY, BUT IT LOOKS LIKE KARASUNO'S HAVING AN OFF DAY TODAY.
*CURRENT ROTATION
SERVE
FUTAKUCHI
ONAGAWA
FUKIAGE (SAKUNAMI)
AONE
KOGANEGAWA
OBARA
NET
AZUMANE
SAWAMURA
HINATA
TSUKKI (NOYA)
KAGEYAMA
TANAKA
FUTAKUCHI SERVE
SUCKS TO BE THEM.

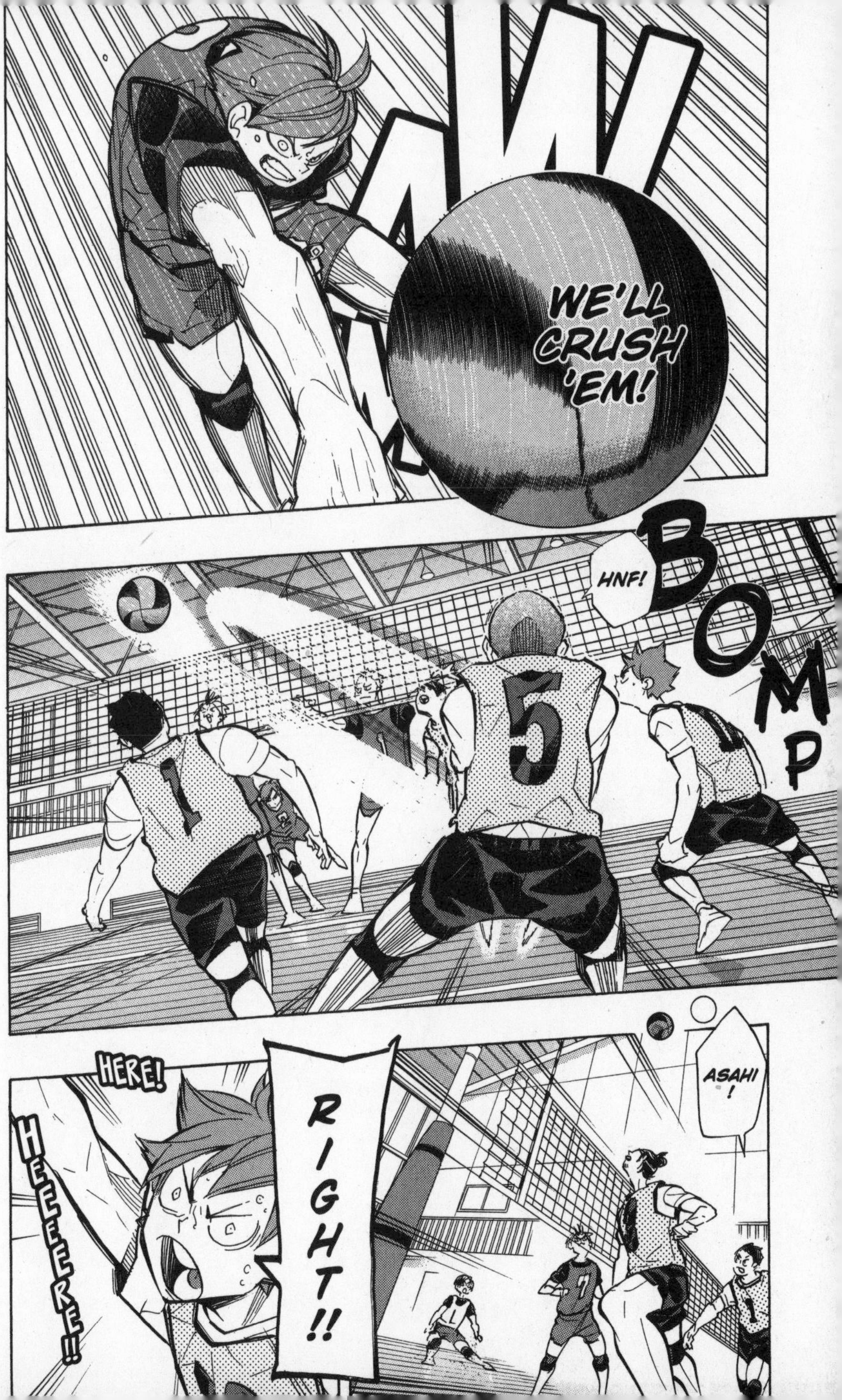

WE'LL CRUSH 'EM!
BOMP
HNF!
ASAHI!
RIGHT!!
HERE!
HEEEERE!!

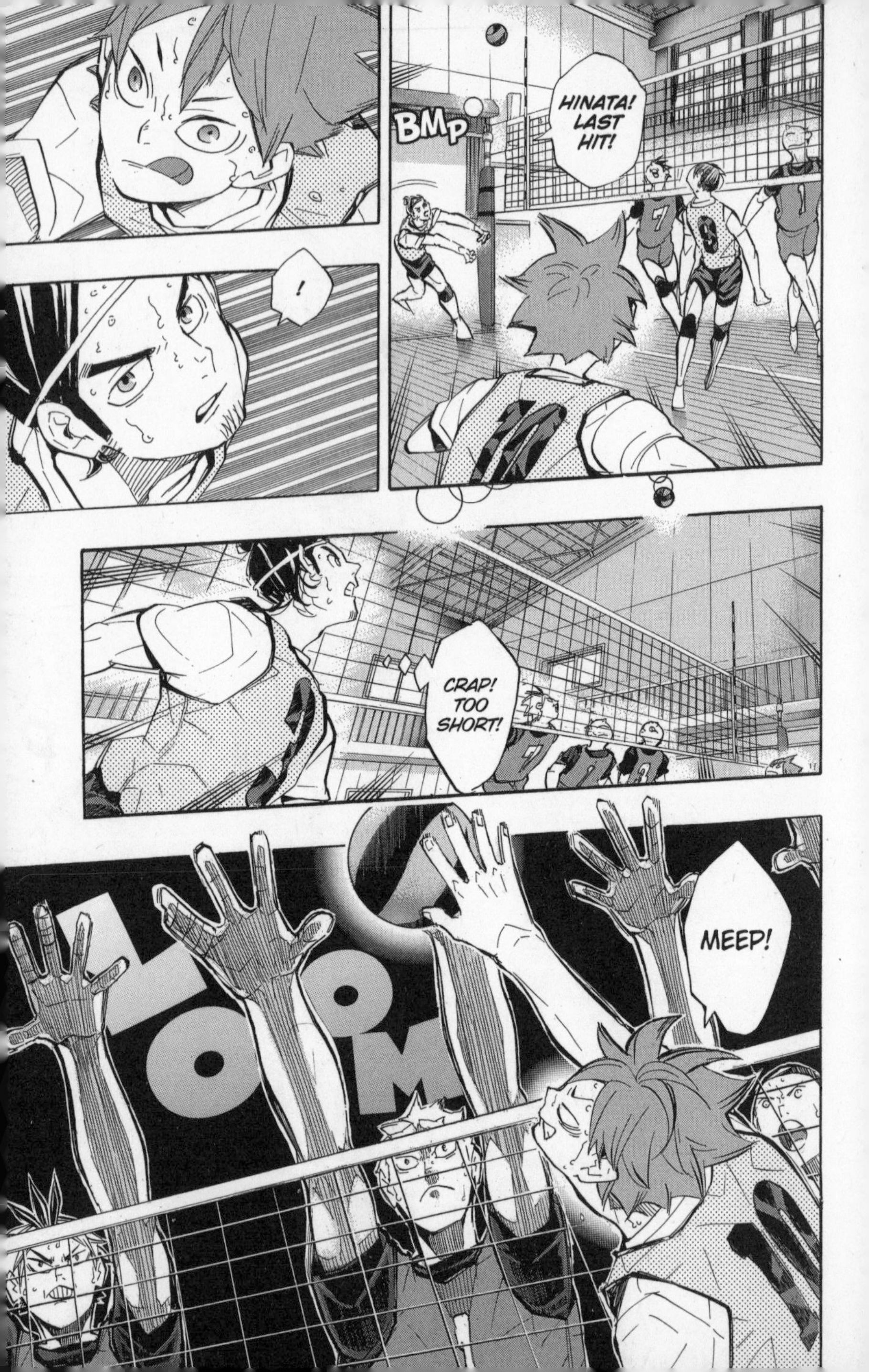
BMP
HINATA! LAST HIT!
!
CRAP! TOO SHORT!
MEEP!

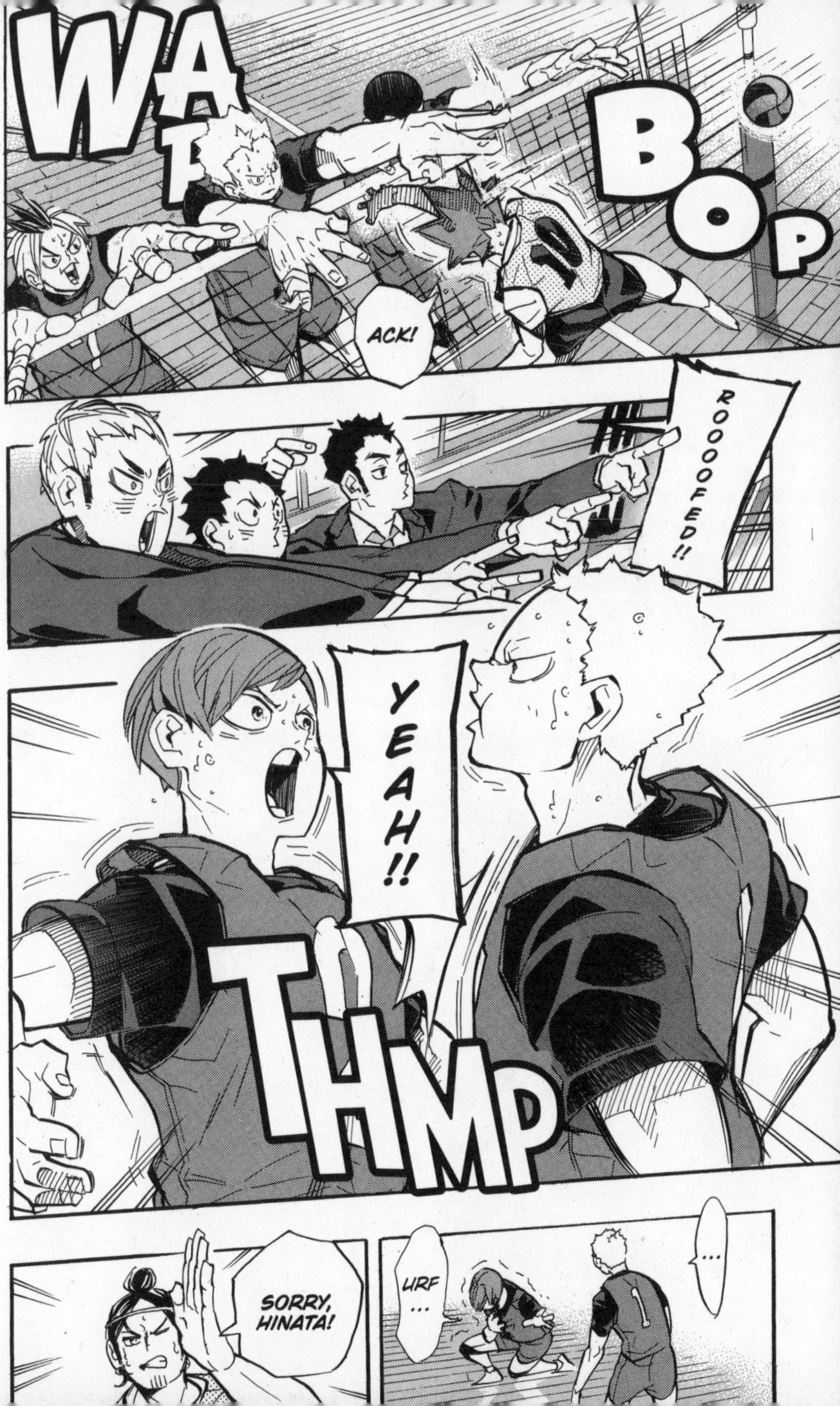
WAP
BOOP
ACK!
ROOOOOFED!!
YEAH!!
THMP
...
URF ...
SORRY, HINATA!

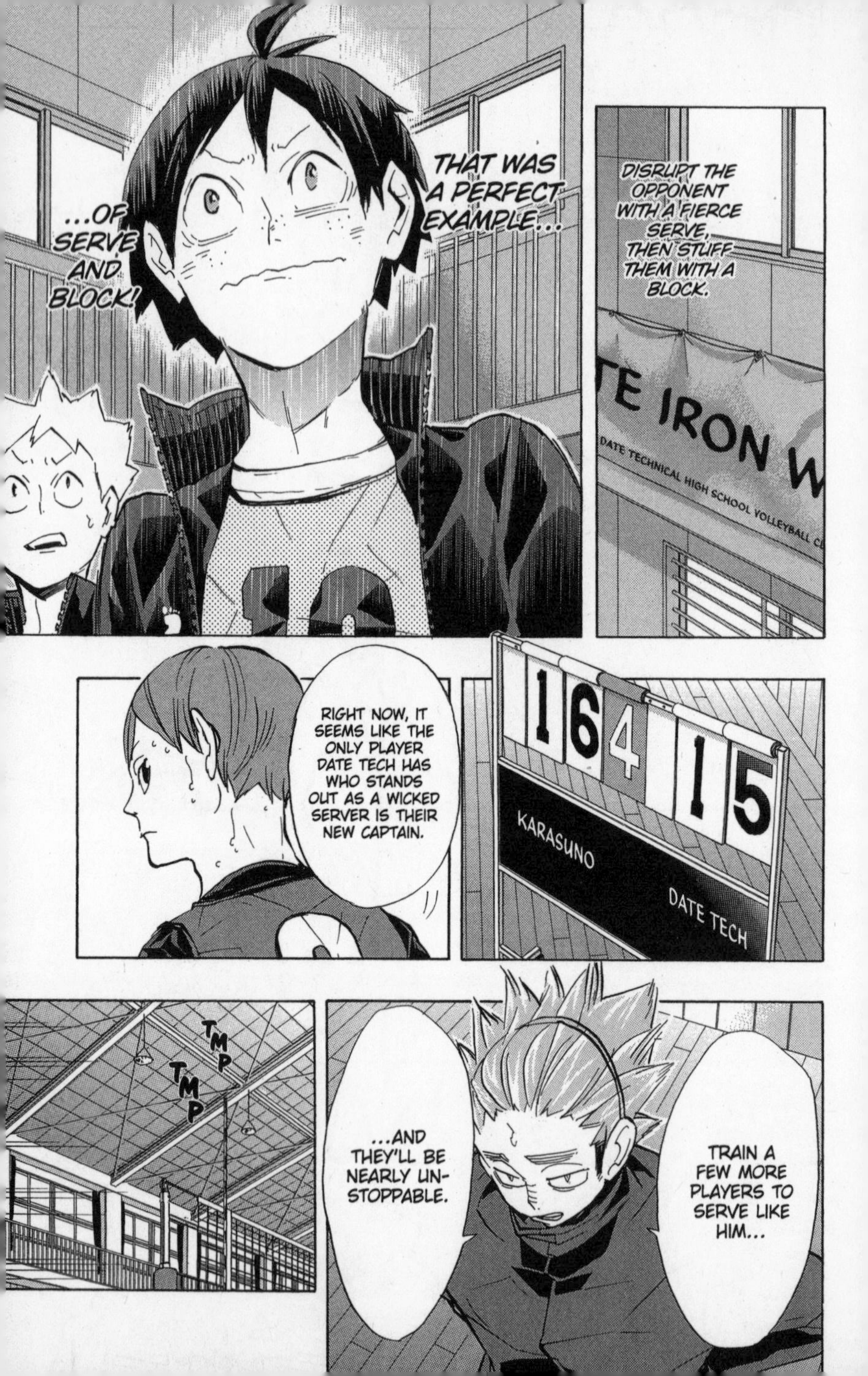
DISRUPT THE OPPONENT WITH A FIERCE SERVE, THEN STUFF THEM WITH A BLOCK.
TE IRON W
DATE TECHNICAL HIGH SCHOOL VOLLEYBALL C
THAT WAS A PERFECT EXAMPLE...
...OF SERVE AND BLOCK!
16 4 15
KARASUNO
DATE TECH
RIGHT NOW, IT SEEMS LIKE THE ONLY PLAYER DATE TECH HAS WHO STANDS OUT AS A WICKED SERVER IS THEIR NEW CAPTAIN.
TRAIN A FEW MORE PLAYERS TO SERVE LIKE HIM...
...AND THEY'LL BE NEARLY UN-STOPPABLE.
TMP
TMP

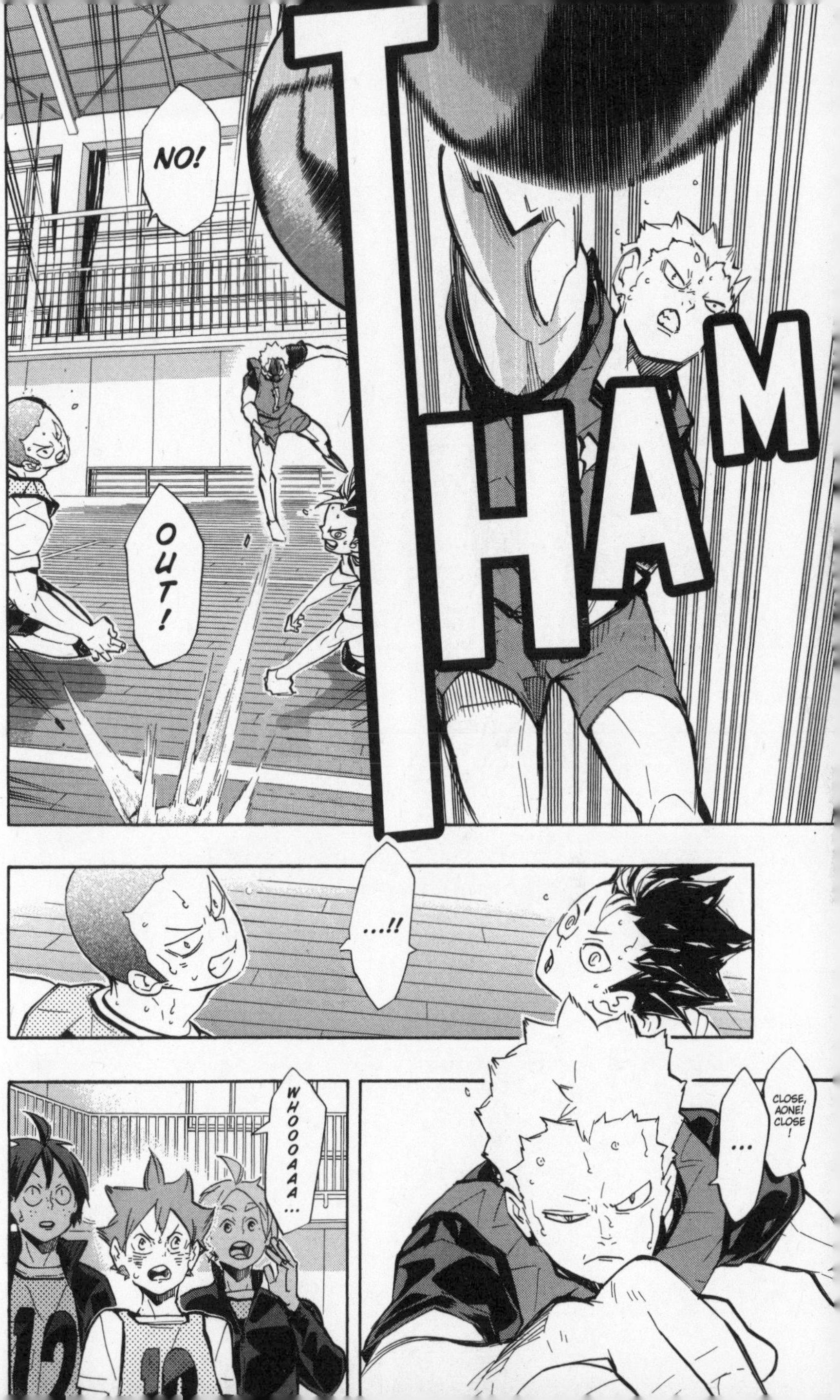
THAM
NO!
OUT!
...!!
CLOSE, AONE! CLOSE!
...
WHOOOAAA...

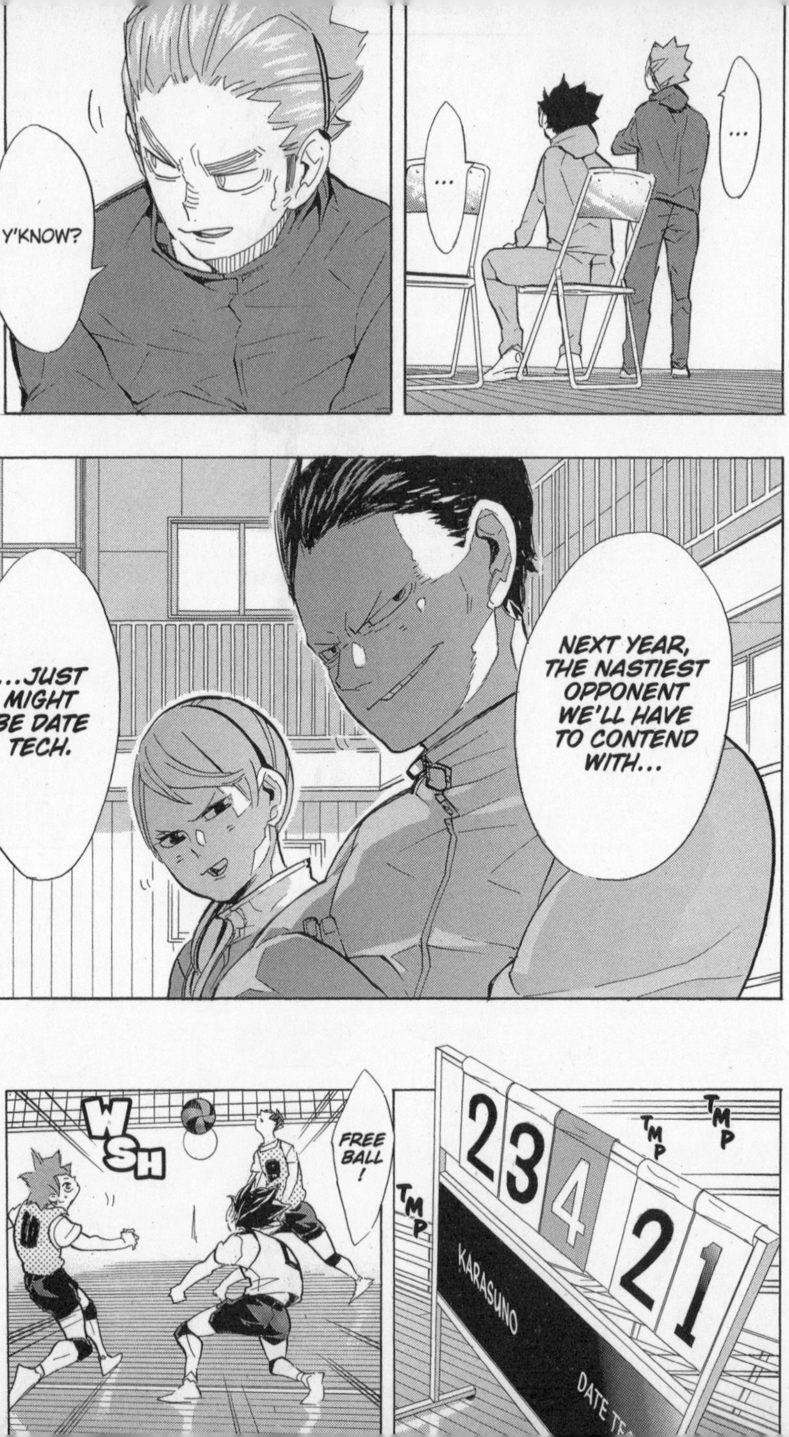
...
...
Y'KNOW?
NEXT YEAR, THE NASTIEST OPPONENT WE'LL HAVE TO CONTEND WITH...
...JUST MIGHT BE DATE TECH.
TMP
TMP
TMP
23
4
21
KARASUNO
FREE BALL!
WSH

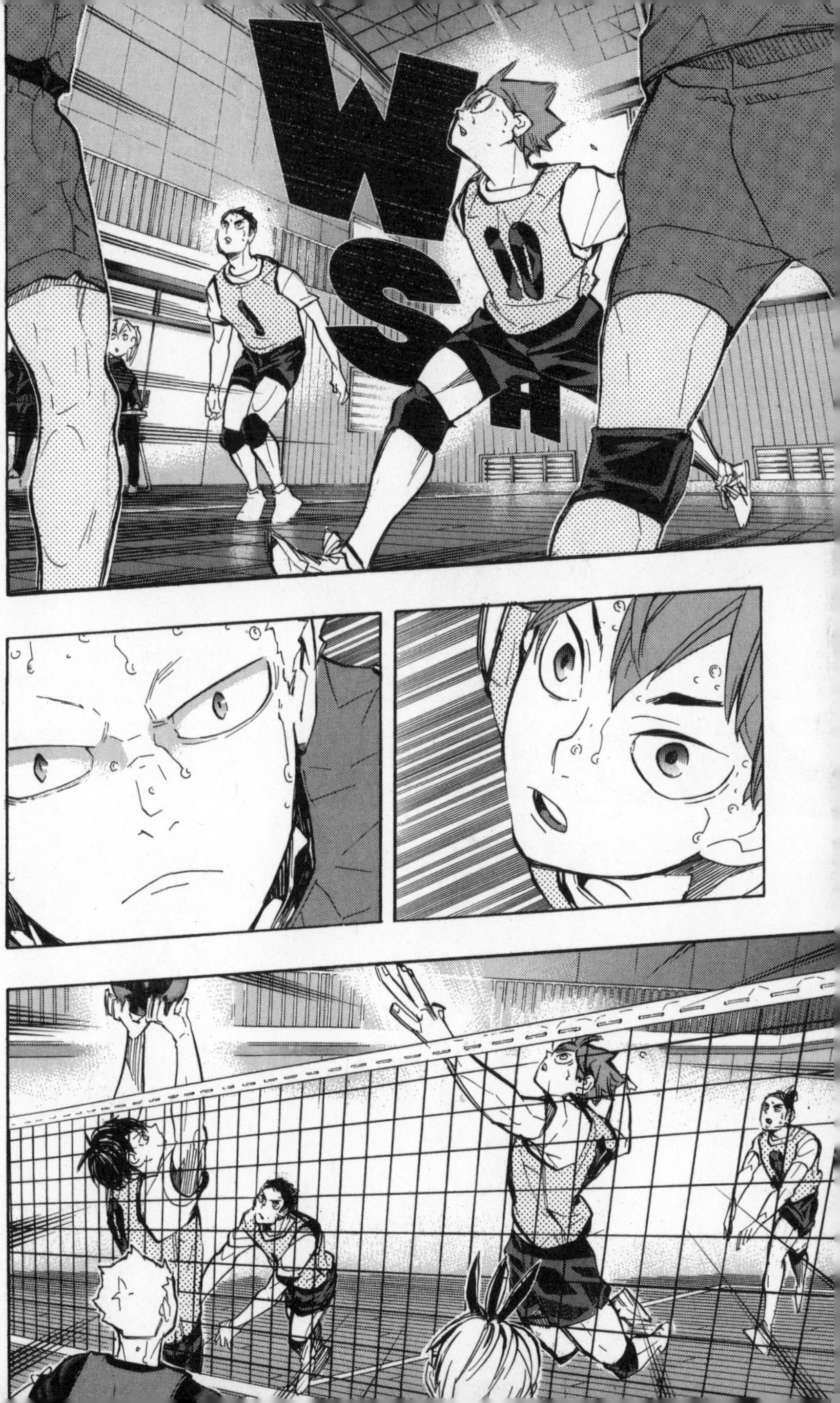
WSH

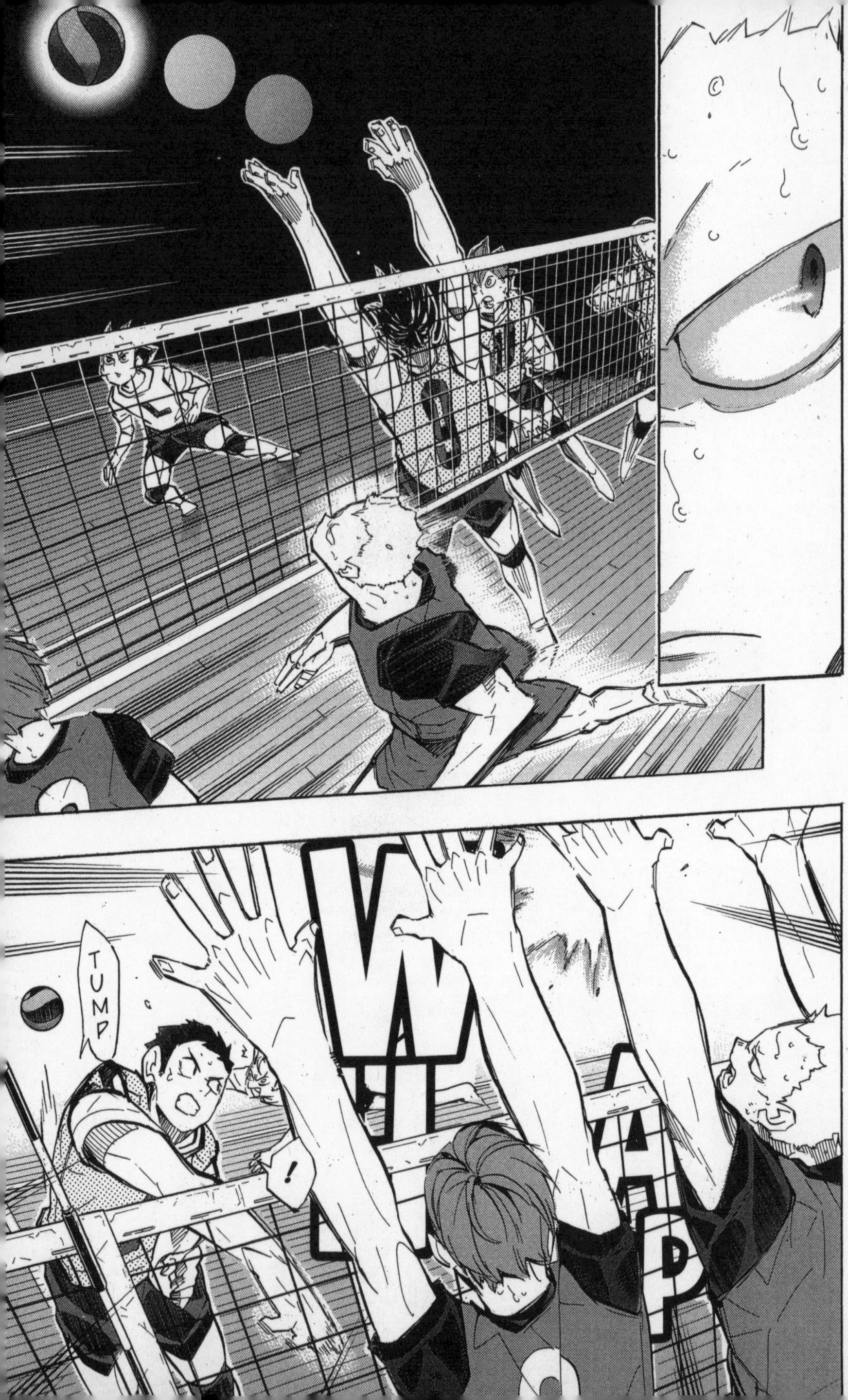
TUMP
!

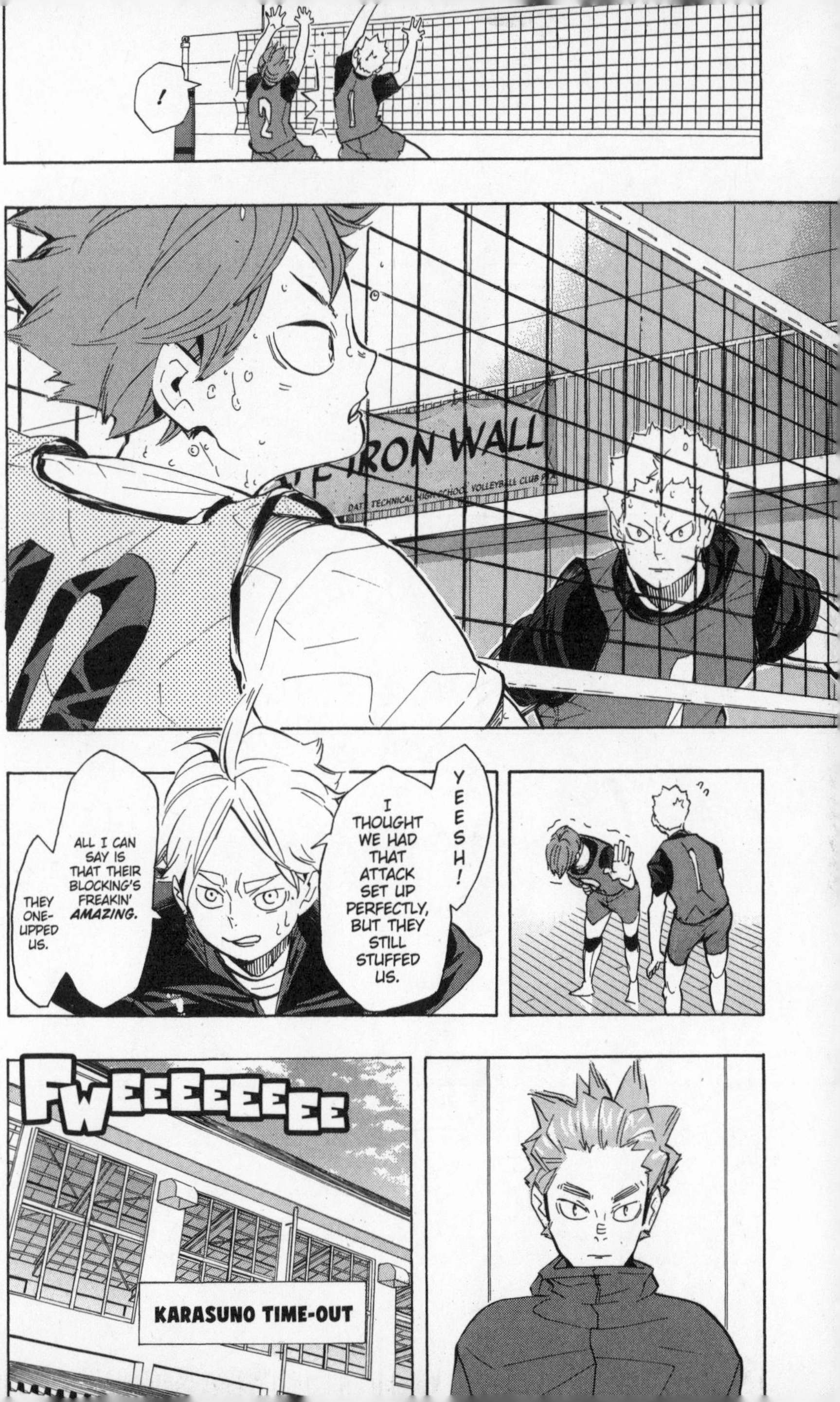
!
IRON WALL
YEESH!
I THOUGHT WE HAD THAT ATTACK SET UP PERFECTLY, BUT THEY STILL STUFFED US.
ALL I CAN SAY IS THAT THEIR BLOCKING'S FREAKIN' *AMAZING*.
THEY ONE-UPPED US.
FWEEEEEEEEE
KARASUNO TIME-OUT

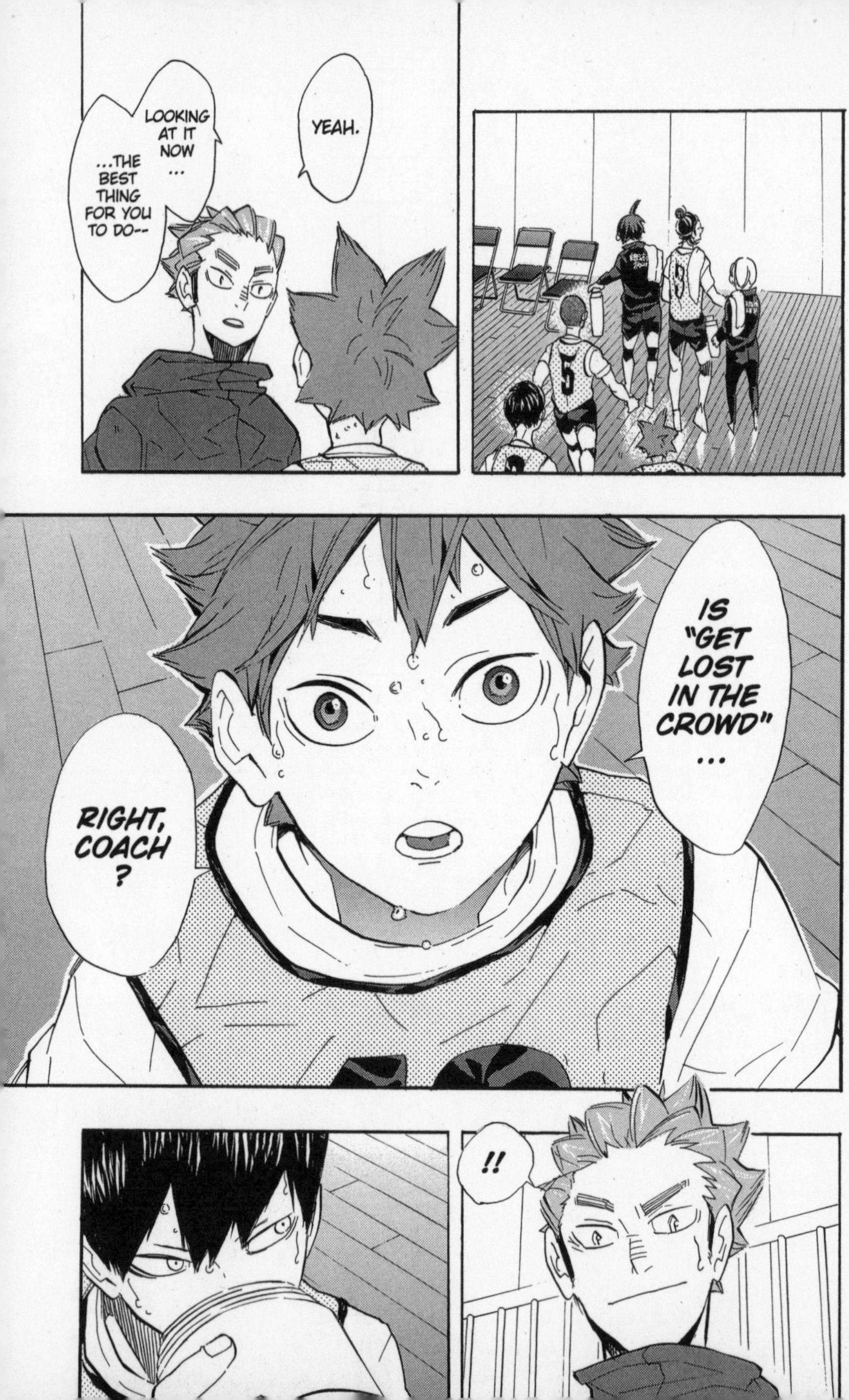
YEAH.
LOOKING AT IT NOW ...
...THE BEST THING FOR YOU TO DO--
IS "GET LOST IN THE CROWD" ...
RIGHT, COACH?
!!

CHAPTER 226: Lost in the Crowd

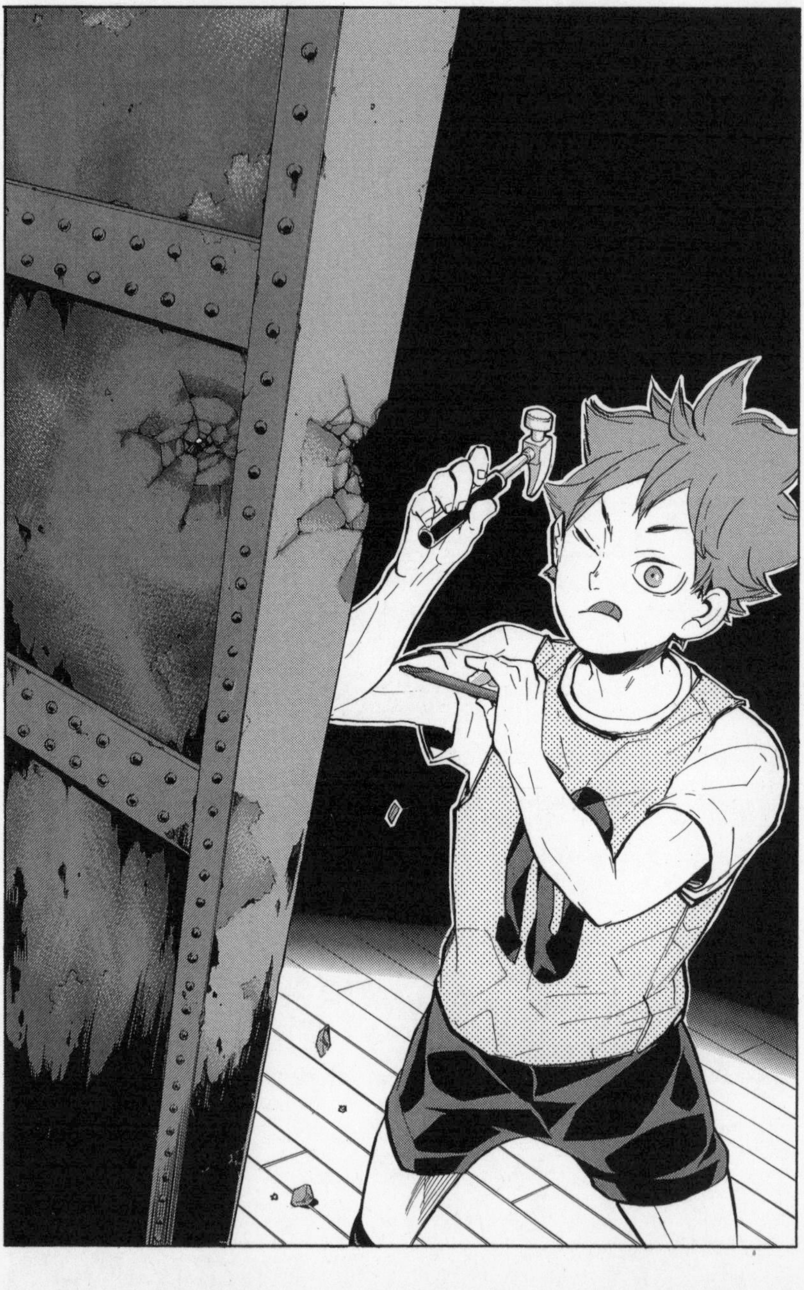

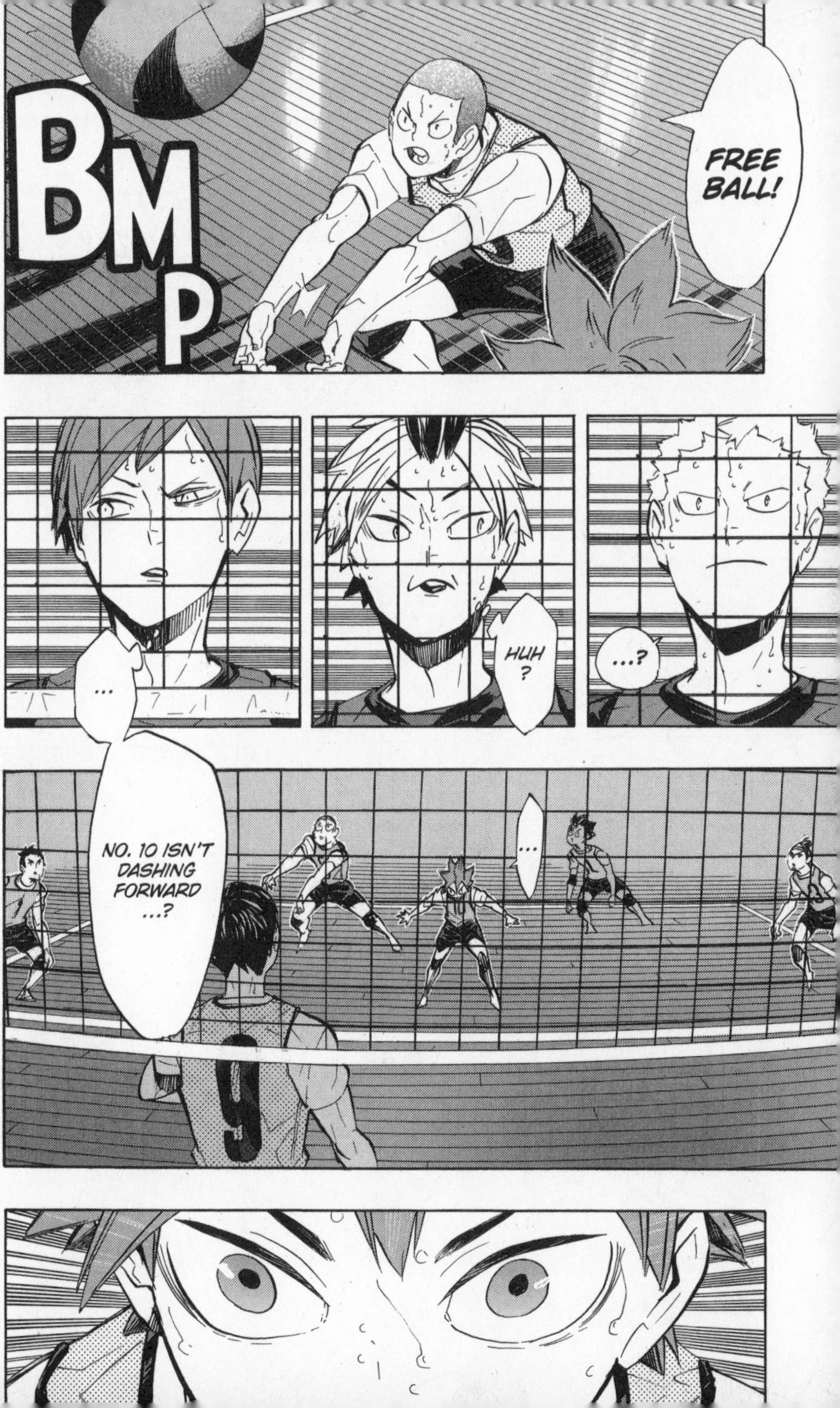
FREE BALL!
BMP
...?
HUH?
...
...
NO. 10 ISN'T DASHING FORWARD ...?

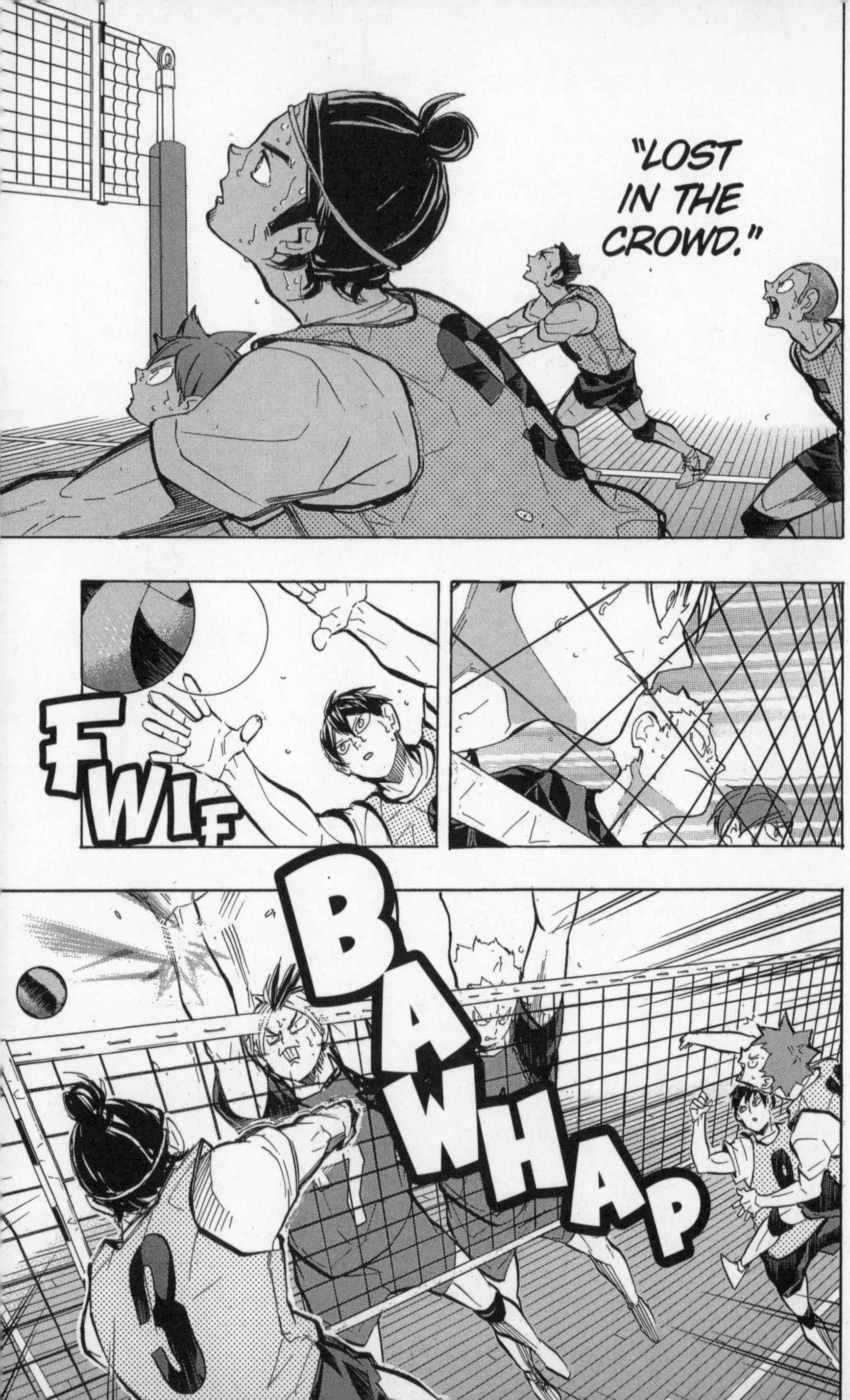
"LOST IN THE CROWD."
FWIF
BAWHAP

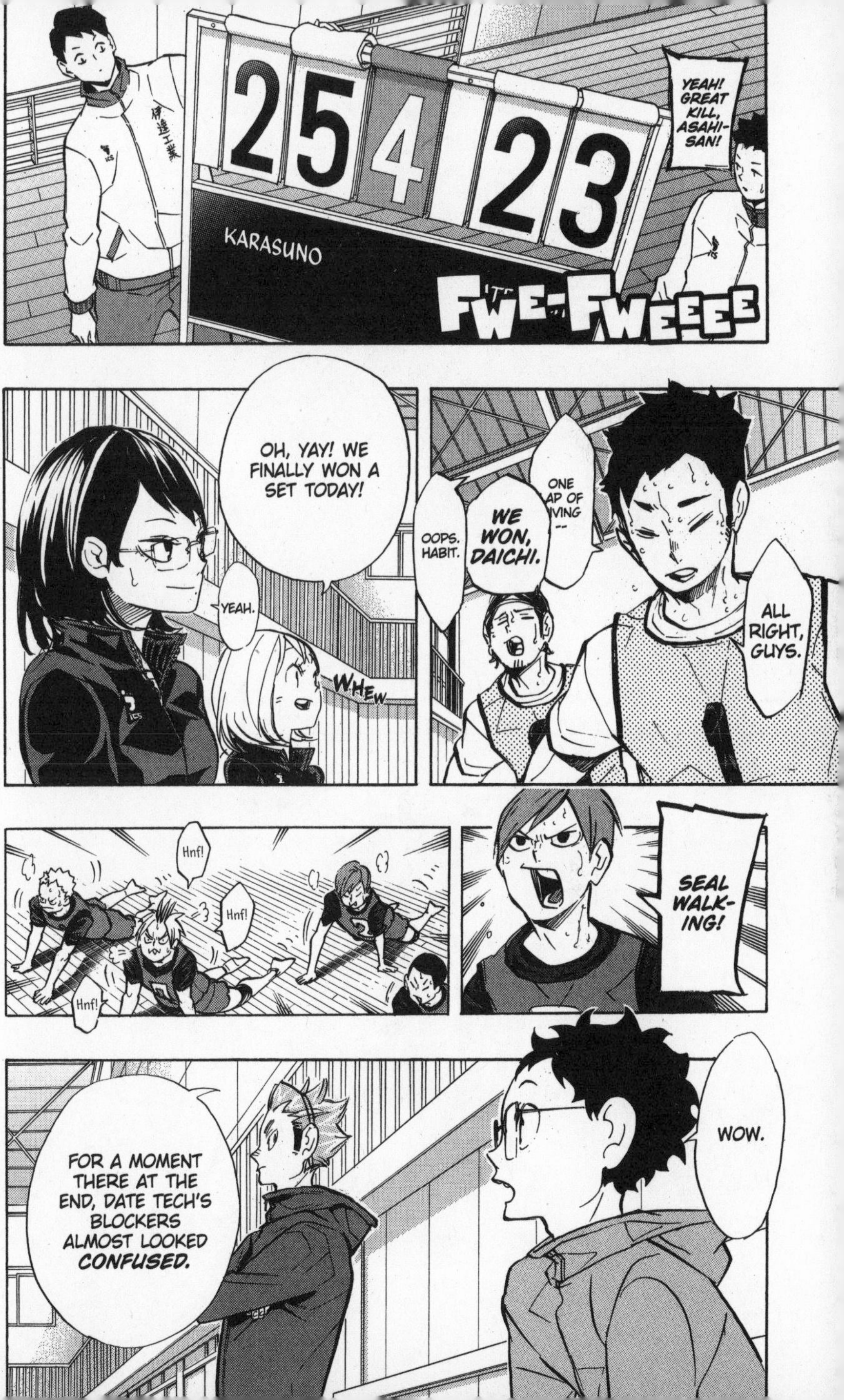
YEAH! GREAT KILL, ASAHI-SAN!
25 4 23
KARASUNO
FWE-FWEEEE
ALL RIGHT, GUYS.
ONE
AP OF
IVING
--
WE WON, DAICHI.
OOPS. HABIT.
OH, YAY! WE FINALLY WON A SET TODAY!
YEAH.
WHEW
SEAL WALK-ING!
Hnf!
Hnf!
Hnf!
WOW.
FOR A MOMENT THERE AT THE END, DATE TECH'S BLOCKERS ALMOST LOOKED CONFUSED.

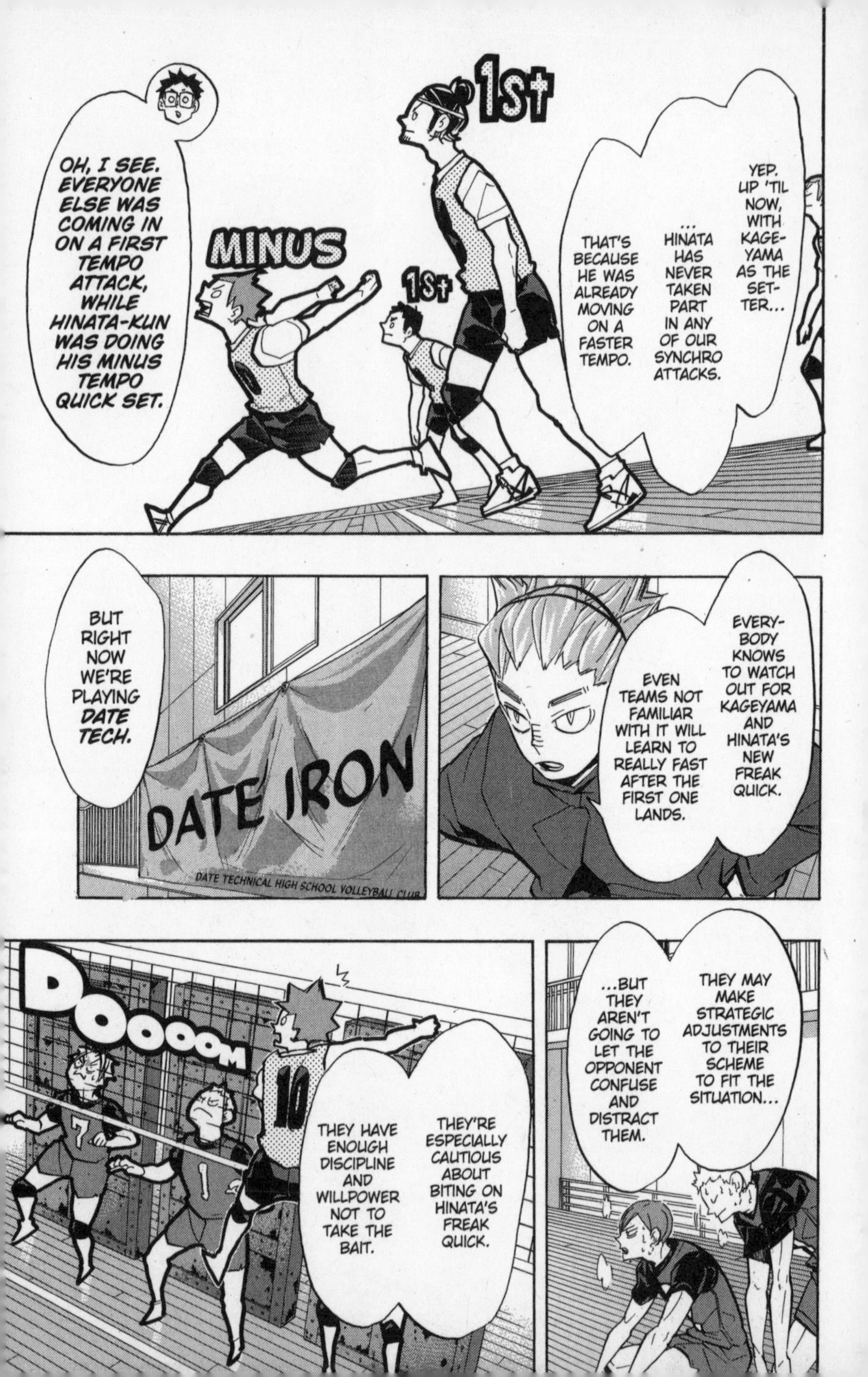
YEP. UP 'TIL NOW, WITH KAGEYAMA AS THE SETTER...
...HINATA HAS NEVER TAKEN PART IN ANY OF OUR SYNCHRO ATTACKS.
THAT'S BECAUSE HE WAS ALREADY MOVING ON A FASTER TEMPO.
1st
1st
MINUS
OH, I SEE. EVERYONE ELSE WAS COMING IN ON A FIRST TEMPO ATTACK, WHILE HINATA-KUN WAS DOING HIS MINUS TEMPO QUICK SET.
EVERYBODY KNOWS TO WATCH OUT FOR KAGEYAMA AND HINATA'S NEW FREAK QUICK.
EVEN TEAMS NOT FAMILIAR WITH IT WILL LEARN TO REALLY FAST AFTER THE FIRST ONE LANDS.
BUT RIGHT NOW WE'RE PLAYING DATE TECH.
DATE IRON
DATE TECHNICAL HIGH SCHOOL VOLLEYBALL CLUB
THEY MAY MAKE STRATEGIC ADJUSTMENTS TO THEIR SCHEME TO FIT THE SITUATION...
...BUT THEY AREN'T GOING TO LET THE OPPONENT CONFUSE AND DISTRACT THEM.
DOOOOOM
THEY'RE ESPECIALLY CAUTIOUS ABOUT BITING ON HINATA'S FREAK QUICK.
THEY HAVE ENOUGH DISCIPLINE AND WILLPOWER NOT TO TAKE THE BAIT.

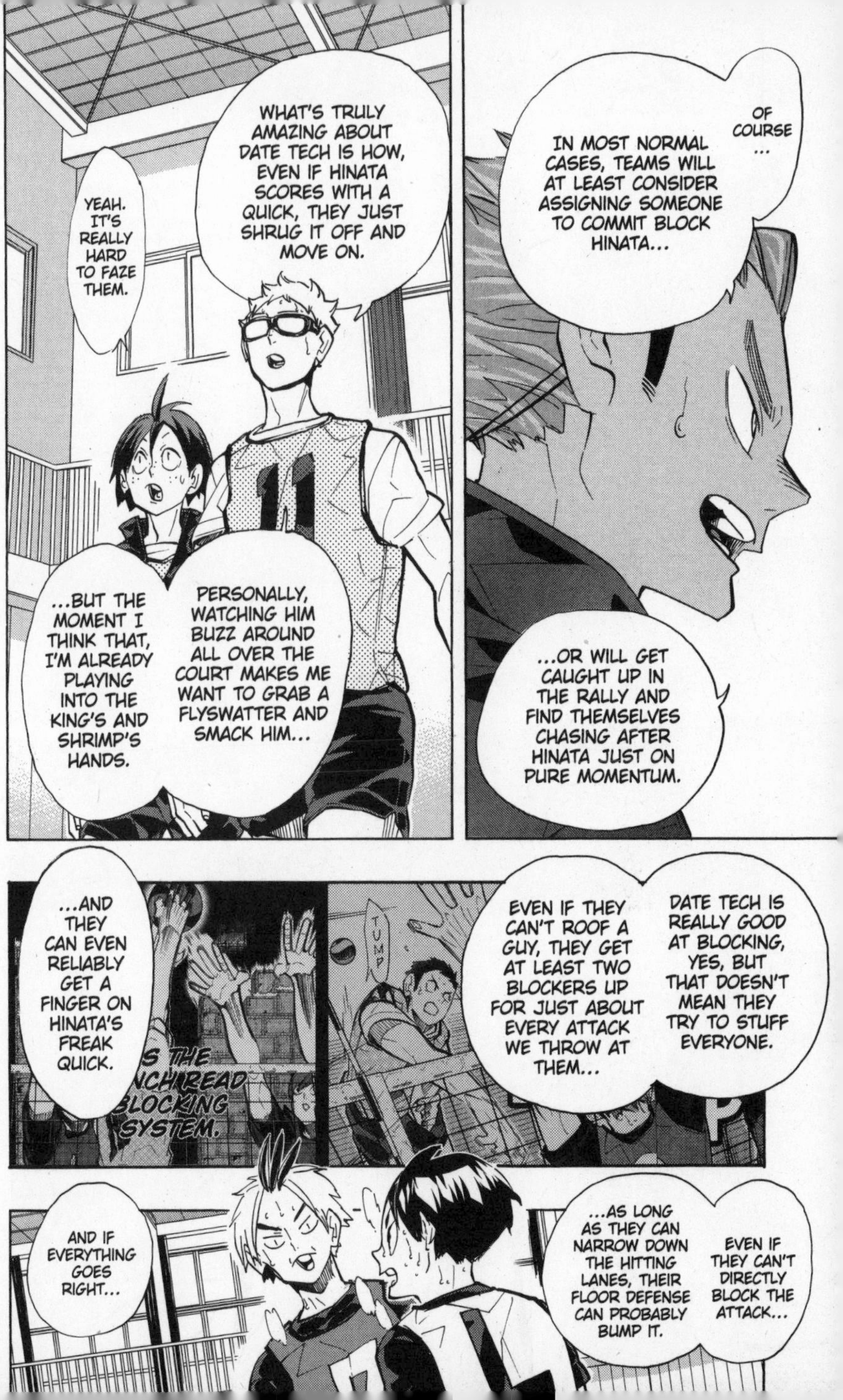
OF COURSE...
IN MOST NORMAL CASES, TEAMS WILL AT LEAST CONSIDER ASSIGNING SOMEONE TO COMMIT BLOCK HINATA...
...OR WILL GET CAUGHT UP IN THE RALLY AND FIND THEMSELVES CHASING AFTER HINATA JUST ON PURE MOMENTUM.
WHAT'S TRULY AMAZING ABOUT DATE TECH IS HOW, EVEN IF HINATA SCORES WITH A QUICK, THEY JUST SHRUG IT OFF AND MOVE ON.
YEAH. IT'S REALLY HARD TO FAZE THEM.
PERSONALLY, WATCHING HIM BUZZ AROUND ALL OVER THE COURT MAKES ME WANT TO GRAB A FLYSWATTER AND SMACK HIM...
...BUT THE MOMENT I THINK THAT, I'M ALREADY PLAYING INTO THE KING'S AND SHRIMP'S HANDS.
DATE TECH IS REALLY GOOD AT BLOCKING, YES, BUT THAT DOESN'T MEAN THEY TRY TO STUFF EVERYONE.
EVEN IF THEY CAN'T ROOF A GUY, THEY GET AT LEAST TWO BLOCKERS UP FOR JUST ABOUT EVERY ATTACK WE THROW AT THEM...
TUMP
...AND THEY CAN EVEN RELIABLY GET A FINGER ON HINATA'S FREAK QUICK.
S THE
NCH READ
BLOCKING
SYSTEM.
EVEN IF THEY CAN'T DIRECTLY BLOCK THE ATTACK...
...AS LONG AS THEY CAN NARROW DOWN THE HITTING LANES, THEIR FLOOR DEFENSE CAN PROBABLY BUMP IT.
AND IF EVERYTHING GOES RIGHT...

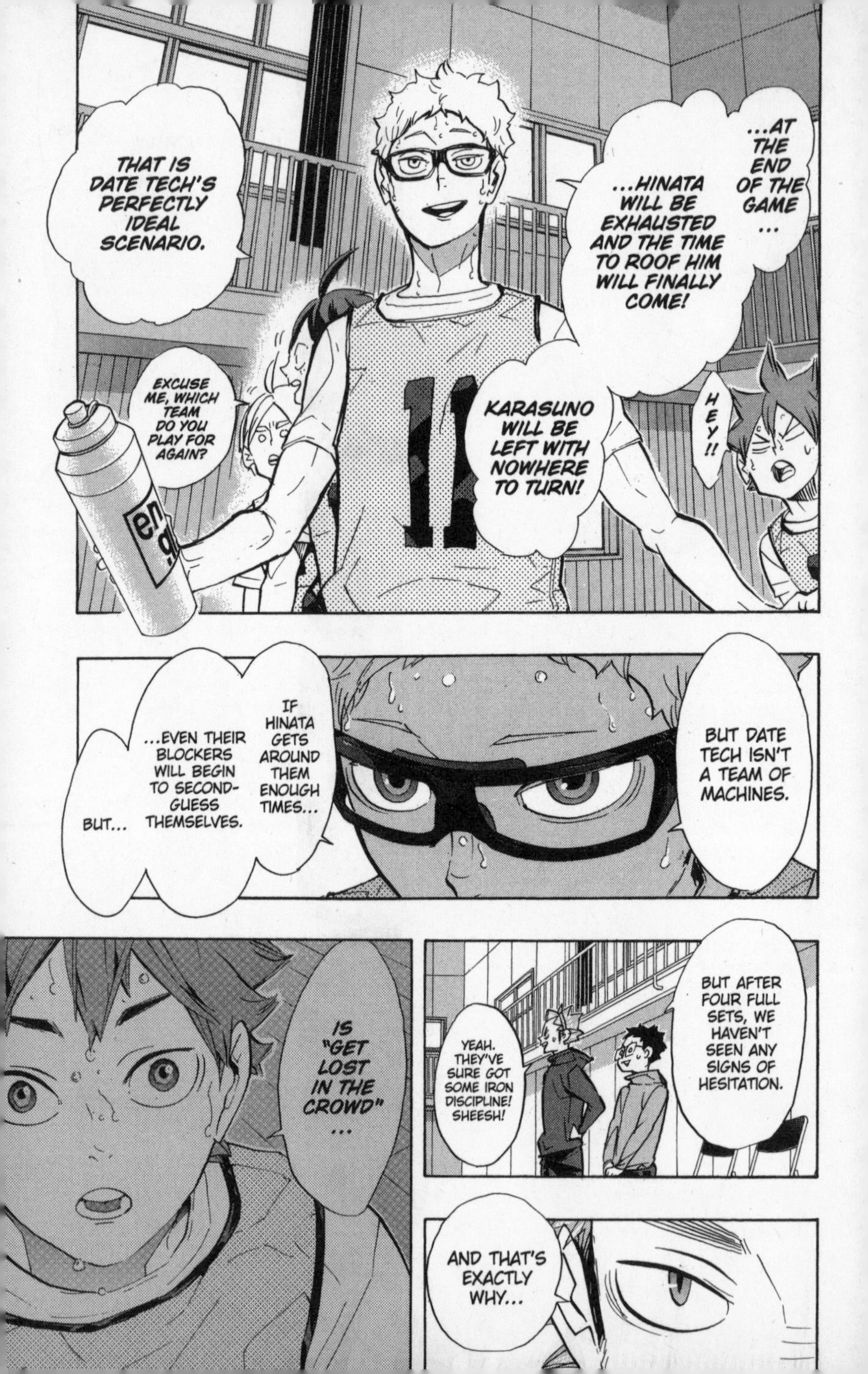
...AT THE END OF THE GAME...
...HINATA WILL BE EXHAUSTED AND THE TIME TO ROOF HIM WILL FINALLY COME!
HEY!!
KARASUNO WILL BE LEFT WITH NOWHERE TO TURN!
THAT IS DATE TECH'S PERFECTLY IDEAL SCENARIO.
EXCUSE ME, WHICH TEAM DO YOU PLAY FOR AGAIN?
BUT DATE TECH ISN'T A TEAM OF MACHINES.
IF HINATA GETS AROUND THEM ENOUGH TIMES...
...EVEN THEIR BLOCKERS WILL BEGIN TO SECOND-GUESS THEMSELVES.
BUT...
BUT AFTER FOUR FULL SETS, WE HAVEN'T SEEN ANY SIGNS OF HESITATION.
YEAH. THEY'VE SURE GOT SOME IRON DISCIPLINE! SHEESH!
AND THAT'S EXACTLY WHY...
IS "GET LOST IN THE CROWD"...

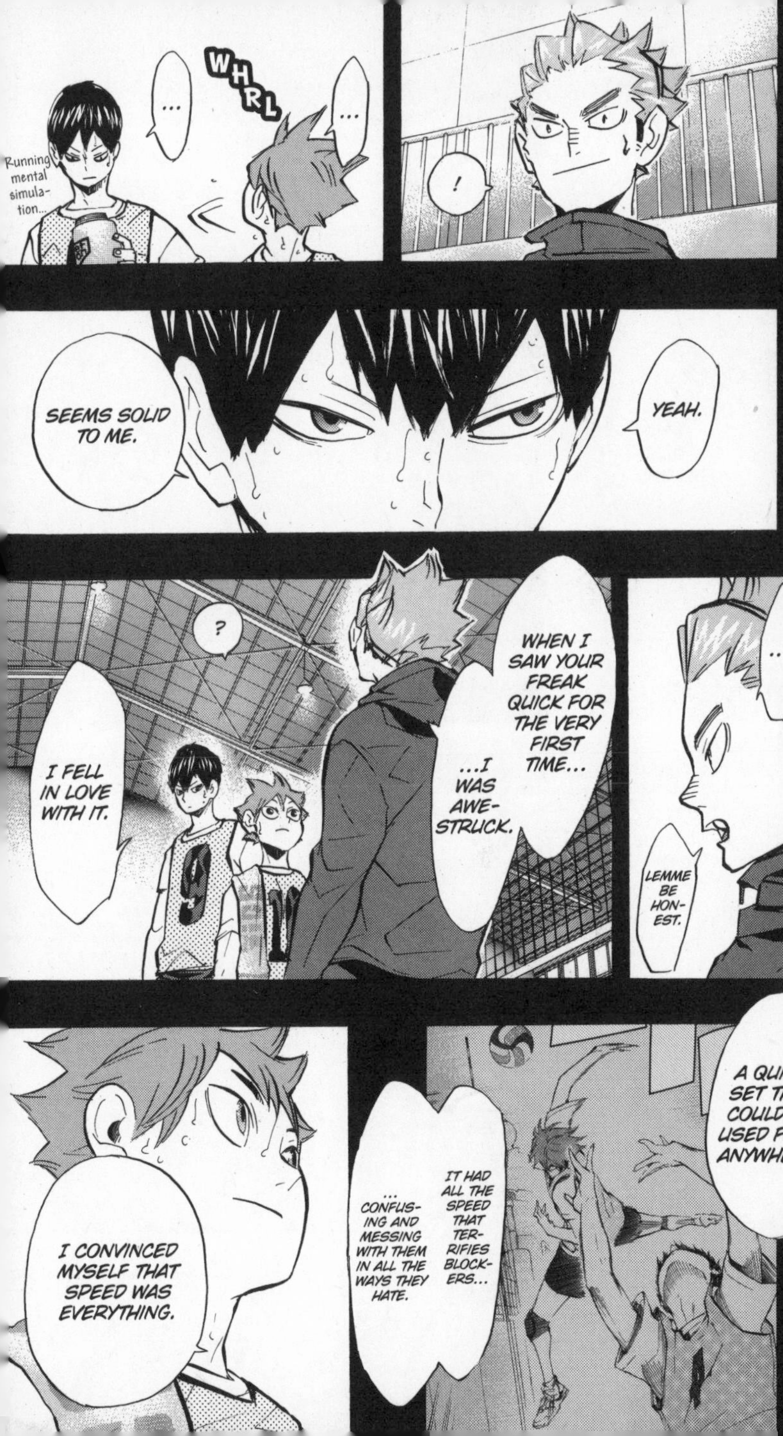
!
...
WHRL
...
Running mental simulation...
YEAH.
SEEMS SOLID TO ME.
...
LEMME BE HONEST.
WHEN I SAW YOUR FREAK QUICK FOR THE VERY FIRST TIME...
...I WAS AWESTRUCK.
?
I FELL IN LOVE WITH IT.
A QUICK SET THAT COULD BE USED FROM ANYWHERE!
IT HAD ALL THE SPEED THAT TERRIFIES BLOCKERS...
...CONFUSING AND MESSING WITH THEM IN ALL THE WAYS THEY HATE.
I CONVINCED MYSELF THAT SPEED WAS EVERYTHING.

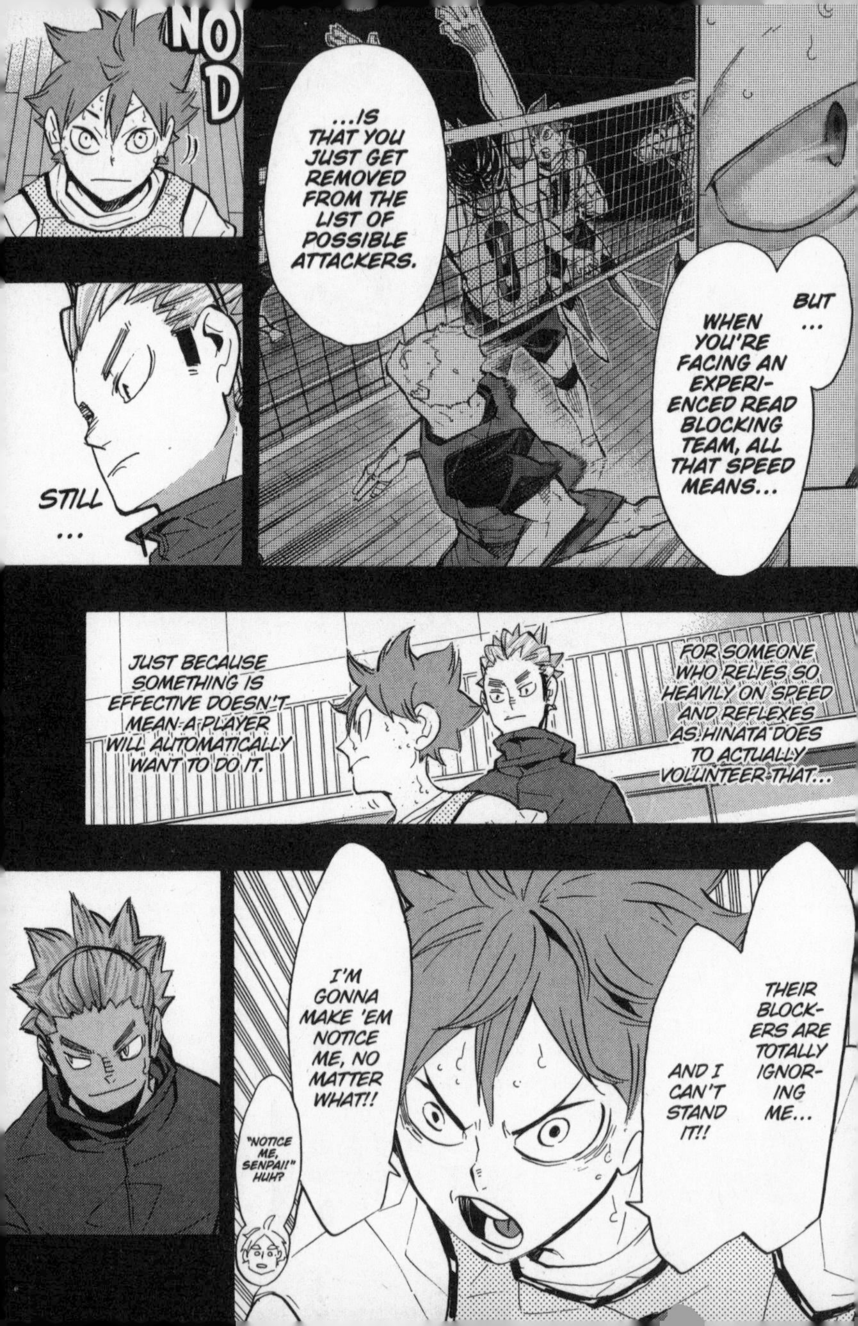
BUT... WHEN YOU'RE FACING AN EXPERI-ENCED READ BLOCKING TEAM, ALL THAT SPEED MEANS...
...IS THAT YOU JUST GET REMOVED FROM THE LIST OF POSSIBLE ATTACKERS.
NOD
STILL...
FOR SOMEONE WHO RELIES SO HEAVILY ON SPEED AND REFLEXES AS HINATA DOES TO ACTUALLY VOLUNTEER THAT...
JUST BECAUSE SOMETHING IS EFFECTIVE DOESN'T MEAN A PLAYER WILL AUTOMATICALLY WANT TO DO IT.
THEIR BLOCK-ERS ARE TOTALLY IGNOR-ING ME...
AND I CAN'T STAND IT!!
I'M GONNA MAKE 'EM NOTICE ME, NO MATTER WHAT!!
"NOTICE ME, SENPAI!" HUH?

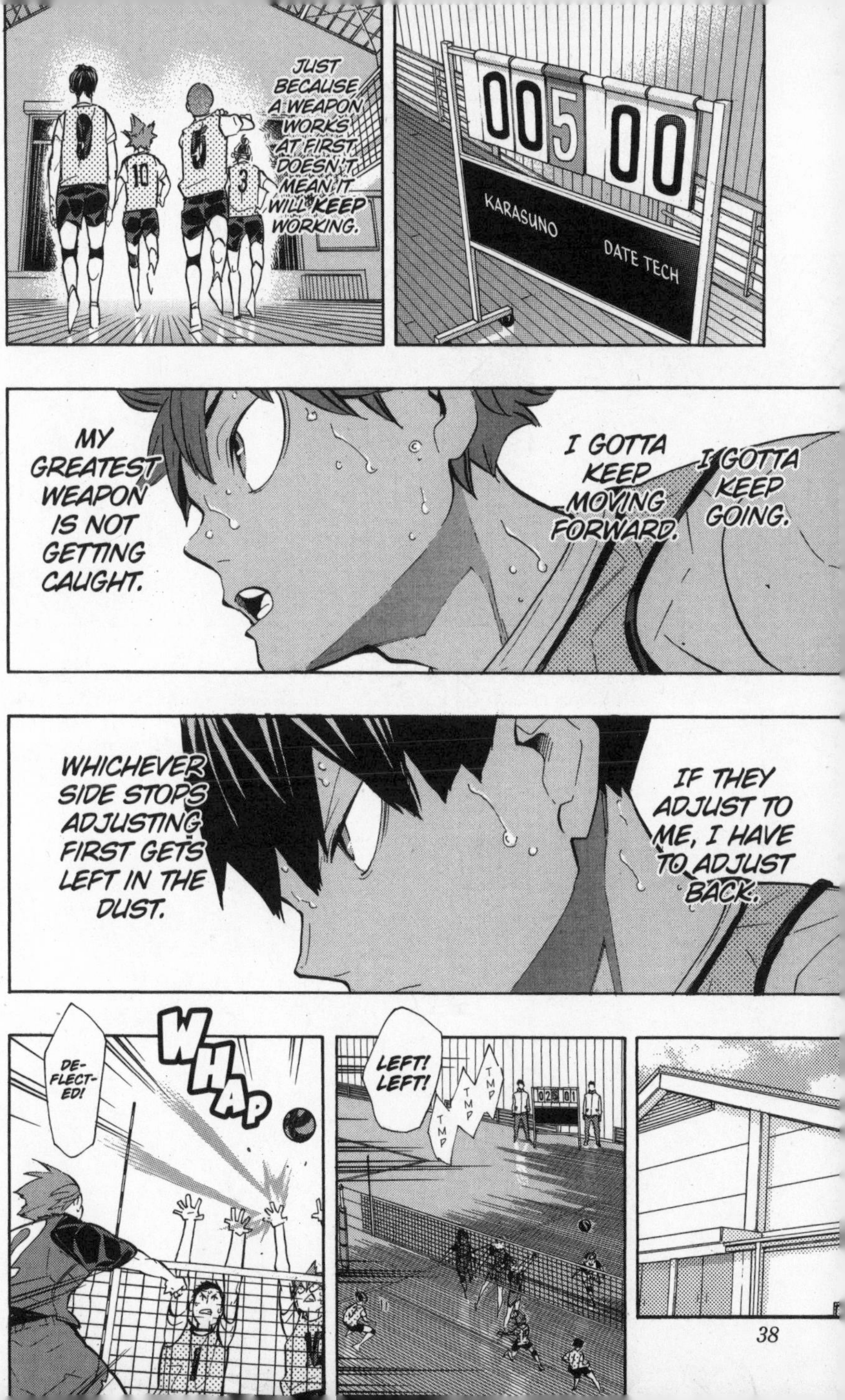
005 00
KARASUNO
DATE TECH
JUST BECAUSE A WEAPON WORKS AT FIRST DOESN'T MEAN IT WILL KEEP WORKING.
I GOTTA KEEP GOING.
I GOTTA KEEP MOVING FORWARD.
MY GREATEST WEAPON IS NOT GETTING CAUGHT.
IF THEY ADJUST TO ME, I HAVE TO ADJUST BACK.
WHICHEVER SIDE STOPS ADJUSTING FIRST GETS LEFT IN THE DUST.
LEFT! LEFT!
TMP TMP TMP
WHAP
DE-FLECT-ED!

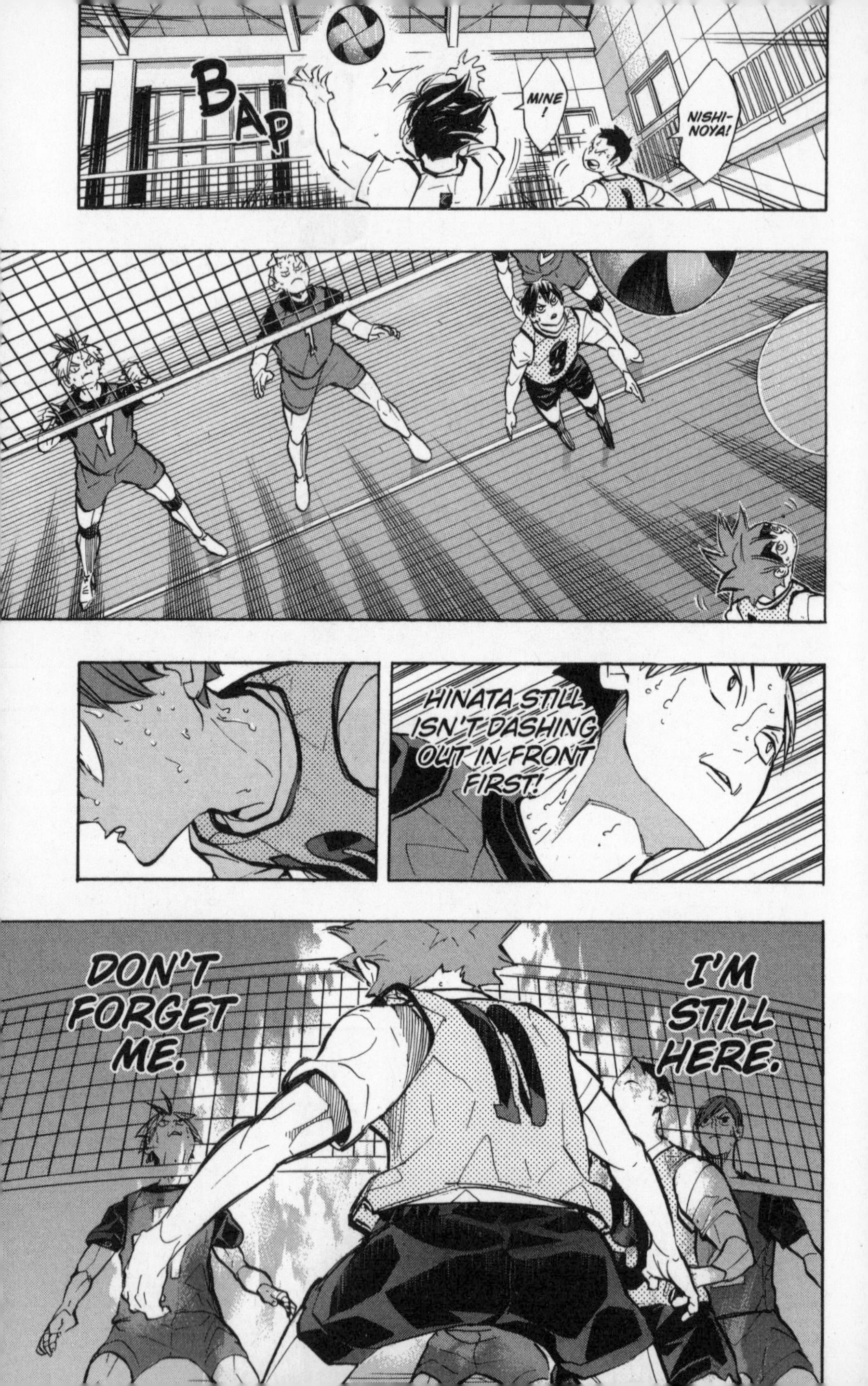
NISHI-NOYA!
MINE!
BAP
HINATA STILL ISN'T DASHING OUT IN FRONT FIRST!
I'M STILL HERE.
DON'T FORGET ME.

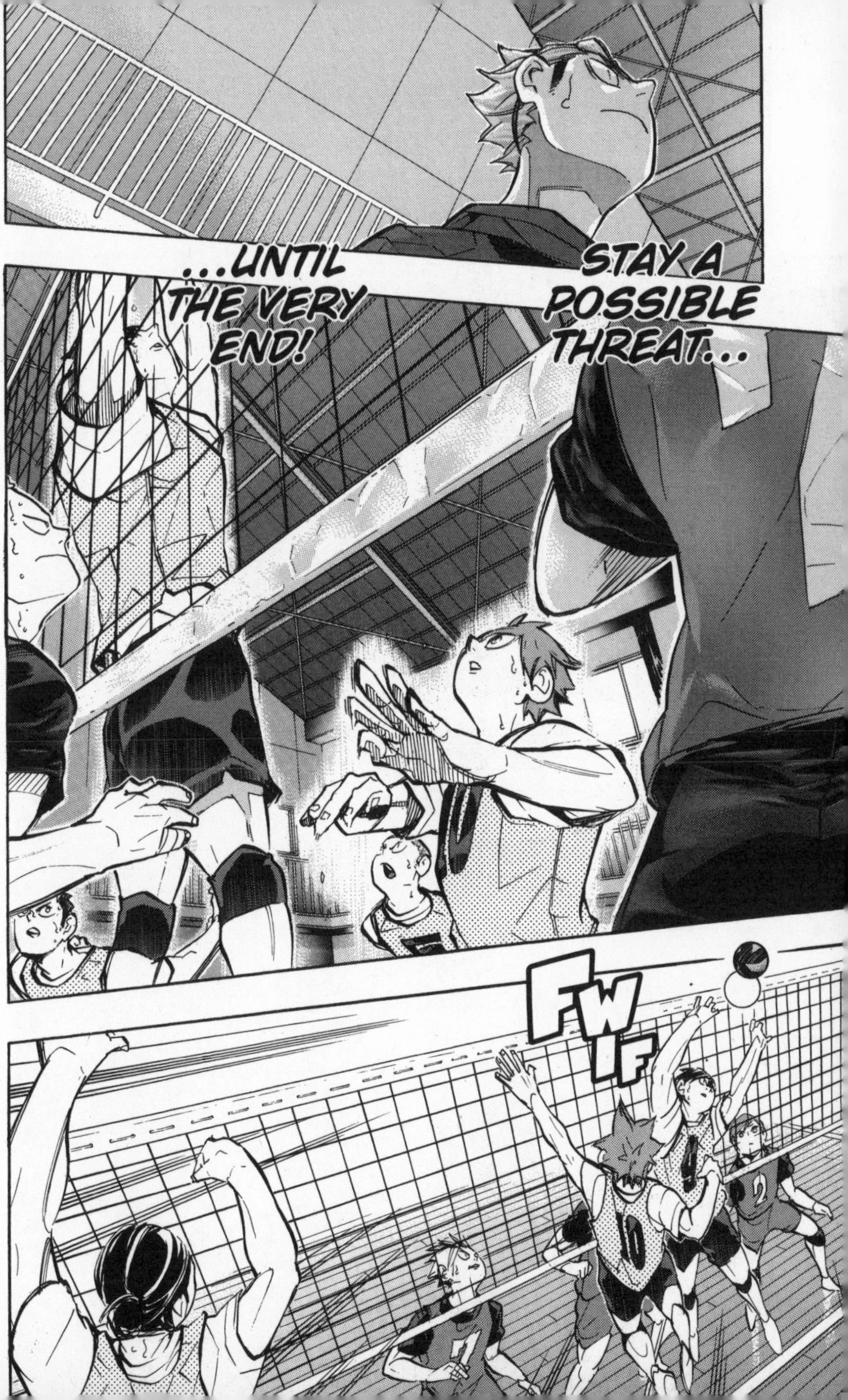
STAY A POSSIBLE THREAT...
...UNTIL THE VERY END!
FWIF

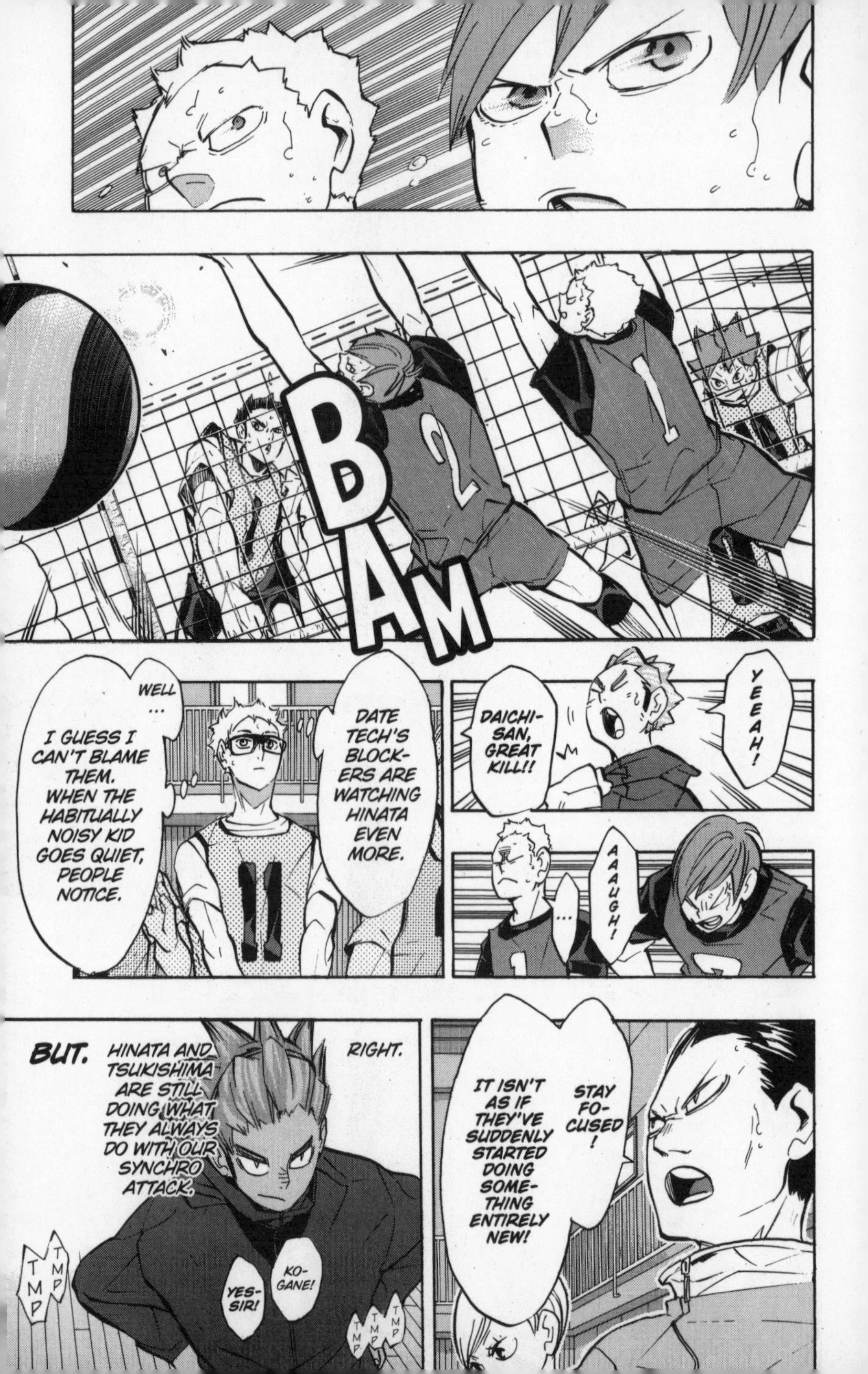
BAM
YEEEAH!
DAICHI-SAN, GREAT KILL!!
AAAUGH!
...
DATE TECH'S BLOCKERS ARE WATCHING HINATA EVEN MORE.
WELL... I GUESS I CAN'T BLAME THEM. WHEN THE HABITUALLY NOISY KID GOES QUIET, PEOPLE NOTICE.
STAY FOCUSED!
IT ISN'T AS IF THEY'VE SUDDENLY STARTED DOING SOMETHING ENTIRELY NEW!
RIGHT.
HINATA AND TSUKISHIMA ARE STILL DOING WHAT THEY ALWAYS DO WITH OUR SYNCHRO ATTACK.
BUT.
KO-GANE!
YES-SIR!
TMP TMP TMP
TMP TMP TMP

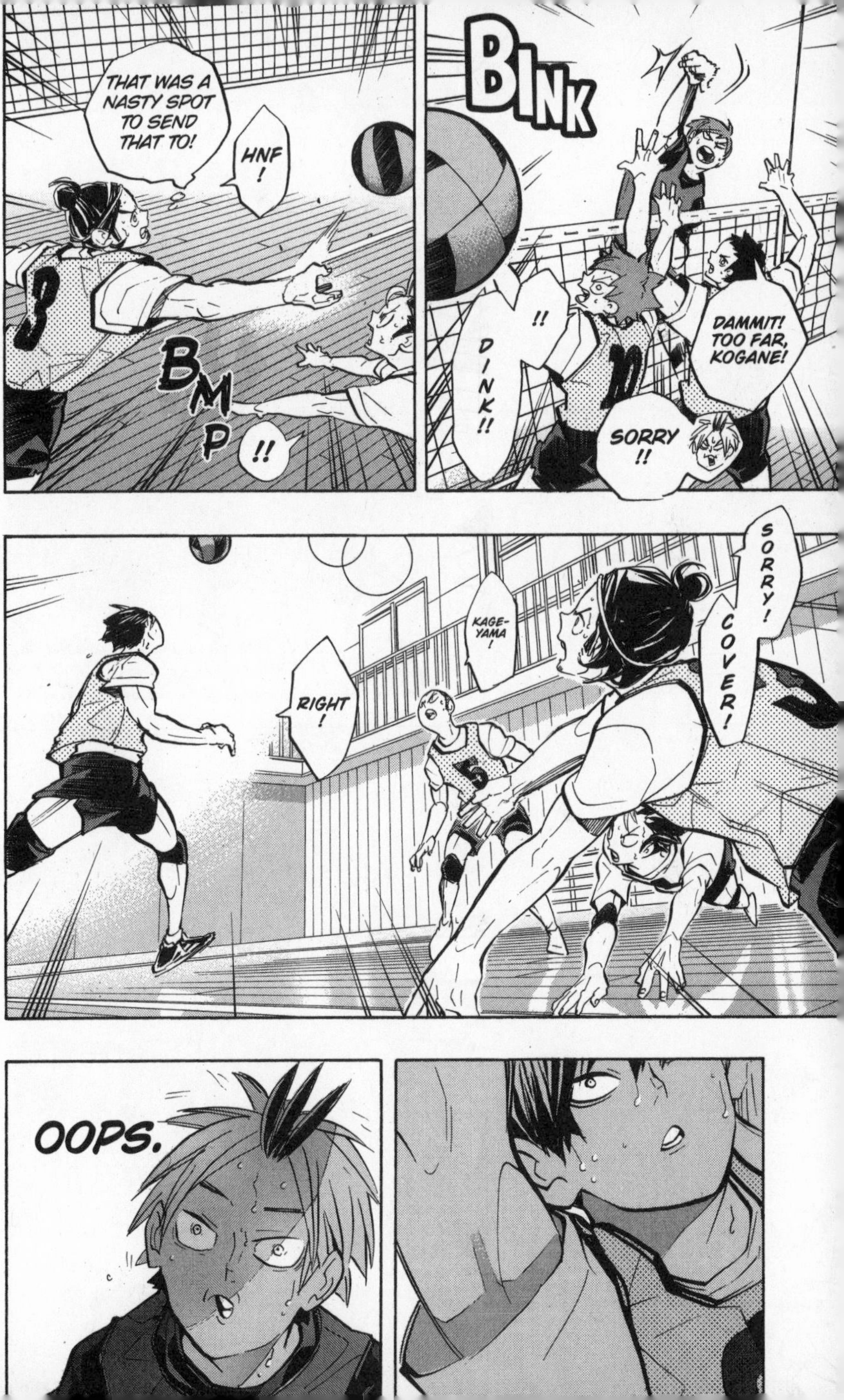
BINK
DAMMIT! TOO FAR, KOGANE!
!!
DINK!!
SORRY!!
THAT WAS A NASTY SPOT TO SEND THAT TO!
HNF!
BMP
!!
SORRY!
COVER!
KAGE-YAMA!
RIGHT!
OOPS.

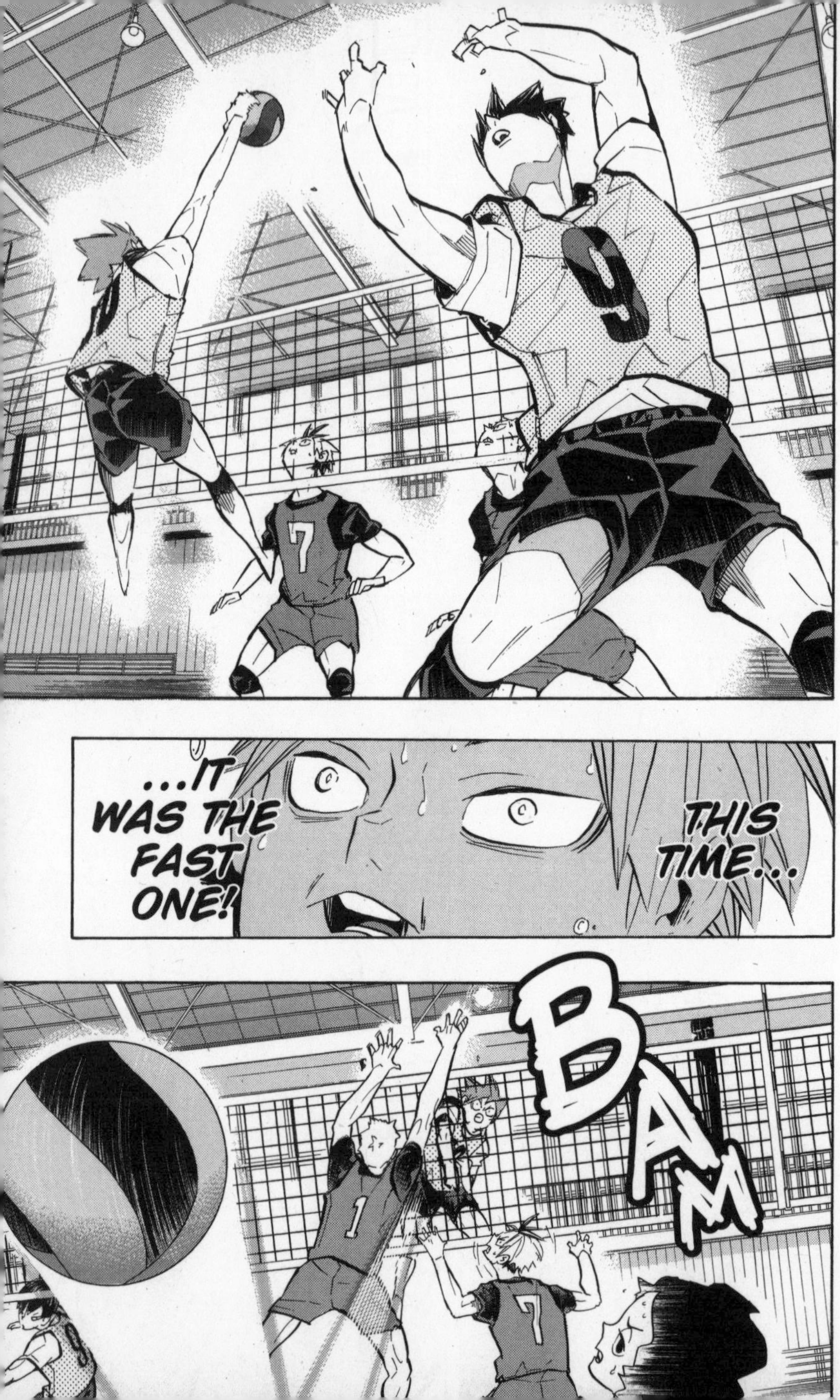
THIS TIME...
...IT WAS THE FAST ONE!
BAM

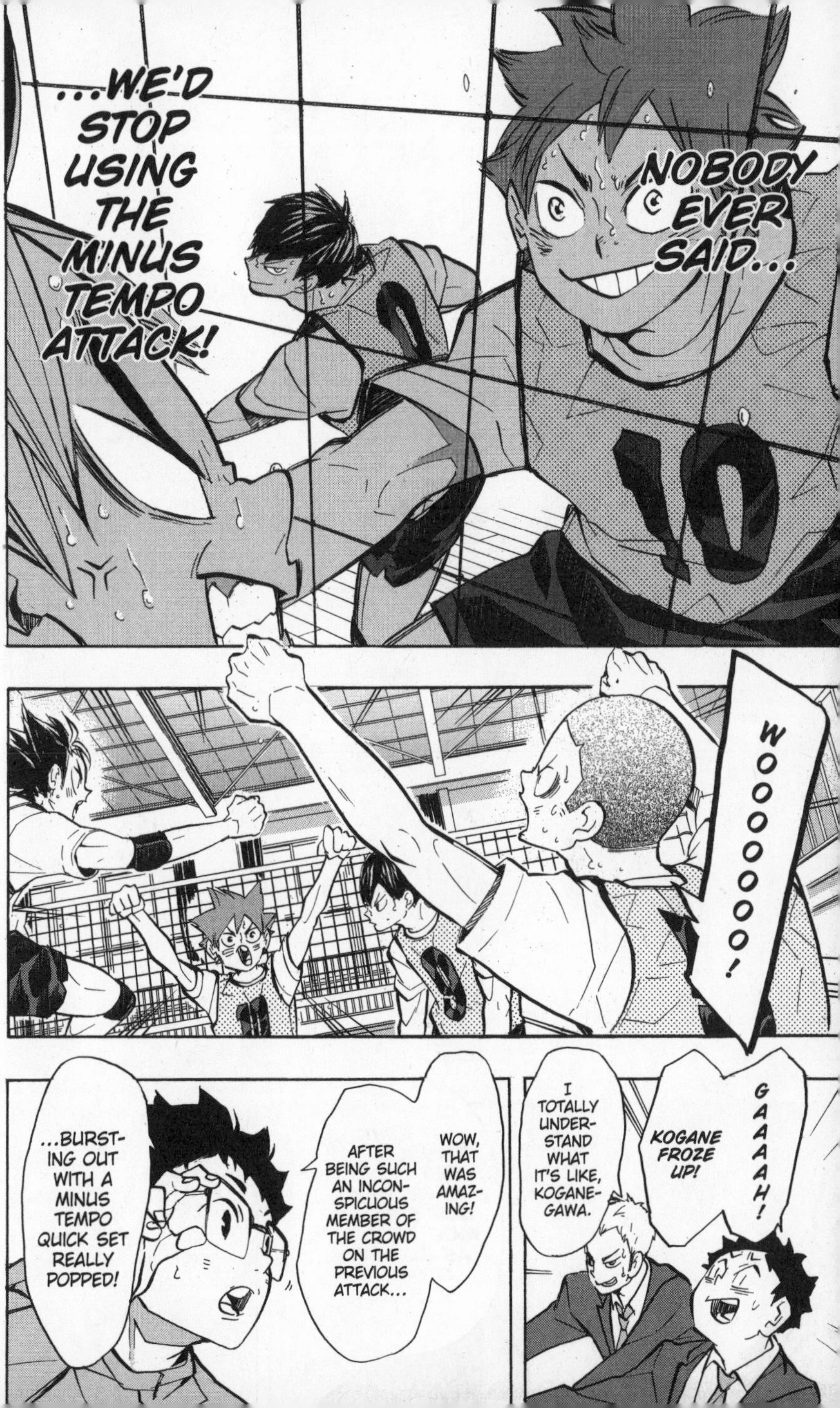

NOBODY EVER SAID...
...WE'D STOP USING THE MINUS TEMPO ATTACK!
WOOOOOOOOO!
GAAAAH!
KOGANE FROZE UP!
I TOTALLY UNDER-STAND WHAT IT'S LIKE, KOGANE-GAWA.
WOW, THAT WAS AMAZ-ING!
AFTER BEING SUCH AN INCON-SPICUOUS MEMBER OF THE CROWD ON THE PREVIOUS ATTACK...
...BURST-ING OUT WITH A MINUS TEMPO QUICK SET REALLY POPPED!

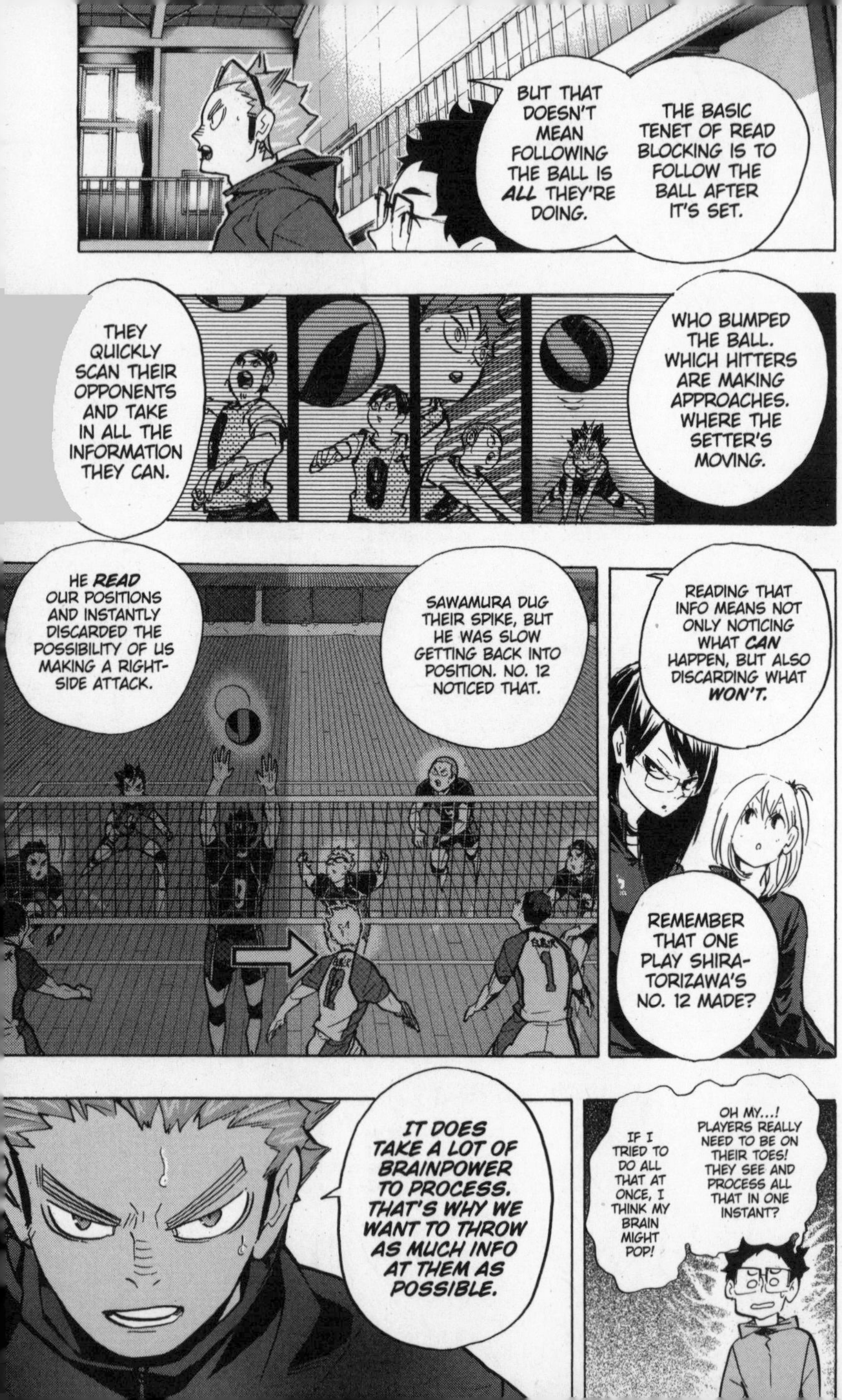
THE BASIC TENET OF READ BLOCKING IS TO FOLLOW THE BALL AFTER IT'S SET.
BUT THAT DOESN'T MEAN FOLLOWING THE BALL IS ***ALL*** THEY'RE DOING.
WHO BUMPED THE BALL. WHICH HITTERS ARE MAKING APPROACHES. WHERE THE SETTER'S MOVING.
THEY QUICKLY SCAN THEIR OPPONENTS AND TAKE IN ALL THE INFORMATION THEY CAN.
READING THAT INFO MEANS NOT ONLY NOTICING WHAT ***CAN*** HAPPEN, BUT ALSO DISCARDING WHAT ***WON'T.***
REMEMBER THAT ONE PLAY SHIRATORIZAWA'S NO. 12 MADE?
SAWAMURA DUG THEIR SPIKE, BUT HE WAS SLOW GETTING BACK INTO POSITION. NO. 12 NOTICED THAT.
HE ***READ*** OUR POSITIONS AND INSTANTLY DISCARDED THE POSSIBILITY OF US MAKING A RIGHT-SIDE ATTACK.
OH MY...! PLAYERS REALLY NEED TO BE ON THEIR TOES! THEY SEE AND PROCESS ALL THAT IN ONE INSTANT?
IF I TRIED TO DO ALL THAT AT ONCE, I THINK MY BRAIN MIGHT POP!
IT DOES TAKE A LOT OF BRAINPOWER TO PROCESS. THAT'S WHY WE WANT TO THROW AS MUCH INFO AT THEM AS POSSIBLE.

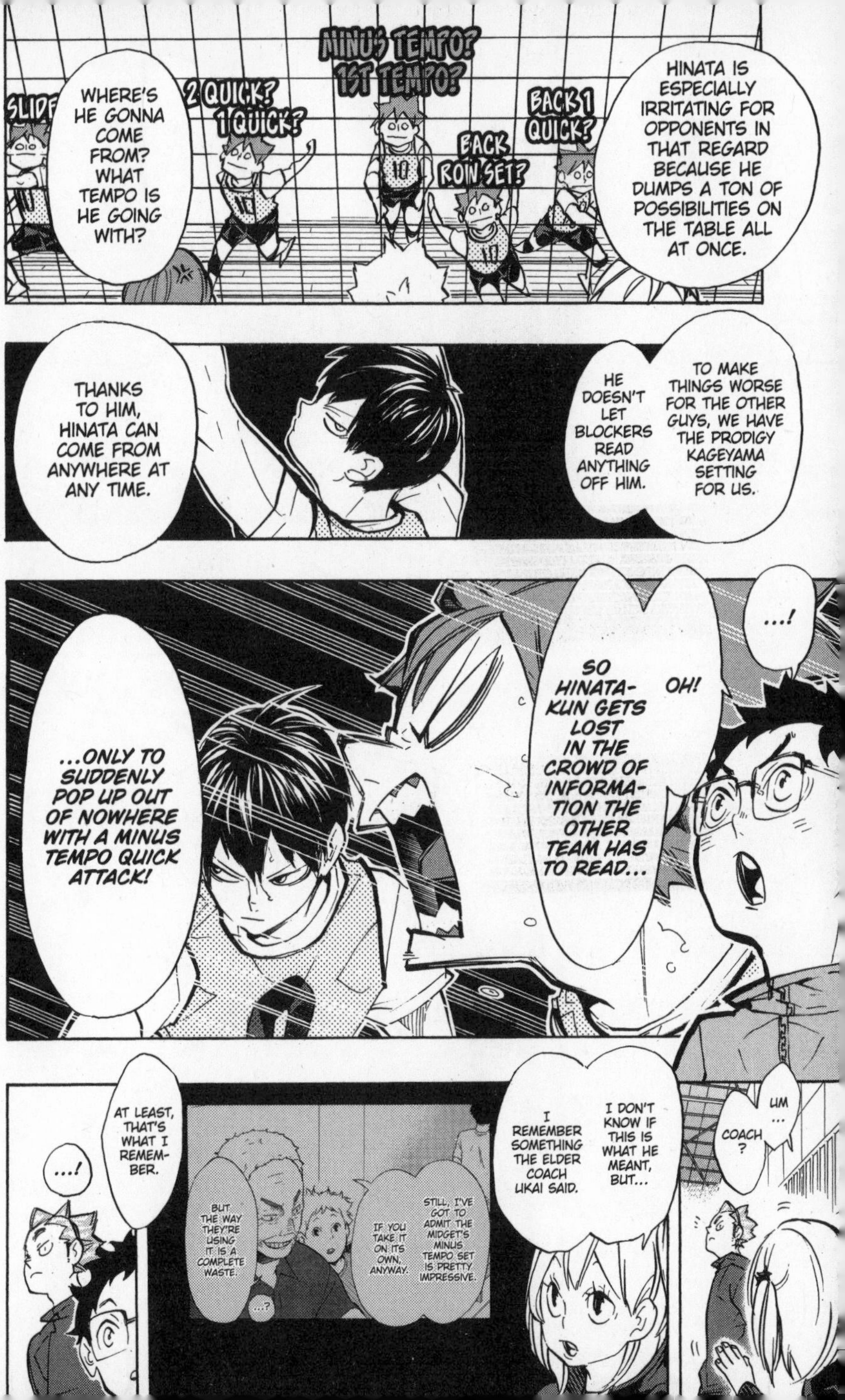
HINATA IS ESPECIALLY IRRITATING FOR OPPONENTS IN THAT REGARD BECAUSE HE DUMPS A TON OF POSSIBILITIES ON THE TABLE ALL AT ONCE.
MINUS TEMPO? 1ST TEMPO?
BACK 1 QUICK?
BACK ROW SET?
2 QUICK? 1 QUICK?
WHERE'S HE GONNA COME FROM? WHAT TEMPO IS HE GOING WITH?
SLIDE
TO MAKE THINGS WORSE FOR THE OTHER GUYS, WE HAVE THE PRODIGY KAGEYAMA SETTING FOR US.
HE DOESN'T LET BLOCKERS READ ANYTHING OFF HIM.
THANKS TO HIM, HINATA CAN COME FROM ANYWHERE AT ANY TIME.
...!
OH!
SO HINATA-KUN GETS LOST IN THE CROWD OF INFORMATION THE OTHER TEAM HAS TO READ...
...ONLY TO SUDDENLY POP UP OUT OF NOWHERE WITH A MINUS TEMPO QUICK ATTACK!
UM ... COACH ?
I DON'T KNOW IF THIS IS WHAT HE MEANT, BUT...
I REMEMBER SOMETHING THE ELDER COACH UKAI SAID.
STILL, I'VE GOT TO ADMIT THE MIDGET'S MINUS TEMPO SET IS PRETTY IMPRESSIVE.
IF YOU TAKE IT ON ITS OWN, ANYWAY.
BUT THE WAY THEY'RE USING IT IS A COMPLETE WASTE.
...?
AT LEAST, THAT'S WHAT I REMEMBER.
...!

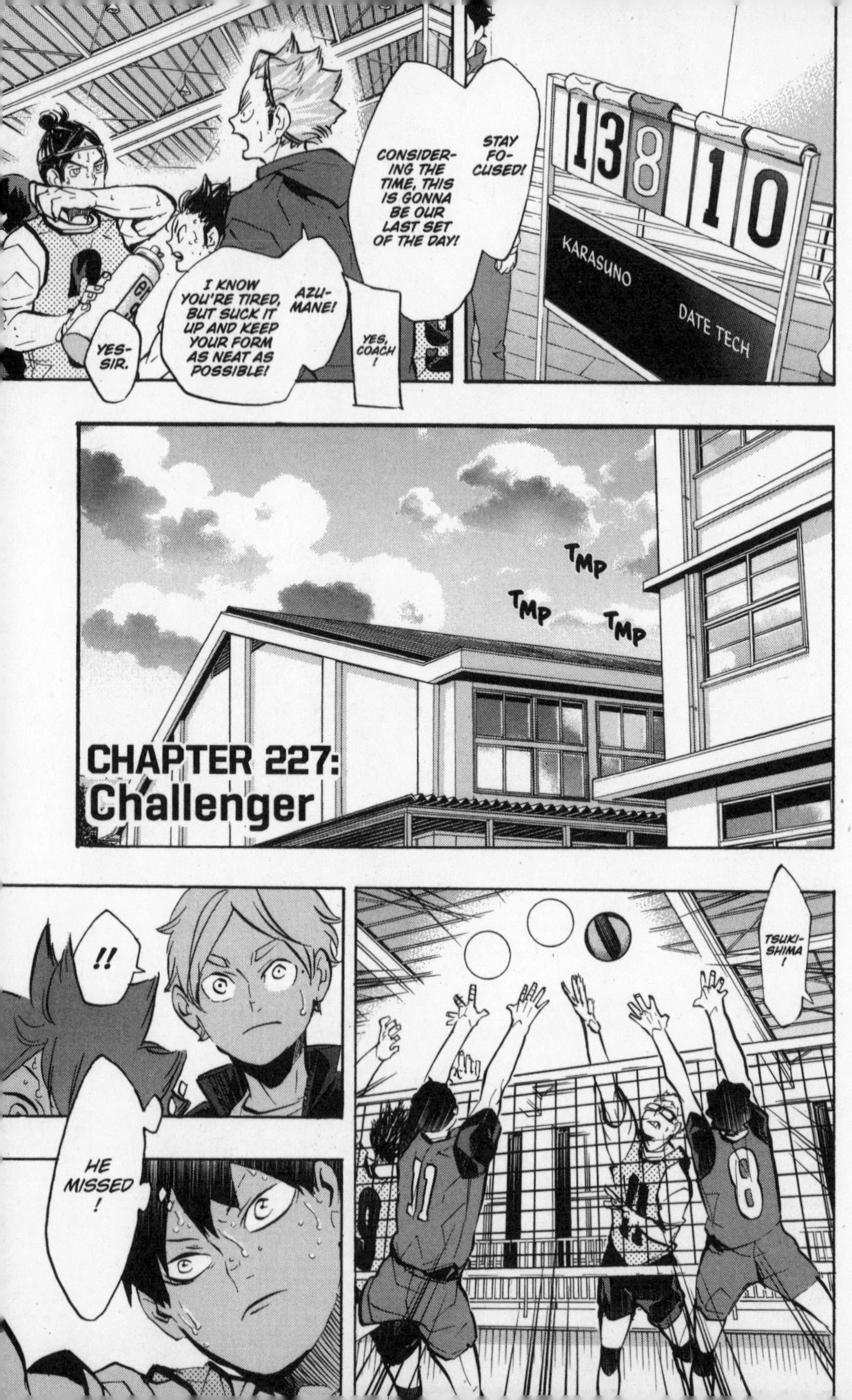
13 8 10
KARASUNO
DATE TECH
STAY FOCUSED!
CONSIDERING THE TIME, THIS IS GONNA BE OUR LAST SET OF THE DAY!
AZUMANE!
I KNOW YOU'RE TIRED, BUT SUCK IT UP AND KEEP YOUR FORM AS NEAT AS POSSIBLE!
YES, COACH!
YES-SIR.
TMP
TMP
TMP
CHAPTER 227: Challenger
TSUKISHIMA!
!!
HE MISSED!

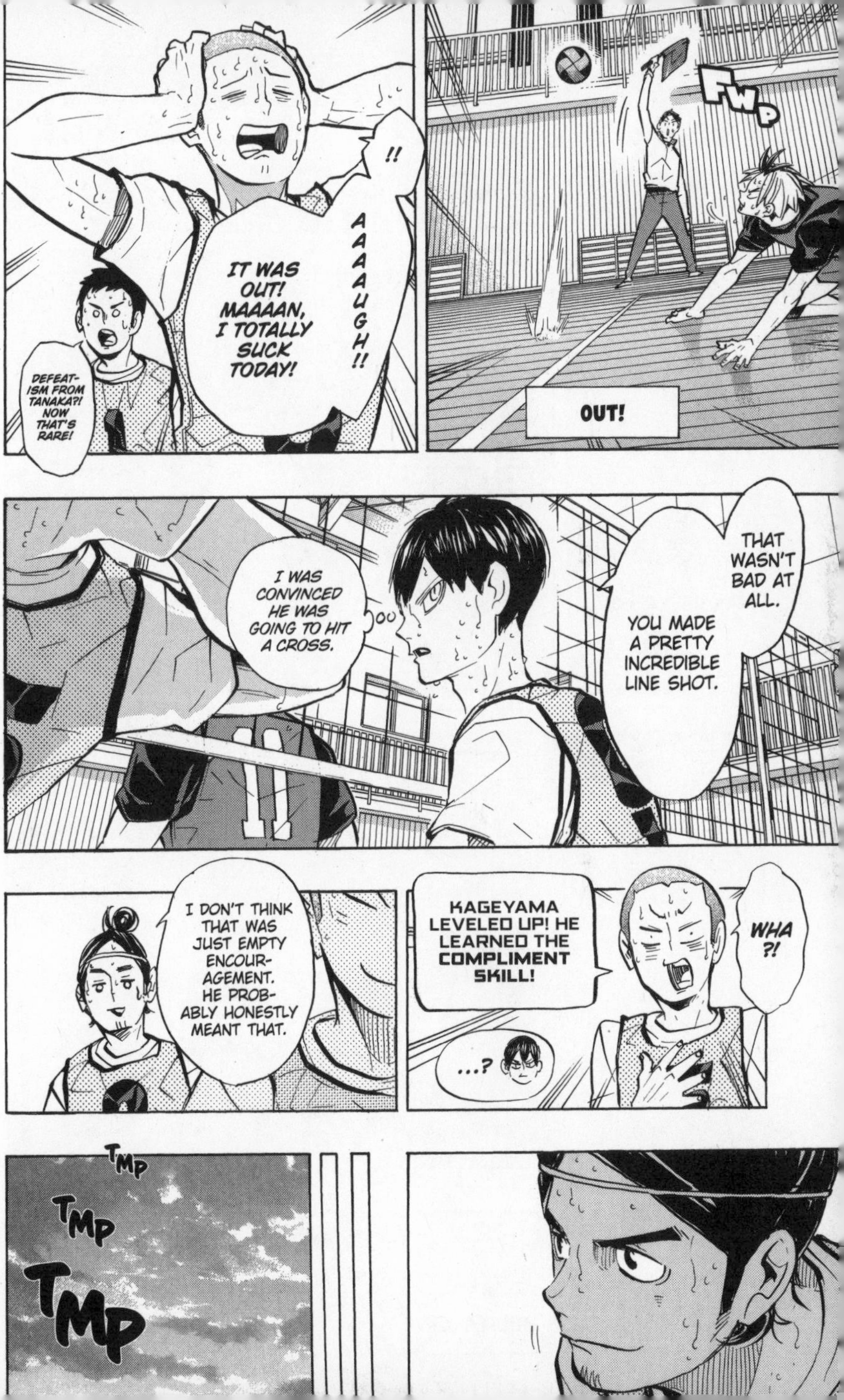
FWP
OUT!
!!
AAAAAUGH!!
IT WAS OUT! MAAAAN, I TOTALLY SUCK TODAY!
DEFEAT-ISM FROM TANAKA?! NOW THAT'S RARE!
THAT WASN'T BAD AT ALL.
YOU MADE A PRETTY INCREDIBLE LINE SHOT.
I WAS CONVINCED HE WAS GOING TO HIT A CROSS.
WHA ?!
KAGEYAMA LEVELED UP! HE LEARNED THE COMPLIMENT SKILL!
...?
I DON'T THINK THAT WAS JUST EMPTY ENCOUR-AGEMENT. HE PROBABLY HONESTLY MEANT THAT.
TMP
TMP
TMP

FUTAKUCHI SERVE

GAAAAAAH!

!!

PLAF

...

OH, DON'T WORRY. WE'VE GOT AAALL DAAAY TO HANG OUT!

WHY DON'T YOU JUST, Y'KNOW, LEAVE?

STILL GOT A LONG WAY TO GO, FUTAKUCHI!

BWAH HA HA!

1 8 8 16

KARASUNO   DAT

OKAY.

SERVE

HINATA (NOYA)   TANAKA   KAGEYAMA

SAWAMURA   AZUMANE   TSUKISHIMA

NET

OBARA   KOGANEGAWA   AONE

FUKIAGE (SAKUNAMI)   ONAGAWA   FUTAKUCHI

HINATA SERVE

*CURRENT ROTATION

IT FEELS GOOD TO KNOW THERE ARE GUYS ON THE SIDELINES READY TO STEP OUT AND PLAY.

BUT...

GEEZ, YAMAGUCHI SURE HAS GROWN SOME GUTS.

Is it my turn yet? Is it? Is it? My turn? Now? Please? Is it my turn?

KINOSHITA!

KINOSHITA IN HINATA OUT

WSH

SHFL

TMP

TA

FWE EEEE

OUT!!

TUMP BOOM

KINOSHITA SERVE (2)

HINATA (NOYA) IN
KINOSHITA OUT

YES, COACH...

QUIT FLINCHING LIKE A SCAREDY-CAT EVERY TIME I CALL ON YOU.

YOU DO REALLY GOOD OUT THERE.

19 8 17

KARASUNO

DATE TECH

Y-YES-SIR...

URK!

TRY TO HIDE FROM ME AGAIN AND I'LL HAVE YOU SIT AT MY ELBOW ALL GAME.

TMP
TMP
Ta
TMP

56

MINUS TEMPO!!

BA

WHAP

THIS TIME NO. 10 DASHED OUT!

OR NOT?!

I'M GONNA STOP YOU!

OH NO, YOU DON'T!

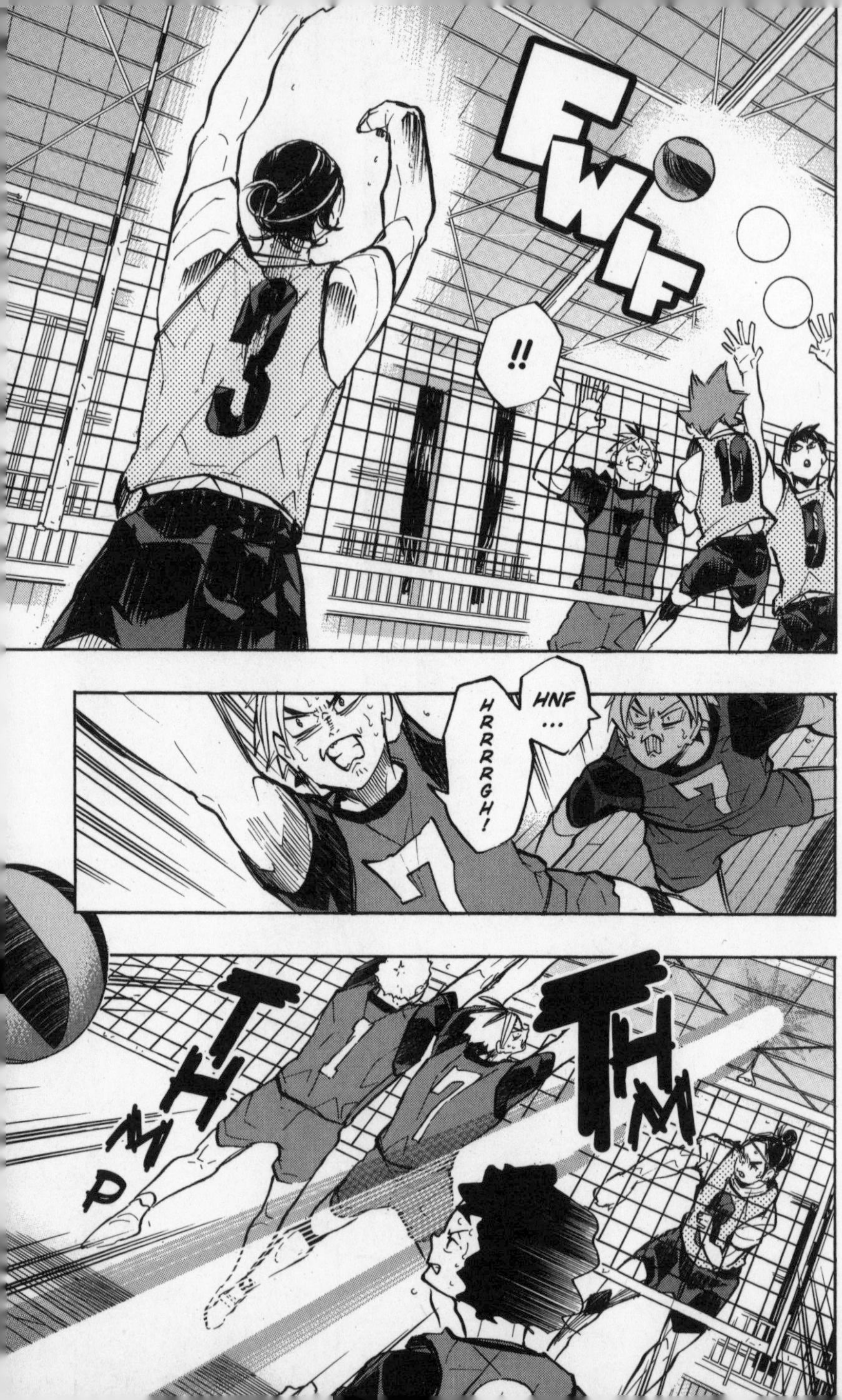
FWIF
!!
HNF...
HRRRRGH!
THM
THMP

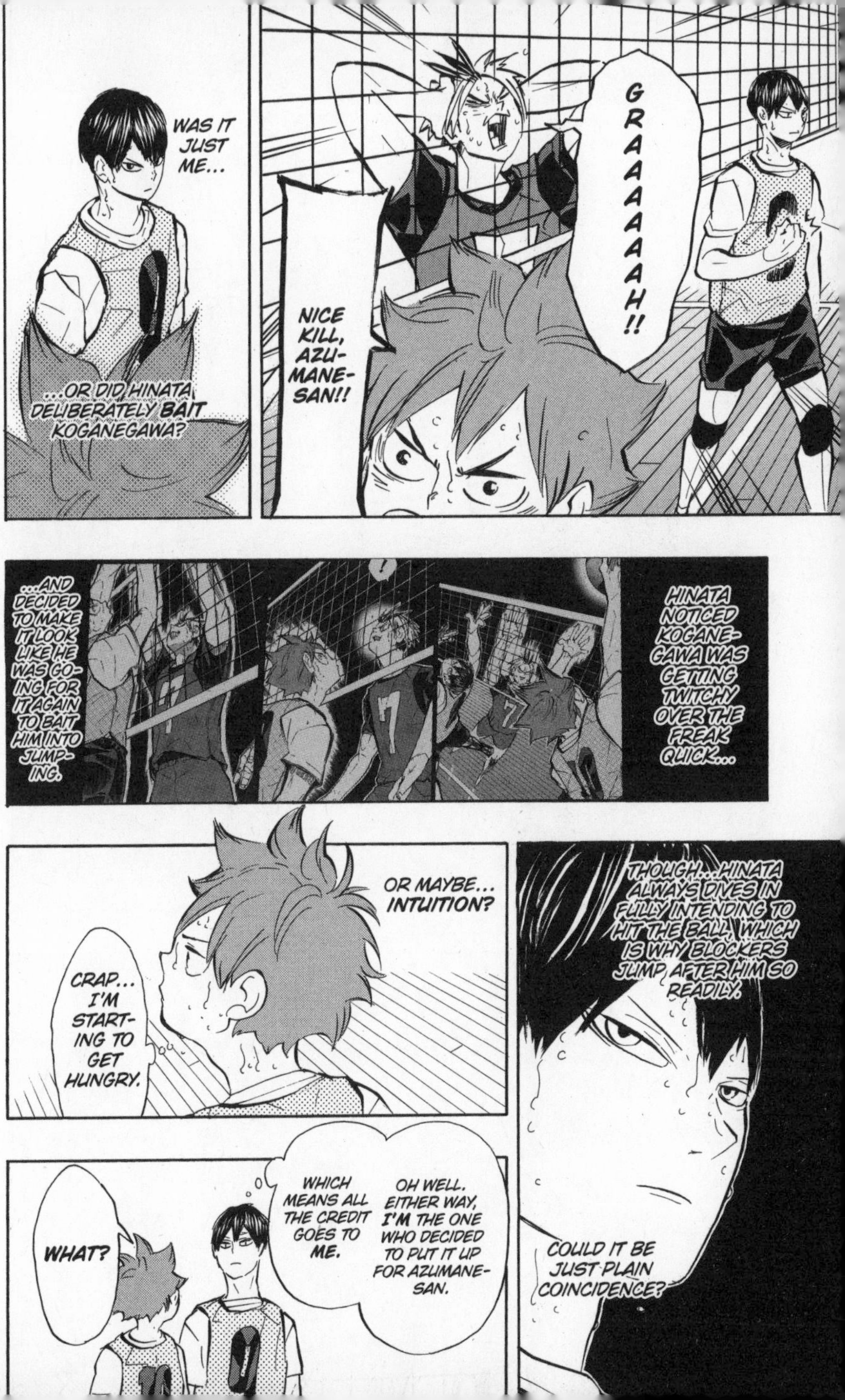
GRAAAAAAAH!!
NICE KILL, AZUMANE-SAN!!
WAS IT JUST ME...
...OR DID HINATA DELIBERATELY BAIT KOGANEGAWA?
HINATA NOTICED KOGANEGAWA WAS GETTING TWITCHY OVER THE FREAK QUICK...
...AND DECIDED TO MAKE IT LOOK LIKE HE WAS GOING FOR IT AGAIN TO BAIT HIM INTO JUMPING.
THOUGH... HINATA ALWAYS DIVES IN FULLY INTENDING TO HIT THE BALL, WHICH IS WHY BLOCKERS JUMP AFTER HIM SO READILY.
COULD IT BE JUST PLAIN COINCIDENCE?
OR MAYBE... INTUITION?
CRAP... I'M STARTING TO GET HUNGRY.
OH WELL. EITHER WAY, I'M THE ONE WHO DECIDED TO PUT IT UP FOR AZUMANE-SAN.
WHICH MEANS ALL THE CREDIT GOES TO ME.
WHAT?

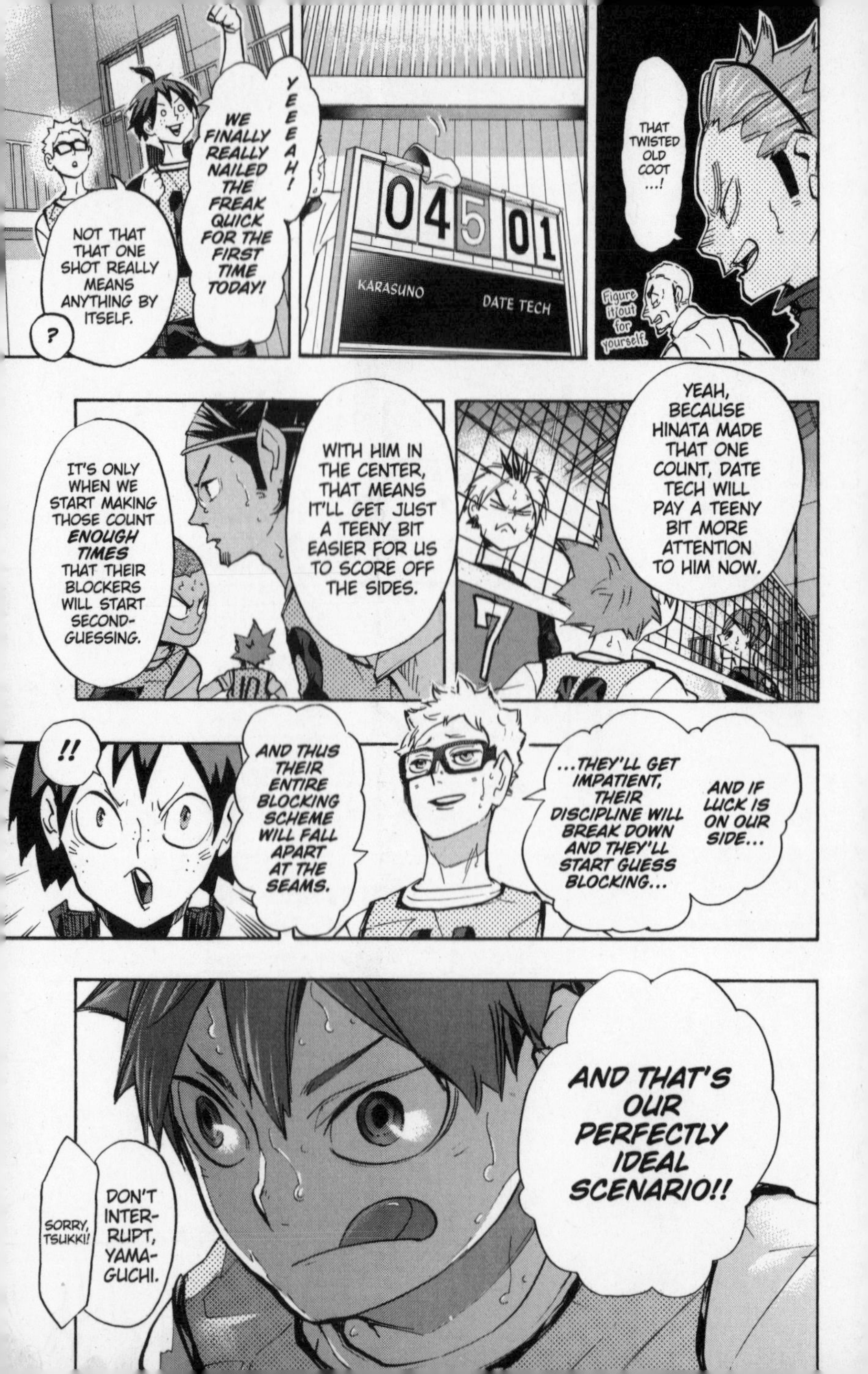
THAT TWISTED OLD COOT ...!
Figure it out for yourself.
04
5
01
KARASUNO
DATE TECH
YEEEAH!
WE FINALLY REALLY NAILED THE FREAK QUICK FOR THE FIRST TIME TODAY!
NOT THAT THAT ONE SHOT REALLY MEANS ANYTHING BY ITSELF.
?
YEAH, BECAUSE HINATA MADE THAT ONE COUNT, DATE TECH WILL PAY A TEENY BIT MORE ATTENTION TO HIM NOW.
WITH HIM IN THE CENTER, THAT MEANS IT'LL GET JUST A TEENY BIT EASIER FOR US TO SCORE OFF THE SIDES.
IT'S ONLY WHEN WE START MAKING THOSE COUNT ENOUGH TIMES THAT THEIR BLOCKERS WILL START SECOND-GUESSING.
AND IF LUCK IS ON OUR SIDE...
...THEY'LL GET IMPATIENT, THEIR DISCIPLINE WILL BREAK DOWN AND THEY'LL START GUESS BLOCKING...
AND THUS THEIR ENTIRE BLOCKING SCHEME WILL FALL APART AT THE SEAMS.
!!
AND THAT'S OUR PERFECTLY IDEAL SCENARIO!!
DON'T INTERRUPT, YAMAGUCHI.
SORRY, TSUKKI!

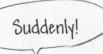

Suddenly!

TOP 3 PLAYERS WITH SMALL APPETITES!	
#1	KENMA KOZUME (NEKOMA)
#2	SATORI TENDO (SHIRATORIZAWA)
#3	KEI TSUKISHIMA (KARASUNO)

I DON'T EAT LIKE A BIRD. I HAVE AN *AVERAGE* APPETITE.
IT'S ALL THE REST OF YOU WHO EAT TOO MUCH.
THE SECOND THEY STOP PLAYING VOLLEYBALL, THEY'RE ALL GONNA GET FAT.
AGREED...
NEK

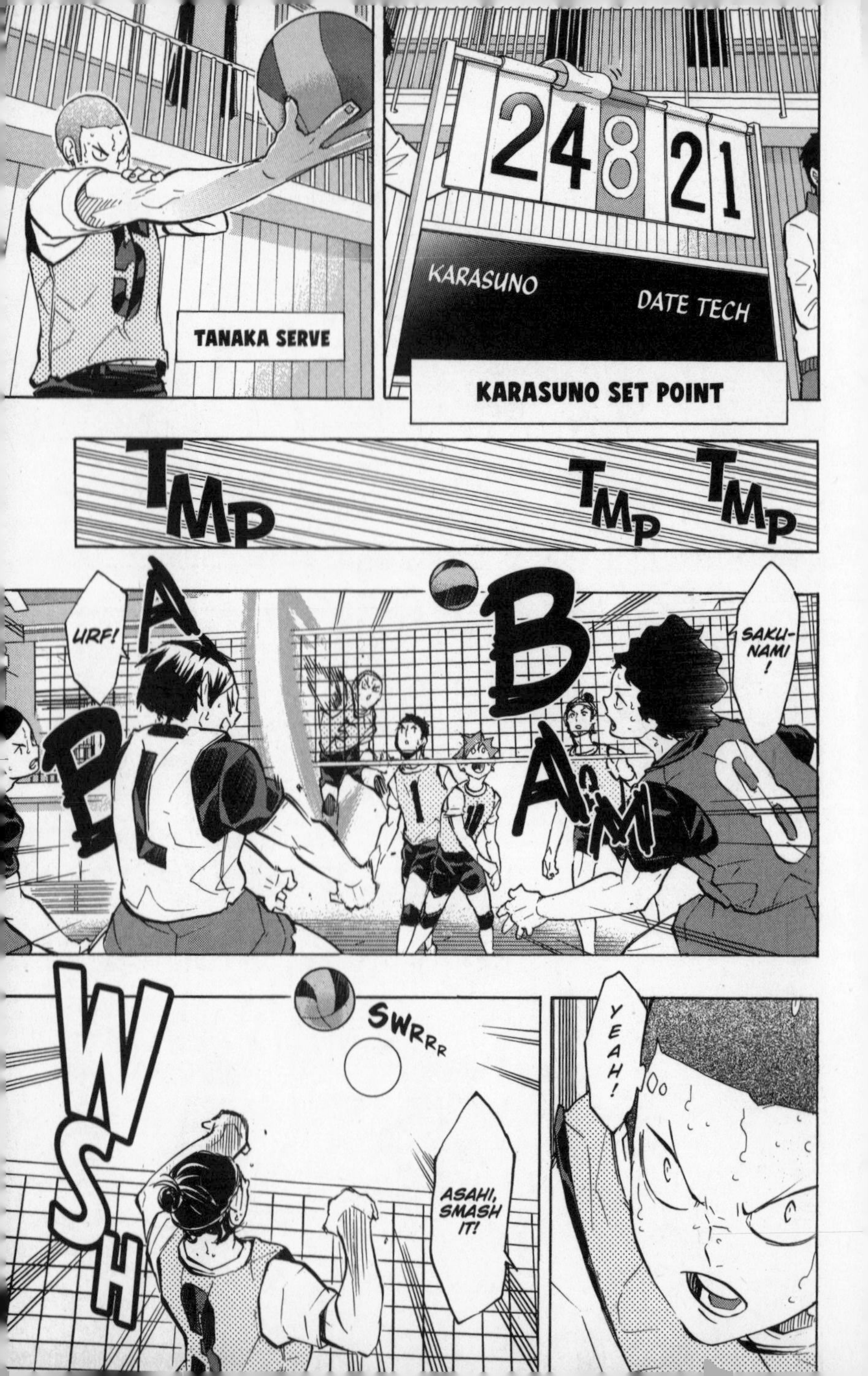

24 8 21
KARASUNO
DATE TECH
KARASUNO SET POINT
TANAKA SERVE
TMP TMP TMP
SAKU-NAMI!
BAM
URF!
YEAH!
ASAHI, SMASH IT!
SWRRR
WSH

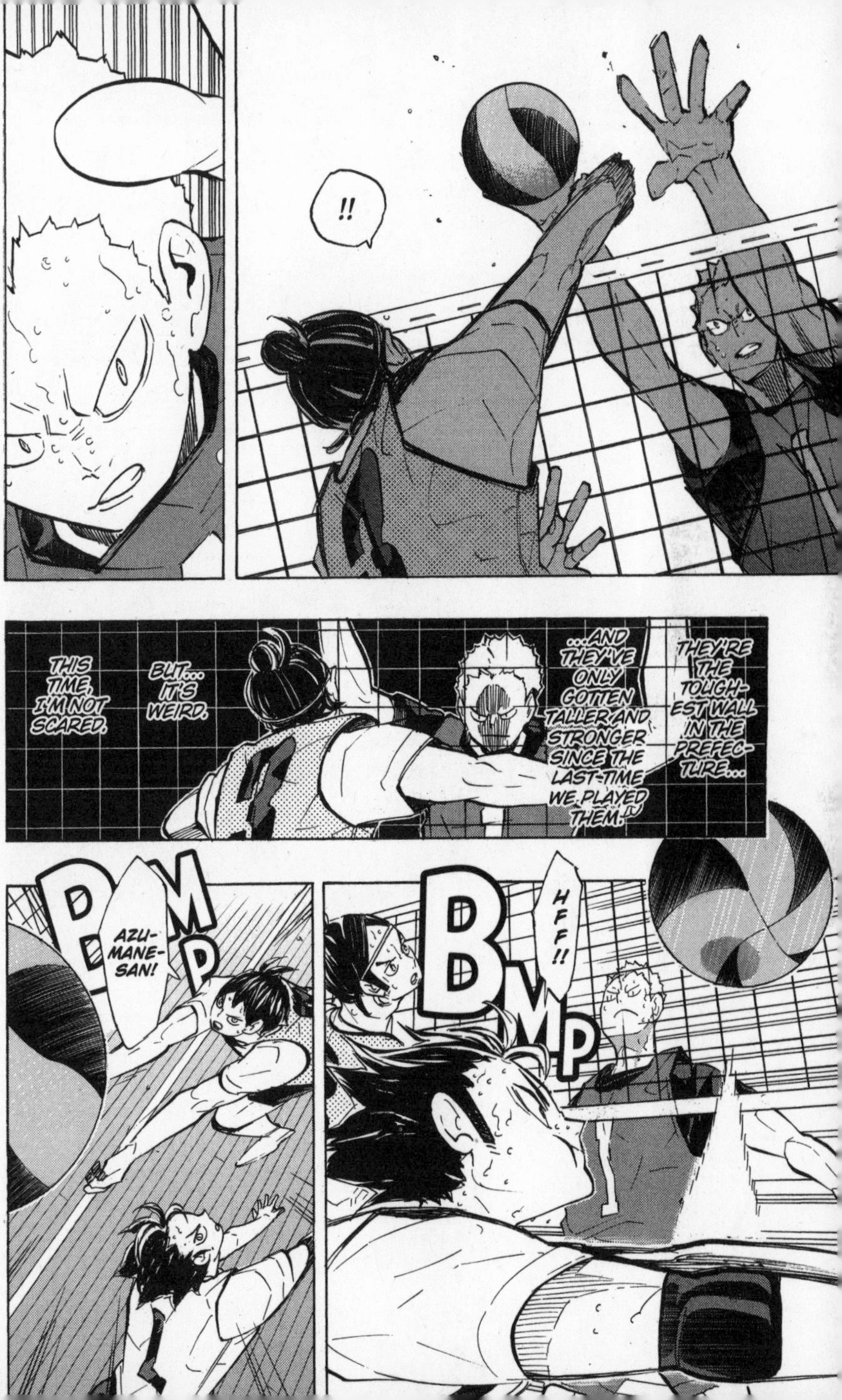
!!
THEY'RE THE TOUGH-EST WALL IN THE PREFEC-TURE...
...AND THEY'VE ONLY GOTTEN TALLER AND STRONGER SINCE THE LAST TIME WE PLAYED THEM.
BUT... IT'S WEIRD.
THIS TIME, I'M NOT SCARED.
BMP
HFF!!
BMP
AZU-MANE-SAN!

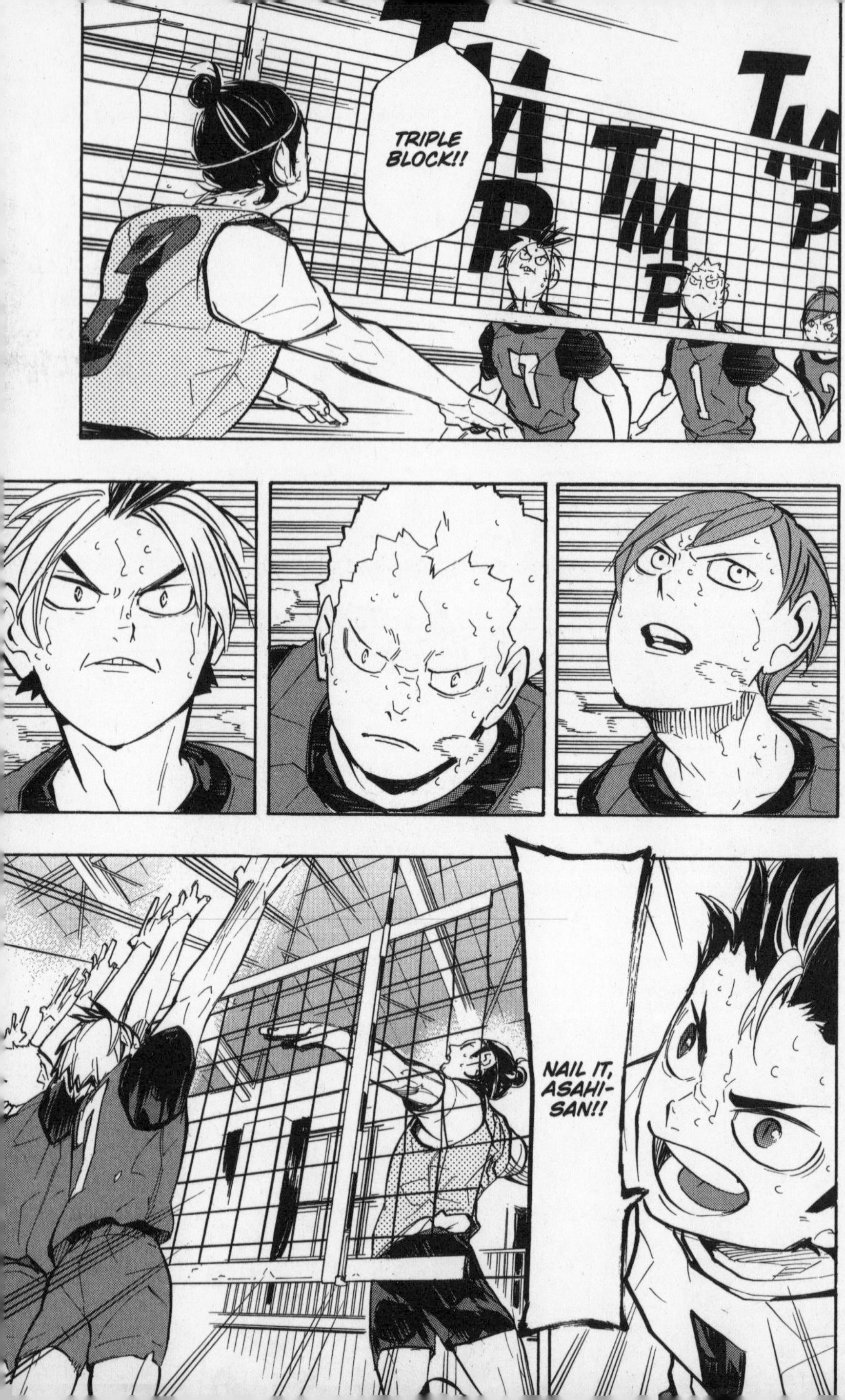
TMP
TMP
TRIPLE BLOCK!!
TMP
NAIL IT, ASAHI-SAN!!

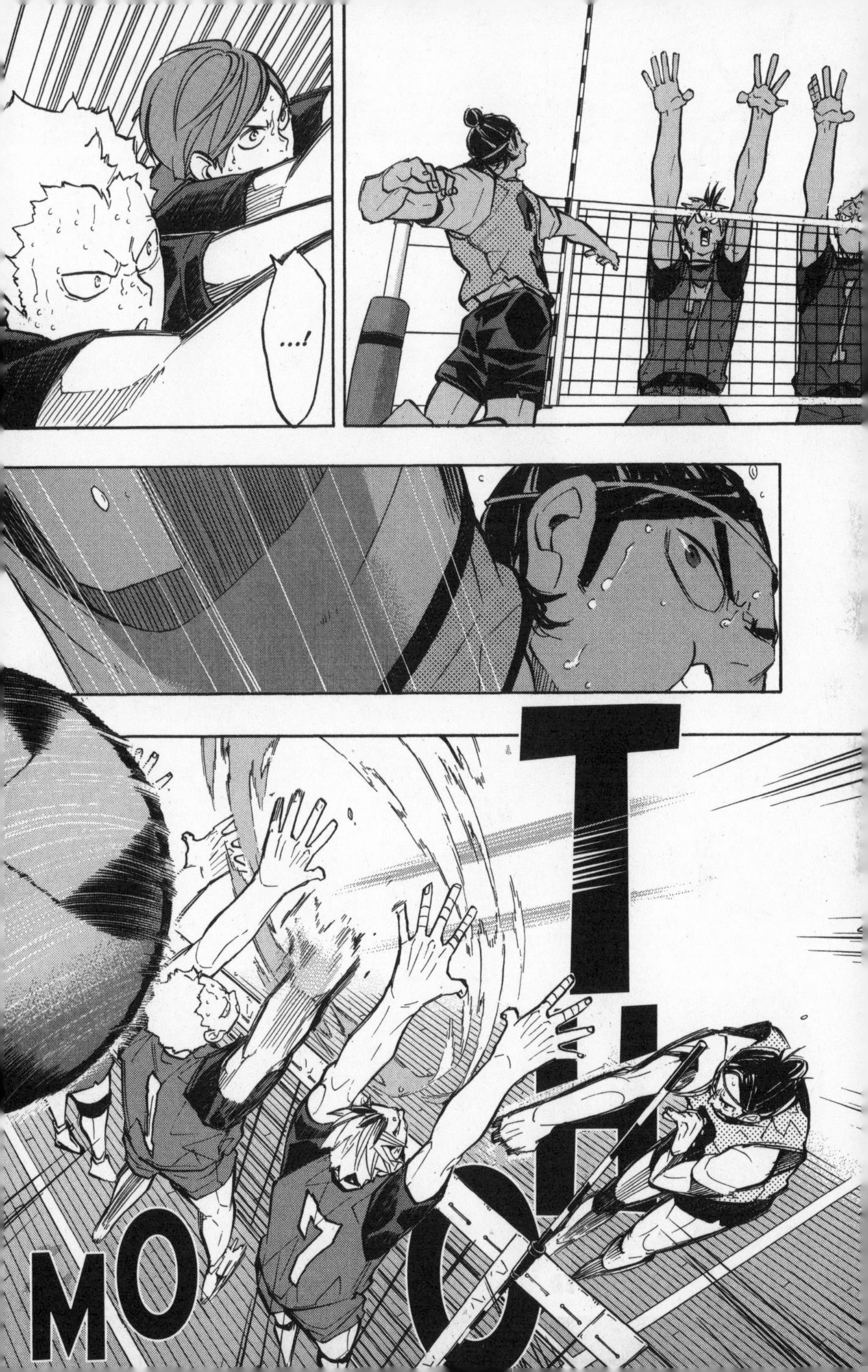
...!
THOOM

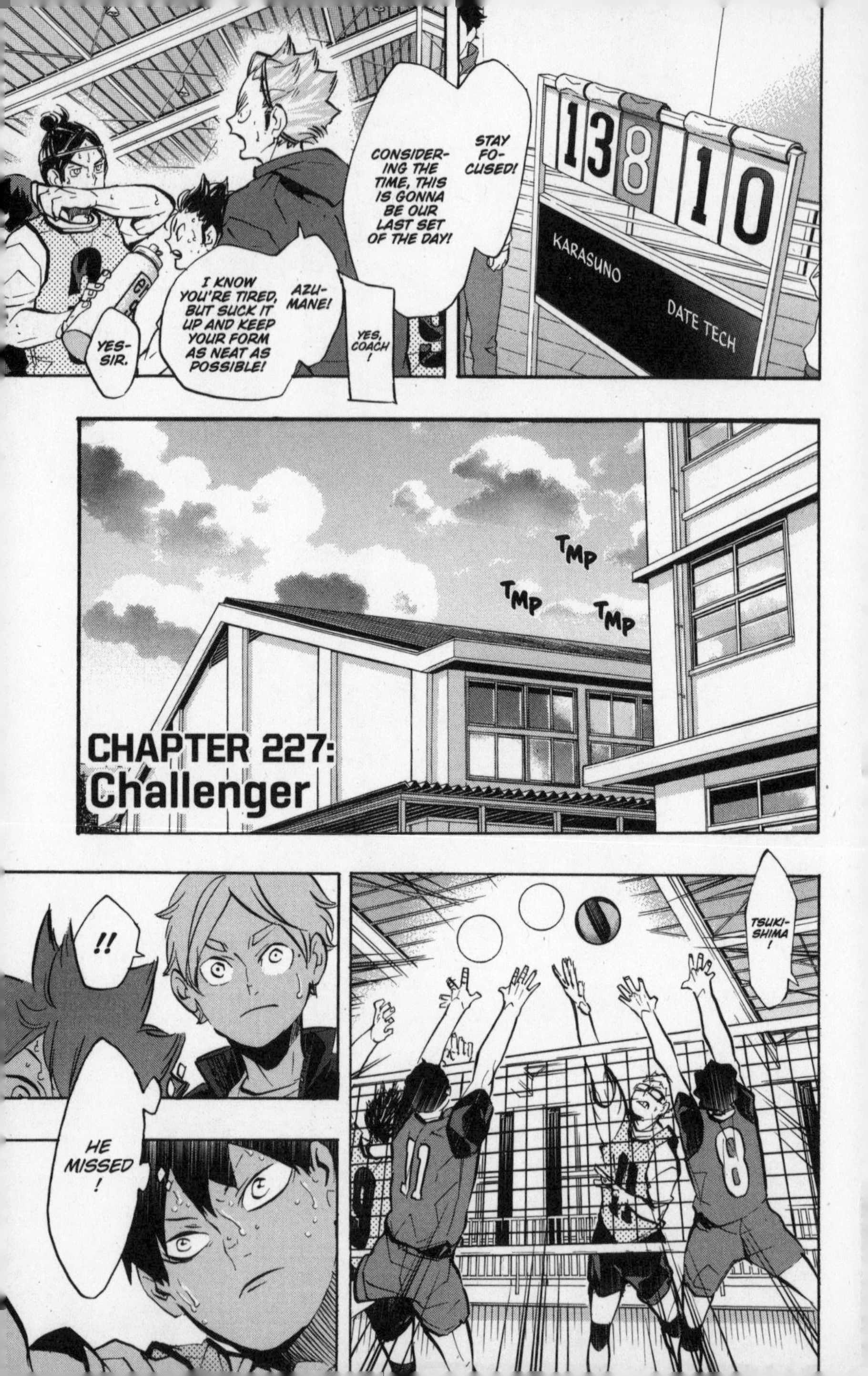
13
8
10
KARASUNO
DATE TECH
STAY FOCUSED!
CONSIDERING THE TIME, THIS IS GONNA BE OUR LAST SET OF THE DAY!
YES, COACH!
AZUMANE!
I KNOW YOU'RE TIRED, BUT SUCK IT UP AND KEEP YOUR FORM AS NEAT AS POSSIBLE!
YES-SIR.
TMP
TMP
TMP
CHAPTER 227:
Challenger
TSUKISHIMA!
!!
HE MISSED!

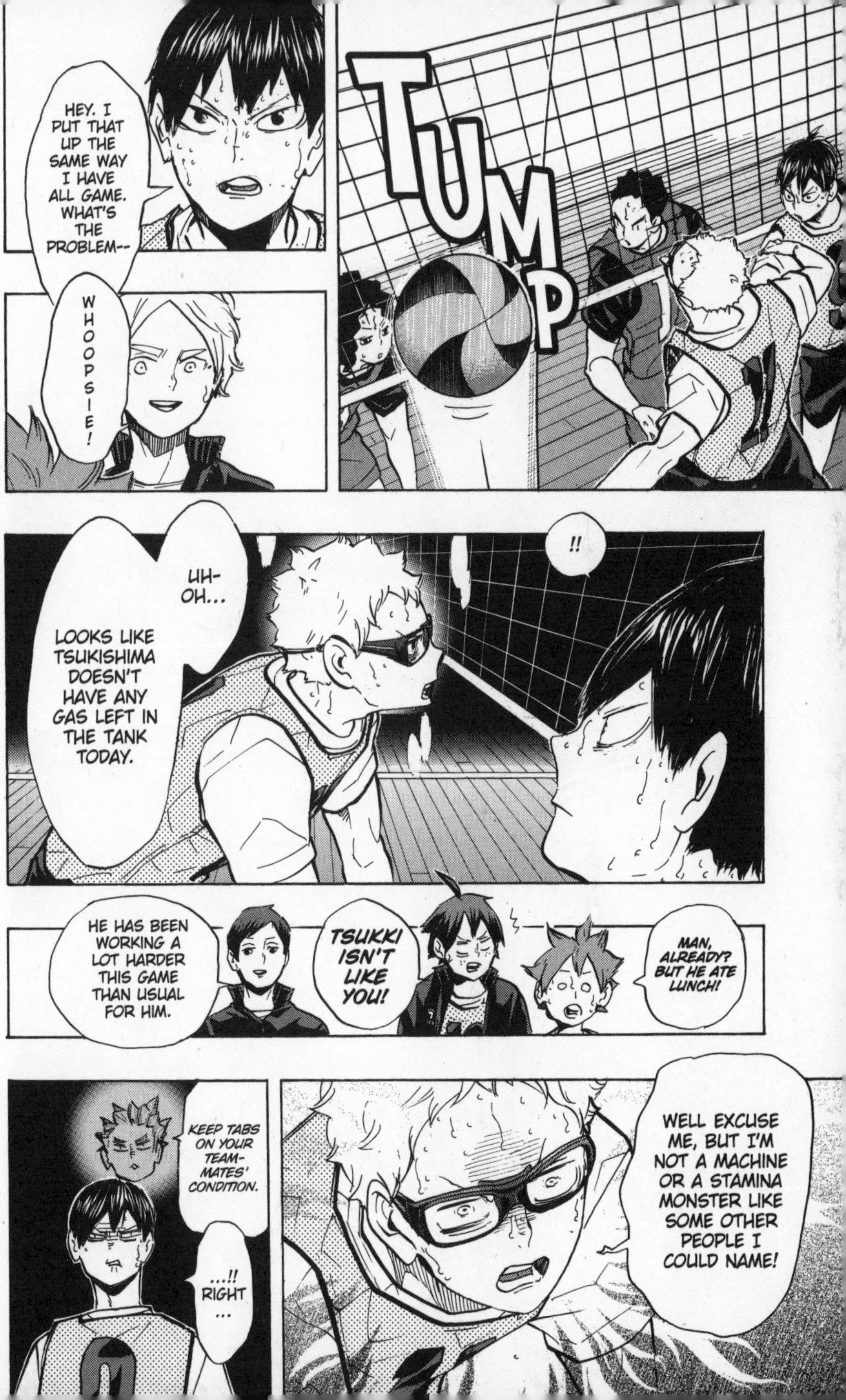
TUMP
HEY. I PUT THAT UP THE SAME WAY I HAVE ALL GAME. WHAT'S THE PROBLEM--
WHOOPSIE!
!!
UH-OH...
LOOKS LIKE TSUKISHIMA DOESN'T HAVE ANY GAS LEFT IN THE TANK TODAY.
MAN, ALREADY? BUT HE ATE LUNCH!
TSUKKI ISN'T LIKE YOU!
HE HAS BEEN WORKING A LOT HARDER THIS GAME THAN USUAL FOR HIM.
WELL EXCUSE ME, BUT I'M NOT A MACHINE OR A STAMINA MONSTER LIKE SOME OTHER PEOPLE I COULD NAME!
KEEP TABS ON YOUR TEAM-MATES' CONDITION.
...!! RIGHT...

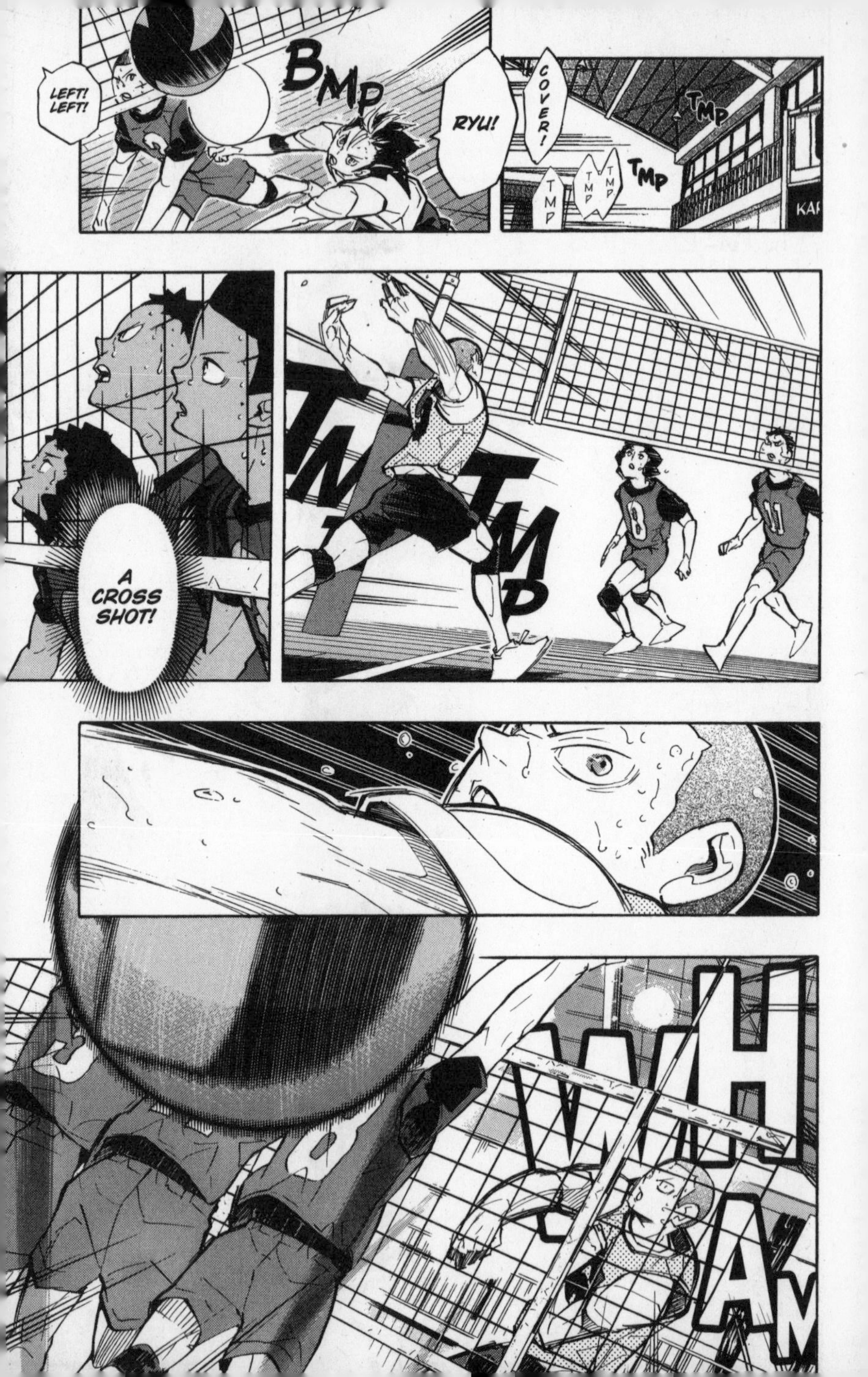
COVER!
TMP
TMP
TMP
TMP
TMP
RYU!
BMP
LEFT! LEFT!
TMP TMP
A CROSS SHOT!
WHAM

IT WAS OUT! MAAAAN, I TOTALLY SUCK TODAY!

AAAAUGH!!

!!

DEFEATISM FROM TANAKA?! NOW THAT'S RARE!

FWP

OUT!

I WAS CONVINCED HE WAS GOING TO HIT A CROSS.

THAT WASN'T BAD AT ALL.

YOU MADE A PRETTY INCREDIBLE LINE SHOT.

I DON'T THINK THAT WAS JUST EMPTY ENCOURAGEMENT. HE PROBABLY HONESTLY MEANT THAT.

KAGEYAMA LEVELED UP! HE LEARNED THE COMPLIMENT SKILL!

WHA?!

...?

TMP

TMP

TMP

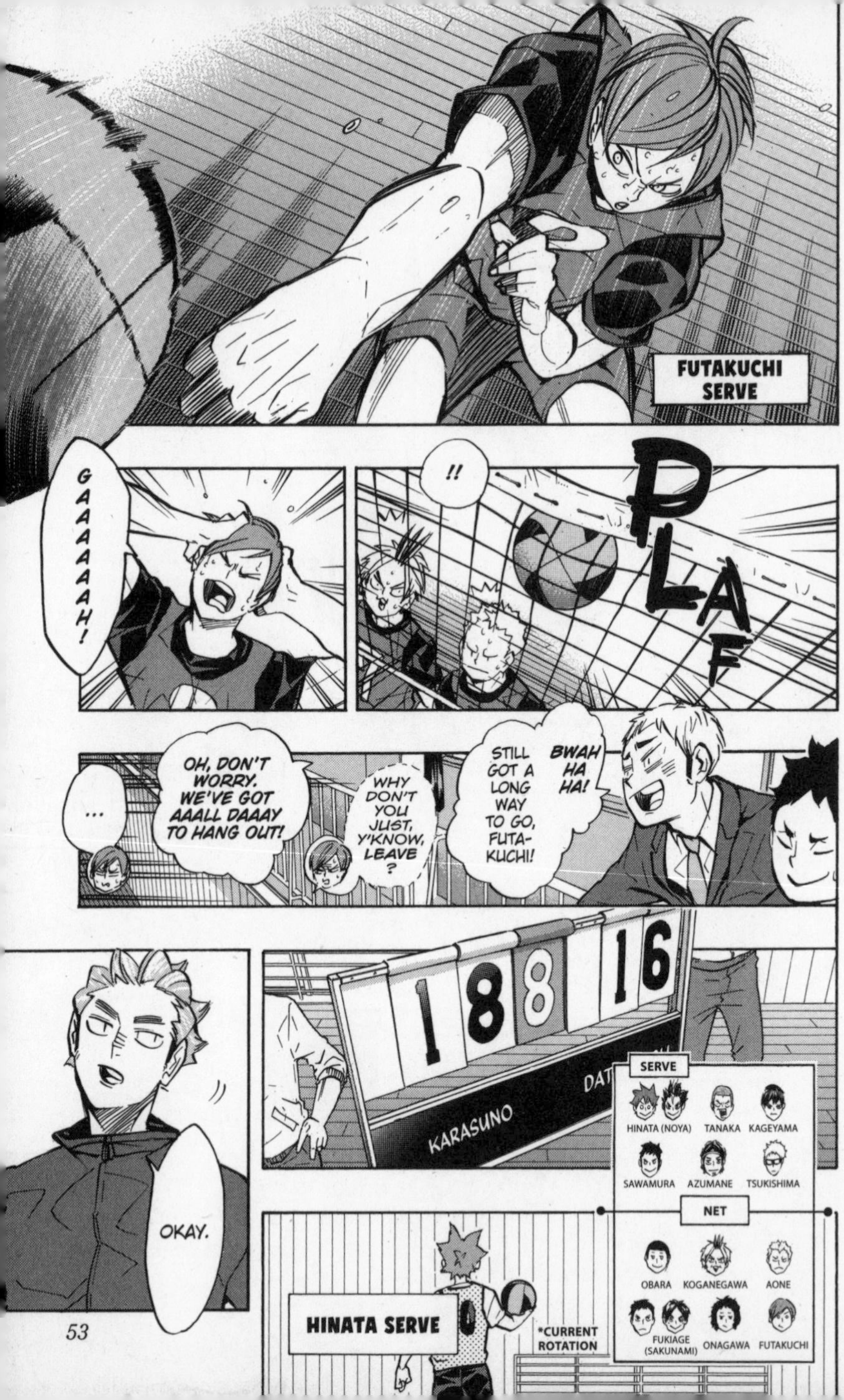
FUTAKUCHI SERVE
!!
PLAF
GAAAAAAAH!
BWAH HA HA!
STILL GOT A LONG WAY TO GO, FUTA-KUCHI!
WHY DON'T YOU JUST, Y'KNOW, LEAVE?
OH, DON'T WORRY. WE'VE GOT AAALL DAAAY TO HANG OUT!
...
18 8 16
KARASUNO
DAT
SERVE
HINATA (NOYA)
TANAKA
KAGEYAMA
SAWAMURA
AZUMANE
TSUKISHIMA
NET
OBARA
KOGANEGAWA
AONE
FUKIAGE (SAKUNAMI)
ONAGAWA
FUTAKUCHI
*CURRENT ROTATION
HINATA SERVE
OKAY.

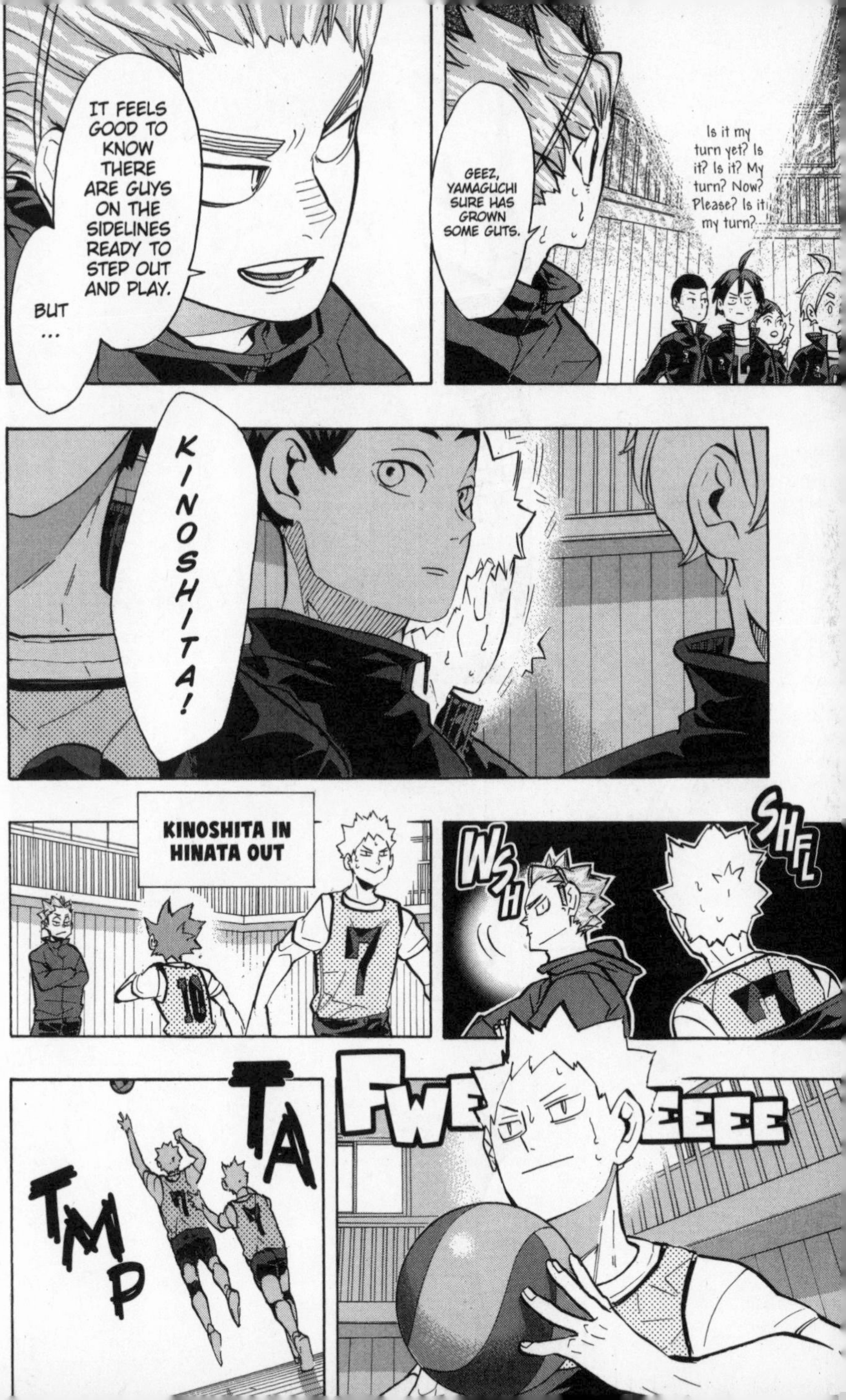

Is it my turn yet? Is it? Is it? My turn? Now? Please? Is it my turn?
GEEZ, YAMAGUCHI SURE HAS GROWN SOME GUTS.
IT FEELS GOOD TO KNOW THERE ARE GUYS ON THE SIDELINES READY TO STEP OUT AND PLAY.
BUT ...
KINOSHITA!
SHFL
WSH
KINOSHITA IN HINATA OUT
FWE EEEE
TA
TMP

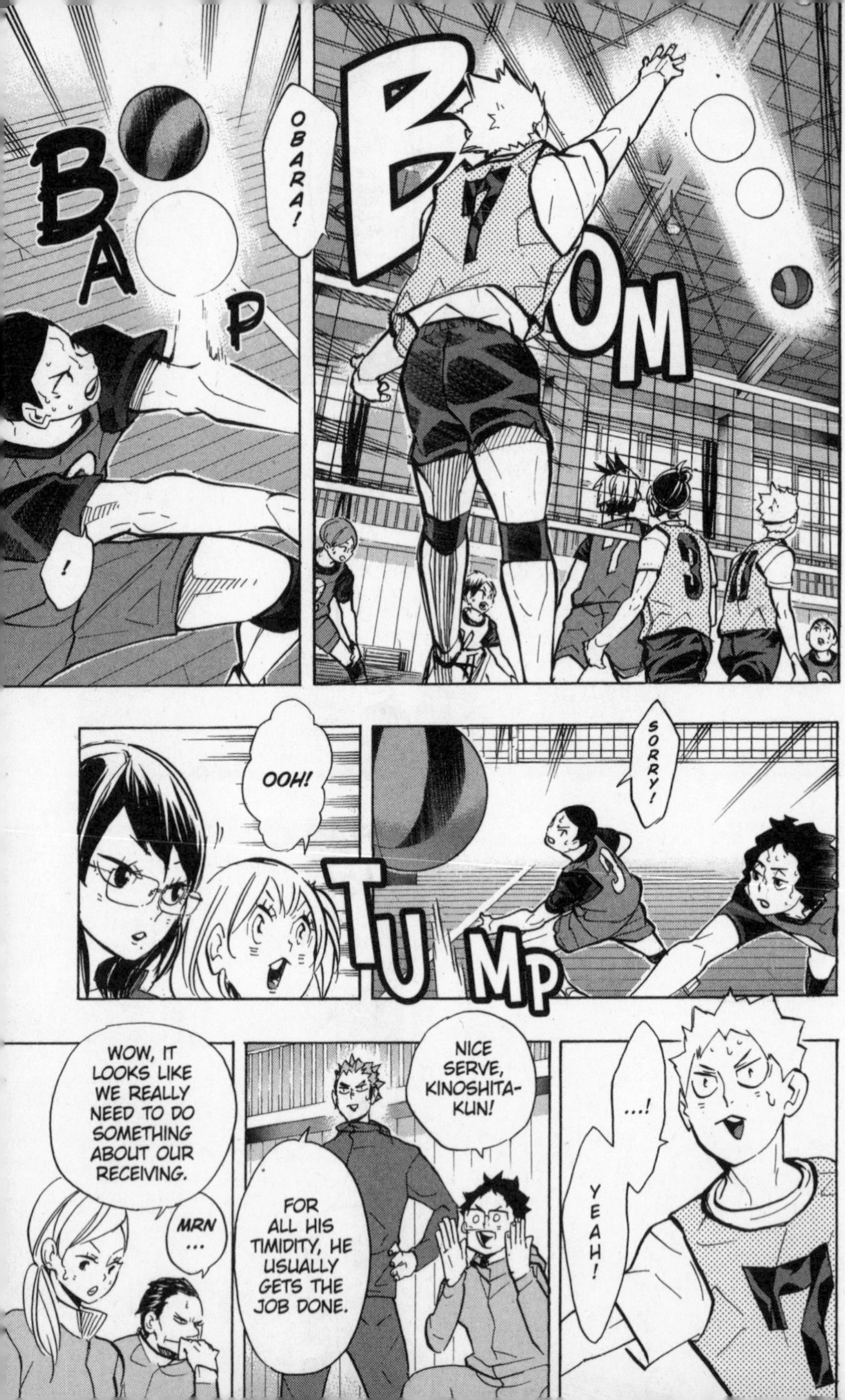
OBARA!
BOOM
BAP
!
SORRY!
TUMP
OOH!
...!
YEAH!
NICE SERVE, KINOSHITA-KUN!
FOR ALL HIS TIMIDITY, HE USUALLY GETS THE JOB DONE.
WOW, IT LOOKS LIKE WE REALLY NEED TO DO SOMETHING ABOUT OUR RECEIVING.
MRN...

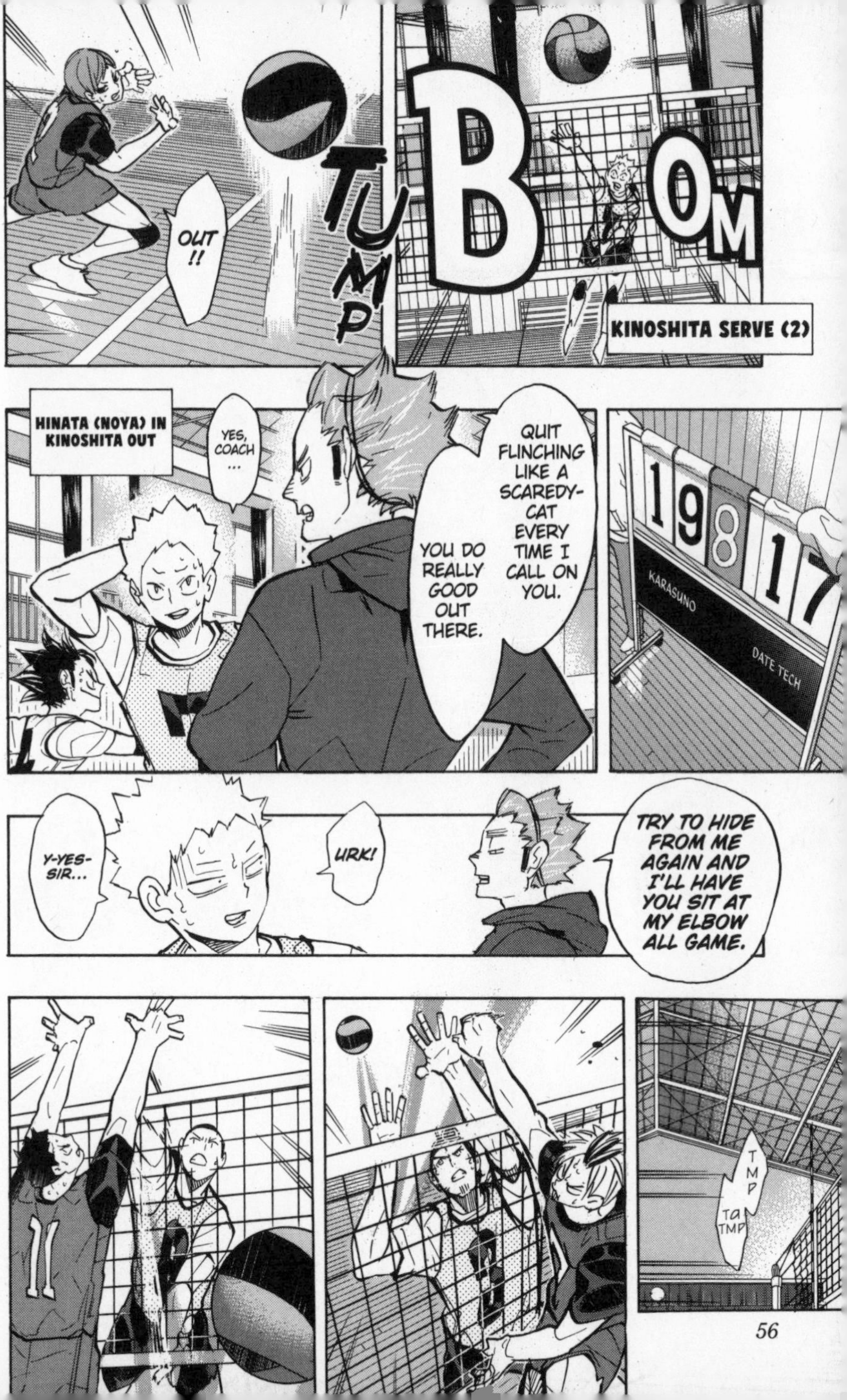
BOOM
KINOSHITA SERVE (2)
TUMP
OUT!!
KARASUNO
19
8
17
DATE TECH
QUIT FLINCHING LIKE A SCAREDY-CAT EVERY TIME I CALL ON YOU.
YOU DO REALLY GOOD OUT THERE.
YES, COACH...
HINATA (NOYA) IN KINOSHITA OUT
TRY TO HIDE FROM ME AGAIN AND I'LL HAVE YOU SIT AT MY ELBOW ALL GAME.
URK!
Y-YES-SIR...
TMP
TA TMP

23 8 21

KARASUNO

DATE

FWEEEEE

ONAGAWA SERVE

KAGEYAMA	NARITA (NOYA)	AZUMANE	
TANAKA	HINATA	SAWAMURA	

NET

KOGANEGAWA	AONE	FUTAKUCHI
OBARA	FUKIAGE (SAKUNAMI)	ONAGAWA

SERVE

*CURRENT ROTATION

BOM

BMP

HNF!

PLAT

!!

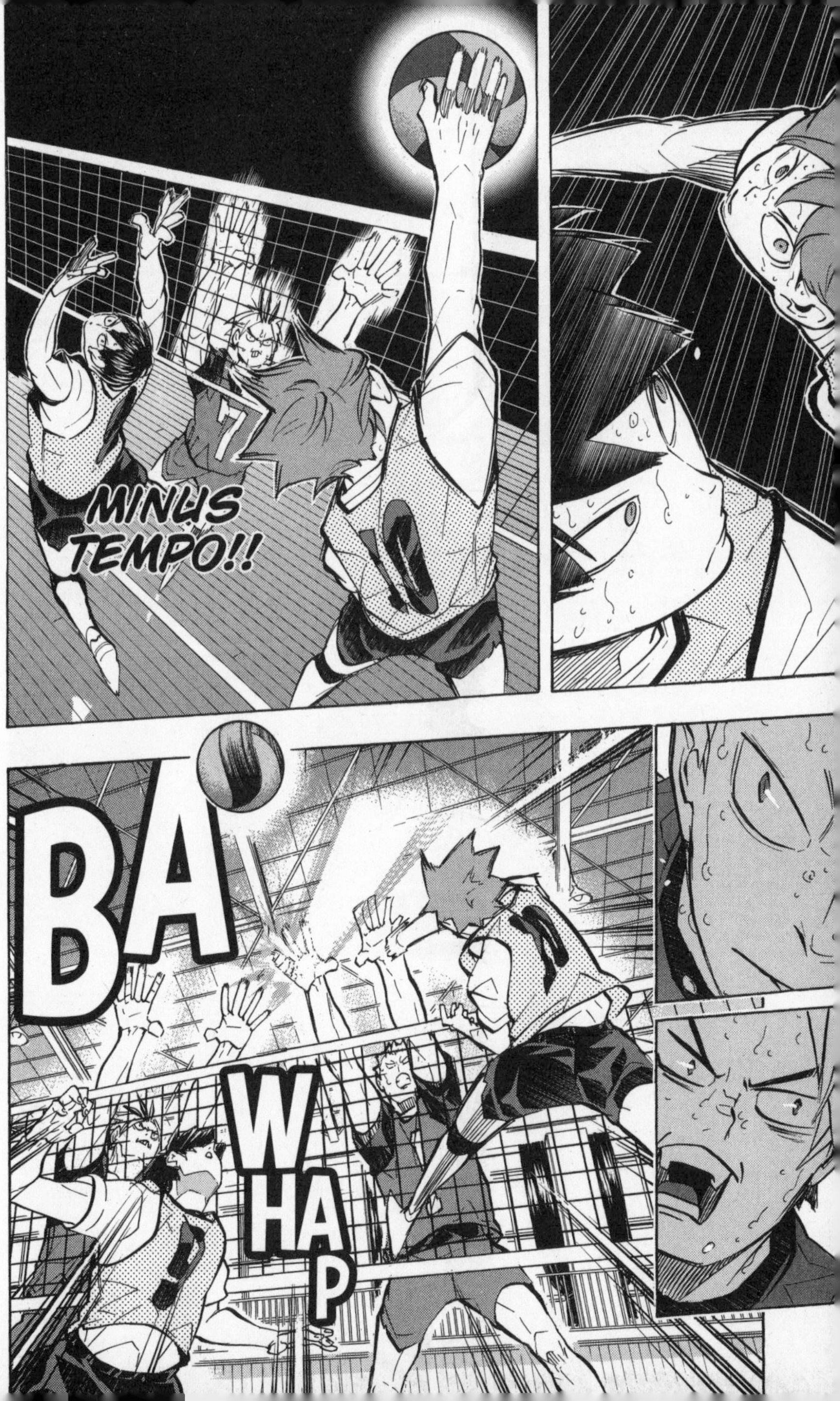
MINUS TEMPO!!
BA
WHAP

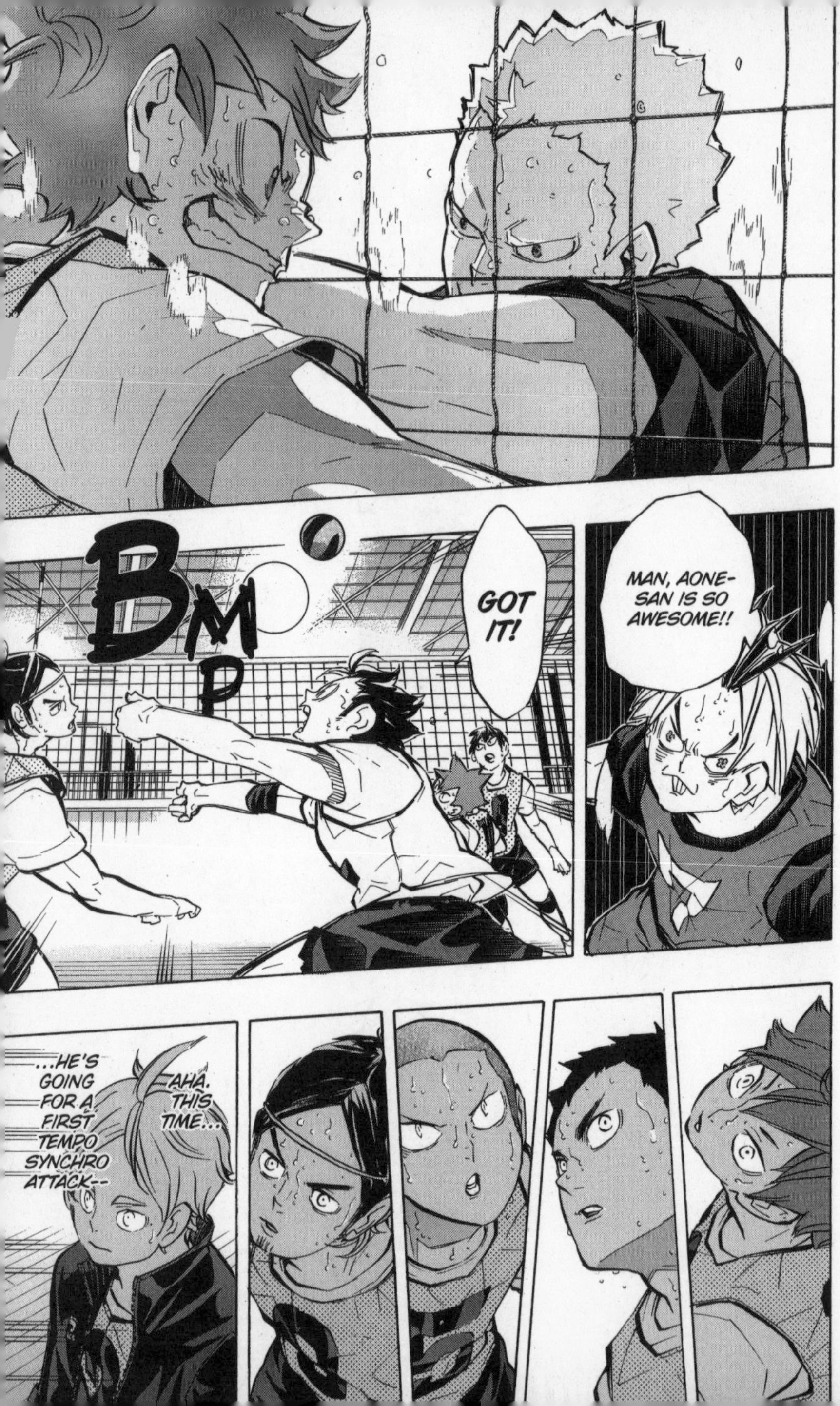
MAN, AONE-SAN IS SO AWESOME!!
GOT IT!
BMP
AHA. THIS TIME...
...HE'S GOING FOR A FIRST TEMPO SYNCHRO ATTACK--

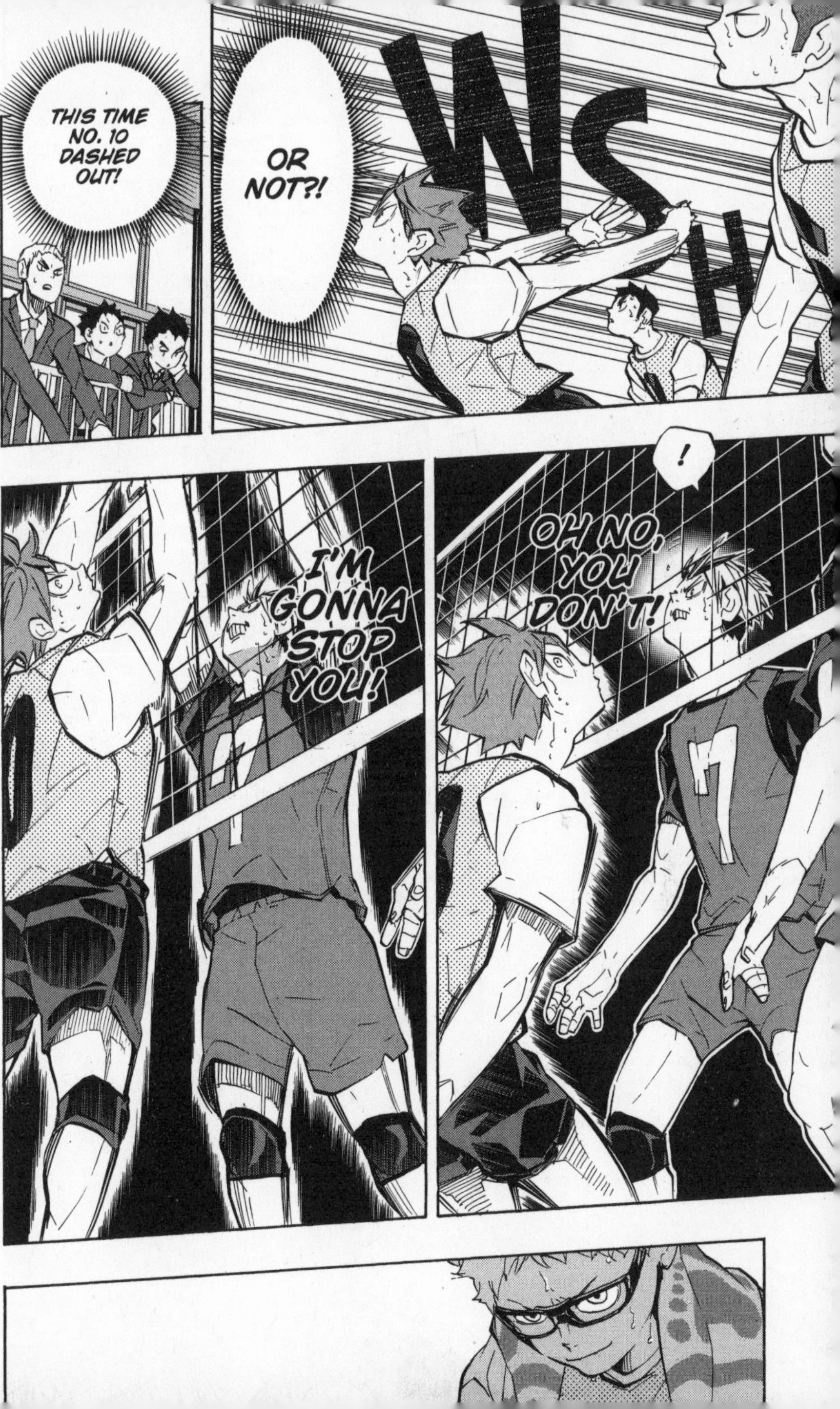
THIS TIME NO. 10 DASHED OUT!
OR NOT?!
WSH
I'M GONNA STOP YOU!
!
OH NO, YOU DON'T!

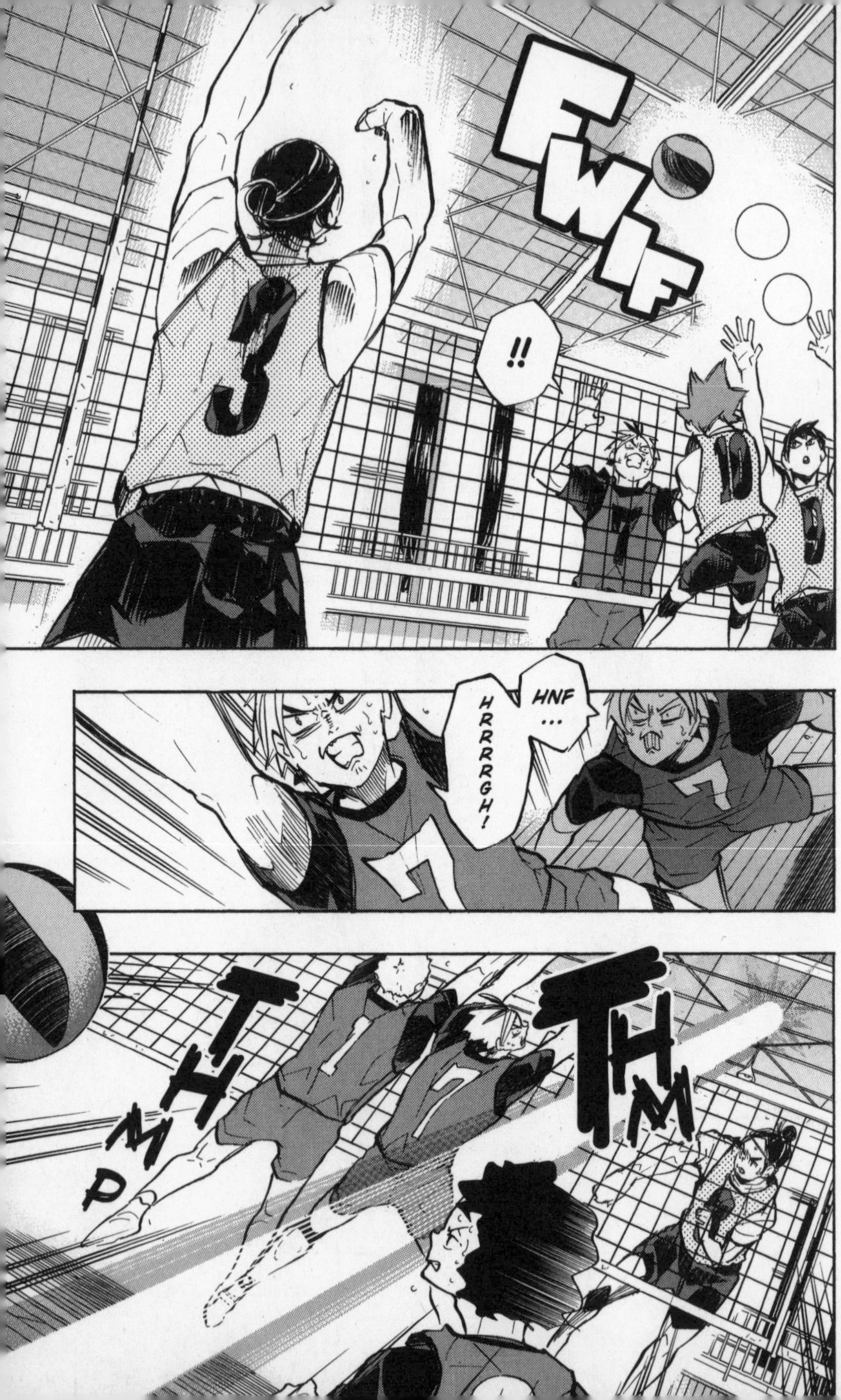
FWIF
!!
HNF...
HRRRRGH!
THM
THMP

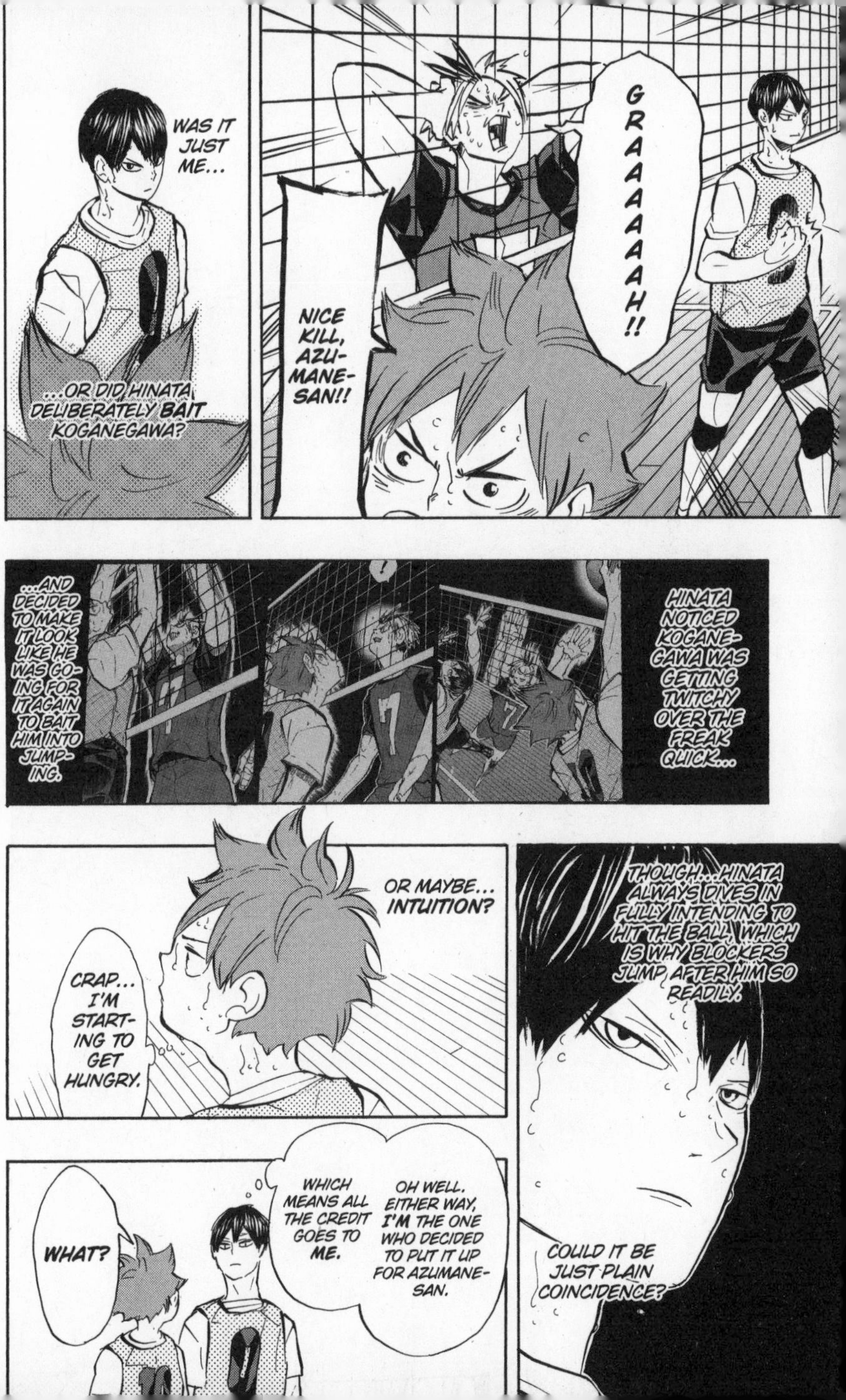
GRAAAAAAAH!!
NICE KILL, AZUMANE-SAN!!
WAS IT JUST ME...
...OR DID HINATA DELIBERATELY BAIT KOGANEGAWA?
HINATA NOTICED KOGANEGAWA WAS GETTING TWITCHY OVER THE FREAK QUICK...
...AND DECIDED TO MAKE IT LOOK LIKE HE WAS GOING FOR IT AGAIN TO BAIT HIM INTO JUMPING.
THOUGH... HINATA ALWAYS DIVES IN FULLY INTENDING TO HIT THE BALL, WHICH IS WHY BLOCKERS JUMP AFTER HIM SO READILY.
COULD IT BE JUST PLAIN COINCIDENCE?
OR MAYBE... INTUITION?
CRAP... I'M STARTING TO GET HUNGRY.
OH WELL. EITHER WAY, I'M THE ONE WHO DECIDED TO PUT IT UP FOR AZUMANE-SAN.
WHICH MEANS ALL THE CREDIT GOES TO ME.
WHAT?

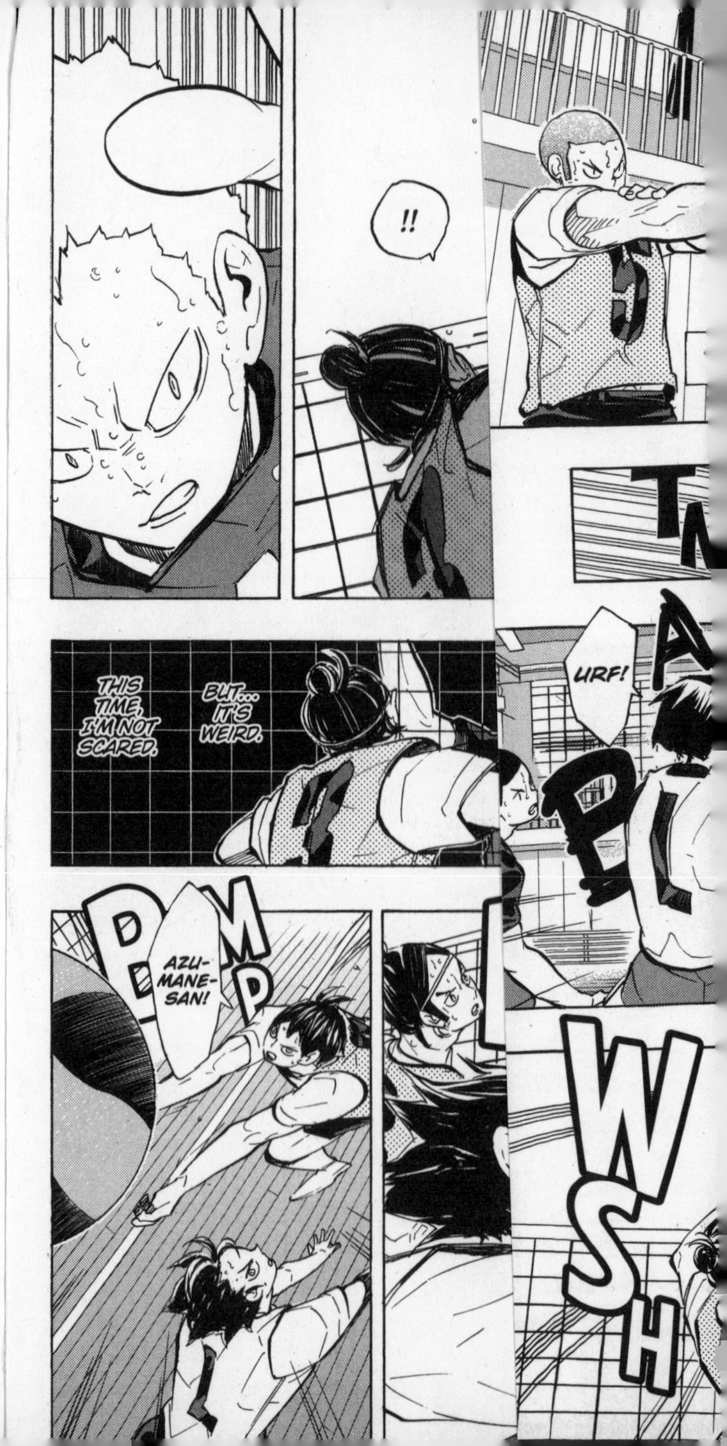

URF!
TMP
WSH
!!
BUT... IT'S WEIRD.
THIS TIME, I'M NOT SCARED.
DMP
AZUMANE-SAN!

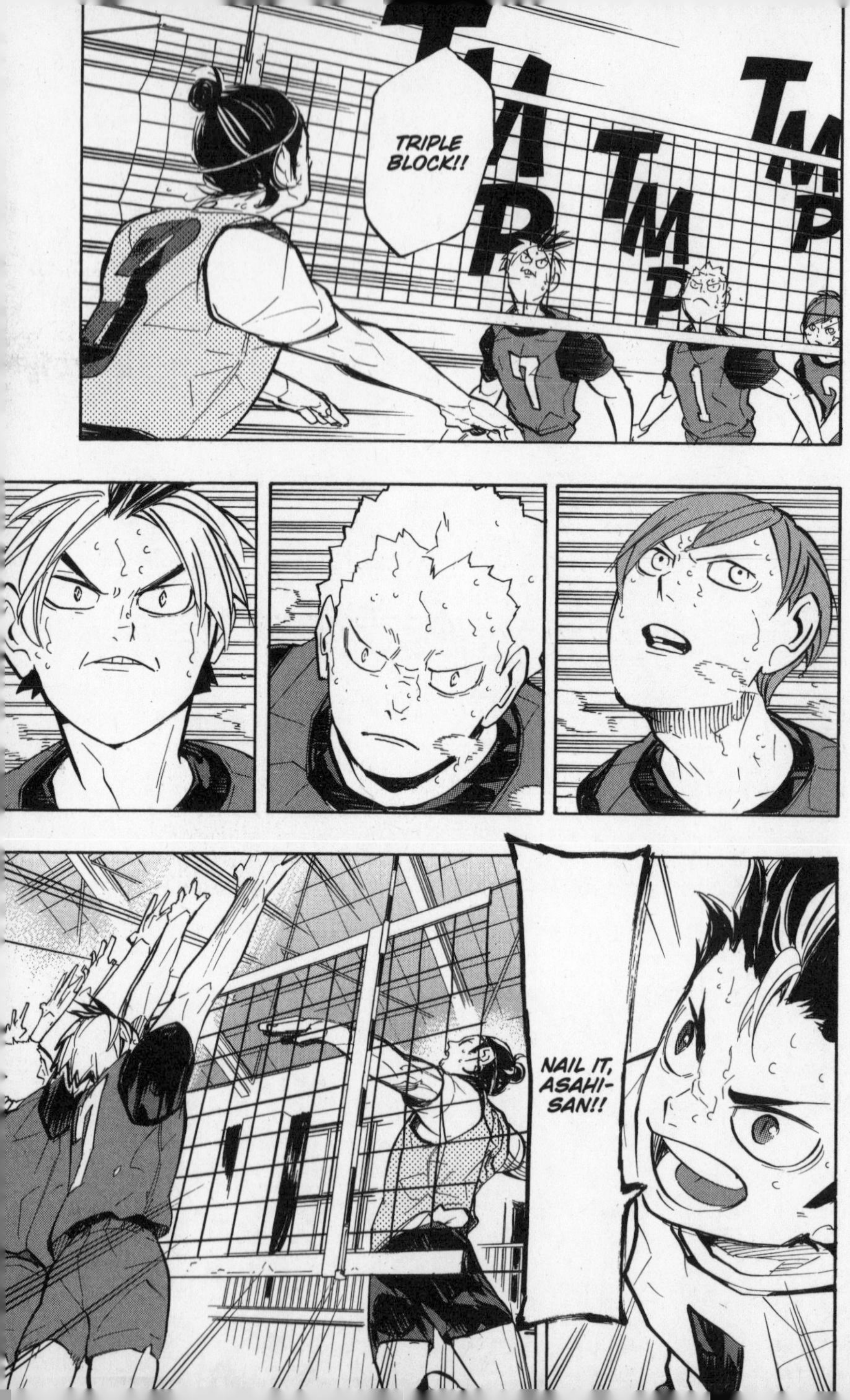

TMP
TMP
TMP
TRIPLE BLOCK!!
NAIL IT, ASAHI-SAN!!

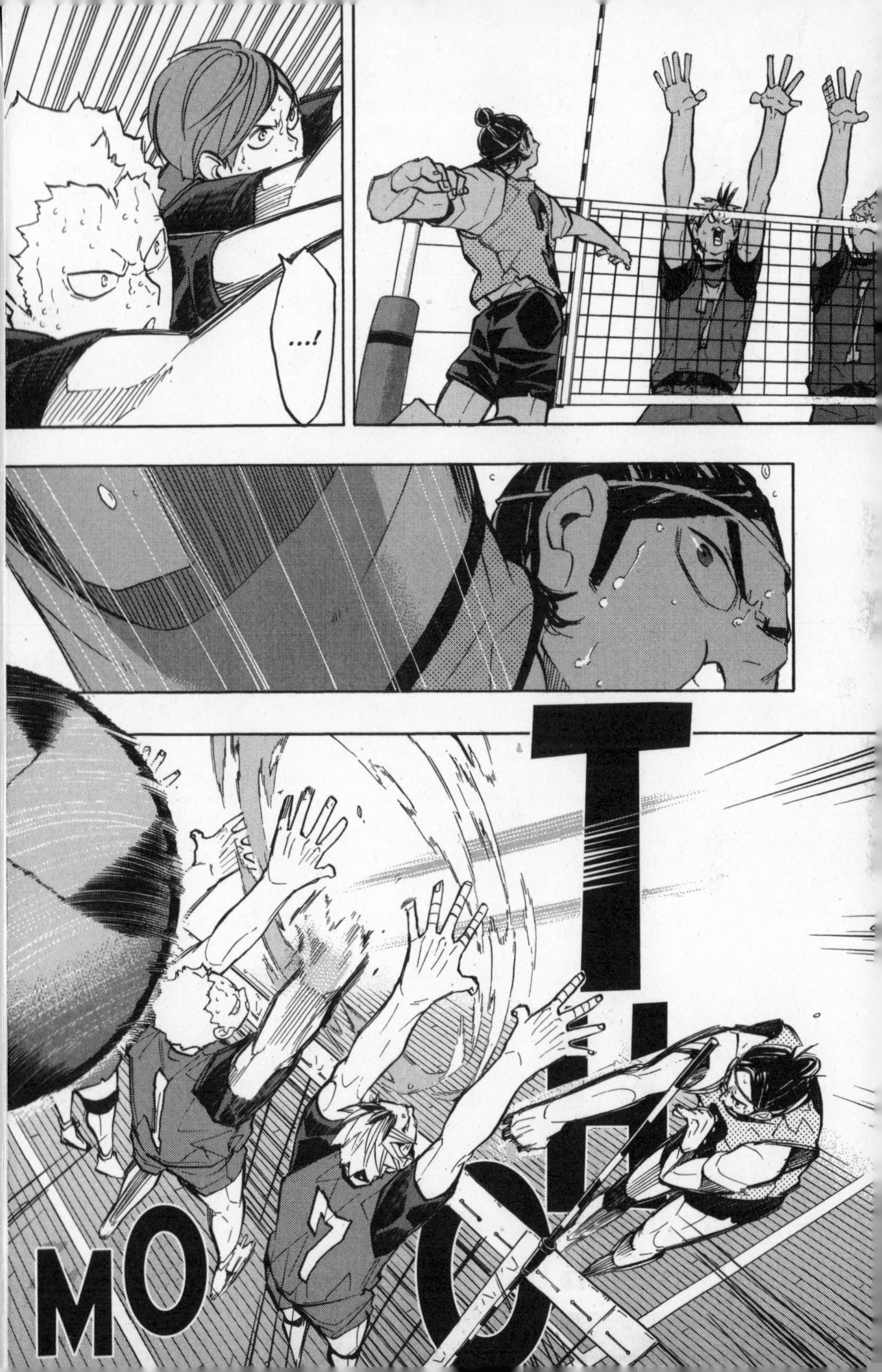
...!
T
H
O
MO

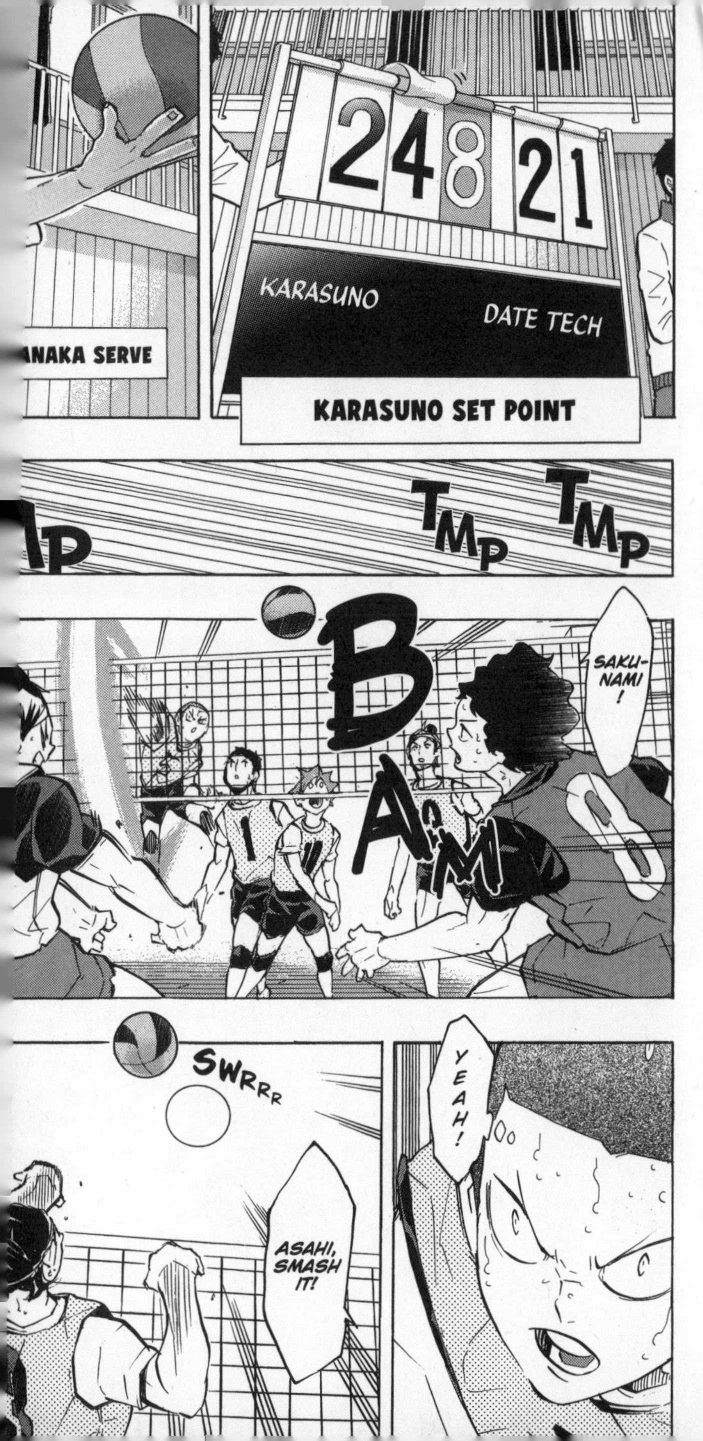
24 8 21
KARASUNO
DATE TECH
KARASUNO SET POINT
ANAKA SERVE
TMP TMP
MP
BAM
SAKUNAMI!
YEAH!
SWRRR
ASAHI, SMASH IT!

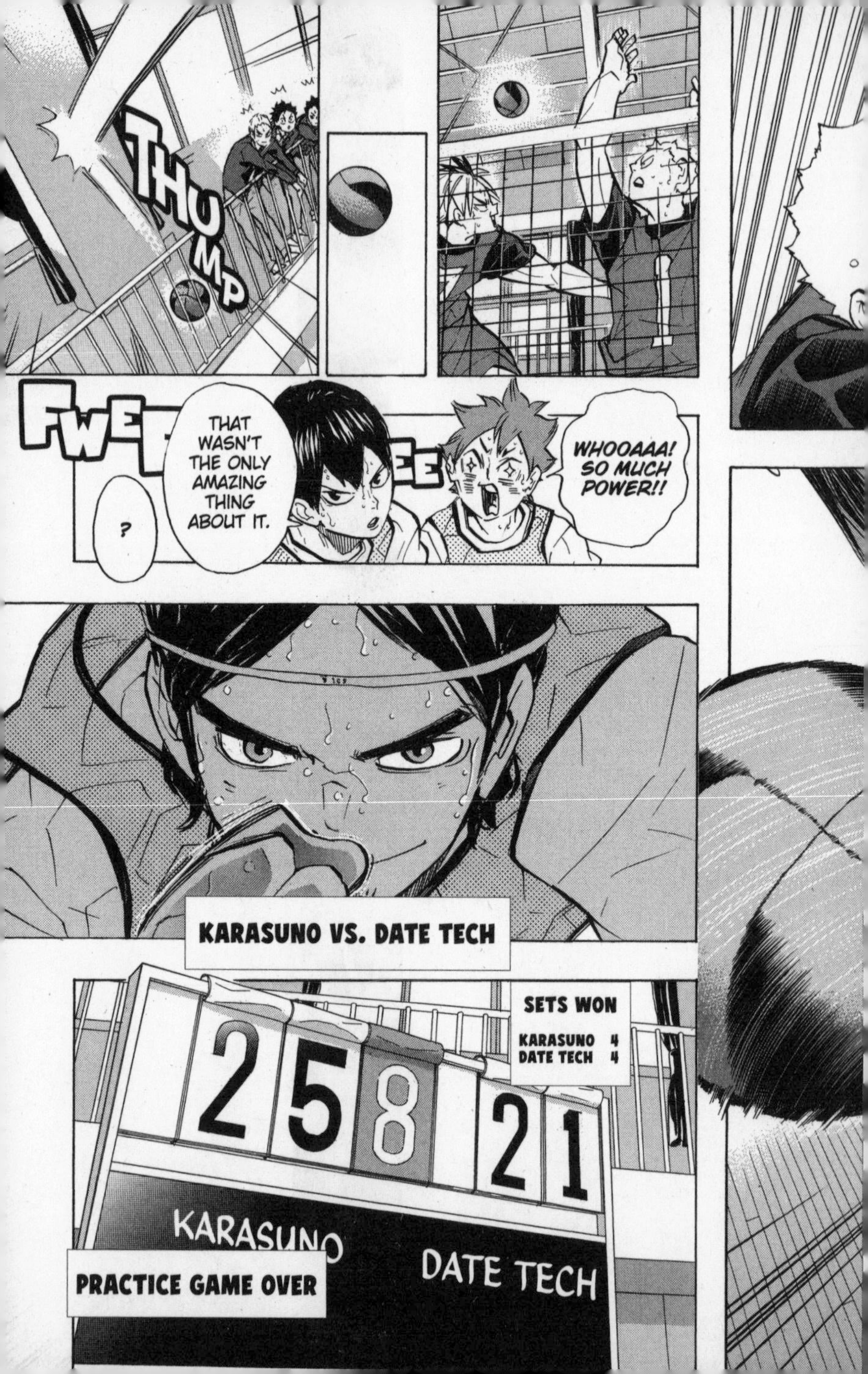
THUMP
FWE
EE
WHOOAAA! SO MUCH POWER!!
THAT WASN'T THE ONLY AMAZING THING ABOUT IT.
?
KARASUNO VS. DATE TECH
SETS WON
KARASUNO 4
DATE TECH 4
25
8
21
KARASUNO
DATE TECH
PRACTICE GAME OVER

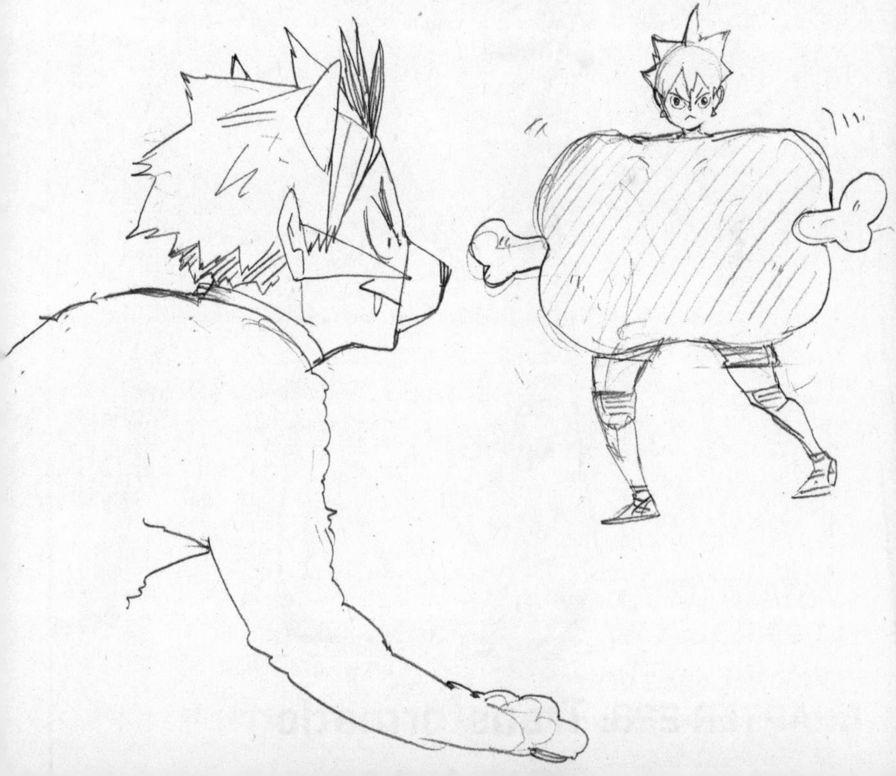

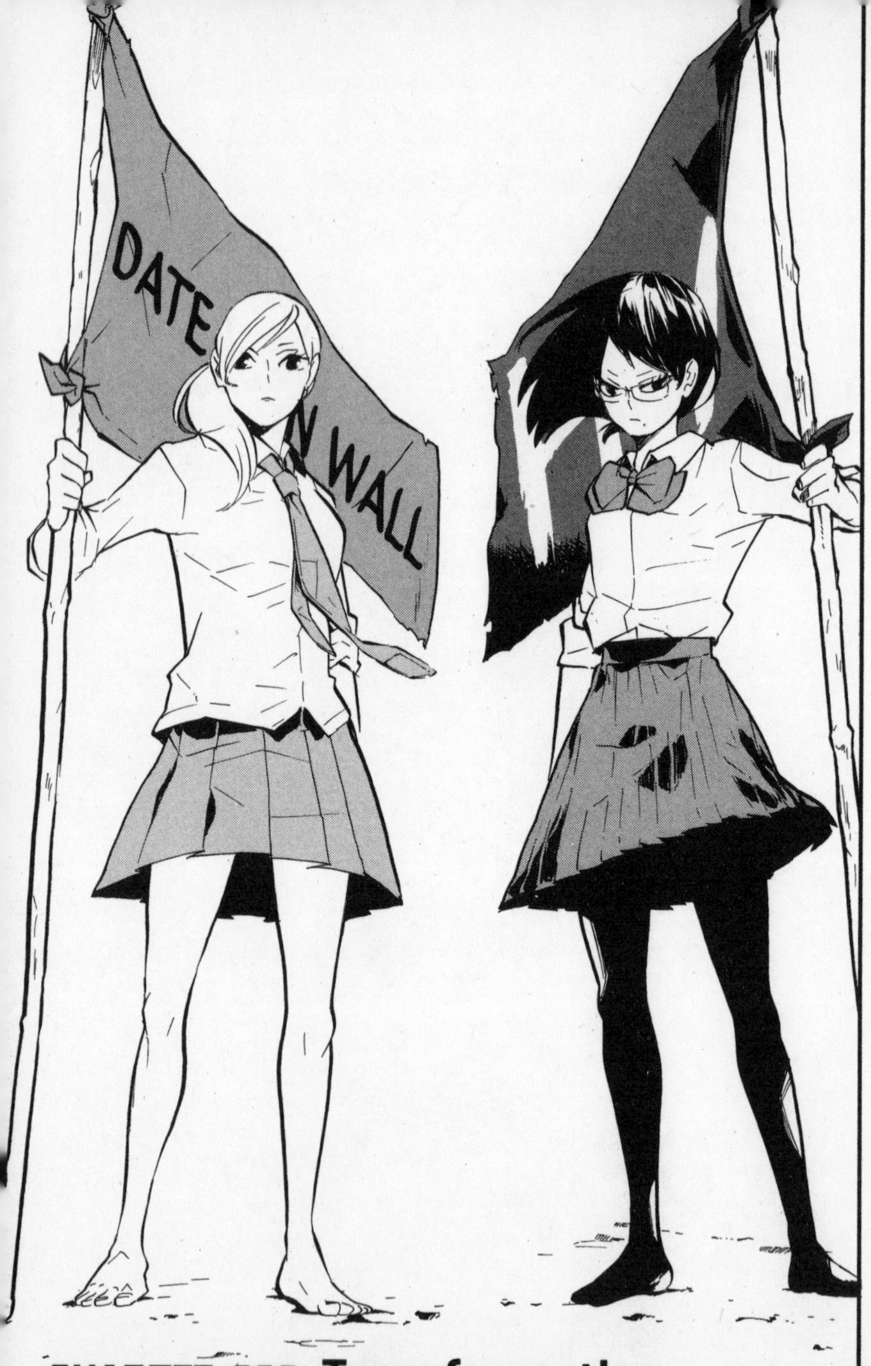
DATE
N WALL

CHAPTER 228: Transformation

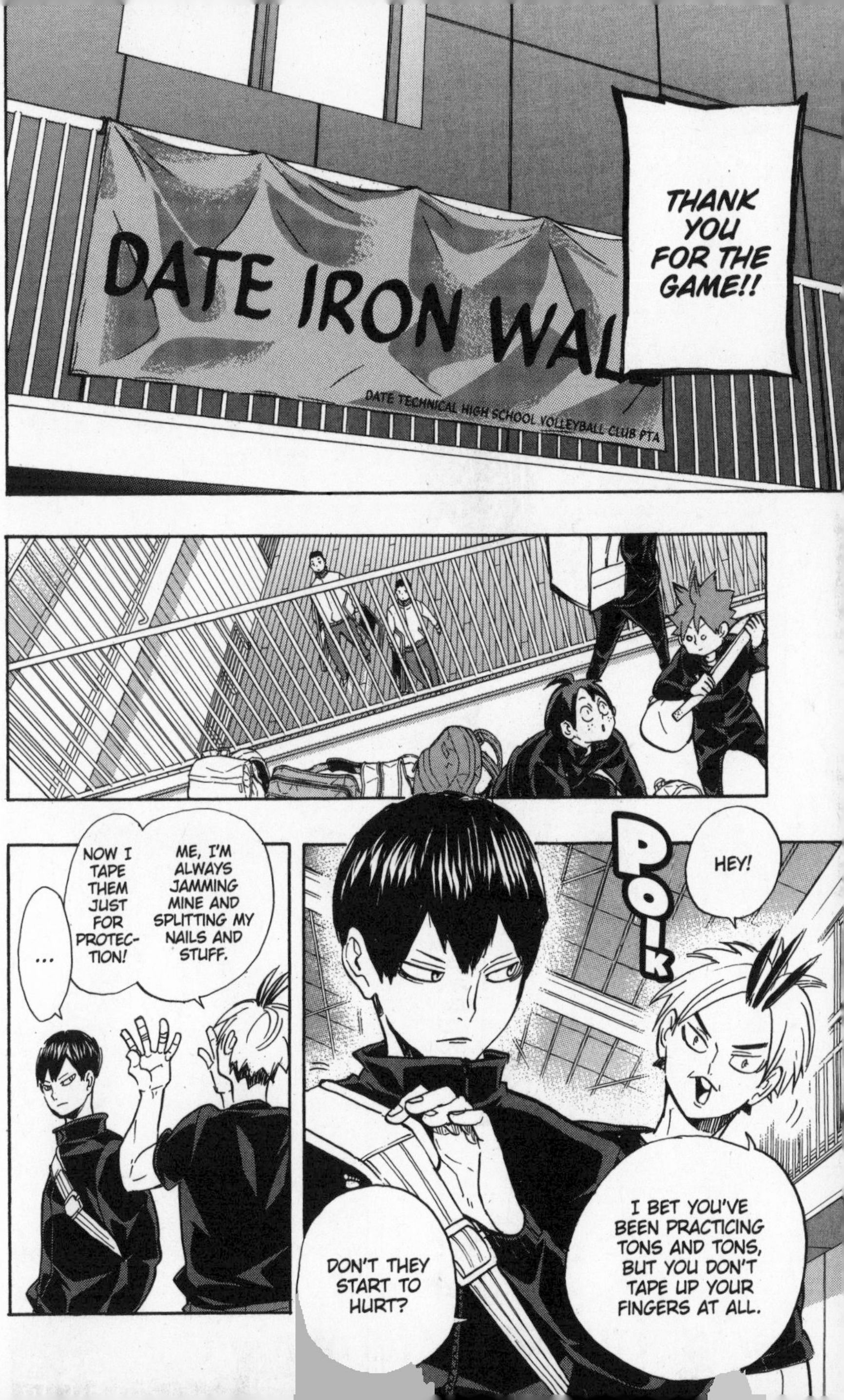
THANK YOU FOR THE GAME!!
DATE IRON WAL
DATE TECHNICAL HIGH SCHOOL VOLLEYBALL CLUB PTA
HEY!
POIK
I BET YOU'VE BEEN PRACTICING TONS AND TONS, BUT YOU DON'T TAPE UP YOUR FINGERS AT ALL.
DON'T THEY START TO HURT?
ME, I'M ALWAYS JAMMING MINE AND SPLITTING MY NAILS AND STUFF.
NOW I TAPE THEM JUST FOR PROTEC-TION!
...

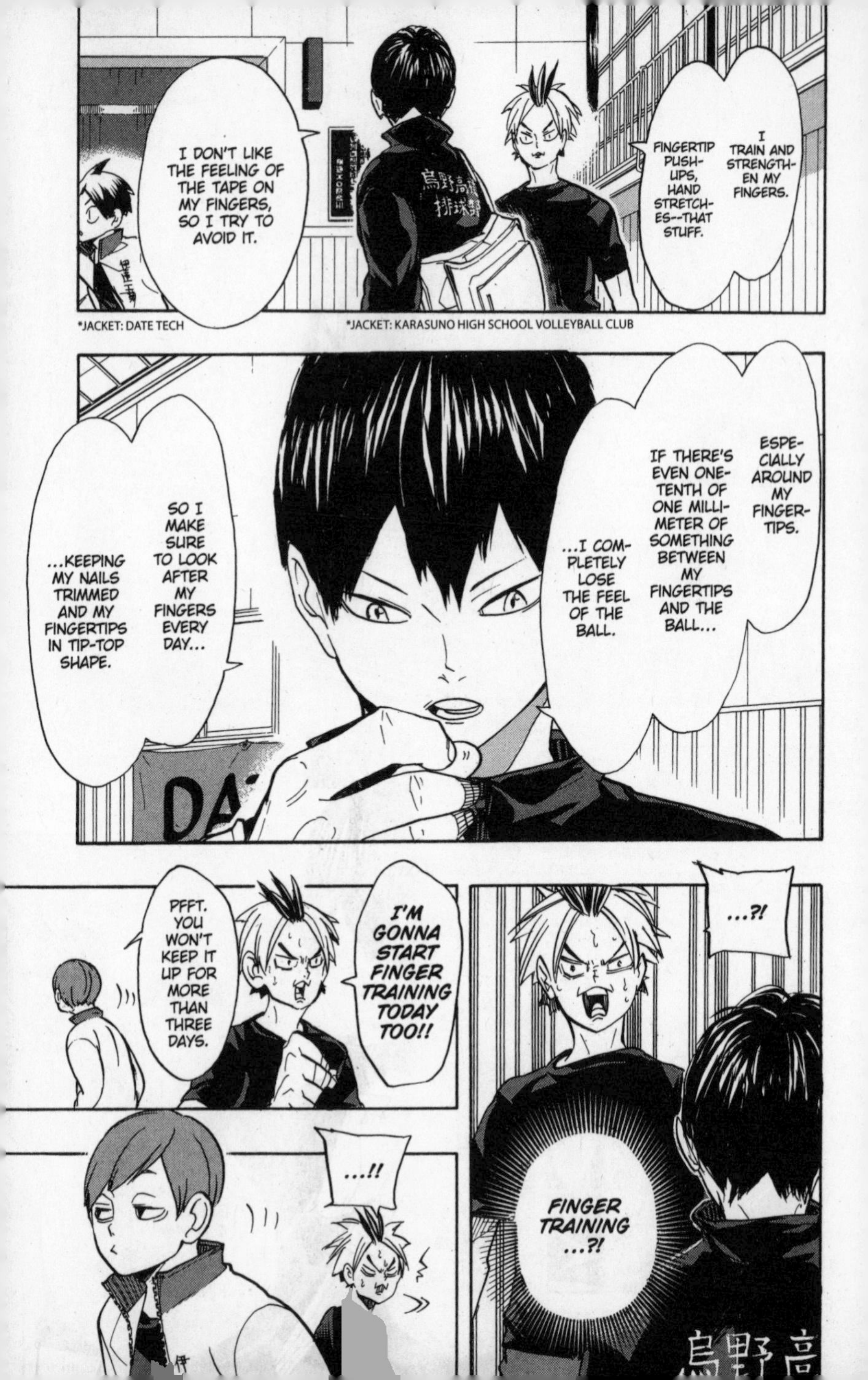
I TRAIN AND STRENGTHEN MY FINGERS.
FINGERTIP PUSH-UPS, HAND STRETCHES--THAT STUFF.
I DON'T LIKE THE FEELING OF THE TAPE ON MY FINGERS, SO I TRY TO AVOID IT.
ESPECIALLY AROUND MY FINGERTIPS.
IF THERE'S EVEN ONE-TENTH OF ONE MILLIMETER OF SOMETHING BETWEEN MY FINGERTIPS AND THE BALL...
...I COMPLETELY LOSE THE FEEL OF THE BALL.
SO I MAKE SURE TO LOOK AFTER MY FINGERS EVERY DAY...
...KEEPING MY NAILS TRIMMED AND MY FINGERTIPS IN TIP-TOP SHAPE.
...?!
FINGER TRAINING ...?!
I'M GONNA START FINGER TRAINING TODAY TOO!!
PFFT. YOU WON'T KEEP IT UP FOR MORE THAN THREE DAYS.
...!!
*JACKET: KARASUNO HIGH SCHOOL VOLLEYBALL CLUB
*JACKET: DATE TECH

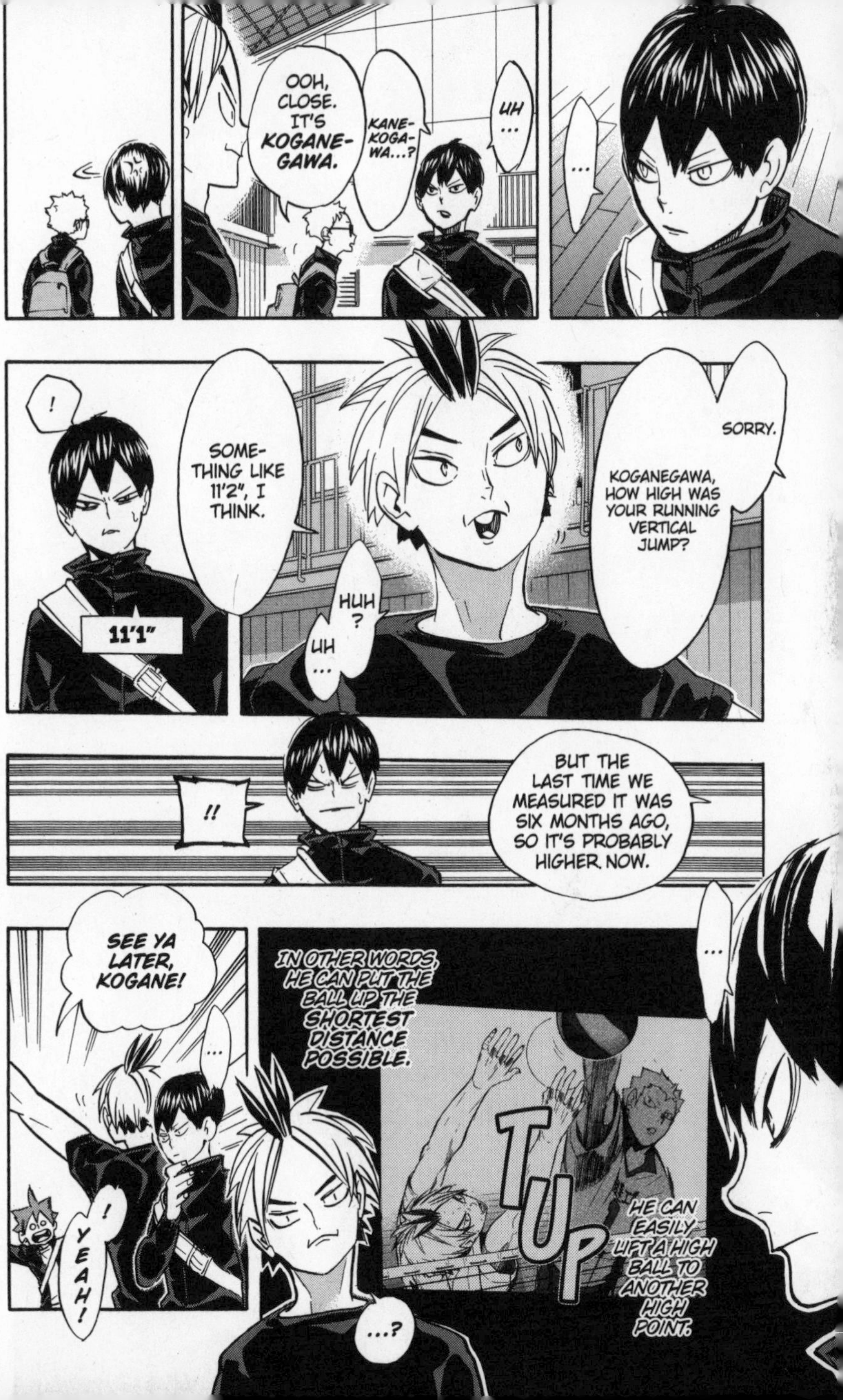
...
UH ...
KANE-KOGAWA...?
OOH, CLOSE. IT'S KOGANE-GAWA.
SORRY.
KOGANEGAWA, HOW HIGH WAS YOUR RUNNING VERTICAL JUMP?
HUH?
UH ...
SOME-THING LIKE 11'2", I THINK.
!
11'1"
BUT THE LAST TIME WE MEASURED IT WAS SIX MONTHS AGO, SO IT'S PROBABLY HIGHER NOW.
!!
...
IN OTHER WORDS, HE CAN PUT THE BALL UP THE SHORTEST DISTANCE POSSIBLE.
TUP
HE CAN EASILY LIFT A HIGH BALL TO ANOTHER HIGH POINT.
...?
SEE YA LATER, KOGANE!
...
! YEAH!

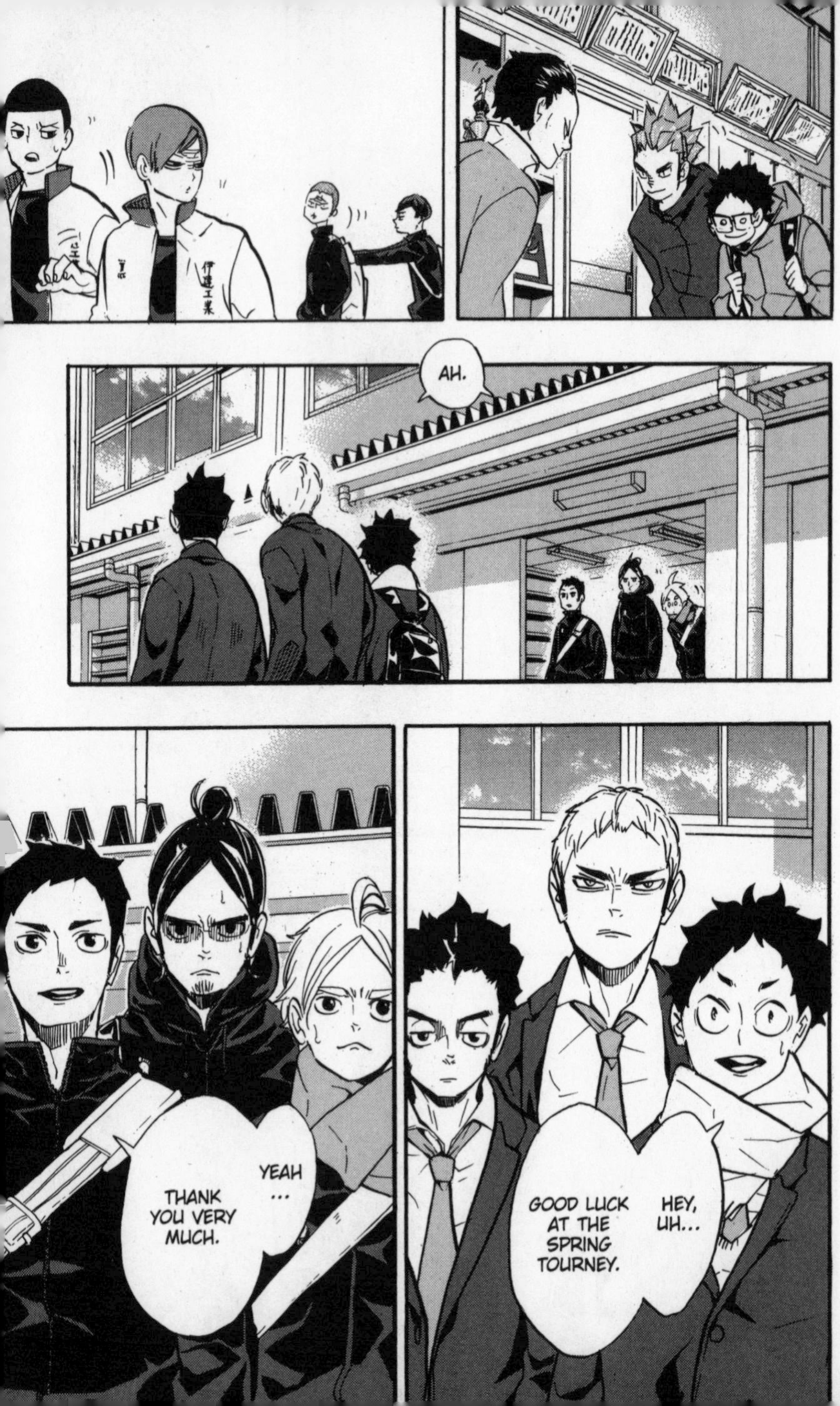
AH.
HEY, UH...
GOOD LUCK AT THE SPRING TOURNEY.
YEAH...
THANK YOU VERY MUCH.

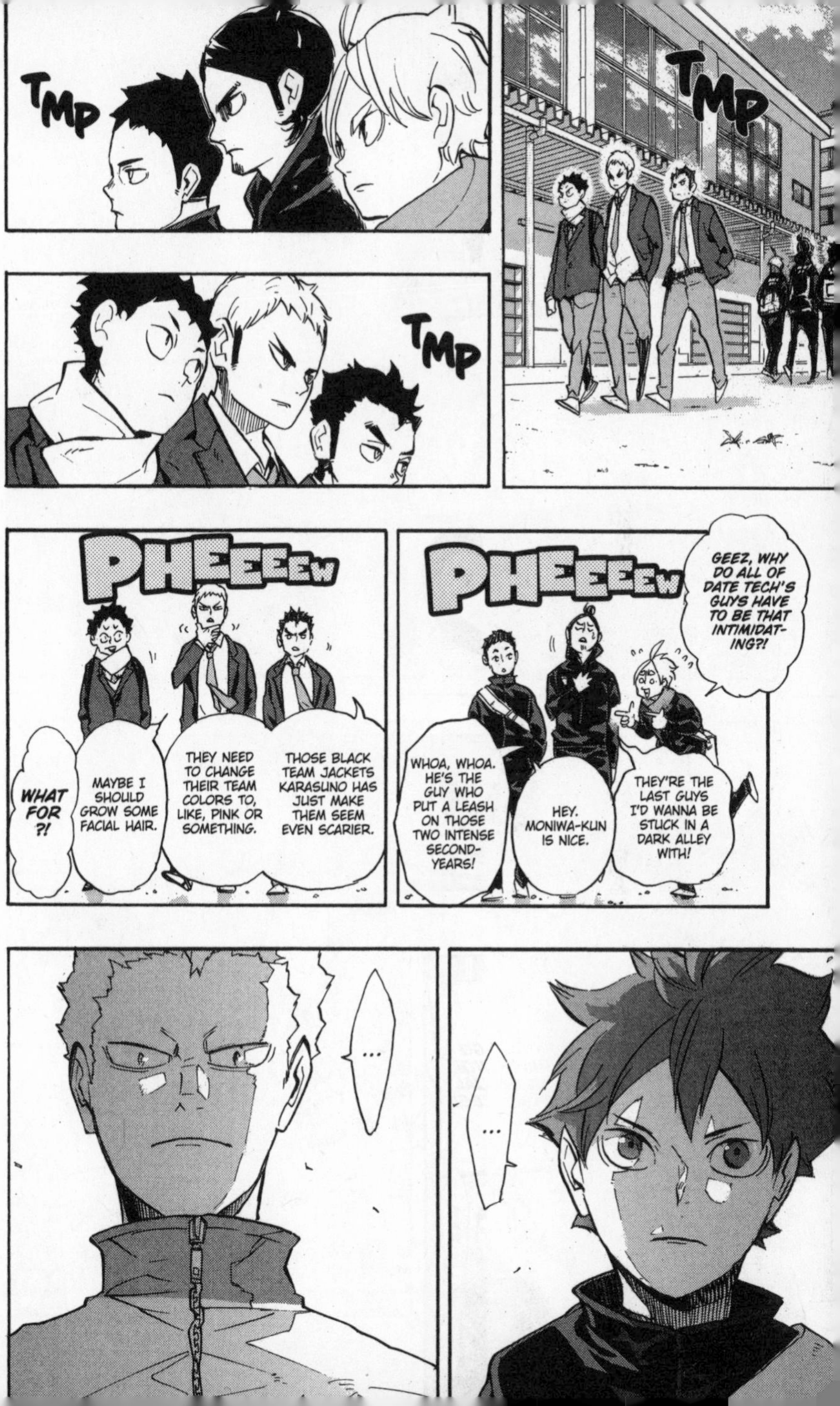
TMP
TMP
TMP
PHEEEEW
GEEZ, WHY DO ALL OF DATE TECH'S GUYS HAVE TO BE THAT INTIMIDATING?!
THEY'RE THE LAST GUYS I'D WANNA BE STUCK IN A DARK ALLEY WITH!
HEY. MONIWA-KUN IS NICE.
WHOA, WHOA. HE'S THE GUY WHO PUT A LEASH ON THOSE TWO INTENSE SECOND-YEARS!
PHEEEEW
THOSE BLACK TEAM JACKETS KARASUNO HAS JUST MAKE THEM SEEM EVEN SCARIER.
THEY NEED TO CHANGE THEIR TEAM COLORS TO, LIKE, PINK OR SOMETHING.
MAYBE I SHOULD GROW SOME FACIAL HAIR.
WHAT FOR?!
...
...

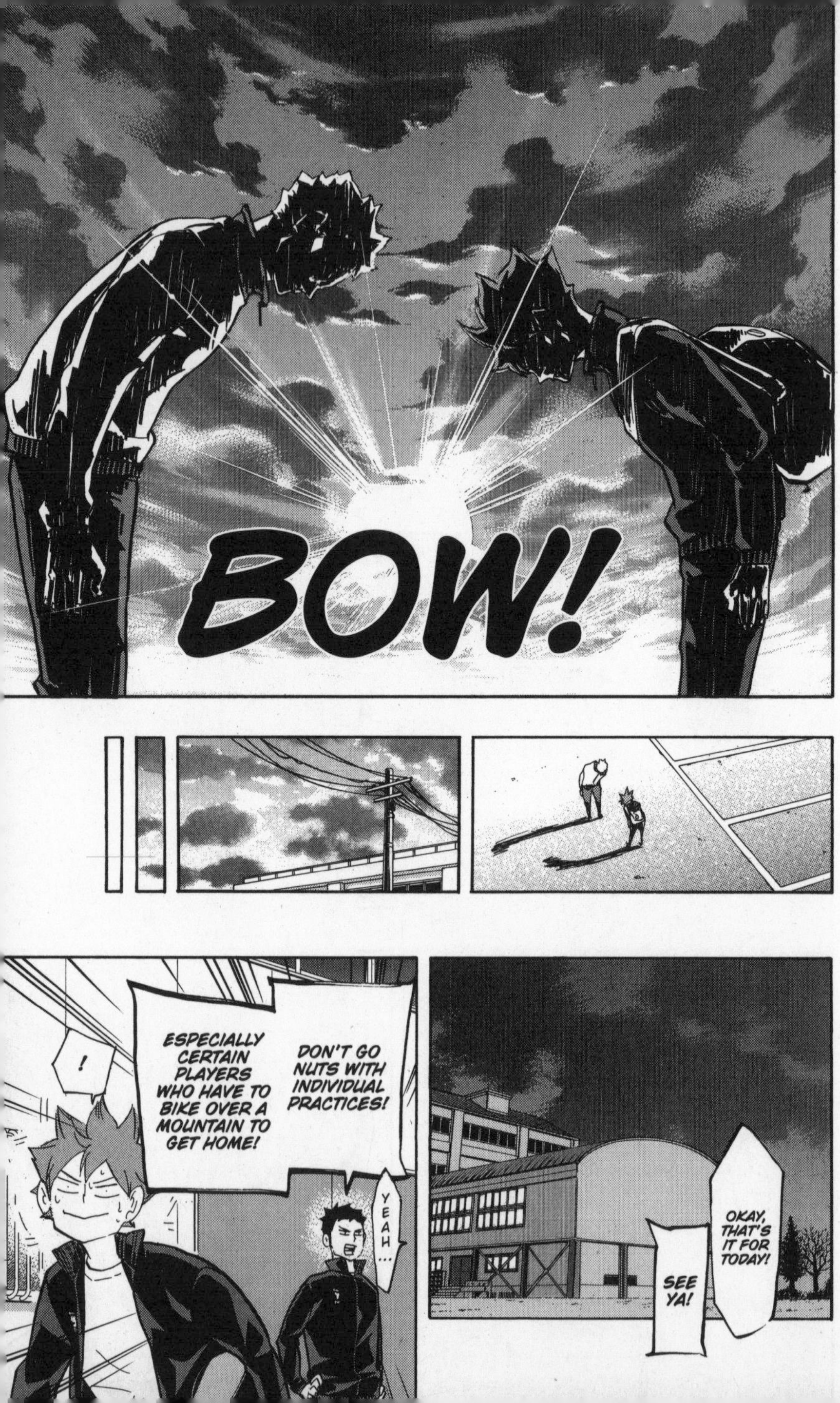
BOW!
OKAY, THAT'S IT FOR TODAY!
SEE YA!
DON'T GO NUTS WITH INDIVIDUAL PRACTICES!
ESPECIALLY CERTAIN PLAYERS WHO HAVE TO BIKE OVER A MOUNTAIN TO GET HOME!
!
YEAH...

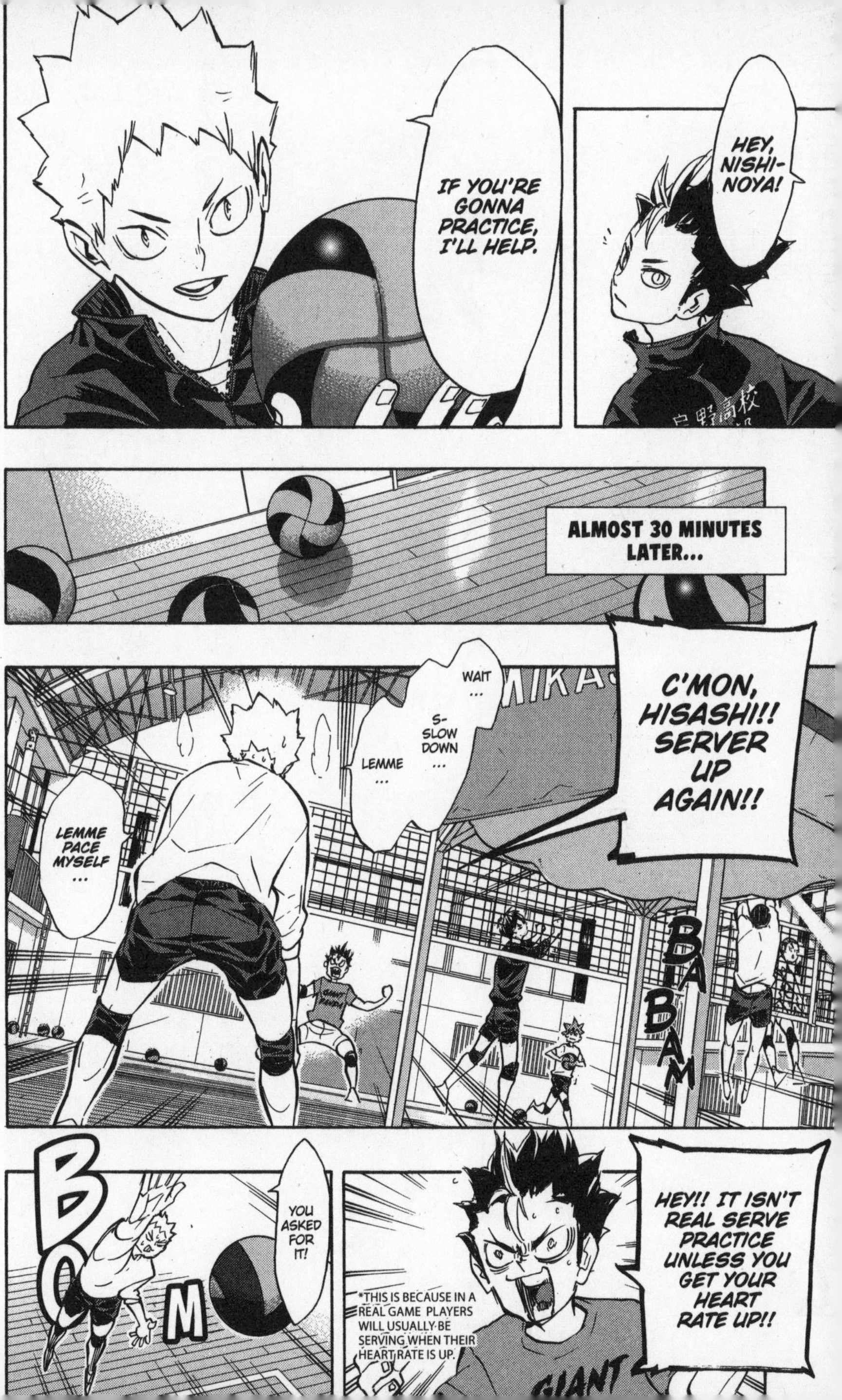
HEY, NISHI-NOYA!
IF YOU'RE GONNA PRACTICE, I'LL HELP.
ALMOST 30 MINUTES LATER...
C'MON, HISASHI!! SERVER UP AGAIN!!
WAIT ...
S-SLOW DOWN ...
LEMME ...
LEMME PACE MYSELF ...
BABAM
HEY!! IT ISN'T REAL SERVE PRACTICE UNLESS YOU GET YOUR HEART RATE UP!!
*THIS IS BECAUSE IN A REAL GAME PLAYERS WILL USUALLY BE SERVING WHEN THEIR HEART RATE IS UP.
YOU ASKED FOR IT!
BOOM

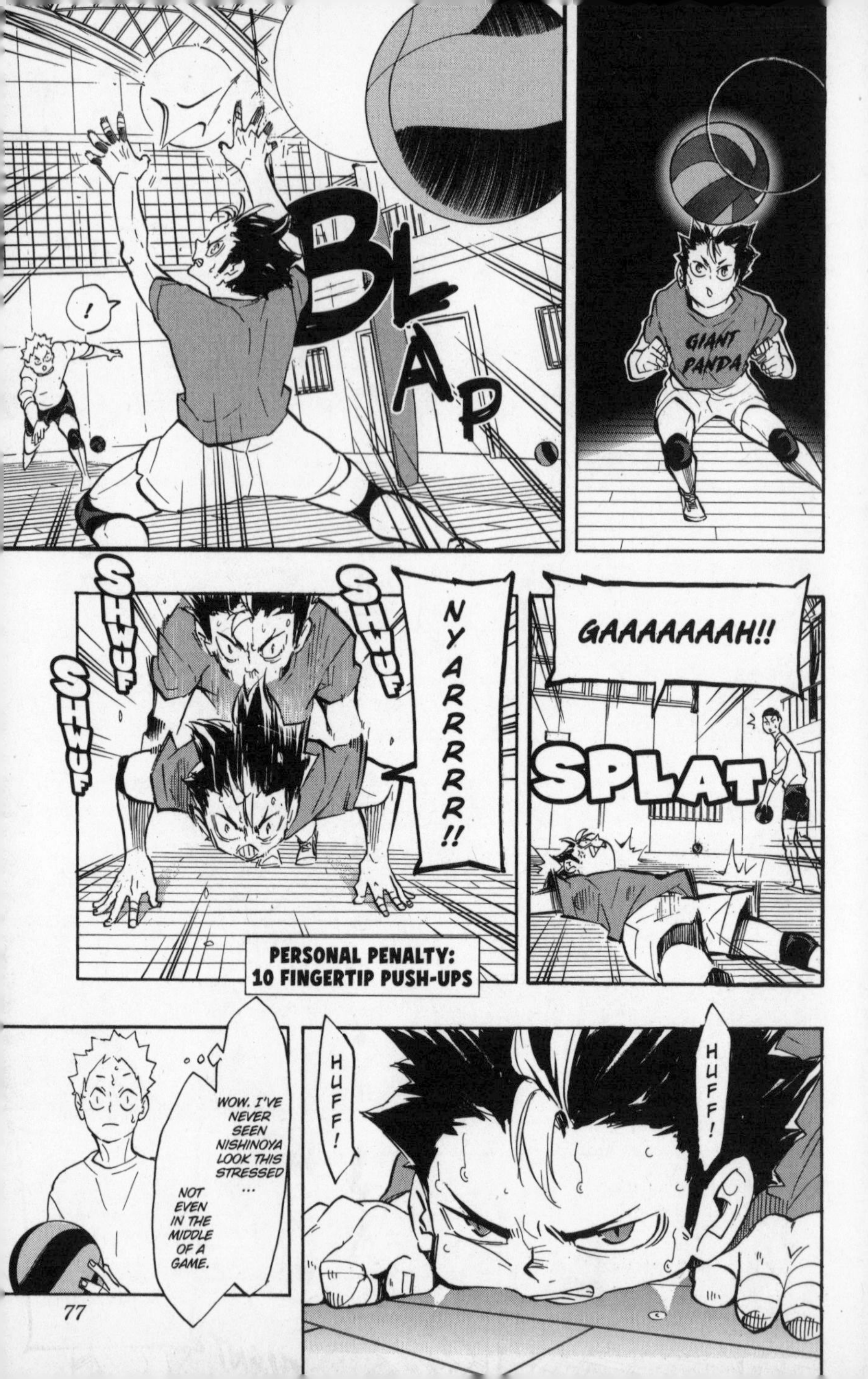
!
BLAP
GAAAAAAAH!!
SPLAT
NYARRRRR!!
SHWUF
SHWUF
SHWUF
PERSONAL PENALTY:
10 FINGERTIP PUSH-UPS
HUFF!
HUFF!
...
WOW. I'VE NEVER SEEN NISHINOYA LOOK THIS STRESSED...
NOT EVEN IN THE MIDDLE OF A GAME.

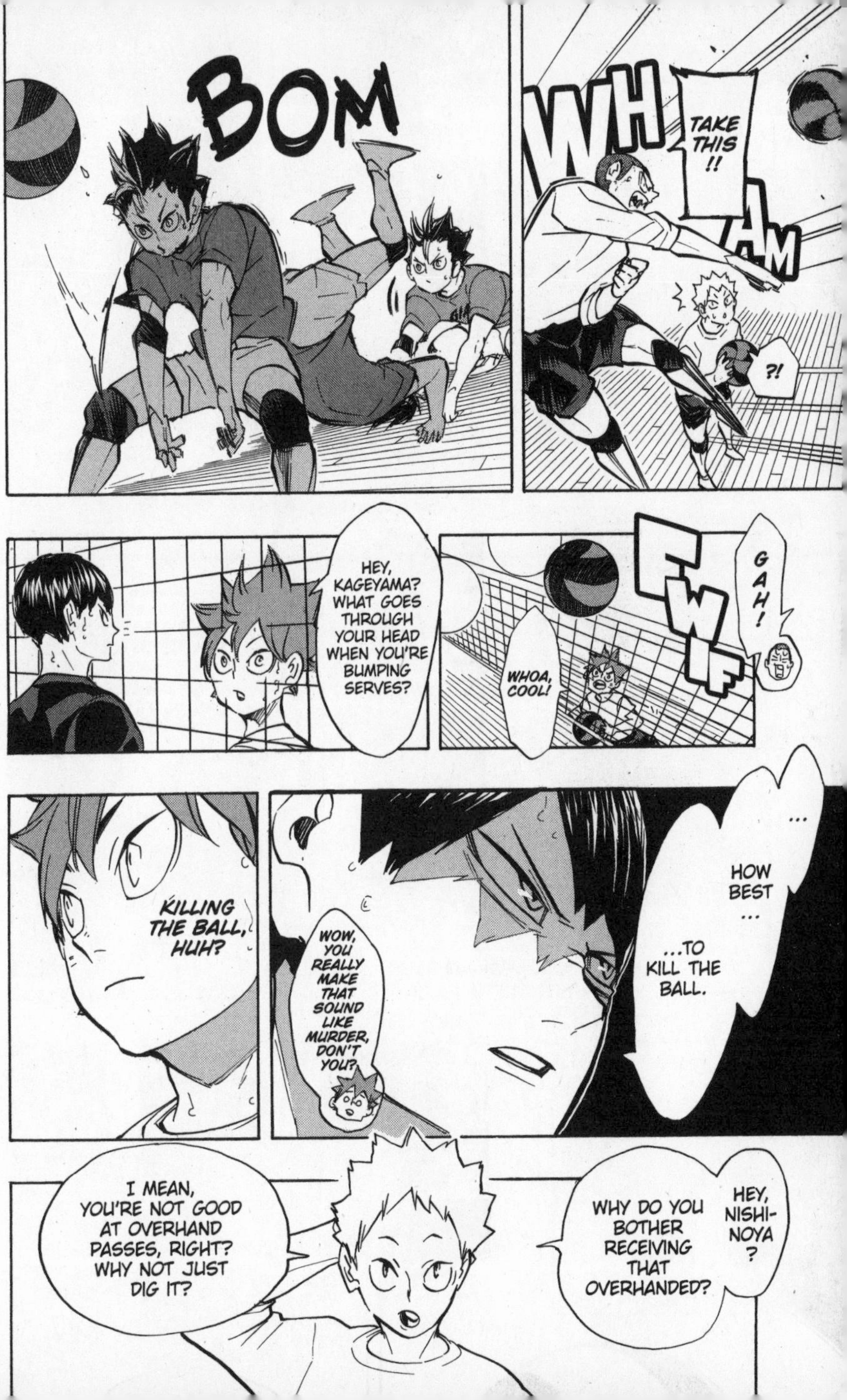
WH
TAKE THIS!!
AM
?!
BOM
GAH!
FWIF
WHOA, COOL!
HEY, KAGEYAMA? WHAT GOES THROUGH YOUR HEAD WHEN YOU'RE BUMPING SERVES?
...
HOW BEST ...
...TO KILL THE BALL.
WOW, YOU REALLY MAKE THAT SOUND LIKE MURDER, DON'T YOU?
KILLING THE BALL, HUH?
HEY, NISHI-NOYA?
WHY DO YOU BOTHER RECEIVING THAT OVERHANDED?
I MEAN, YOU'RE NOT GOOD AT OVERHAND PASSES, RIGHT? WHY NOT JUST DIG IT?

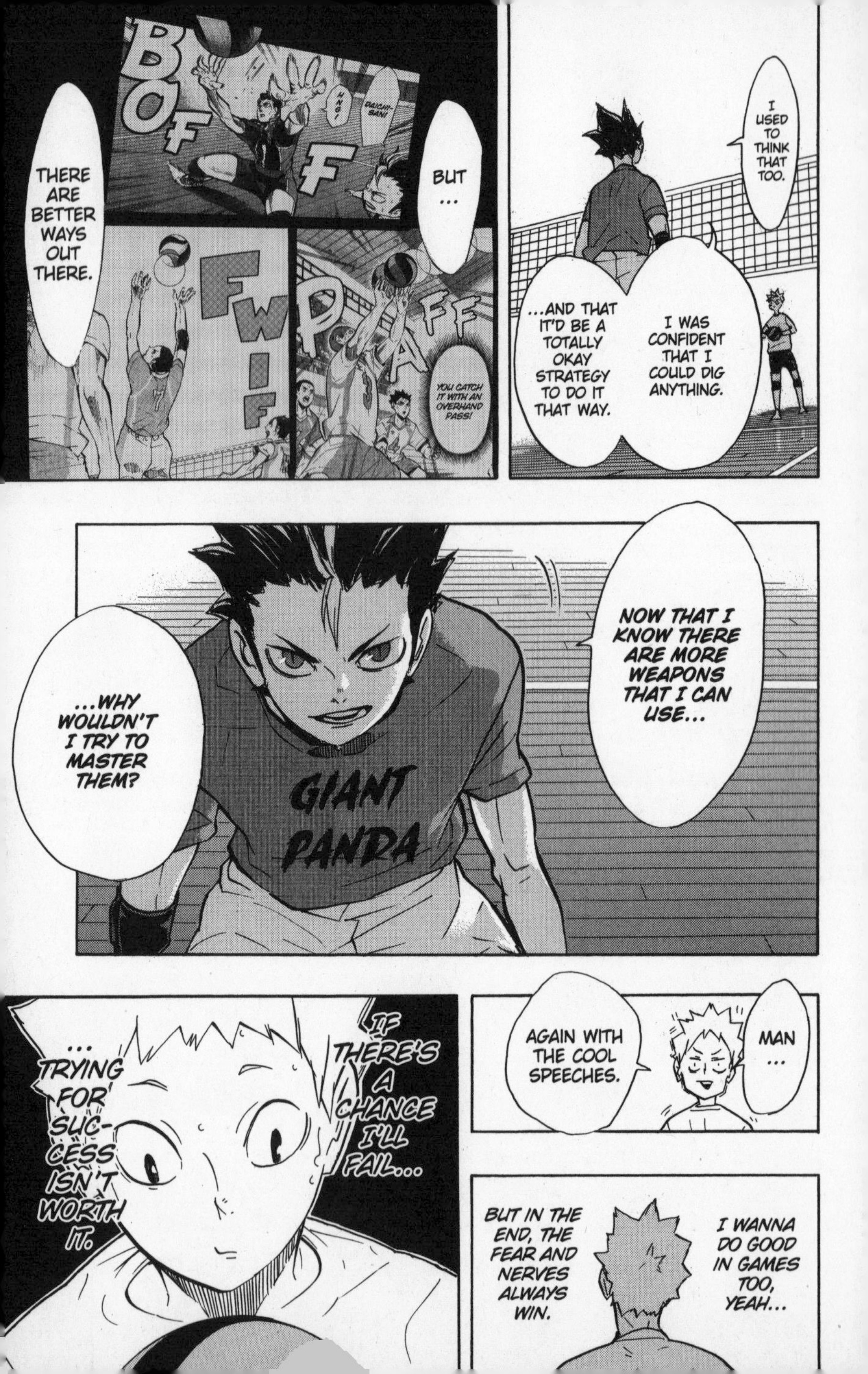
I USED TO THINK THAT TOO.
I WAS CONFIDENT THAT I COULD DIG ANYTHING.
...AND THAT IT'D BE A TOTALLY OKAY STRATEGY TO DO IT THAT WAY.
BOFF
DAICHI-SAN!
HNG!
BUT ...
THERE ARE BETTER WAYS OUT THERE.
PAFF
YOU CATCH IT WITH AN OVERHAND PASS!
FWIF
NOW THAT I KNOW THERE ARE MORE WEAPONS THAT I CAN USE...
...WHY WOULDN'T I TRY TO MASTER THEM?
GIANT PANDA
MAN ...
AGAIN WITH THE COOL SPEECHES.
I WANNA DO GOOD IN GAMES TOO, YEAH...
BUT IN THE END, THE FEAR AND NERVES ALWAYS WIN.
IF THERE'S A CHANCE I'LL FAIL...
...TRYING FOR SUC-CESS ISN'T WORTH IT.

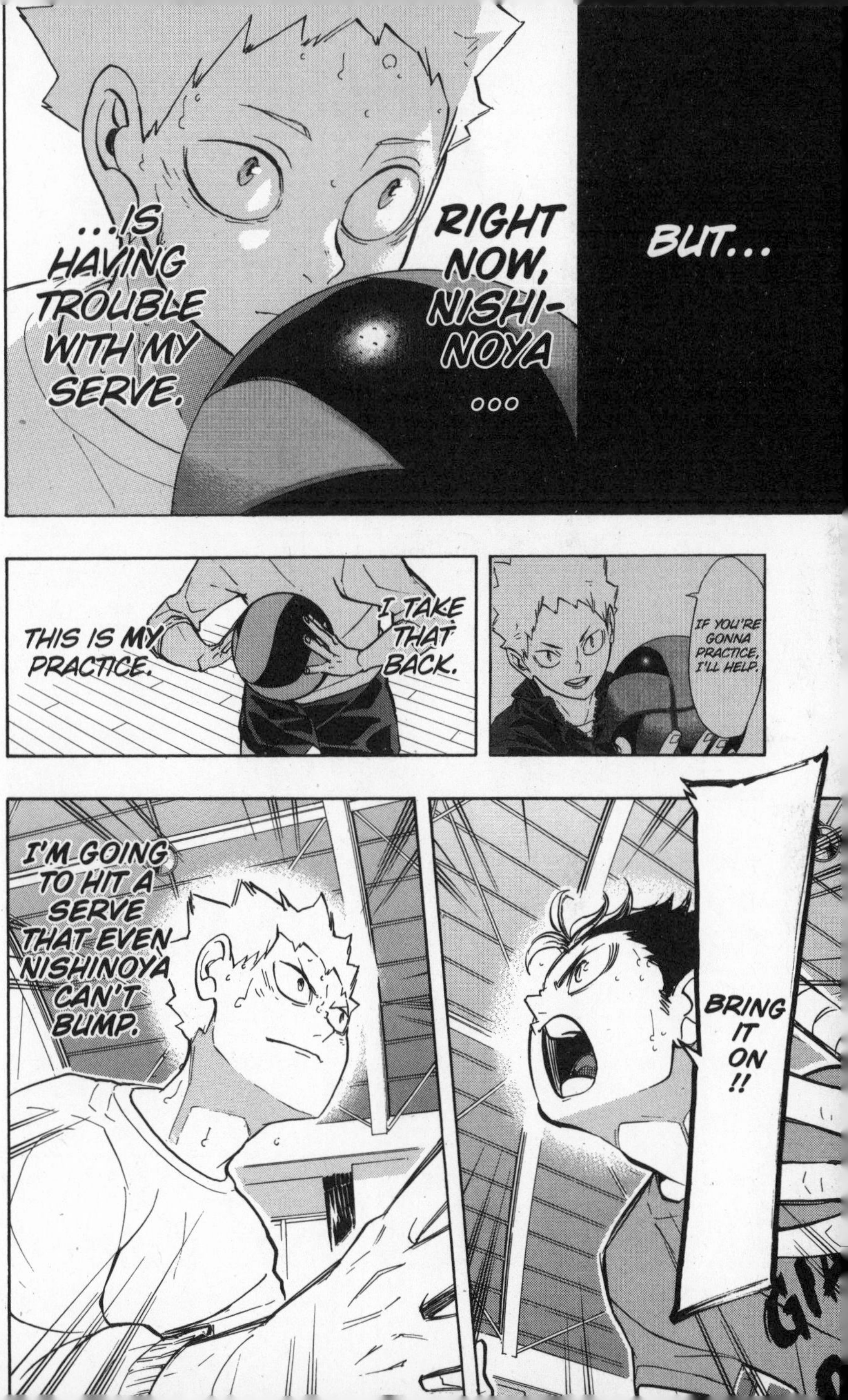
BUT...
RIGHT NOW, NISHI-NOYA ...
...IS HAVING TROUBLE WITH MY SERVE.
IF YOU'RE GONNA PRACTICE, I'LL HELP.
I TAKE THAT BACK.
THIS IS MY PRACTICE.
BRING IT ON !!
I'M GOING TO HIT A SERVE THAT EVEN NISHINOYA CAN'T BUMP.

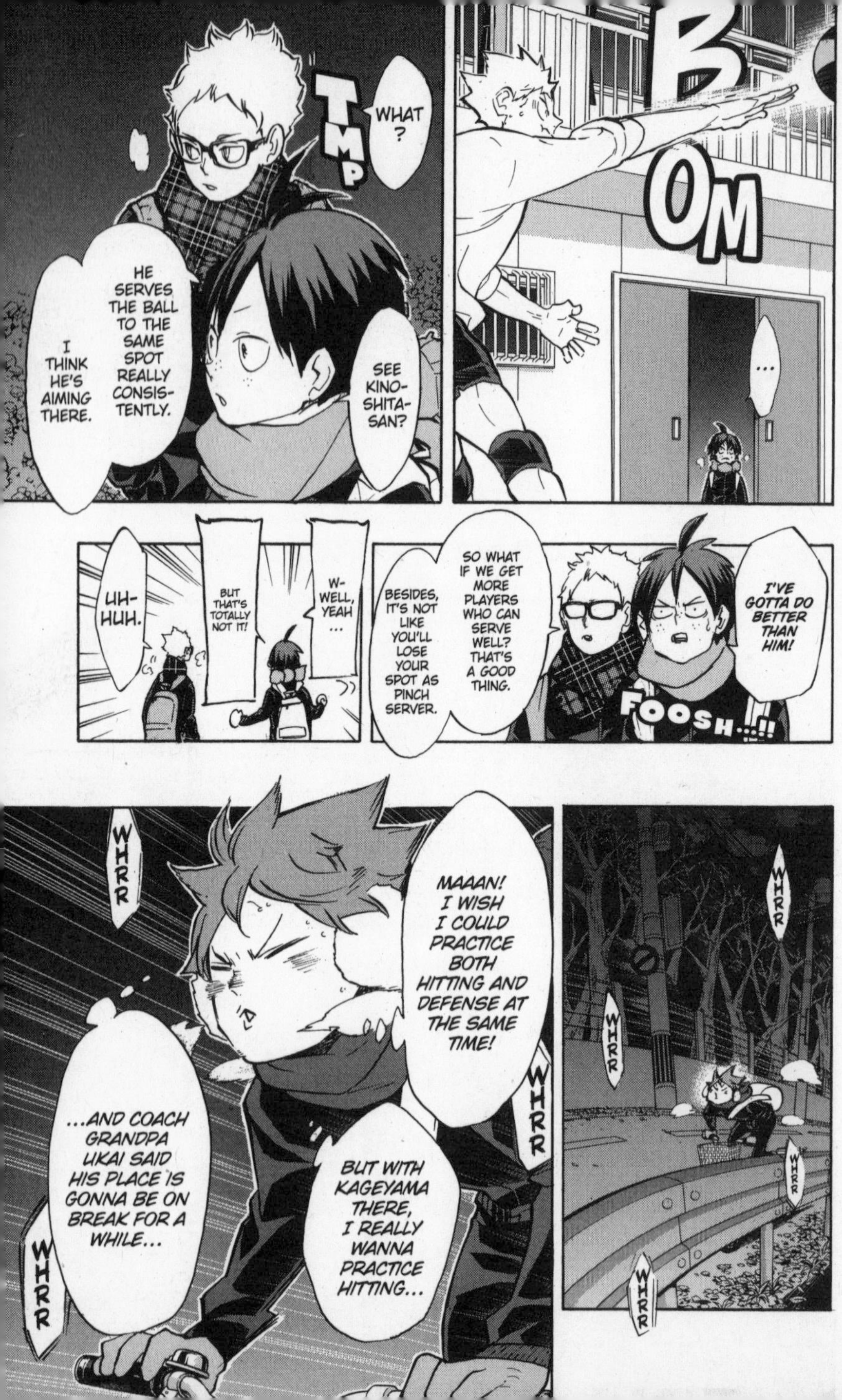
BOOM
...
TMP
WHAT?
SEE KINO-SHITA-SAN?
HE SERVES THE BALL TO THE SAME SPOT REALLY CONSIS-TENTLY.
I THINK HE'S AIMING THERE.
I'VE GOTTA DO BETTER THAN HIM!
FOOSH...!!
SO WHAT IF WE GET MORE PLAYERS WHO CAN SERVE WELL? THAT'S A GOOD THING.
BESIDES, IT'S NOT LIKE YOU'LL LOSE YOUR SPOT AS PINCH SERVER.
W-WELL, YEAH...
BUT THAT'S TOTALLY NOT IT!
UH-HUH.
WHRR
WHRR
WHRR
WHRR
MAAAN! I WISH I COULD PRACTICE BOTH HITTING AND DEFENSE AT THE SAME TIME!
WHRR
WHRR
BUT WITH KAGEYAMA THERE, I REALLY WANNA PRACTICE HITTING...
...AND COACH GRANDPA UKAI SAID HIS PLACE IS GONNA BE ON BREAK FOR A WHILE...
WHRR
WHRR

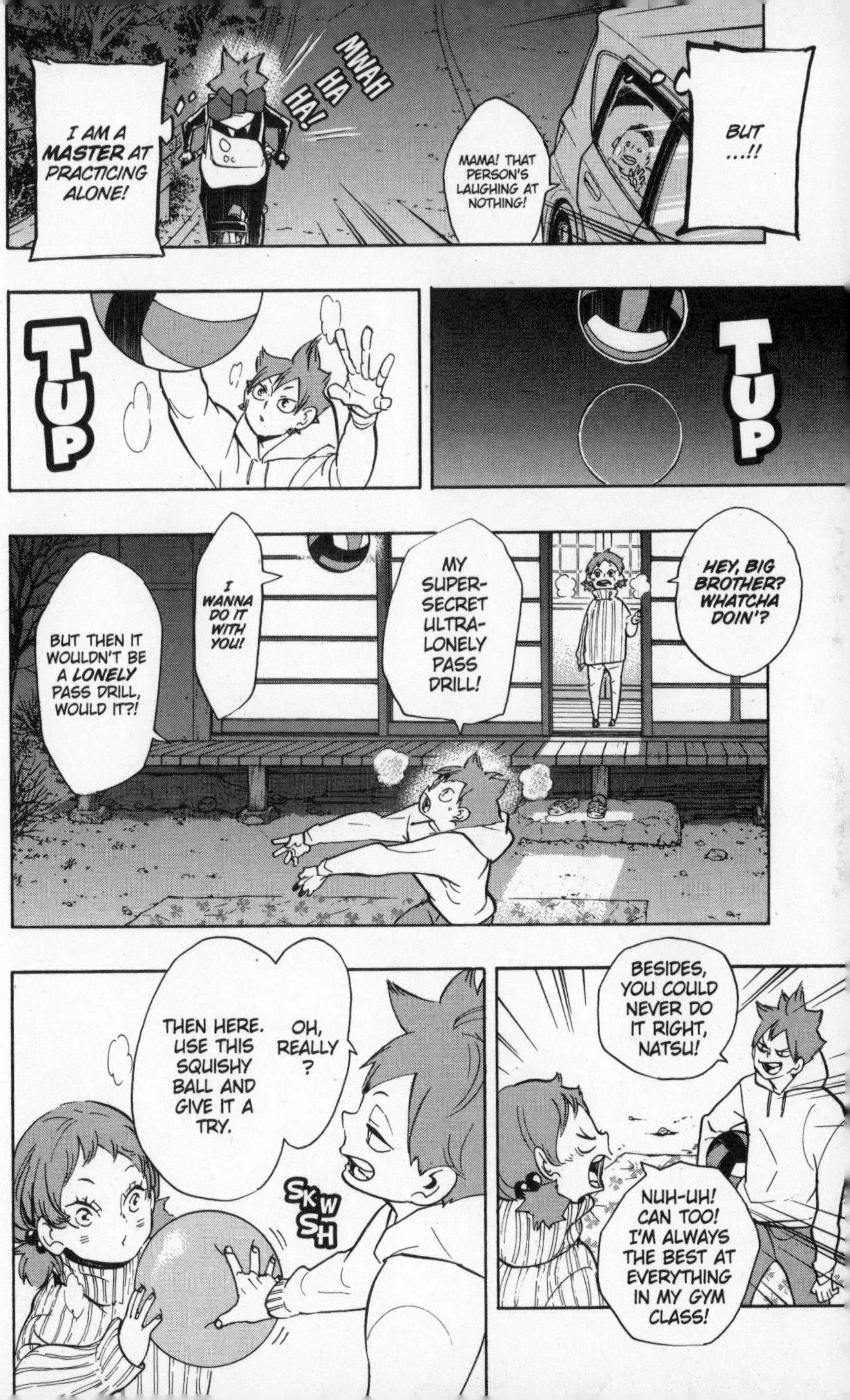
BUT ...!!
MAMA! THAT PERSON'S LAUGHING AT NOTHING!
MWAH HA HA!
I AM A MASTER AT PRACTICING ALONE!
TUP
TUP
HEY, BIG BROTHER? WHATCHA DOIN'?
MY SUPER-SECRET ULTRA-LONELY PASS DRILL!
I WANNA DO IT WITH YOU!
BUT THEN IT WOULDN'T BE A LONELY PASS DRILL, WOULD IT?!
BESIDES, YOU COULD NEVER DO IT RIGHT, NATSU!
NUH-UH! CAN TOO! I'M ALWAYS THE BEST AT EVERYTHING IN MY GYM CLASS!
OH, REALLY?
THEN HERE. USE THIS SQUISHY BALL AND GIVE IT A TRY.
SKWSH

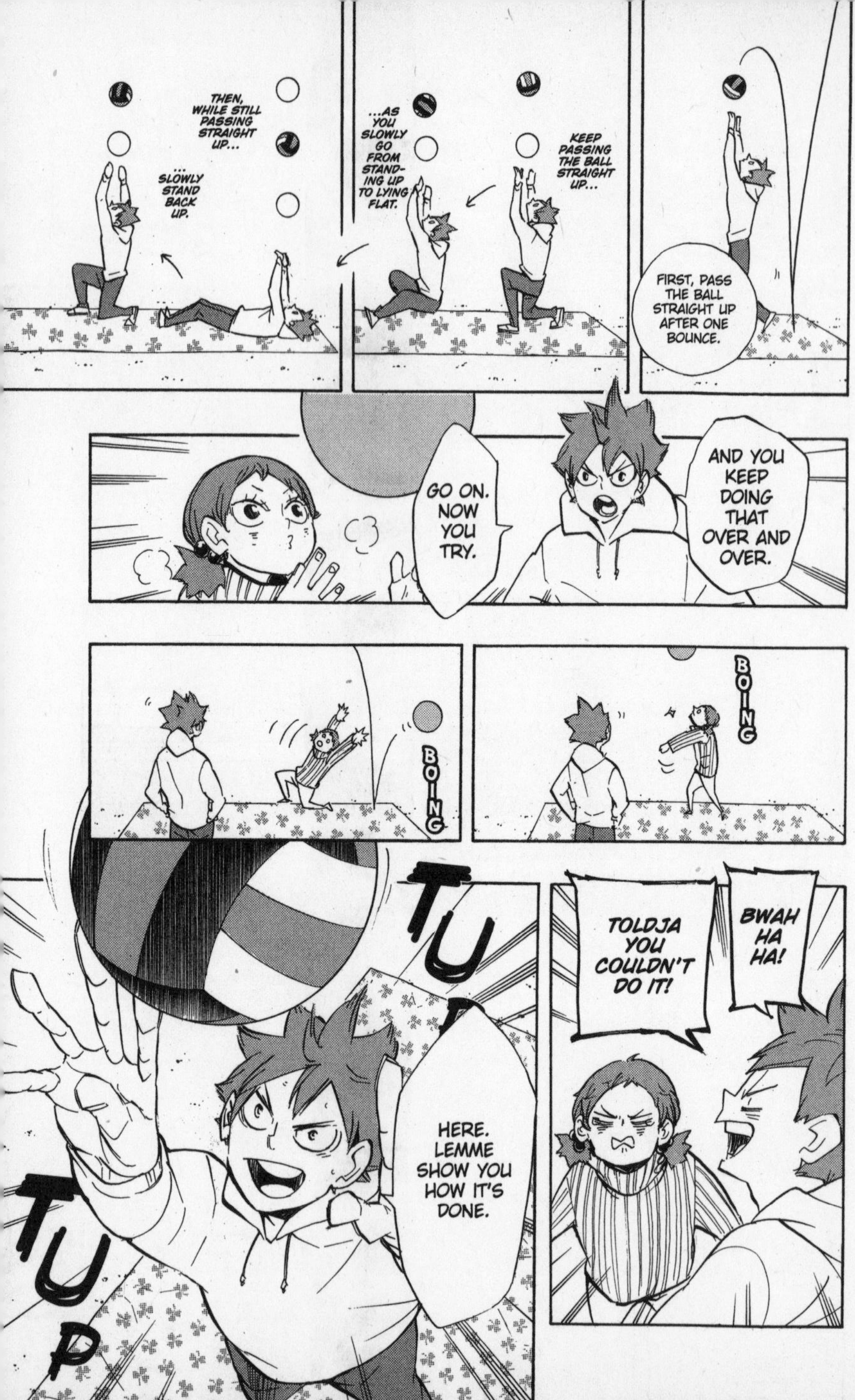
FIRST, PASS THE BALL STRAIGHT UP AFTER ONE BOUNCE.
KEEP PASSING THE BALL STRAIGHT UP...
...AS YOU SLOWLY GO FROM STANDING UP TO LYING FLAT.
THEN, WHILE STILL PASSING STRAIGHT UP...
...SLOWLY STAND BACK UP.
AND YOU KEEP DOING THAT OVER AND OVER.
GO ON. NOW YOU TRY.
BOING
BOING
BWAH HA HA!
TOLDJA YOU COULDN'T DO IT!
TUP
HERE. LEMME SHOW YOU HOW IT'S DONE.
TUP

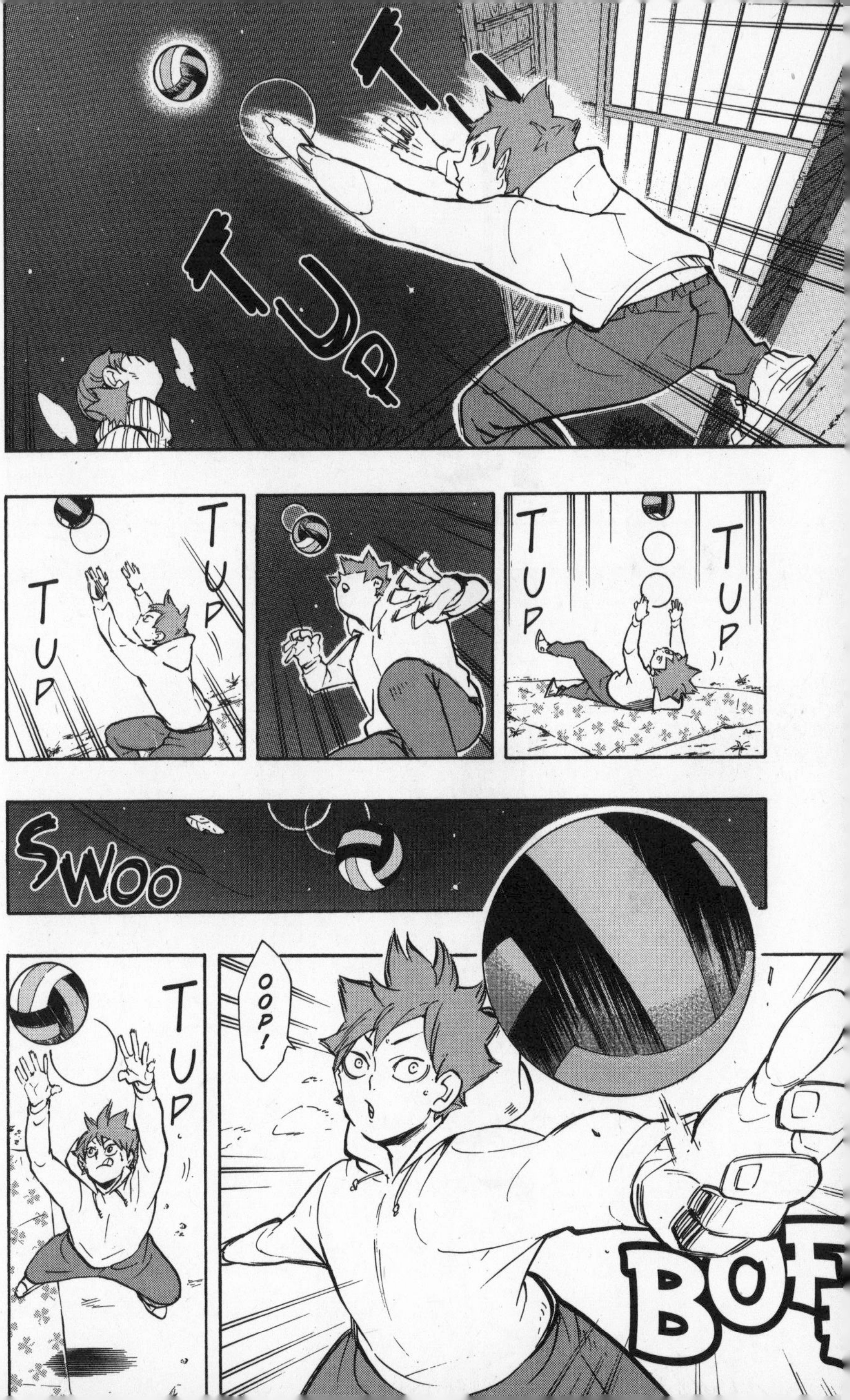

TUP
TUP
TUP
TUP
TUP
SWOO
OOP!
BOF
TUP

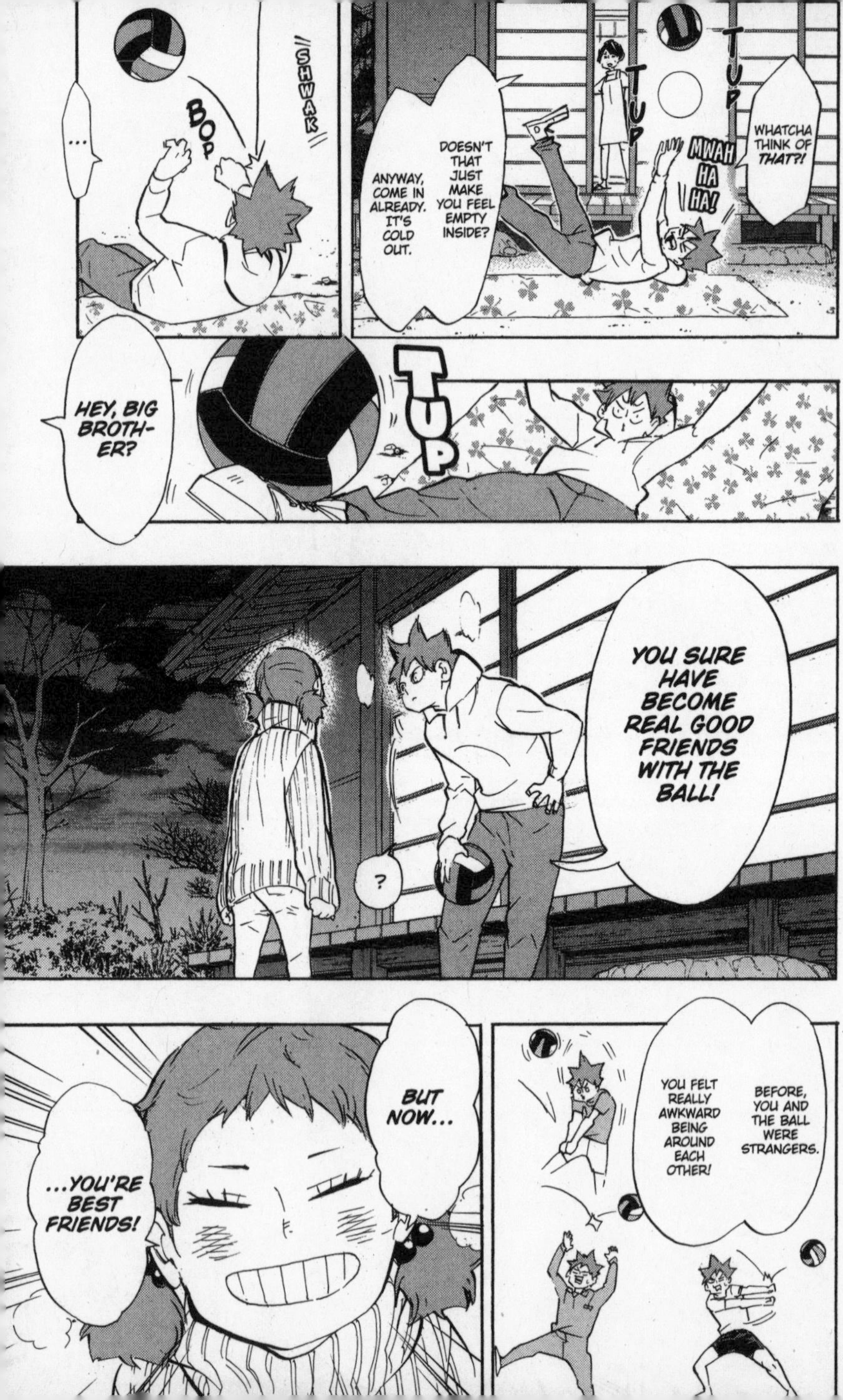
TUP TUP
WHATCHA THINK OF THAT?!
MWAH HA HA!
DOESN'T THAT JUST MAKE YOU FEEL EMPTY INSIDE?
ANYWAY, COME IN ALREADY. IT'S COLD OUT.
SHWAK
BOP
...
TUP TUP
HEY, BIG BROTH-ER?
YOU SURE HAVE BECOME REAL GOOD FRIENDS WITH THE BALL!
?
BEFORE, YOU AND THE BALL WERE STRANGERS.
YOU FELT REALLY AWKWARD BEING AROUND EACH OTHER!
BUT NOW...
...YOU'RE BEST FRIENDS!

MC
MVP200
MIKASA
MUR
MUR
REALLY ?
THANK YOU VERY MUCH!
UWARI

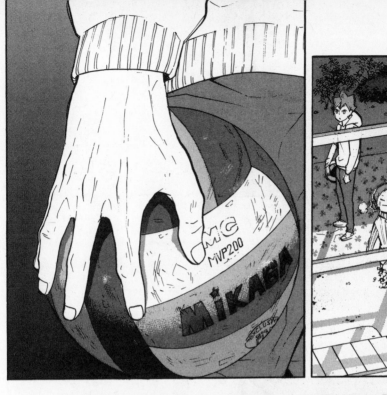

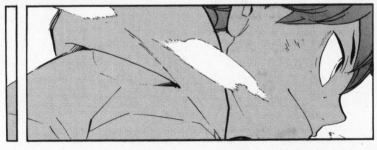

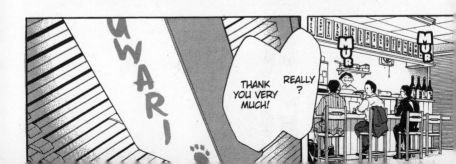

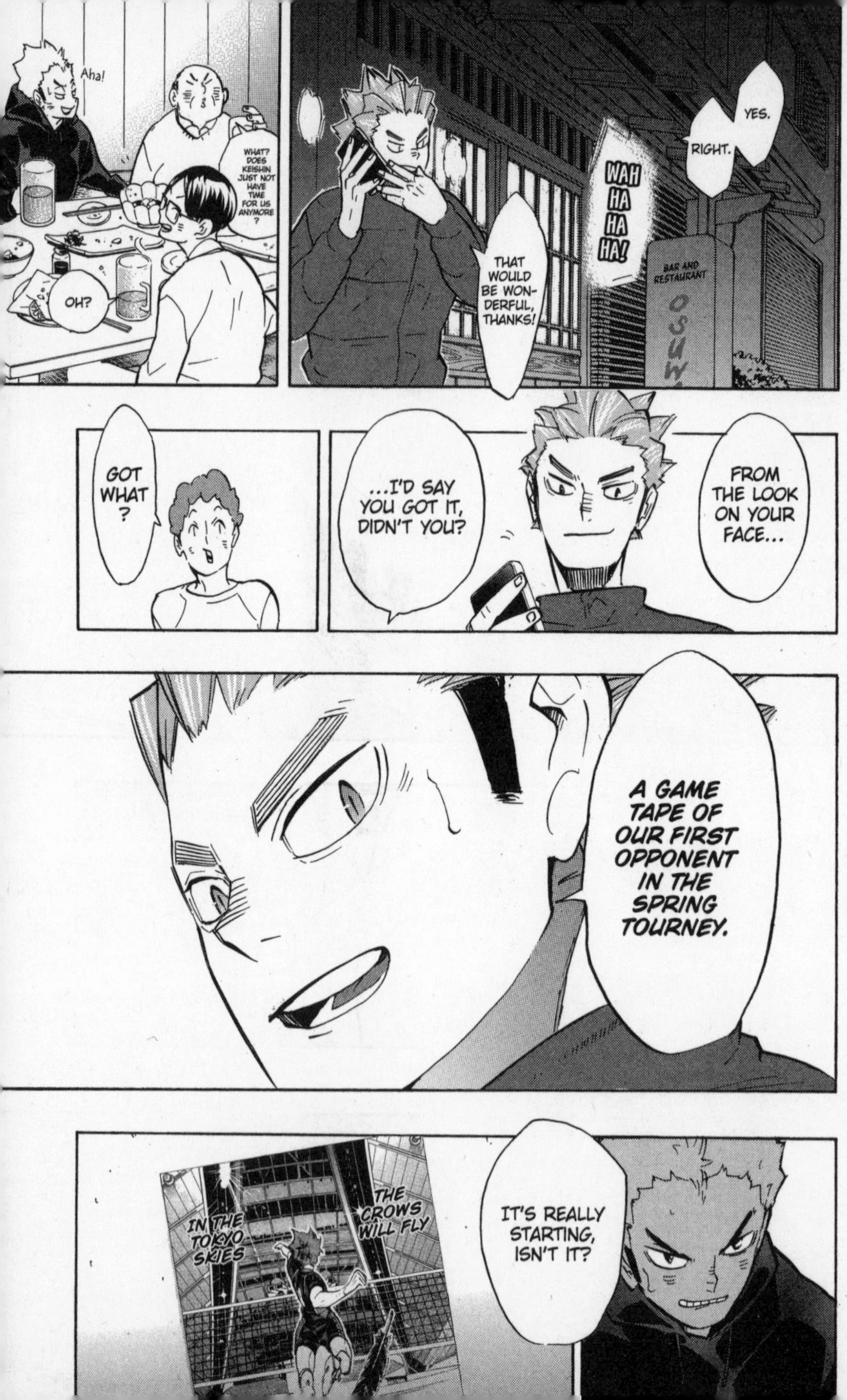
YES.
RIGHT.
WAH HA HA HA!
BAR AND RESTAURANT
THAT WOULD BE WONDERFUL, THANKS!
Aha!
WHAT? DOES KEISHIN JUST NOT HAVE TIME FOR US ANYMORE?
OH?
FROM THE LOOK ON YOUR FACE...
...I'D SAY YOU GOT IT, DIDN'T YOU?
GOT WHAT?
A GAME TAPE OF OUR FIRST OPPONENT IN THE SPRING TOURNEY.
IT'S REALLY STARTING, ISN'T IT?
THE CROWS WILL FLY
IN THE TOKYO SKIES

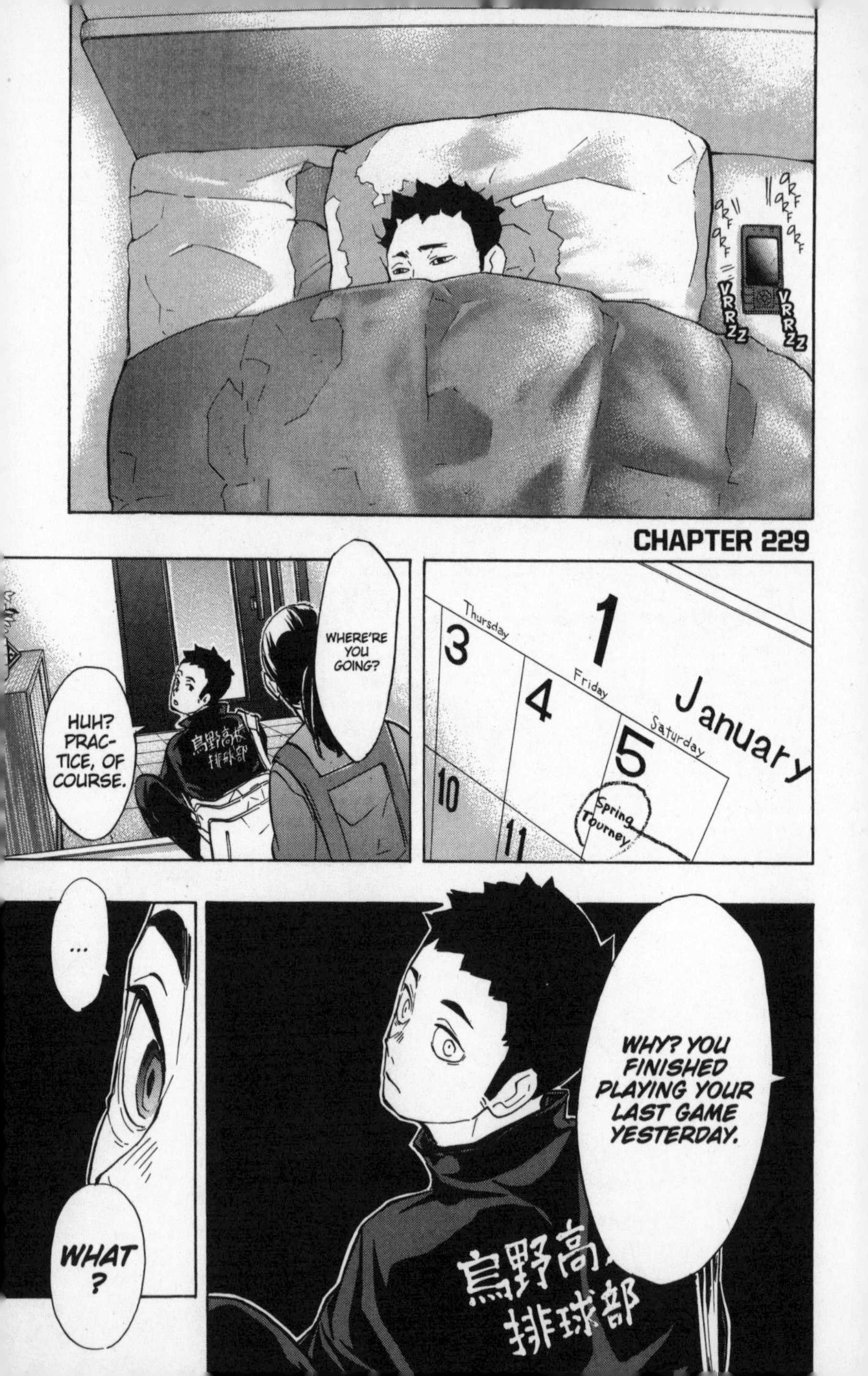
ARF ARF ARF ARF
VRRZZ VRRZZ
CHAPTER 229
3 Thursday
1
4 Friday
January
5 Saturday
10
11
Spring Tourney
WHERE'RE YOU GOING?
HUH? PRACTICE, OF COURSE.
烏野高校 排球部
WHY? YOU FINISHED PLAYING YOUR LAST GAME YESTERDAY.
排球部
...
WHAT?

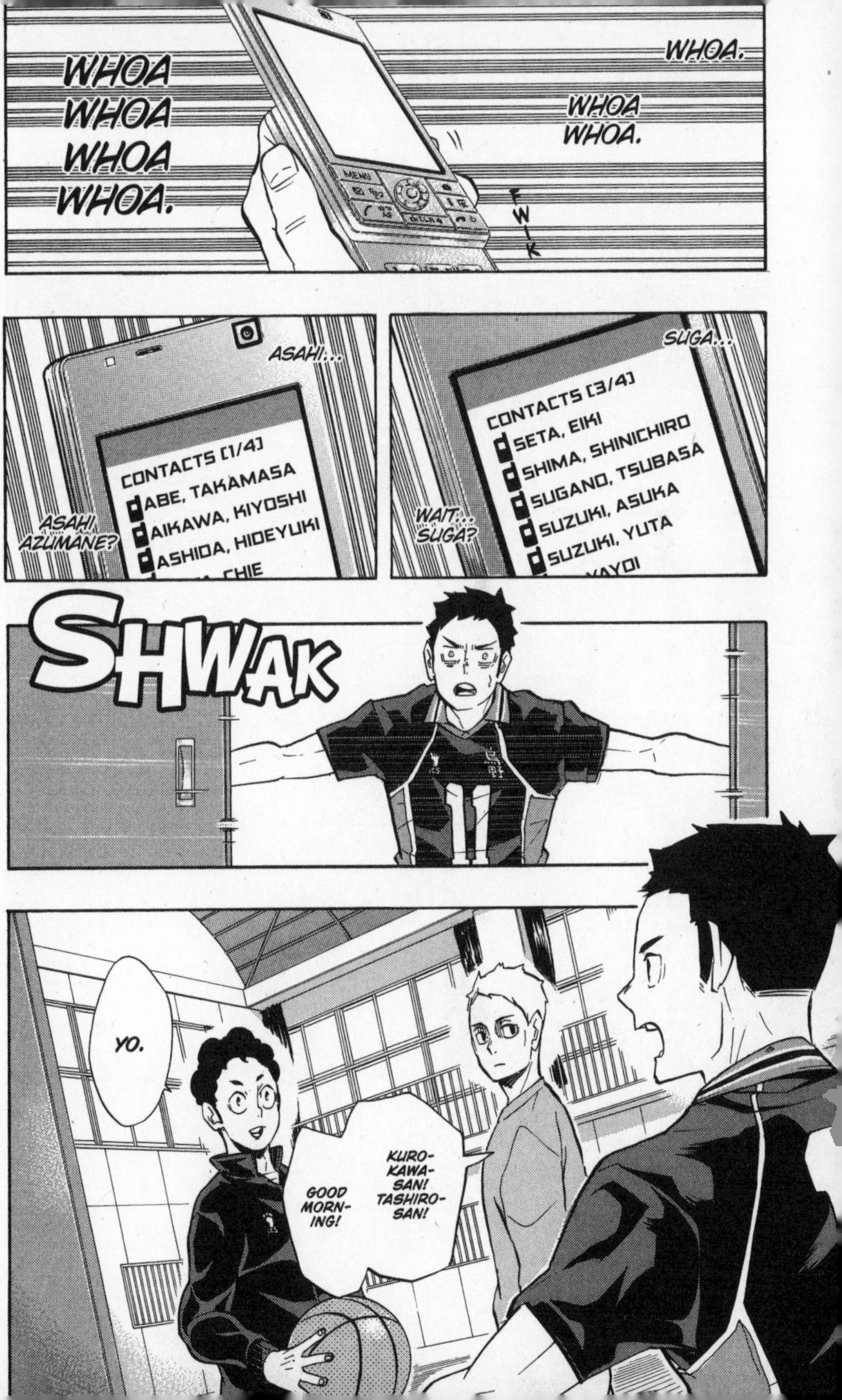
WHOA.
WHOA WHOA.
FWIK
WHOA WHOA WHOA WHOA.
SUGA...
CONTACTS [3/4]
SETA, EIKI
SHIMA, SHINICHIRO
SUGANO, TSUBASA
SUZUKI, ASUKA
SUZUKI, YUTA
WAIT... SUGA?
ASAHI...
CONTACTS [1/4]
ABE, TAKAMASA
AIKAWA, KIYOSHI
ASHIDA, HIDEYUKI
ASAHI AZUMANE?
SHWAK
KURO-KAWA-SAN! TASHIRO-SAN!
GOOD MORN-ING!
YO.

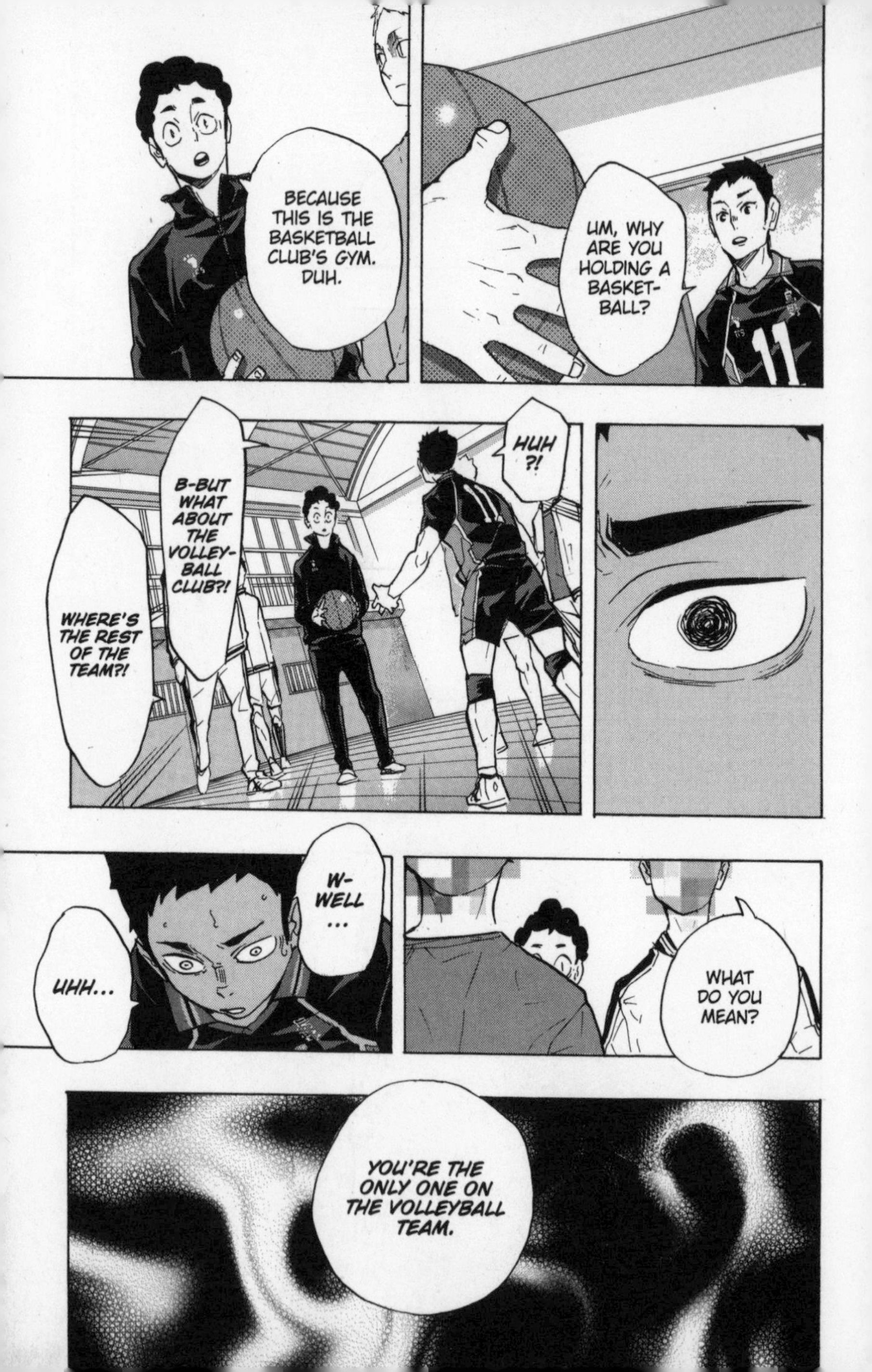
UM, WHY ARE YOU HOLDING A BASKETBALL?
BECAUSE THIS IS THE BASKETBALL CLUB'S GYM. DUH.
HUH?!
B-BUT WHAT ABOUT THE VOLLEYBALL CLUB?!
WHERE'S THE REST OF THE TEAM?!
WHAT DO YOU MEAN?
W-WELL...
UHH...
YOU'RE THE ONLY ONE ON THE VOLLEYBALL TEAM.

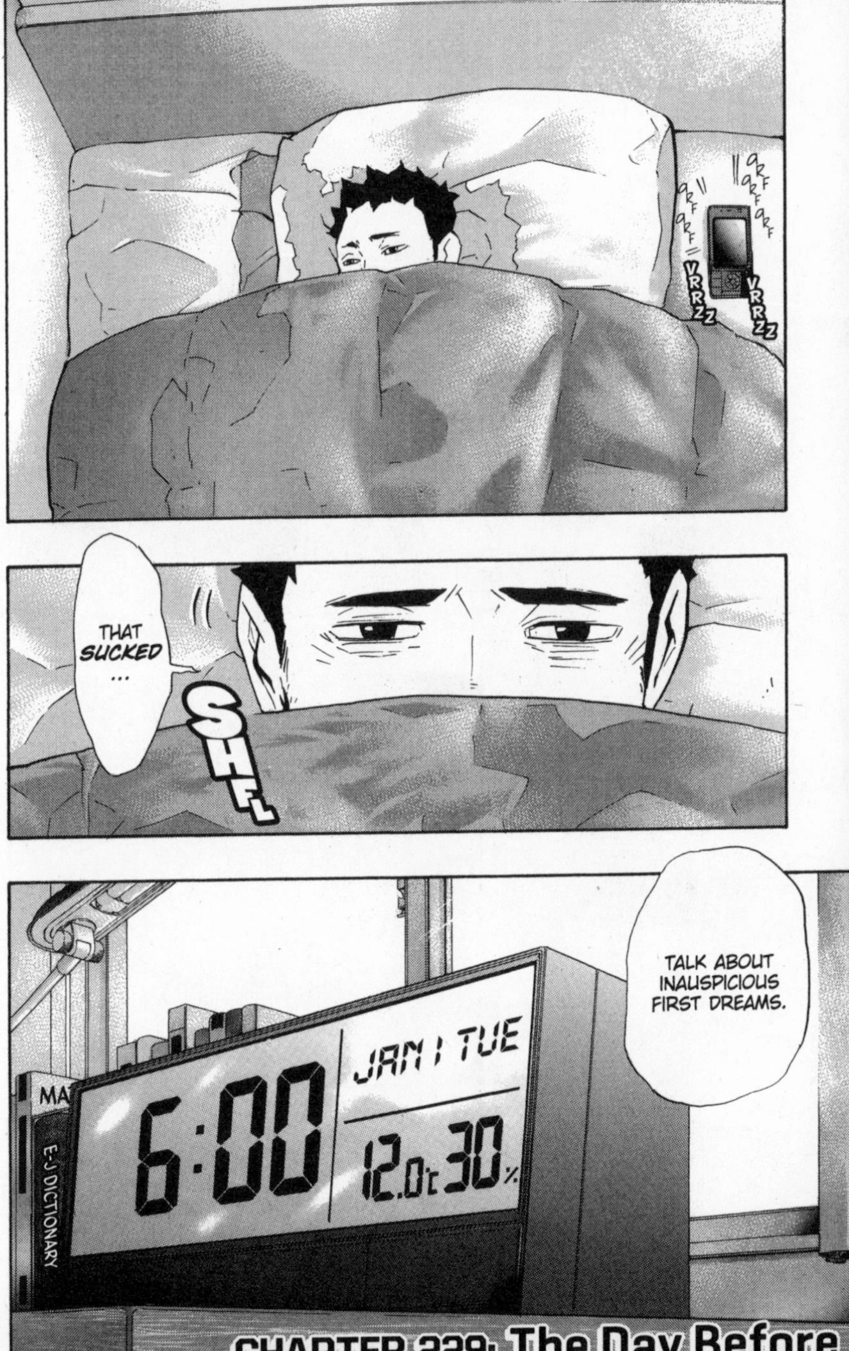
VRRZZ
VRRZZ
ARF ARF ARF
ARF ARF ARF
THAT SUCKED ...
SHFL
TALK ABOUT INAUSPICIOUS FIRST DREAMS.
JAN 1 TUE
6:00
12.0°C 30%
MA
E-J DICTIONARY

CHAPTER 229: The Day Before

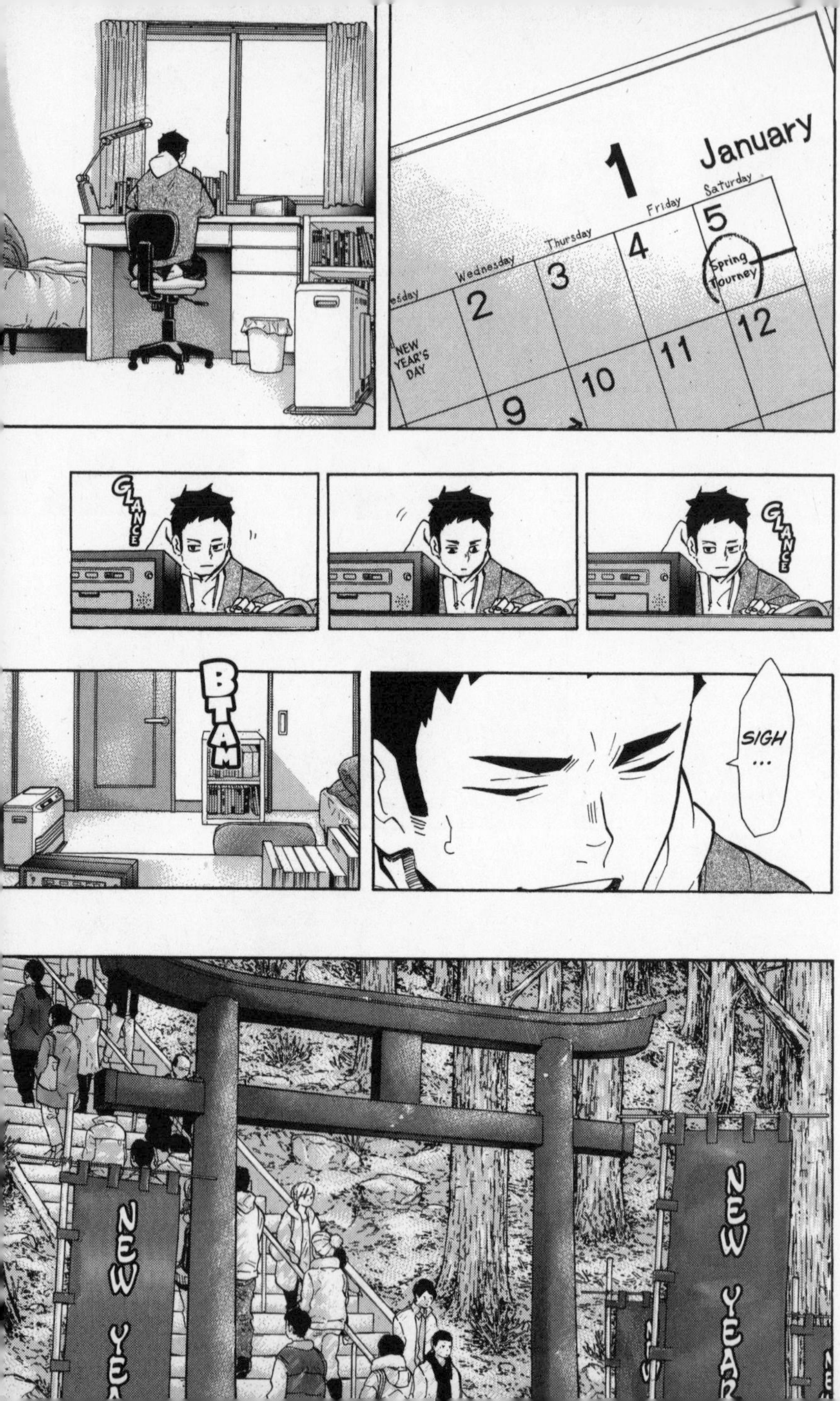
1
January
Saturday
Friday
Thursday
Wednesday
5
Spring Tourney
4
3
2
NEW YEAR'S DAY
12
11
10
9
GLANCE
GLANCE
SIGH...
BTAM
NEW
NEW

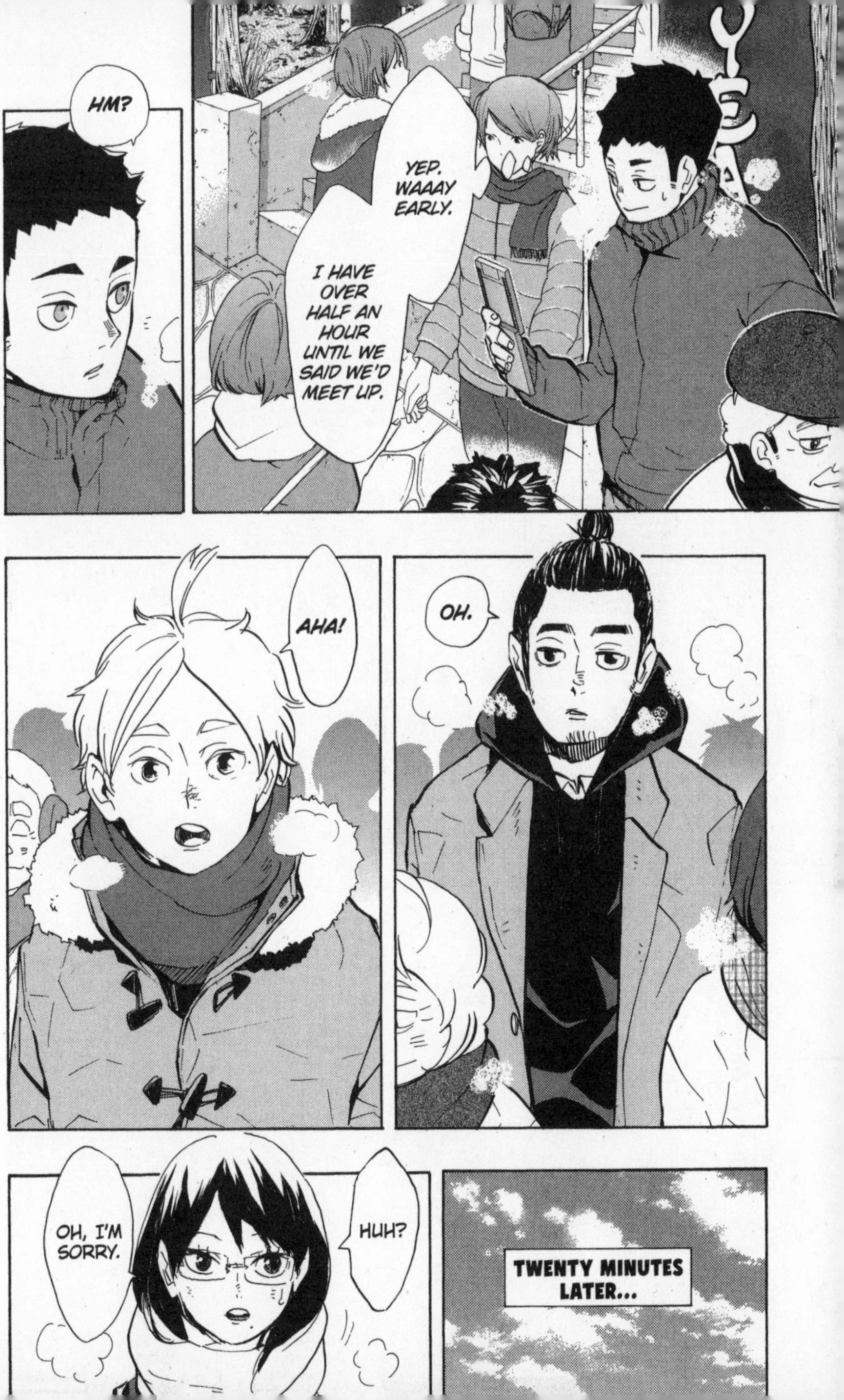
YEP. WAAAY EARLY.
I HAVE OVER HALF AN HOUR UNTIL WE SAID WE'D MEET UP.
HM?
OH.
AHA!
TWENTY MINUTES LATER...
HUH?
OH, I'M SORRY.

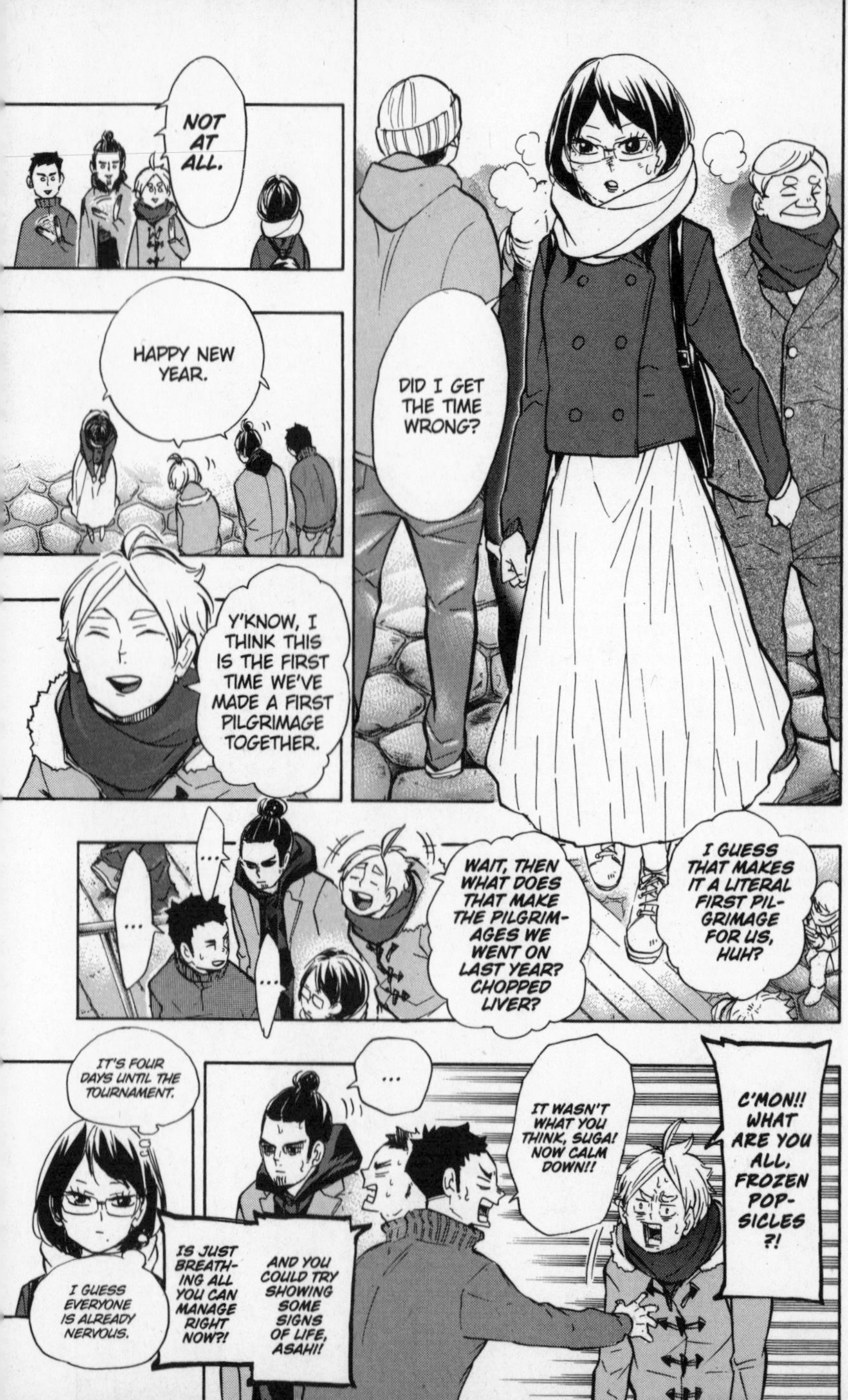
DID I GET THE TIME WRONG?
NOT AT ALL.
HAPPY NEW YEAR.
Y'KNOW, I THINK THIS IS THE FIRST TIME WE'VE MADE A FIRST PILGRIMAGE TOGETHER.
I GUESS THAT MAKES IT A LITERAL FIRST PIL-GRIMAGE FOR US, HUH?
WAIT, THEN WHAT DOES THAT MAKE THE PILGRIM-AGES WE WENT ON LAST YEAR? CHOPPED LIVER?
...
...
...
C'MON!! WHAT ARE YOU ALL, FROZEN POP-SICLES ?!
IS JUST BREATH-ING ALL YOU CAN MANAGE RIGHT NOW?!
AND YOU COULD TRY SHOWING SOME SIGNS OF LIFE, ASAHI!
IT WASN'T WHAT YOU THINK, SUGA! NOW CALM DOWN!!
...
IT'S FOUR DAYS UNTIL THE TOURNAMENT.
I GUESS EVERYONE IS ALREADY NERVOUS.

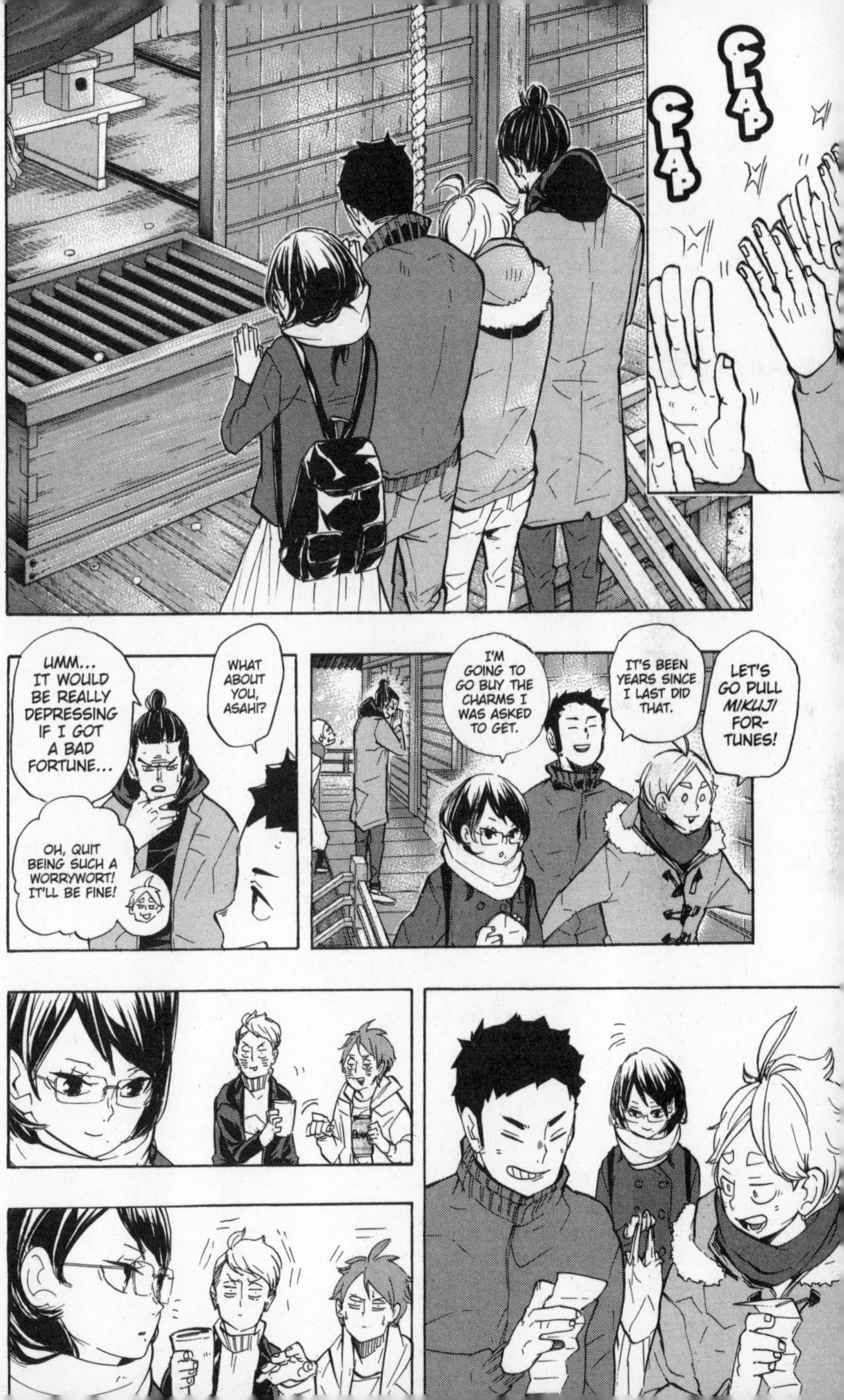
CLAP
CLAP
LET'S GO PULL MIKUJI FORTUNES!
IT'S BEEN YEARS SINCE I LAST DID THAT.
I'M GOING TO GO BUY THE CHARMS I WAS ASKED TO GET.
WHAT ABOUT YOU, ASAHI?
UMM... IT WOULD BE REALLY DEPRESSING IF I GOT A BAD FORTUNE...
OH, QUIT BEING SUCH A WORRYWORT! IT'LL BE FINE!

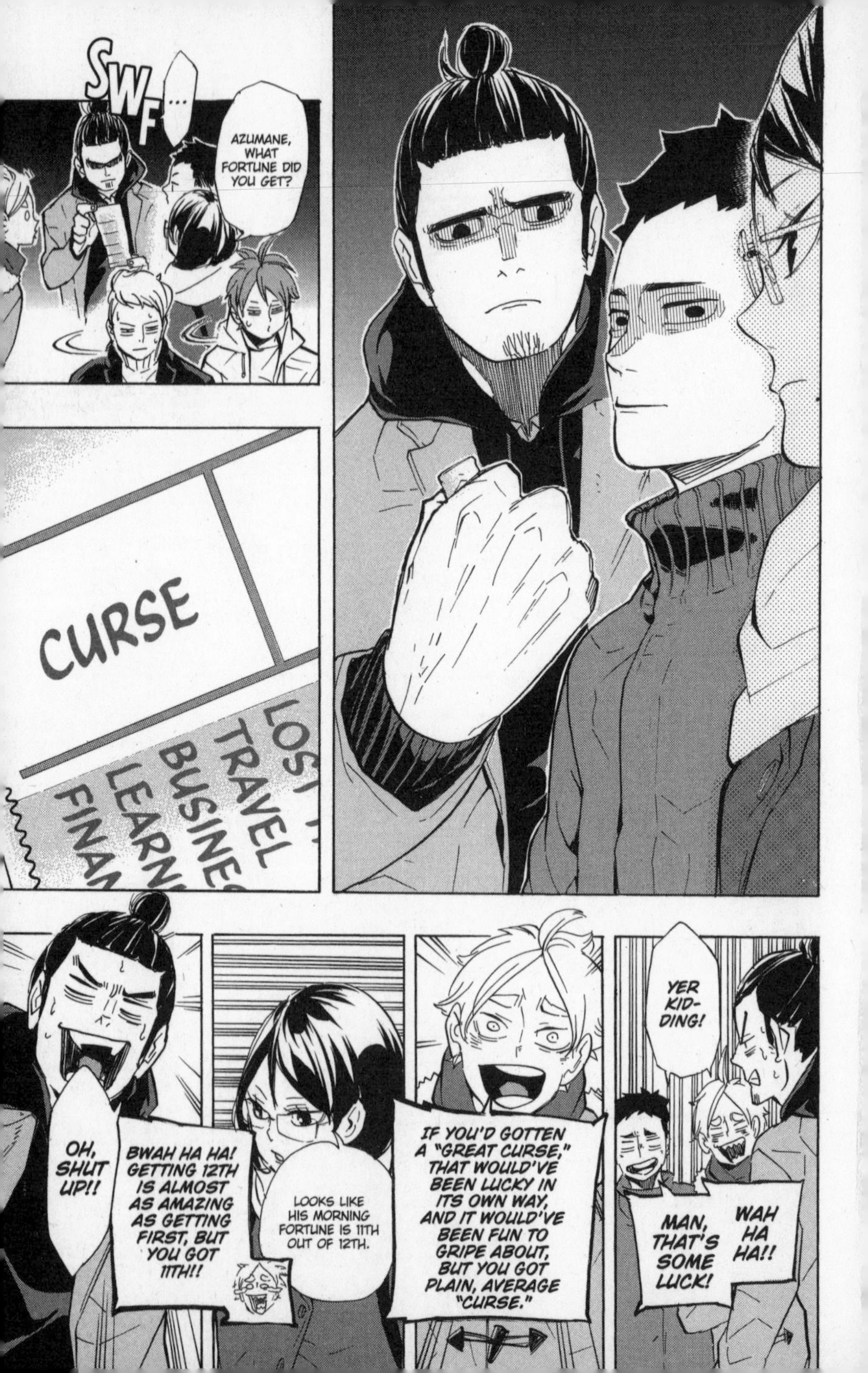
SWF
...
AZUMANE, WHAT FORTUNE DID YOU GET?
CURSE
LOST
TRAVEL
YER KID-DING!
WAH HA HA!!
MAN, THAT'S SOME LUCK!
IF YOU'D GOTTEN A "GREAT CURSE," THAT WOULD'VE BEEN LUCKY IN ITS OWN WAY, AND IT WOULD'VE BEEN FUN TO GRIPE ABOUT, BUT YOU GOT PLAIN, AVERAGE "CURSE."
LOOKS LIKE HIS MORNING FORTUNE IS 11TH OUT OF 12TH.
BWAH HA HA! GETTING 12TH IS ALMOST AS AMAZING AS GETTING FIRST, BUT YOU GOT 11TH!!
OH, SHUT UP!!

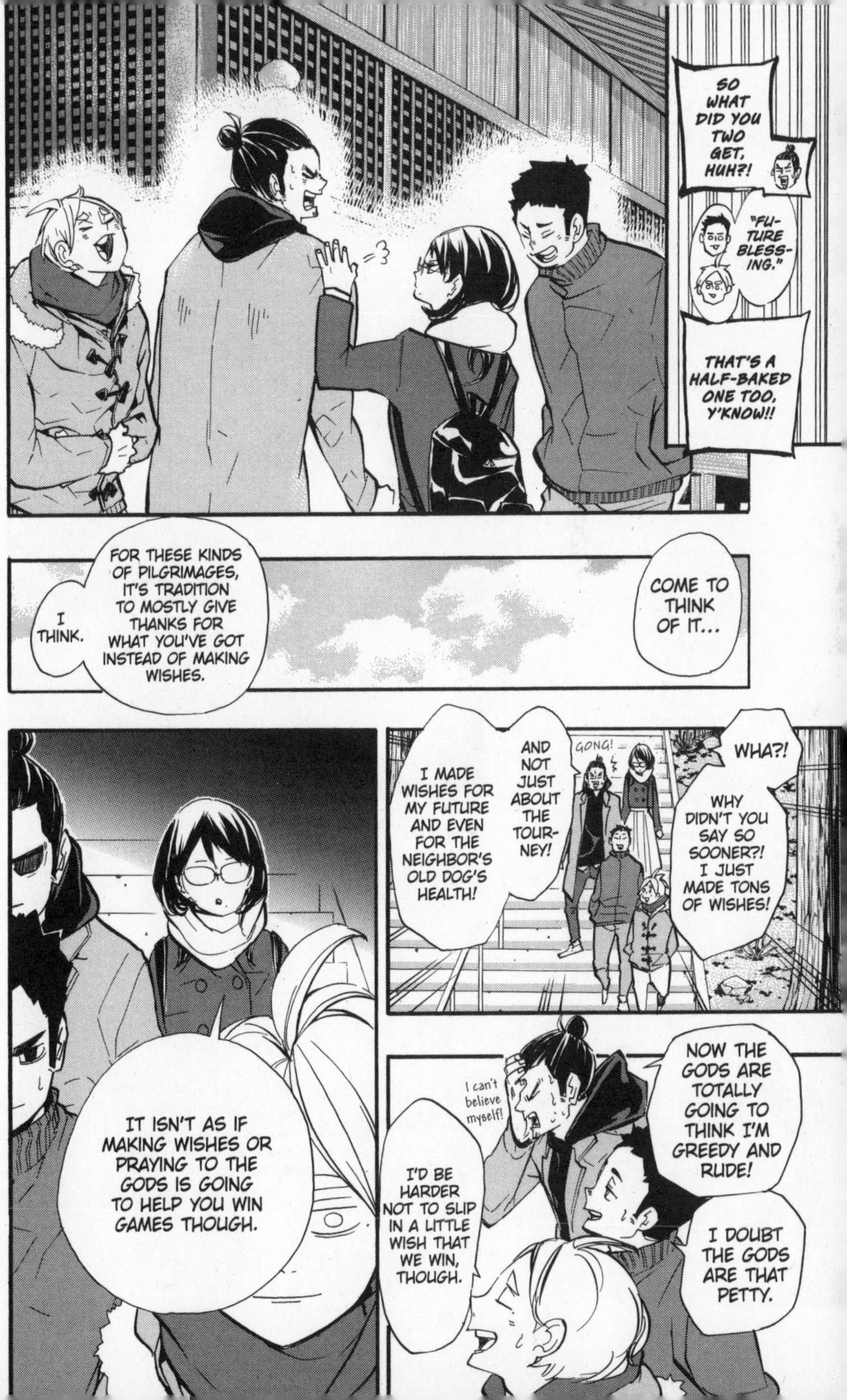
SO WHAT DID YOU TWO GET, HUH?!
"FUTURE BLESSING."
THAT'S A HALF-BAKED ONE TOO, Y'KNOW!!
COME TO THINK OF IT...
FOR THESE KINDS OF PILGRIMAGES, IT'S TRADITION TO MOSTLY GIVE THANKS FOR WHAT YOU'VE GOT INSTEAD OF MAKING WISHES.
I THINK.
WHA?!
WHY DIDN'T YOU SAY SO SOONER?! I JUST MADE TONS OF WISHES!
GONG!
AND NOT JUST ABOUT THE TOURNEY!
I MADE WISHES FOR MY FUTURE AND EVEN FOR THE NEIGHBOR'S OLD DOG'S HEALTH!
NOW THE GODS ARE TOTALLY GOING TO THINK I'M GREEDY AND RUDE!
I can't believe myself!
I DOUBT THE GODS ARE THAT PETTY.
I'D BE HARDER NOT TO SLIP IN A LITTLE WISH THAT WE WIN, THOUGH.
IT ISN'T AS IF MAKING WISHES OR PRAYING TO THE GODS IS GOING TO HELP YOU WIN GAMES THOUGH.

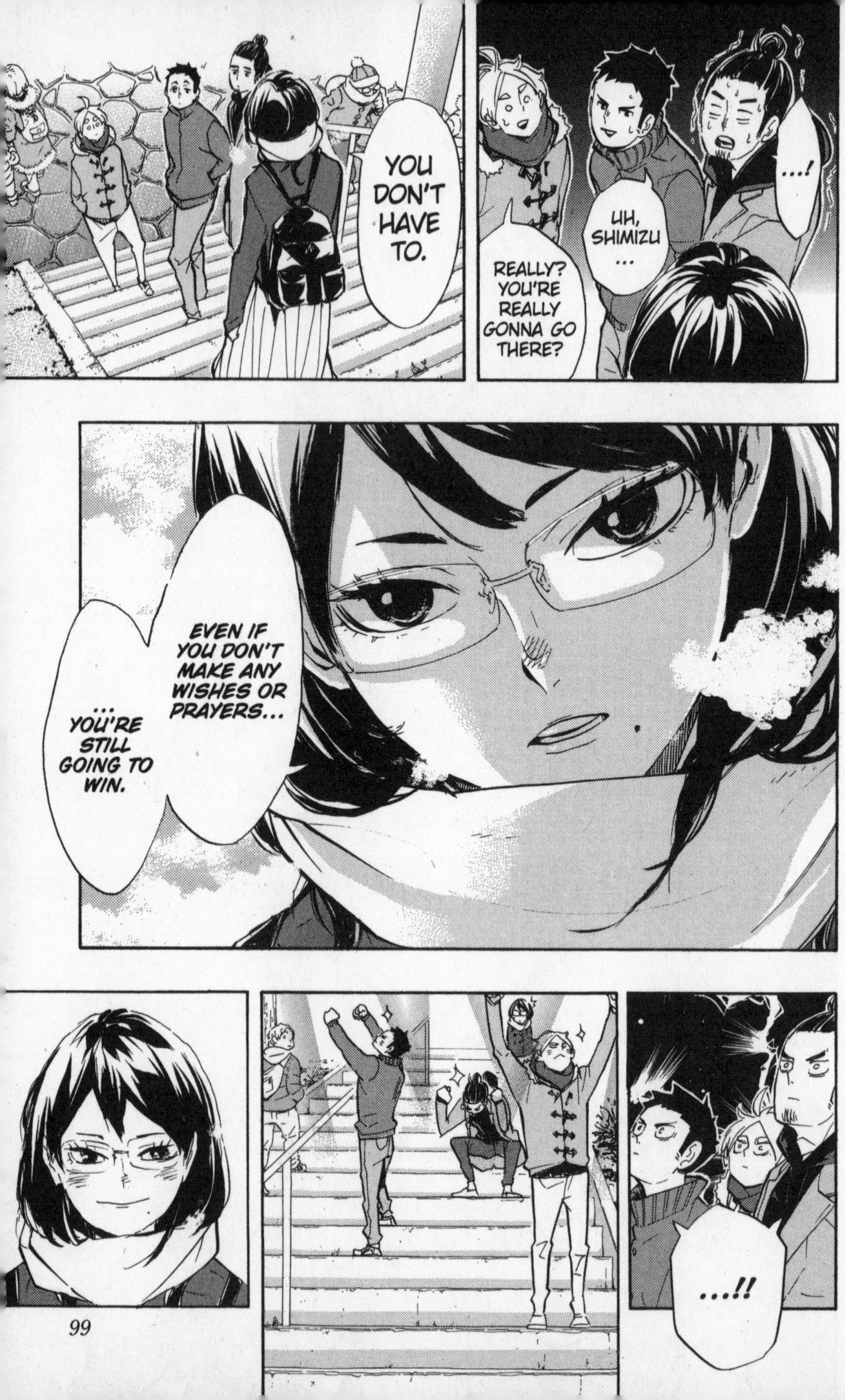
...!
UH, SHIMIZU...
REALLY? YOU'RE REALLY GONNA GO THERE?
YOU DON'T HAVE TO.
EVEN IF YOU DON'T MAKE ANY WISHES OR PRAYERS...
...YOU'RE STILL GOING TO WIN.
...!!

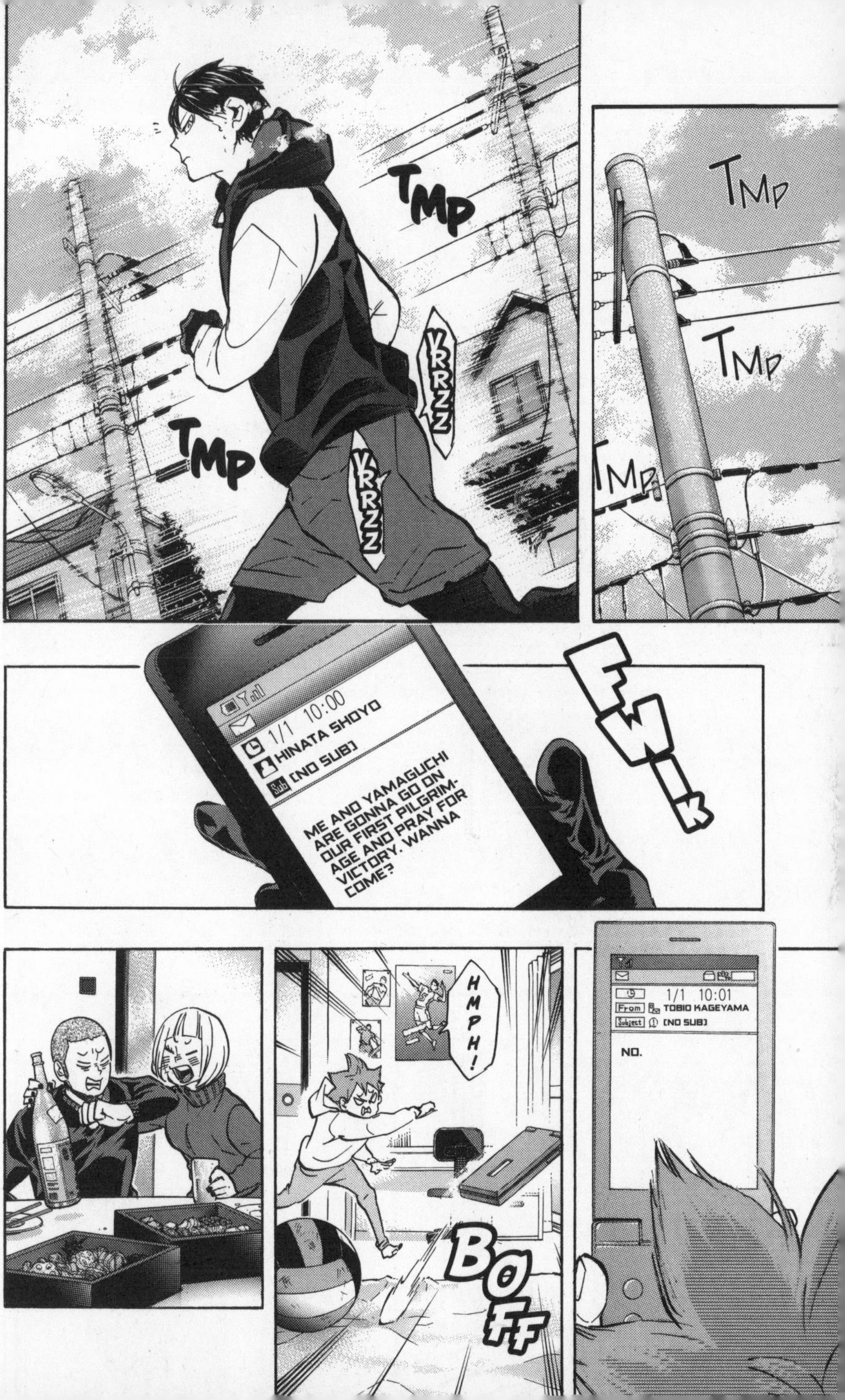

TMP
TMP
TMP
TMP
VRRZZ
VRRZZ
TMP
FWIK
1/1 10:00
HINATA SHOYO
[NO SUB]
ME AND YAMAGUCHI ARE GONNA GO ON OUR FIRST PILGRIMAGE AND PRAY FOR VICTORY. WANNA COME?
1/1 10:01
From TOBIO KAGEYAMA
Subject [NO SUB]
NO.
HMPH!
BOFF

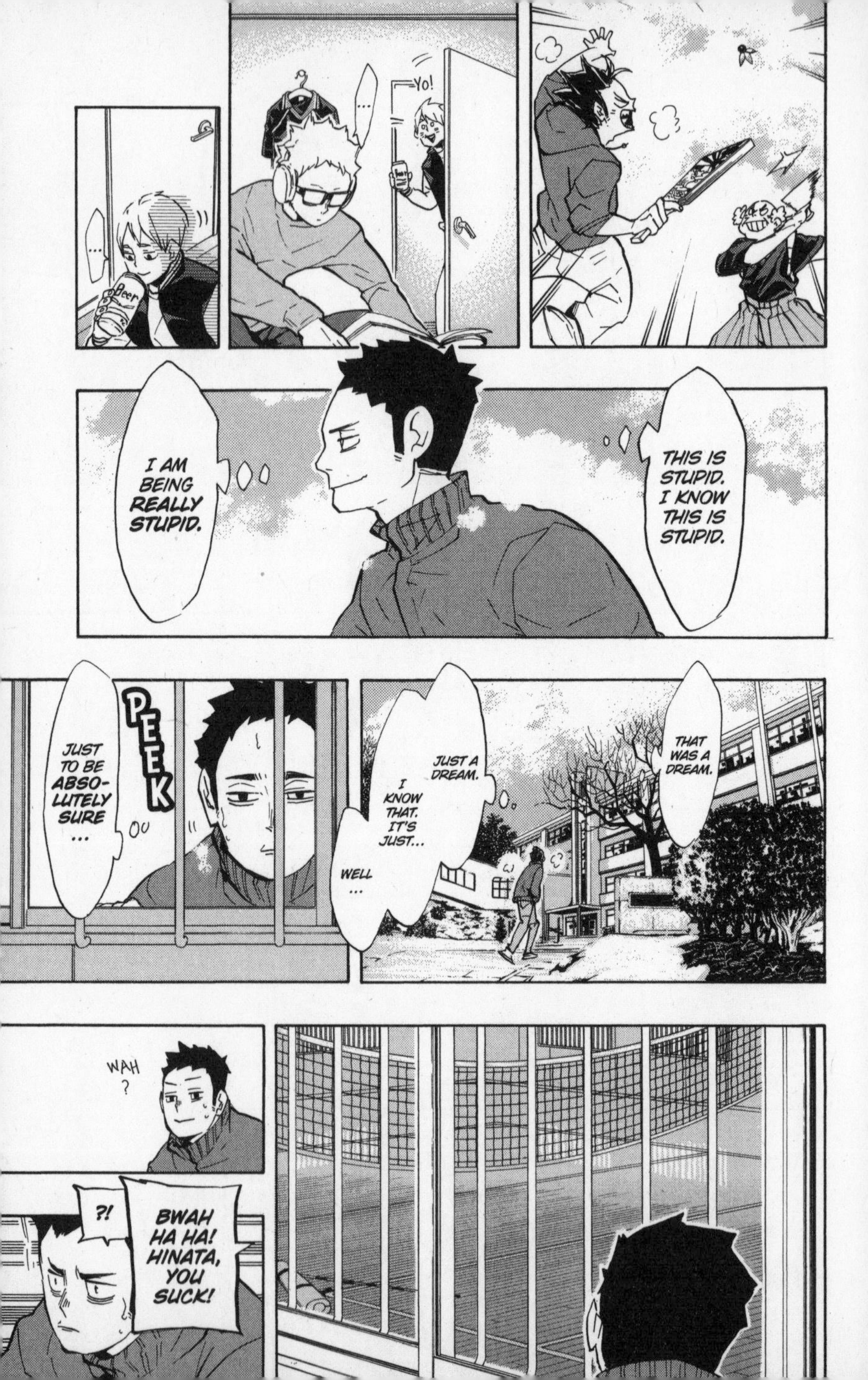
Yo!
...
...
THIS IS STUPID. I KNOW THIS IS STUPID.
I AM BEING REALLY STUPID.
THAT WAS A DREAM.
JUST A DREAM.
I KNOW THAT. IT'S JUST...
WELL ...
PEEK
JUST TO BE ABSO-LUTELY SURE ...
WAH ?
BWAH HA HA! HINATA, YOU SUCK!
?!

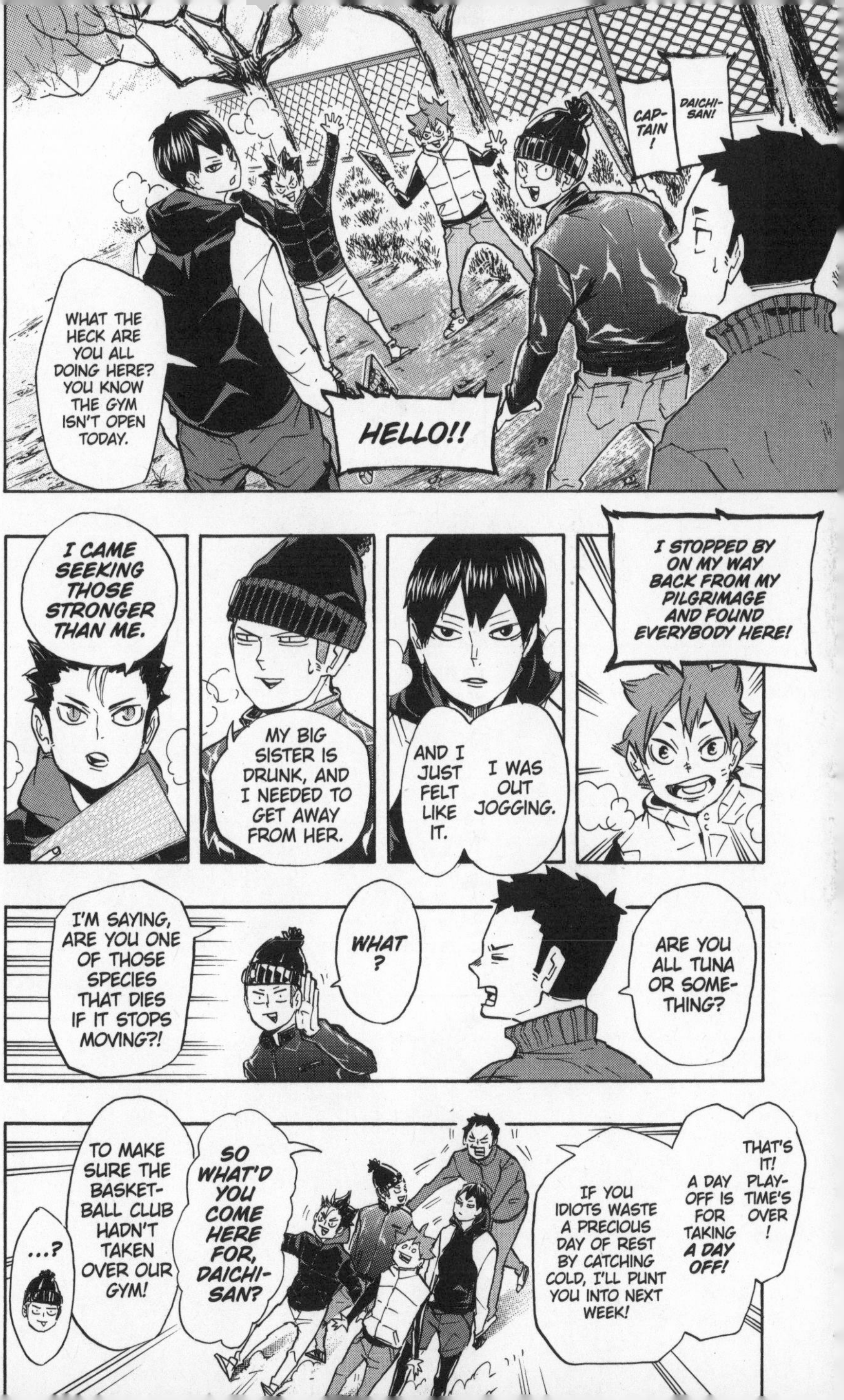
DAICHI-SAN!
CAP-TAIN!
HELLO!!
WHAT THE HECK ARE YOU ALL DOING HERE? YOU KNOW THE GYM ISN'T OPEN TODAY.
I STOPPED BY ON MY WAY BACK FROM MY PILGRIMAGE AND FOUND EVERYBODY HERE!
I WAS OUT JOGGING.
AND I JUST FELT LIKE IT.
MY BIG SISTER IS DRUNK, AND I NEEDED TO GET AWAY FROM HER.
I CAME SEEKING THOSE STRONGER THAN ME.
ARE YOU ALL TUNA OR SOME-THING?
WHAT?
I'M SAYING, ARE YOU ONE OF THOSE SPECIES THAT DIES IF IT STOPS MOVING?!
THAT'S IT! PLAY-TIME'S OVER!
A DAY OFF IS FOR TAKING A DAY OFF!
IF YOU IDIOTS WASTE A PRECIOUS DAY OF REST BY CATCHING COLD, I'LL PUNT YOU INTO NEXT WEEK!
SO WHAT'D YOU COME HERE FOR, DAICHI-SAN?
TO MAKE SURE THE BASKET-BALL CLUB HADN'T TAKEN OVER OUR GYM!
...?

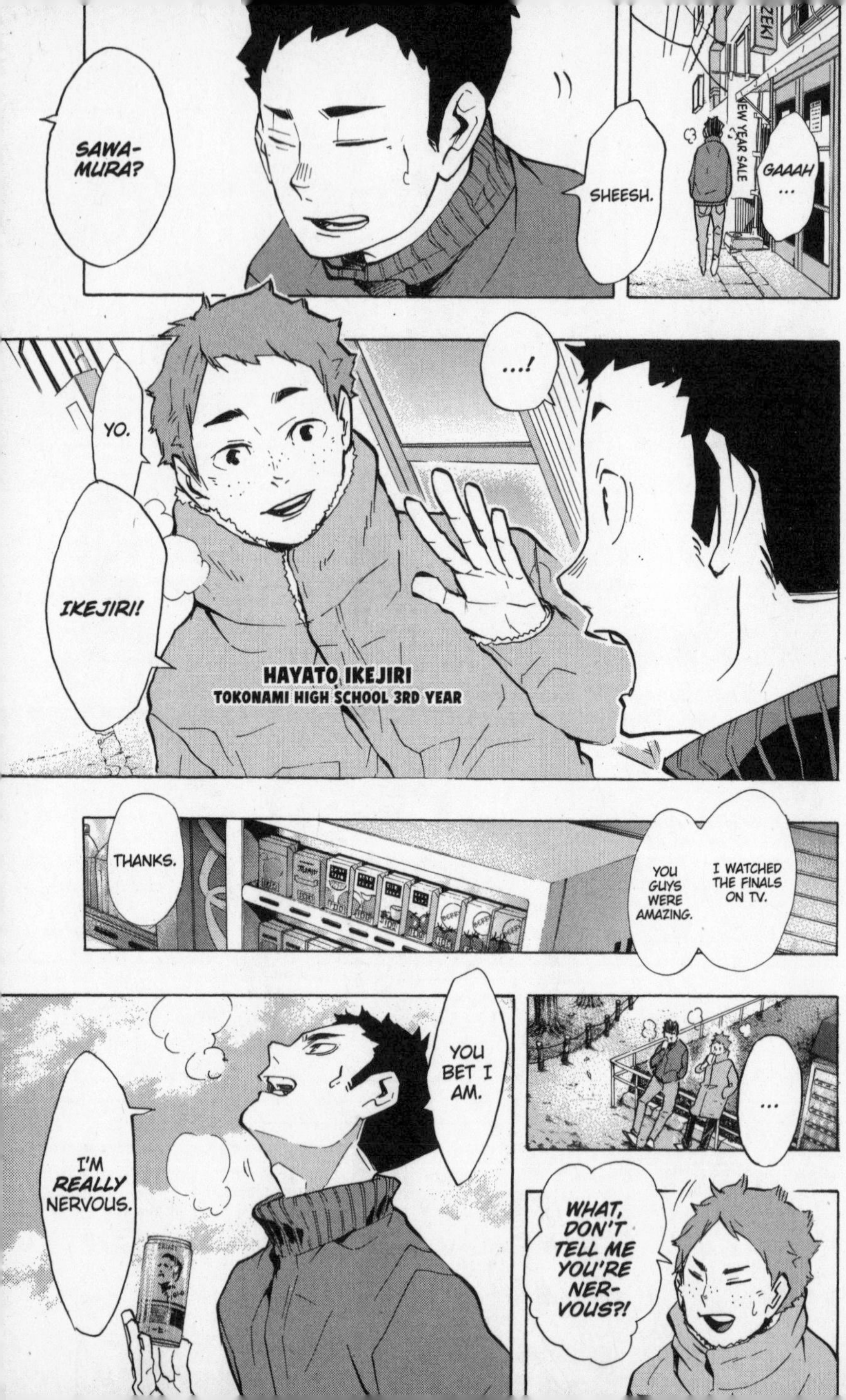
NEW YEAR SALE
GAAAH ...
SHEESH.
SAWA-MURA?
...!
YO.
IKEJIRI!
HAYATO IKEJIRI
TOKONAMI HIGH SCHOOL 3RD YEAR
I WATCHED THE FINALS ON TV.
YOU GUYS WERE AMAZING.
THANKS.
...
WHAT, DON'T TELL ME YOU'RE NER-VOUS?!
YOU BET I AM.
I'M REALLY NERVOUS.

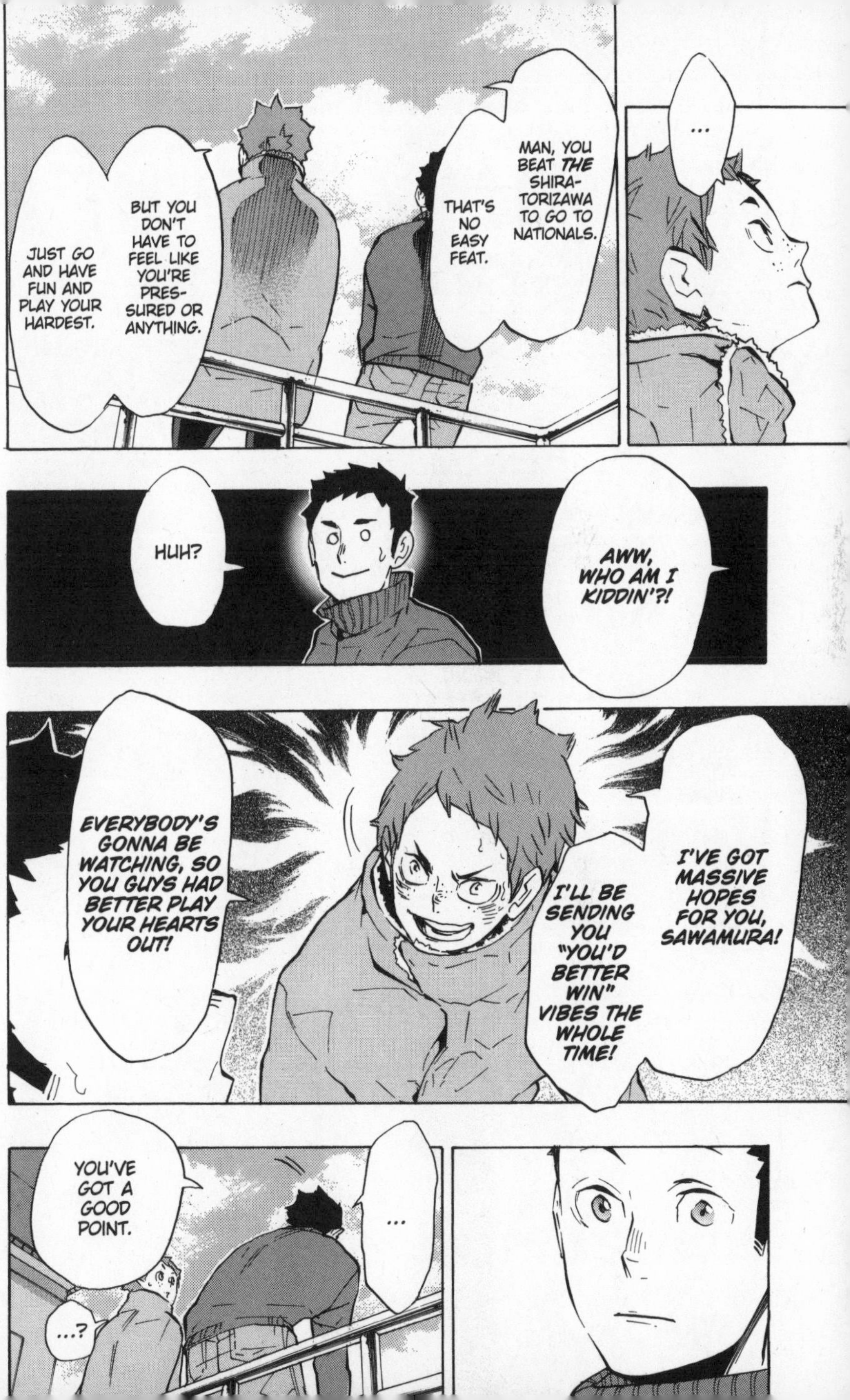
...
MAN, YOU BEAT *THE* SHIRATORIZAWA TO GO TO NATIONALS.
THAT'S NO EASY FEAT.
BUT YOU DON'T HAVE TO FEEL LIKE YOU'RE PRESSURED OR ANYTHING.
JUST GO AND HAVE FUN AND PLAY YOUR HARDEST.
AWW, WHO AM I KIDDIN'?!
HUH?
I'VE GOT MASSIVE HOPES FOR YOU, SAWAMURA!
I'LL BE SENDING YOU "YOU'D BETTER WIN" VIBES THE WHOLE TIME!
EVERYBODY'S GONNA BE WATCHING, SO YOU GUYS HAD BETTER PLAY YOUR HEARTS OUT!
...
YOU'VE GOT A GOOD POINT.
...?

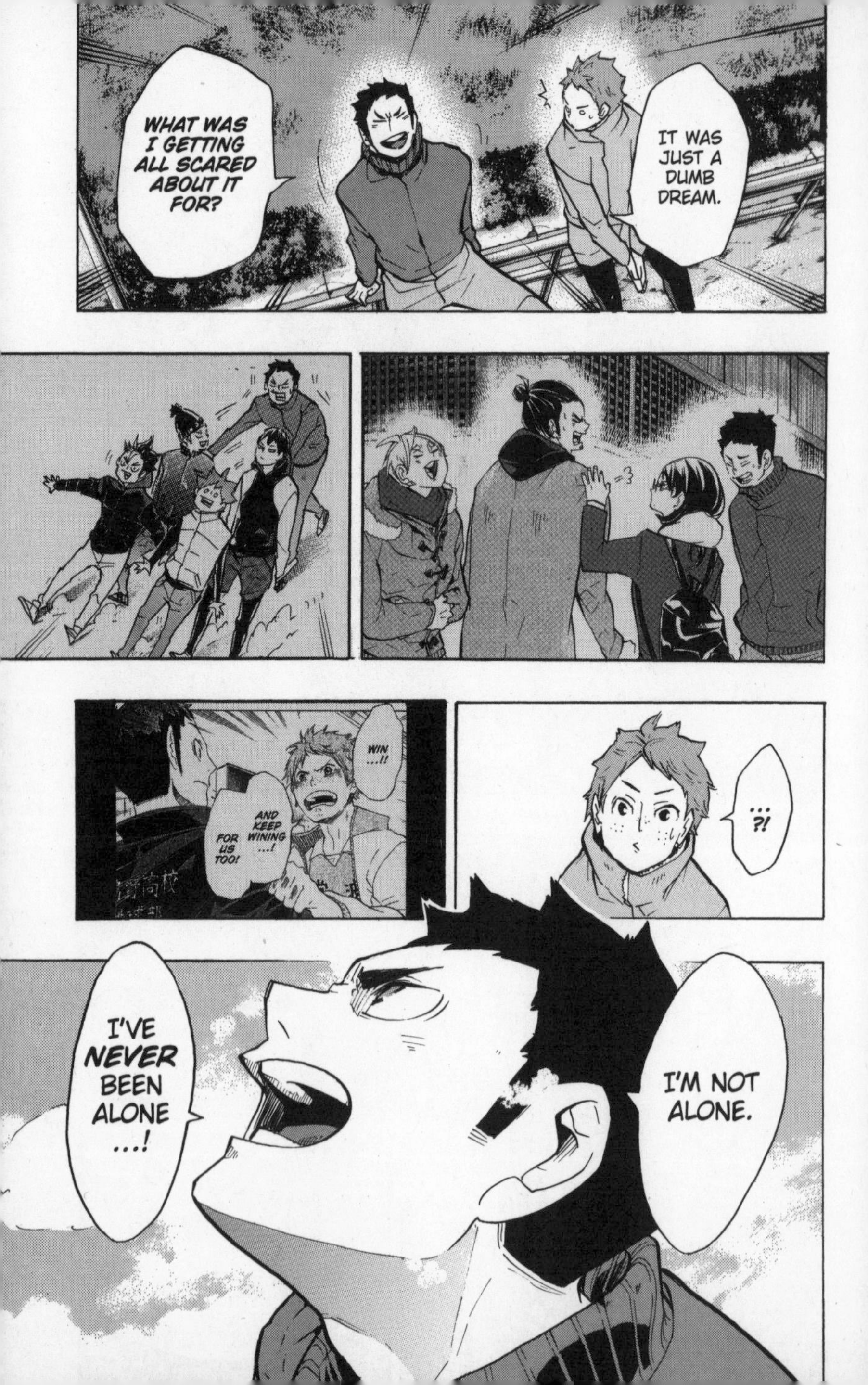
IT WAS JUST A DUMB DREAM.
WHAT WAS I GETTING ALL SCARED ABOUT IT FOR?
...?!
WIN ...!!
AND KEEP WINING ...!
FOR US TOO!
I'M NOT ALONE.
I'VE NEVER BEEN ALONE ...!

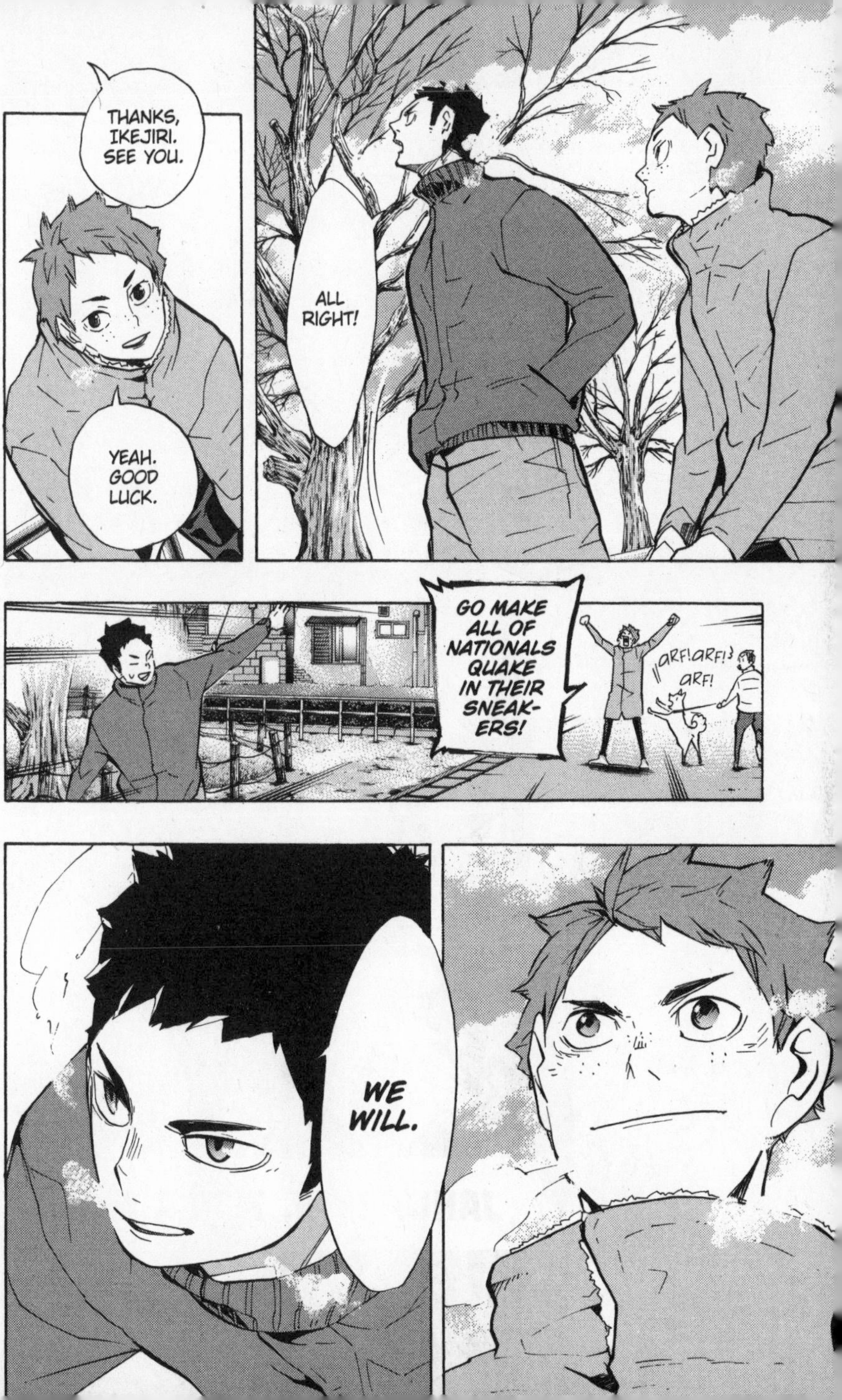
ALL RIGHT!
THANKS, IKEJIRI. SEE YOU.
YEAH. GOOD LUCK.
GO MAKE ALL OF NATIONALS QUAKE IN THEIR SNEAKERS!
ARF! ARF! ARF!
WE WILL.

SEE YOU LATER!

SPRING TOHRNAMENT!! WE'RE GOING!!

JANUARY

FRI	SAT
3 LEAVE!! 4	TOURNEY!! 5
10	

JANUARY 4, 7:30 A.M.

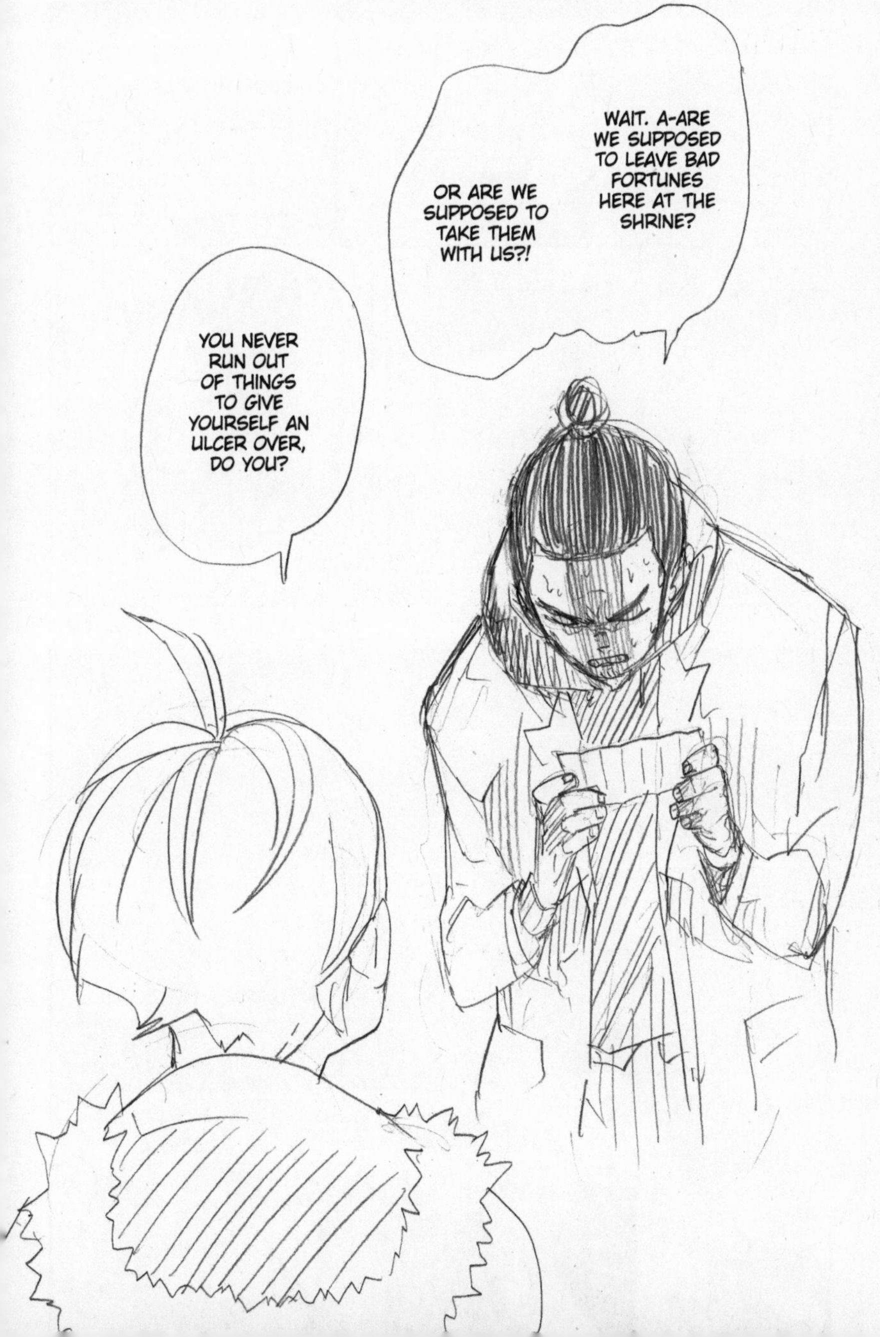
WAIT. A-ARE WE SUPPOSED TO LEAVE BAD FORTUNES HERE AT THE SHRINE?
OR ARE WE SUPPOSED TO TAKE THEM WITH US?!
YOU NEVER RUN OUT OF THINGS TO GIVE YOURSELF AN ULCER OVER, DO YOU?

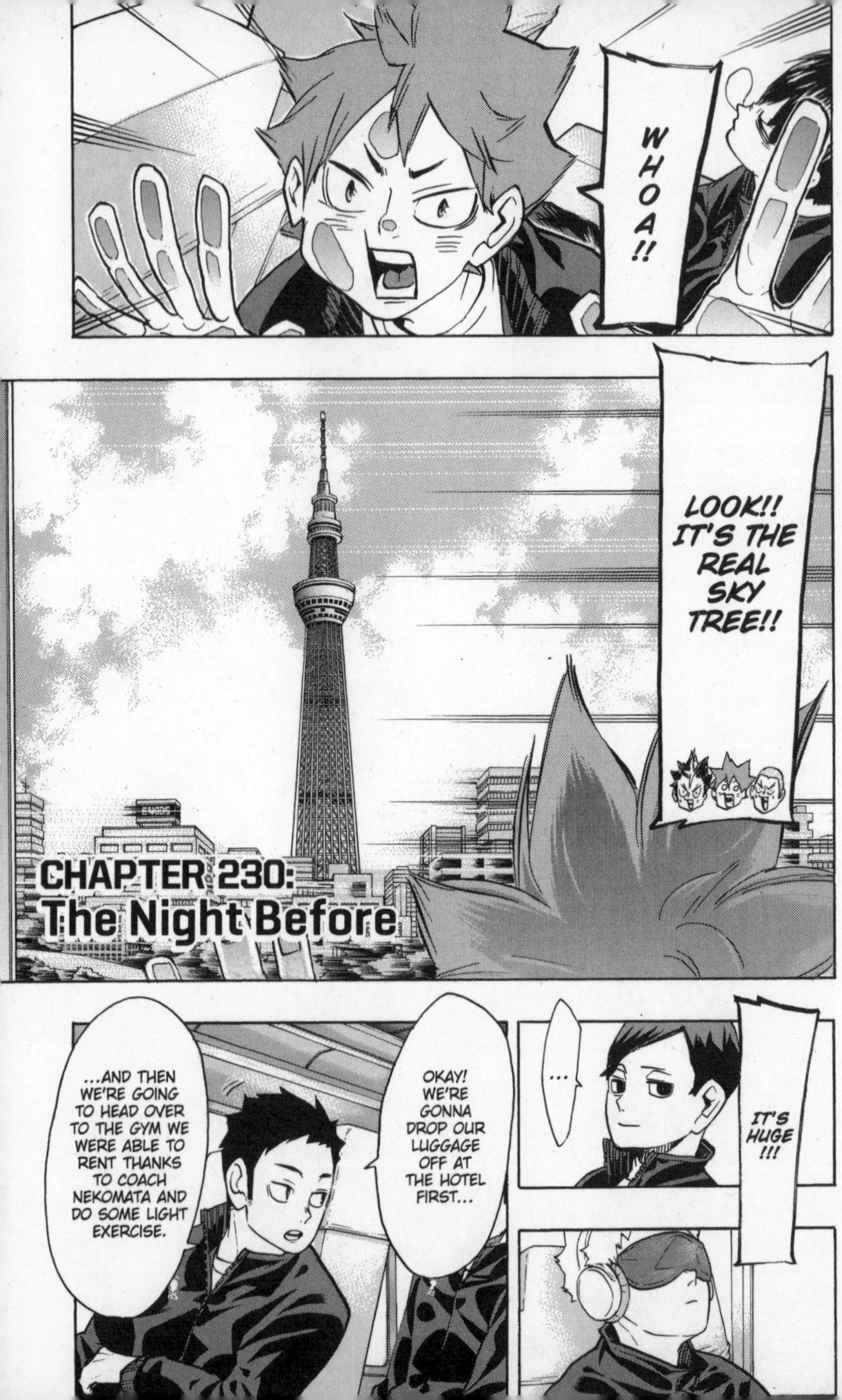
WHOA!!
LOOK!! IT'S THE REAL SKY TREE!!
CHAPTER 230:
The Night Before
IT'S HUGE!!!
...
OKAY! WE'RE GONNA DROP OUR LUGGAGE OFF AT THE HOTEL FIRST...
...AND THEN WE'RE GOING TO HEAD OVER TO THE GYM WE WERE ABLE TO RENT THANKS TO COACH NEKOMATA AND DO SOME LIGHT EXERCISE.

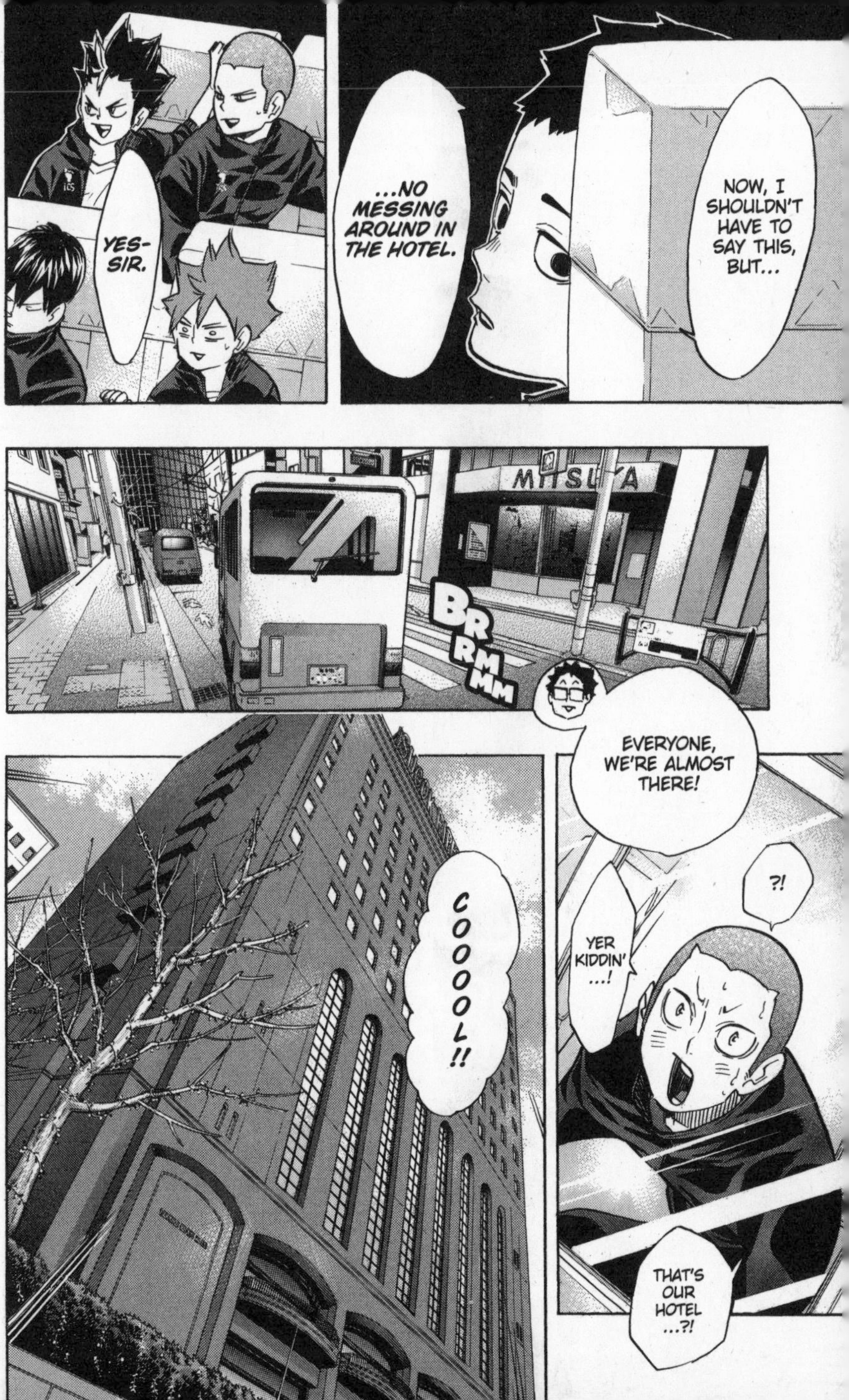
NOW, I SHOULDN'T HAVE TO SAY THIS, BUT...
...NO MESSING AROUND IN THE HOTEL.
YES-SIR.
MITSUYA
BRRMMMM
EVERYONE, WE'RE ALMOST THERE!
?!
YER KIDDIN' ...!
THAT'S OUR HOTEL ...?!
COOOOOL!!

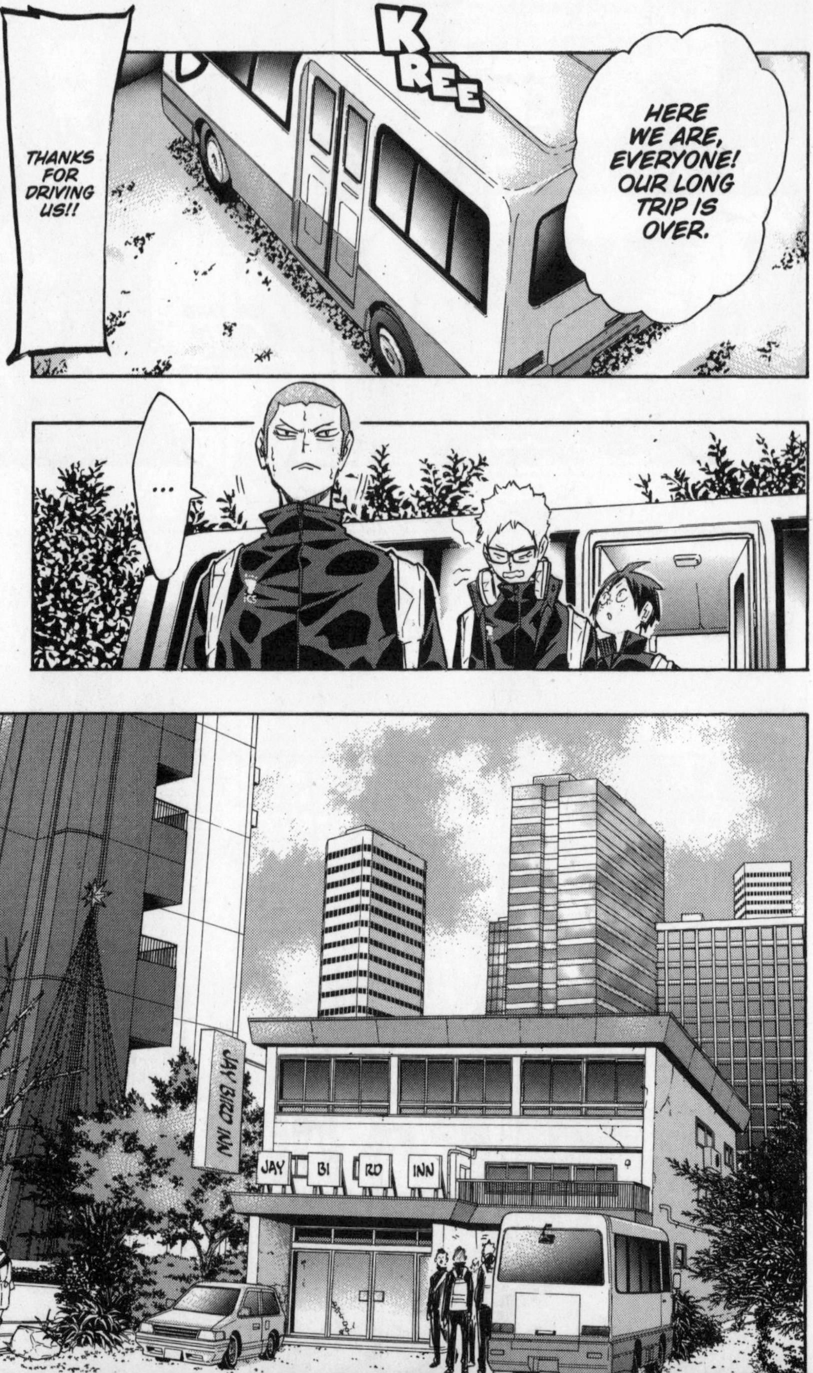
KREE
HERE WE ARE, EVERYONE! OUR LONG TRIP IS OVER.
THANKS FOR DRIVING US!!
...
JAY BIRD INN
JAY BI RD INN

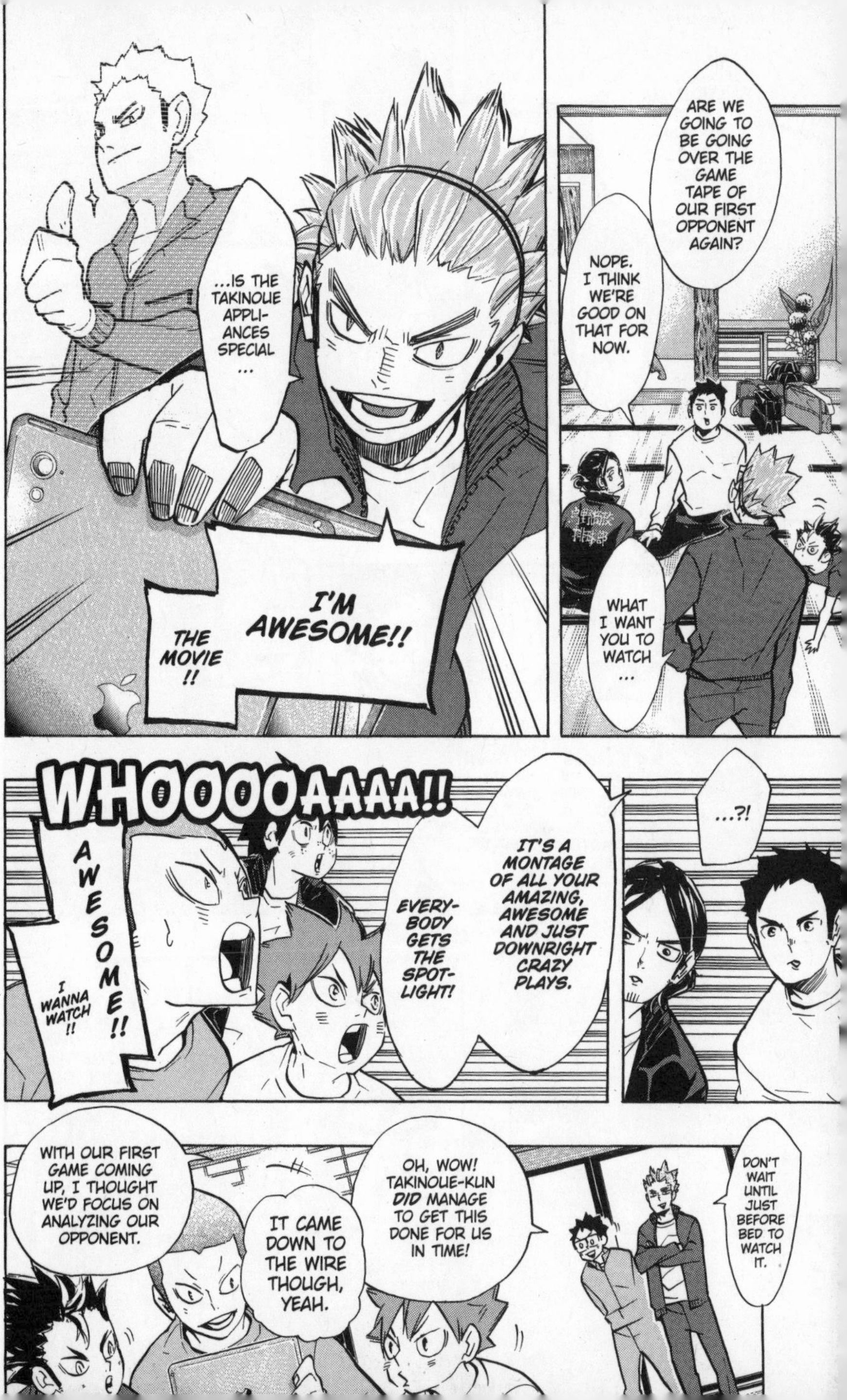
ARE WE GOING TO BE GOING OVER THE GAME TAPE OF OUR FIRST OPPONENT AGAIN?
NOPE. I THINK WE'RE GOOD ON THAT FOR NOW.
WHAT I WANT YOU TO WATCH ...
...IS THE TAKINOUE APPLI-ANCES SPECIAL ...
I'M AWESOME!!
THE MOVIE !!
...?!
IT'S A MONTAGE OF ALL YOUR AMAZING, AWESOME AND JUST DOWNRIGHT CRAZY PLAYS.
EVERY-BODY GETS THE SPOT-LIGHT!
WHOOOOAAAA!!
AWESOME!!
I WANNA WATCH !!
DON'T WAIT UNTIL JUST BEFORE BED TO WATCH IT.
OH, WOW! TAKINOUE-KUN DID MANAGE TO GET THIS DONE FOR US IN TIME!
IT CAME DOWN TO THE WIRE THOUGH, YEAH.
WITH OUR FIRST GAME COMING UP, I THOUGHT WE'D FOCUS ON ANALYZING OUR OPPONENT.

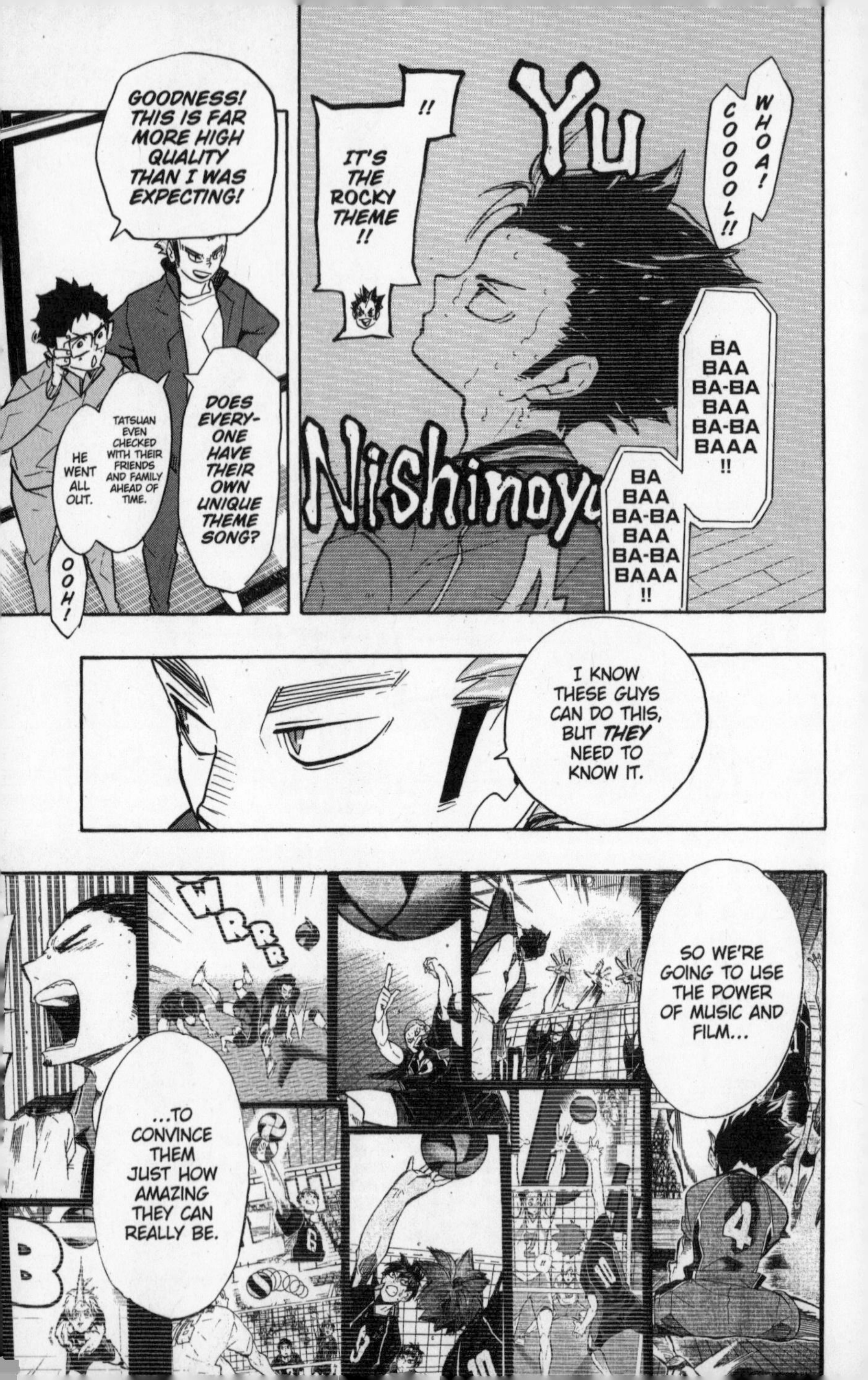
WHOA! COOOOOL!!
Yu Nishinoya
BA BAA BA-BA BAA BA-BA BAAA !!
BA BAA BA-BA BAA BA-BA BAAA !!
!!
IT'S THE ROCKY THEME !!
GOODNESS! THIS IS FAR MORE HIGH QUALITY THAN I WAS EXPECTING!
DOES EVERY-ONE HAVE THEIR OWN UNIQUE THEME SONG?
TATSUAN EVEN CHECKED WITH THEIR FRIENDS AND FAMILY AHEAD OF TIME.
HE WENT ALL OUT.
OOH!
I KNOW THESE GUYS CAN DO THIS, BUT *THEY* NEED TO KNOW IT.
SO WE'RE GOING TO USE THE POWER OF MUSIC AND FILM...
WRRR
...TO CONVINCE THEM JUST HOW AMAZING THEY CAN REALLY BE.

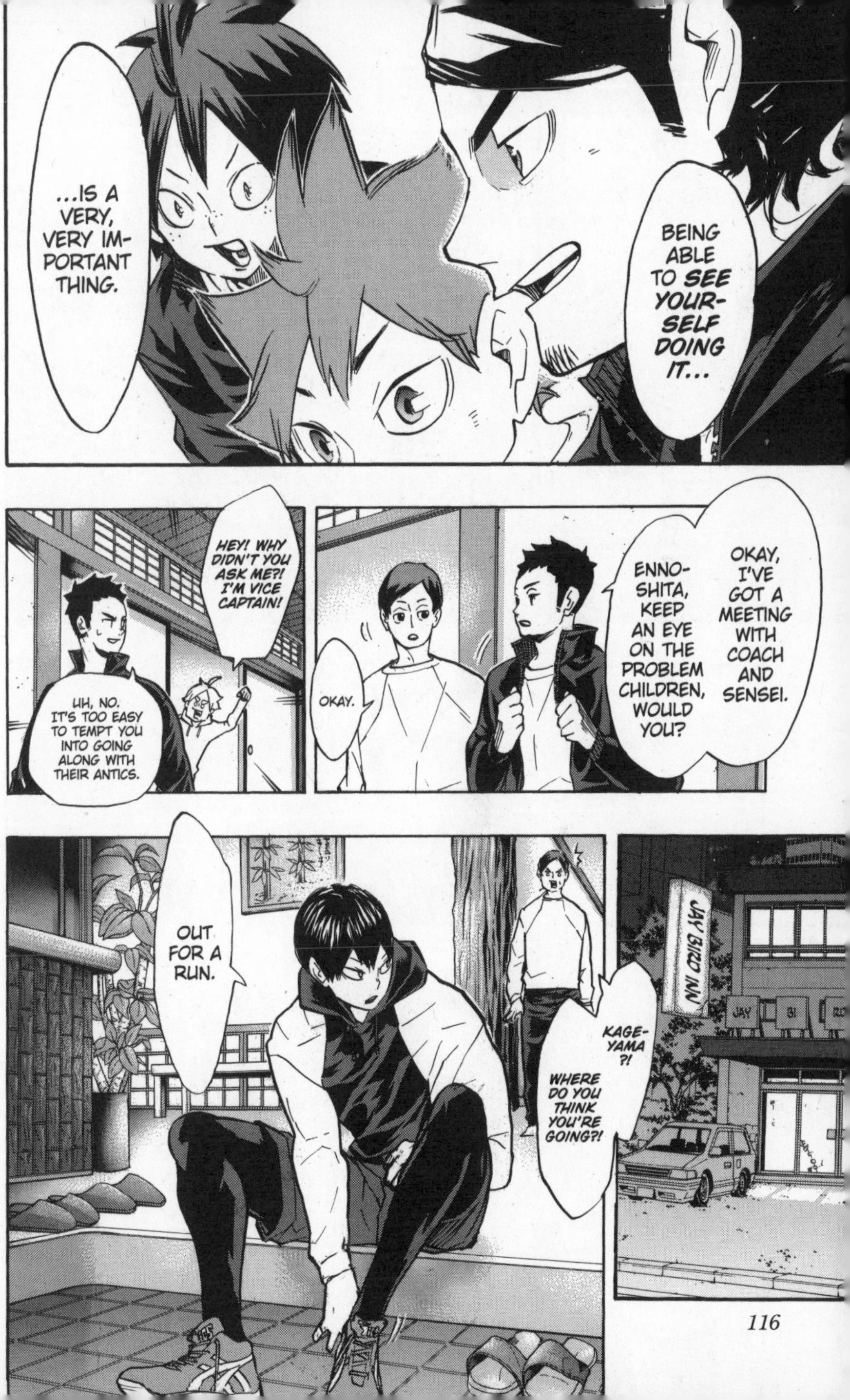
BEING ABLE TO SEE YOURSELF DOING IT...
...IS A VERY, VERY IMPORTANT THING.
OKAY, I'VE GOT A MEETING WITH COACH AND SENSEI.
ENNOSHITA, KEEP AN EYE ON THE PROBLEM CHILDREN, WOULD YOU?
OKAY.
HEY! WHY DIDN'T YOU ASK ME?! I'M VICE CAPTAIN!
UH, NO. IT'S TOO EASY TO TEMPT YOU INTO GOING ALONG WITH THEIR ANTICS.
JAY BIRD INN
KAGEYAMA?!
WHERE DO YOU THINK YOU'RE GOING?!
OUT FOR A RUN.

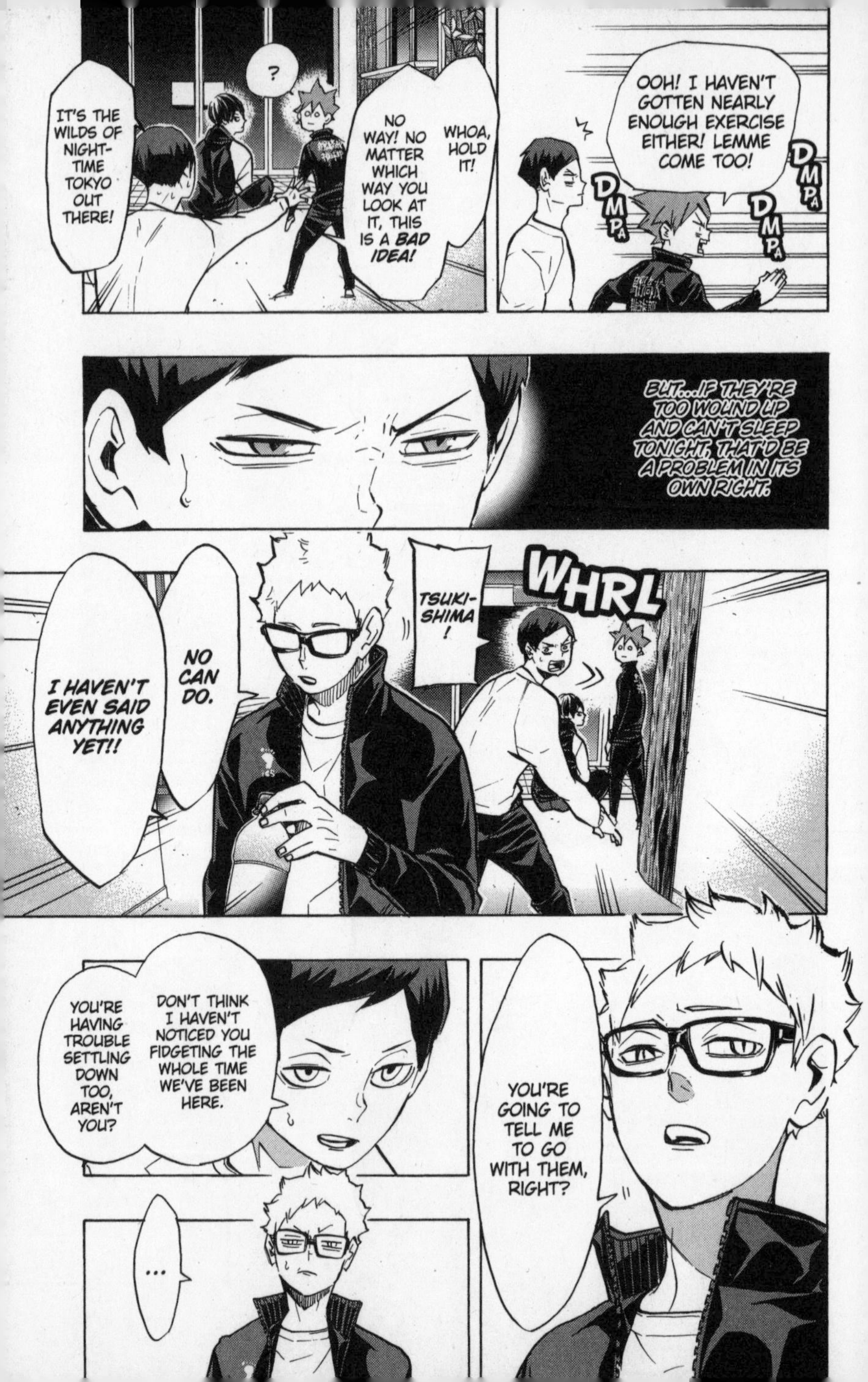
OOH! I HAVEN'T GOTTEN NEARLY ENOUGH EXERCISE EITHER! LEMME COME TOO!
DMPA DMPA DMPA
?
WHOA, HOLD IT!
NO WAY! NO MATTER WHICH WAY YOU LOOK AT IT, THIS IS A BAD IDEA!
IT'S THE WILDS OF NIGHT-TIME TOKYO OUT THERE!
BUT...IF THEY'RE TOO WOUND UP AND CAN'T SLEEP TONIGHT, THAT'D BE A PROBLEM IN ITS OWN RIGHT.
WHRL
TSUKI-SHIMA!
NO CAN DO.
I HAVEN'T EVEN SAID ANYTHING YET!!
YOU'RE GOING TO TELL ME TO GO WITH THEM, RIGHT?
DON'T THINK I HAVEN'T NOTICED YOU FIDGETING THE WHOLE TIME WE'VE BEEN HERE.
YOU'RE HAVING TROUBLE SETTLING DOWN TOO, AREN'T YOU?
...

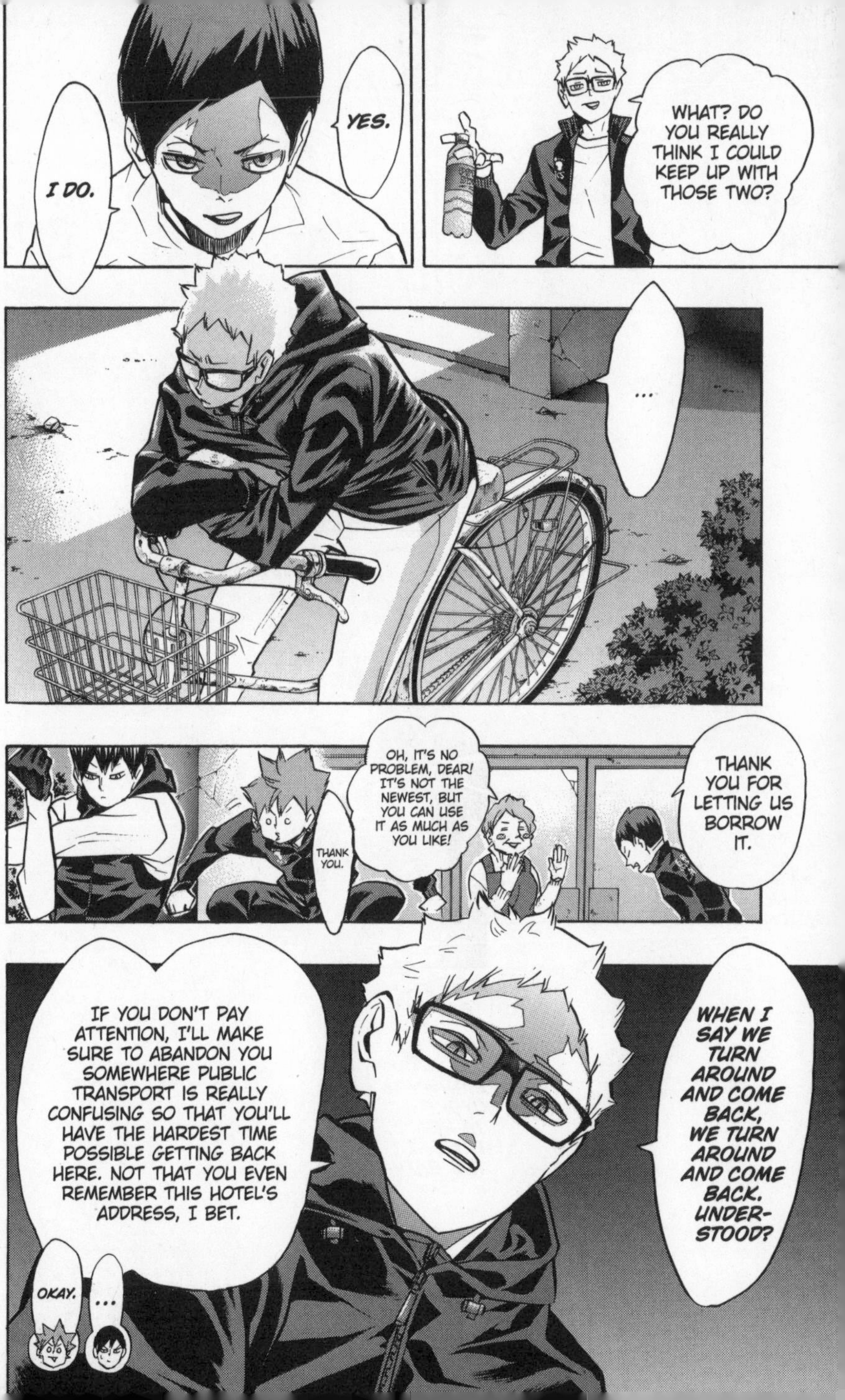
WHAT? DO YOU REALLY THINK I COULD KEEP UP WITH THOSE TWO?
YES.
I DO.
...
THANK YOU FOR LETTING US BORROW IT.
OH, IT'S NO PROBLEM, DEAR! IT'S NOT THE NEWEST, BUT YOU CAN USE IT AS MUCH AS YOU LIKE!
THANK YOU.
WHEN I SAY WE TURN AROUND AND COME BACK, WE TURN AROUND AND COME BACK. UNDER-STOOD?
IF YOU DON'T PAY ATTENTION, I'LL MAKE SURE TO ABANDON YOU SOMEWHERE PUBLIC TRANSPORT IS REALLY CONFUSING SO THAT YOU'LL HAVE THE HARDEST TIME POSSIBLE GETTING BACK HERE. NOT THAT YOU EVEN REMEMBER THIS HOTEL'S ADDRESS, I BET.
...
OKAY.

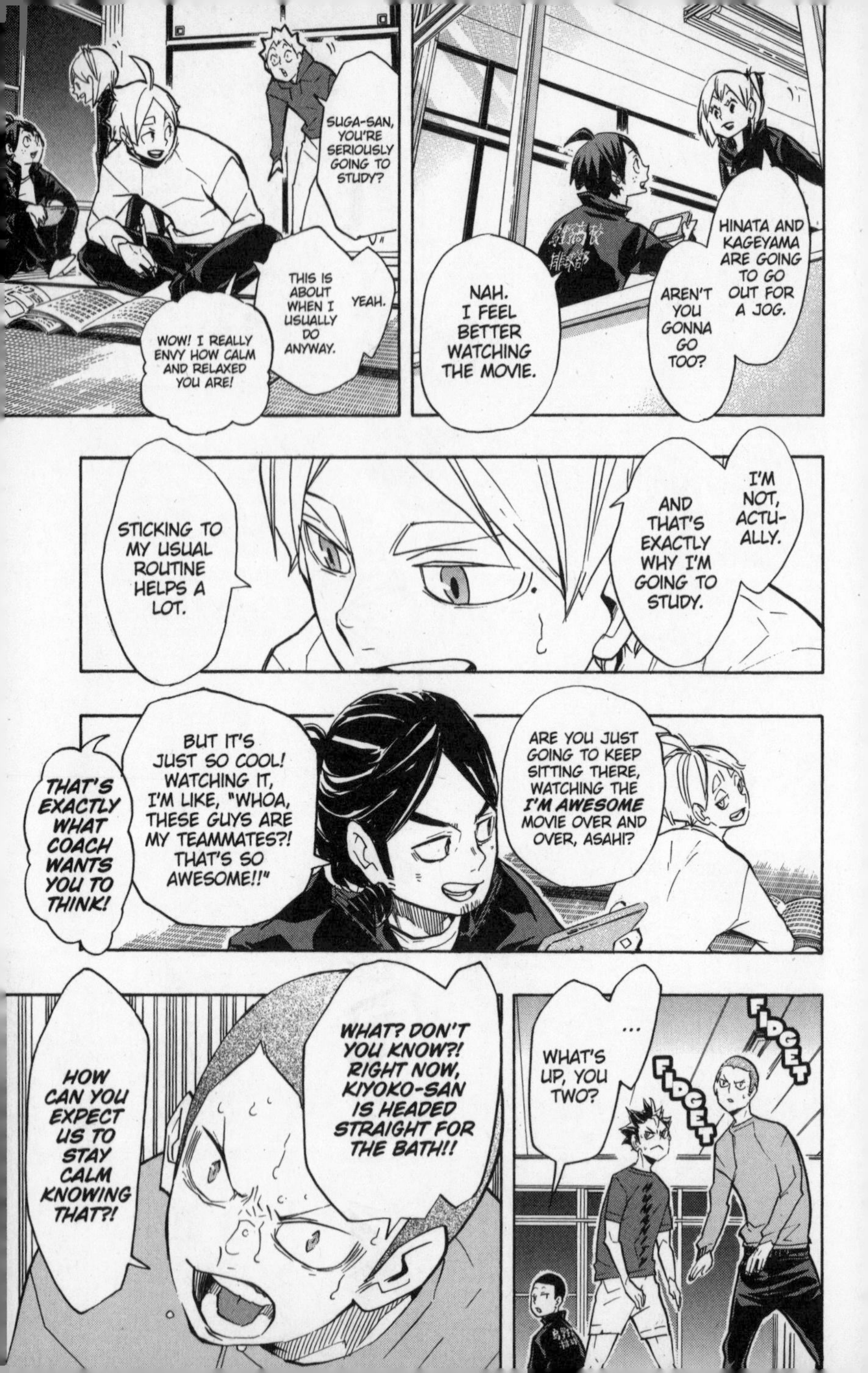
HINATA AND KAGEYAMA ARE GOING TO GO OUT FOR A JOG.
AREN'T YOU GONNA GO TOO?
NAH. I FEEL BETTER WATCHING THE MOVIE.
SUGA-SAN, YOU'RE SERIOUSLY GOING TO STUDY?
YEAH.
THIS IS ABOUT WHEN I USUALLY DO ANYWAY.
WOW! I REALLY ENVY HOW CALM AND RELAXED YOU ARE!
I'M NOT, ACTUALLY.
AND THAT'S EXACTLY WHY I'M GOING TO STUDY.
STICKING TO MY USUAL ROUTINE HELPS A LOT.
ARE YOU JUST GOING TO KEEP SITTING THERE, WATCHING THE *I'M AWESOME* MOVIE OVER AND OVER, ASAHI?
BUT IT'S JUST SO COOL! WATCHING IT, I'M LIKE, "WHOA, THESE GUYS ARE MY TEAMMATES?! THAT'S SO AWESOME!!"
THAT'S EXACTLY WHAT COACH WANTS YOU TO THINK!
FIDGET
FIDGET
...
WHAT'S UP, YOU TWO?
WHAT? DON'T YOU KNOW?! RIGHT NOW, KIYOKO-SAN IS HEADED STRAIGHT FOR THE BATH!!
HOW CAN YOU EXPECT US TO STAY CALM KNOWING THAT?!

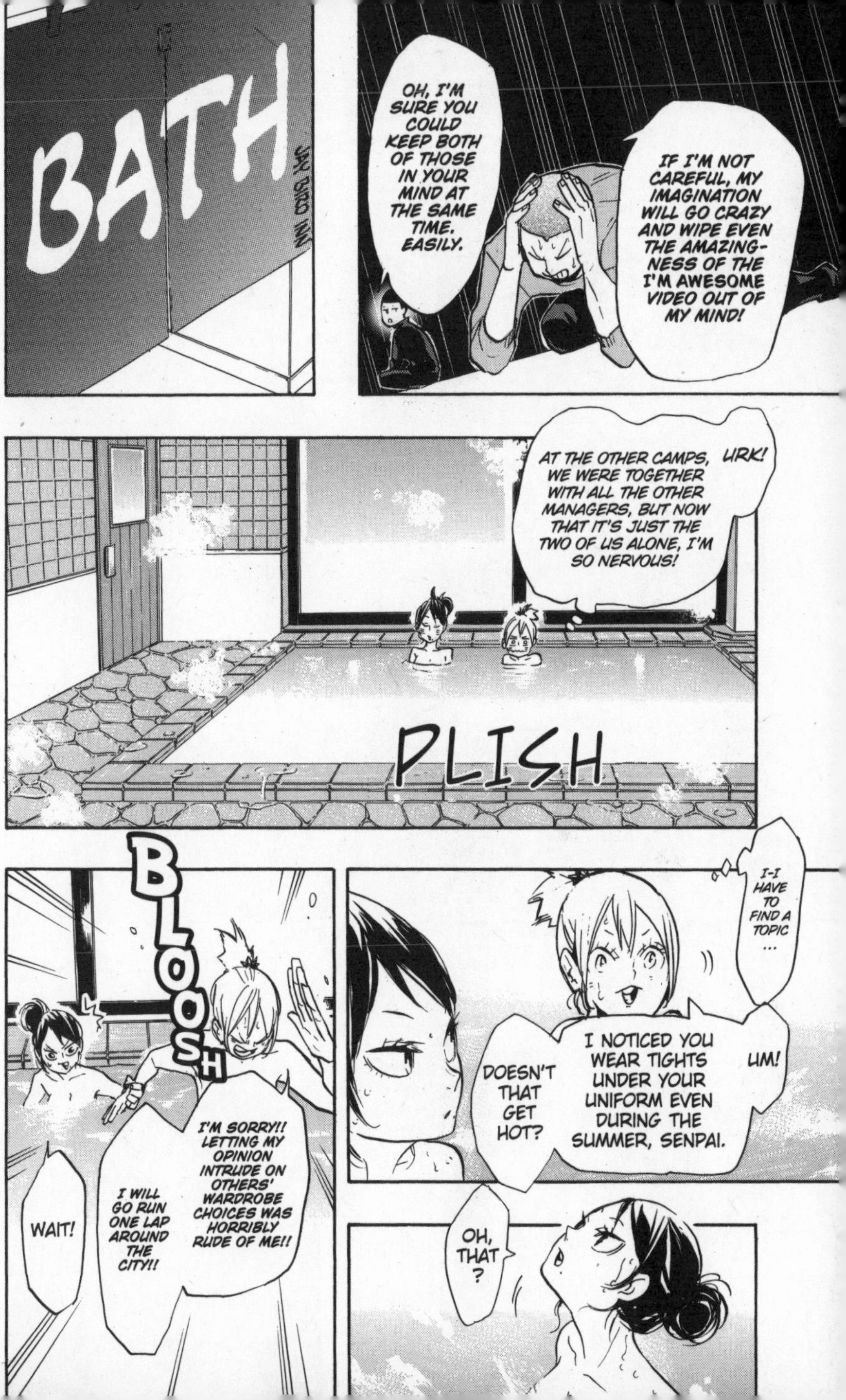
IF I'M NOT CAREFUL, MY IMAGINATION WILL GO CRAZY AND WIPE EVEN THE AMAZINGNESS OF THE I'M AWESOME VIDEO OUT OF MY MIND!
OH, I'M SURE YOU COULD KEEP BOTH OF THOSE IN YOUR MIND AT THE SAME TIME. EASILY.
BATH
URK!
AT THE OTHER CAMPS, WE WERE TOGETHER WITH ALL THE OTHER MANAGERS, BUT NOW THAT IT'S JUST THE TWO OF US ALONE, I'M SO NERVOUS!
PLISH
I-I HAVE TO FIND A TOPIC...
UM!
I NOTICED YOU WEAR TIGHTS UNDER YOUR UNIFORM EVEN DURING THE SUMMER, SENPAI.
DOESN'T THAT GET HOT?
OH, THAT?
BLOOSH
I'M SORRY!! LETTING MY OPINION INTRUDE ON OTHERS' WARDROBE CHOICES WAS HORRIBLY RUDE OF ME!!
I WILL GO RUN ONE LAP AROUND THE CITY!!
WAIT!

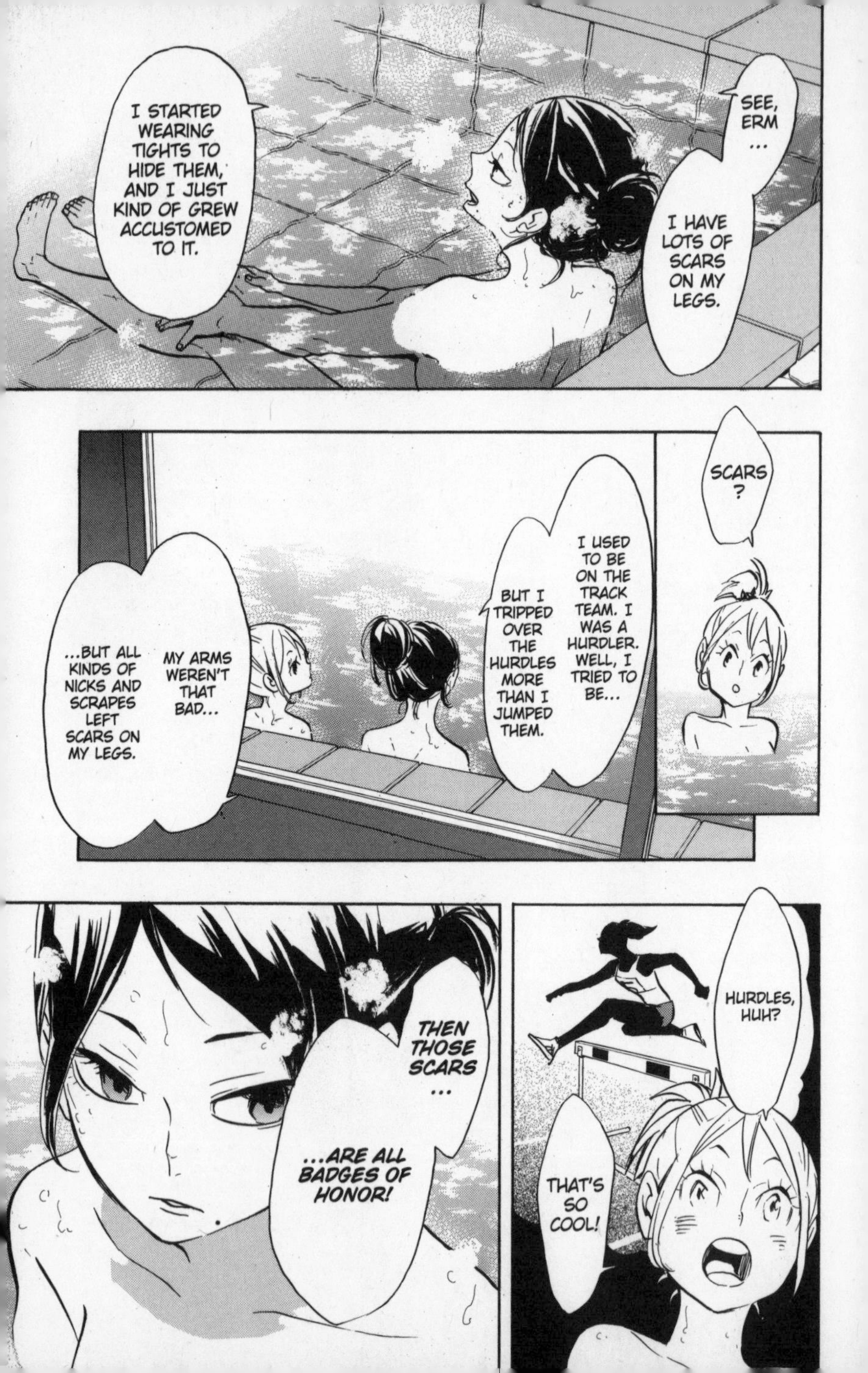
SEE, ERM...
I HAVE LOTS OF SCARS ON MY LEGS.
I STARTED WEARING TIGHTS TO HIDE THEM, AND I JUST KIND OF GREW ACCUSTOMED TO IT.
SCARS?
I USED TO BE ON THE TRACK TEAM. I WAS A HURDLER. WELL, I TRIED TO BE...
BUT I TRIPPED OVER THE HURDLES MORE THAN I JUMPED THEM.
MY ARMS WEREN'T THAT BAD...
...BUT ALL KINDS OF NICKS AND SCRAPES LEFT SCARS ON MY LEGS.
HURDLES, HUH?
THAT'S SO COOL!
THEN THOSE SCARS...
...ARE ALL BADGES OF HONOR!

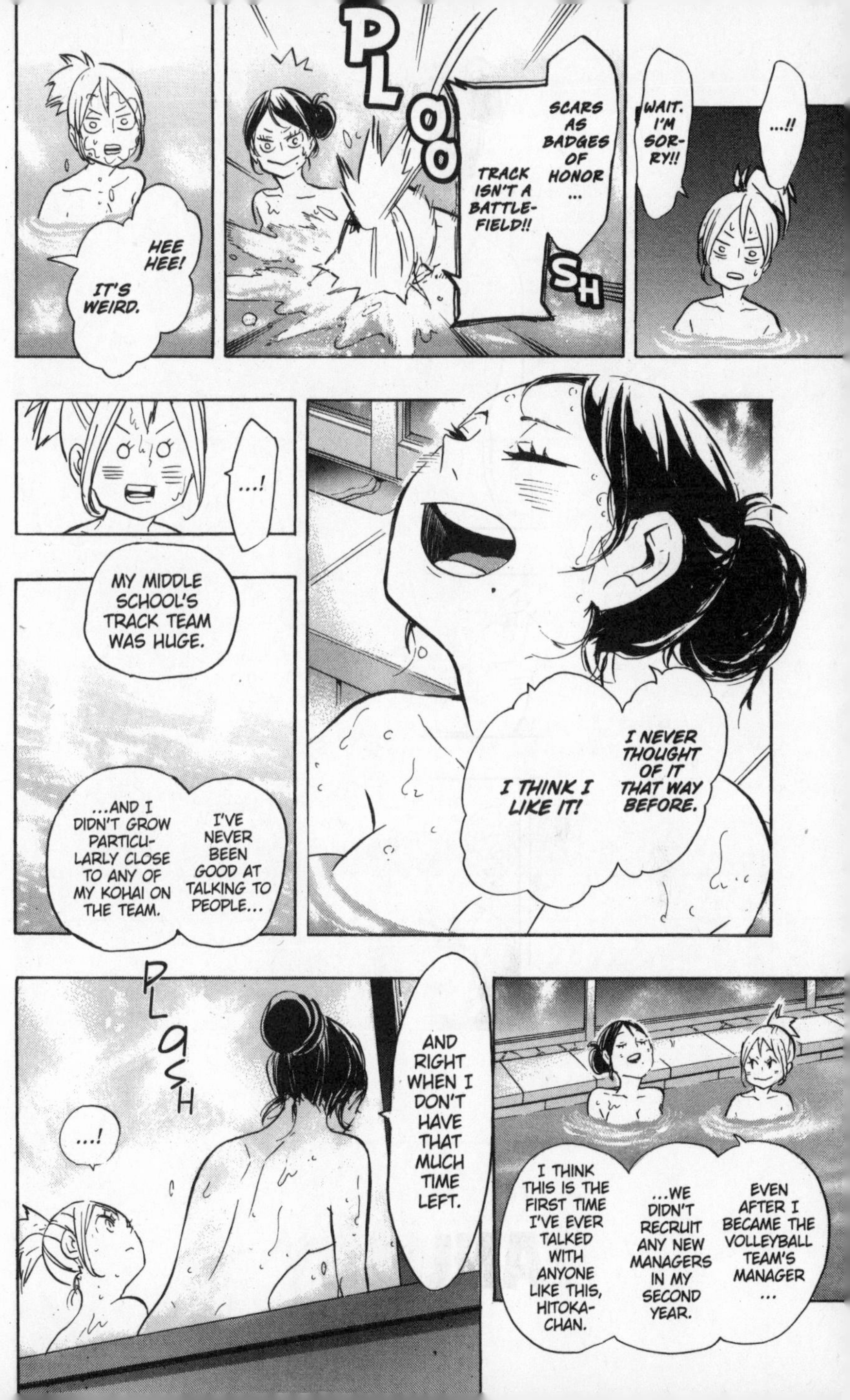
...!!
WAIT. I'M SORRY!!
SCARS AS BADGES OF HONOR...
TRACK ISN'T A BATTLEFIELD!!
PLOO
SH
HEE HEE!
IT'S WEIRD.
I NEVER THOUGHT OF IT THAT WAY BEFORE.
I THINK I LIKE IT!
...!
MY MIDDLE SCHOOL'S TRACK TEAM WAS HUGE.
I'VE NEVER BEEN GOOD AT TALKING TO PEOPLE...
...AND I DIDN'T GROW PARTICULARLY CLOSE TO ANY OF MY KOHAI ON THE TEAM.
EVEN AFTER I BECAME THE VOLLEYBALL TEAM'S MANAGER...
...WE DIDN'T RECRUIT ANY NEW MANAGERS IN MY SECOND YEAR.
I THINK THIS IS THE FIRST TIME I'VE EVER TALKED WITH ANYONE LIKE THIS, HITOKA-CHAN.
AND RIGHT WHEN I DON'T HAVE THAT MUCH TIME LEFT.
PLASH
...!

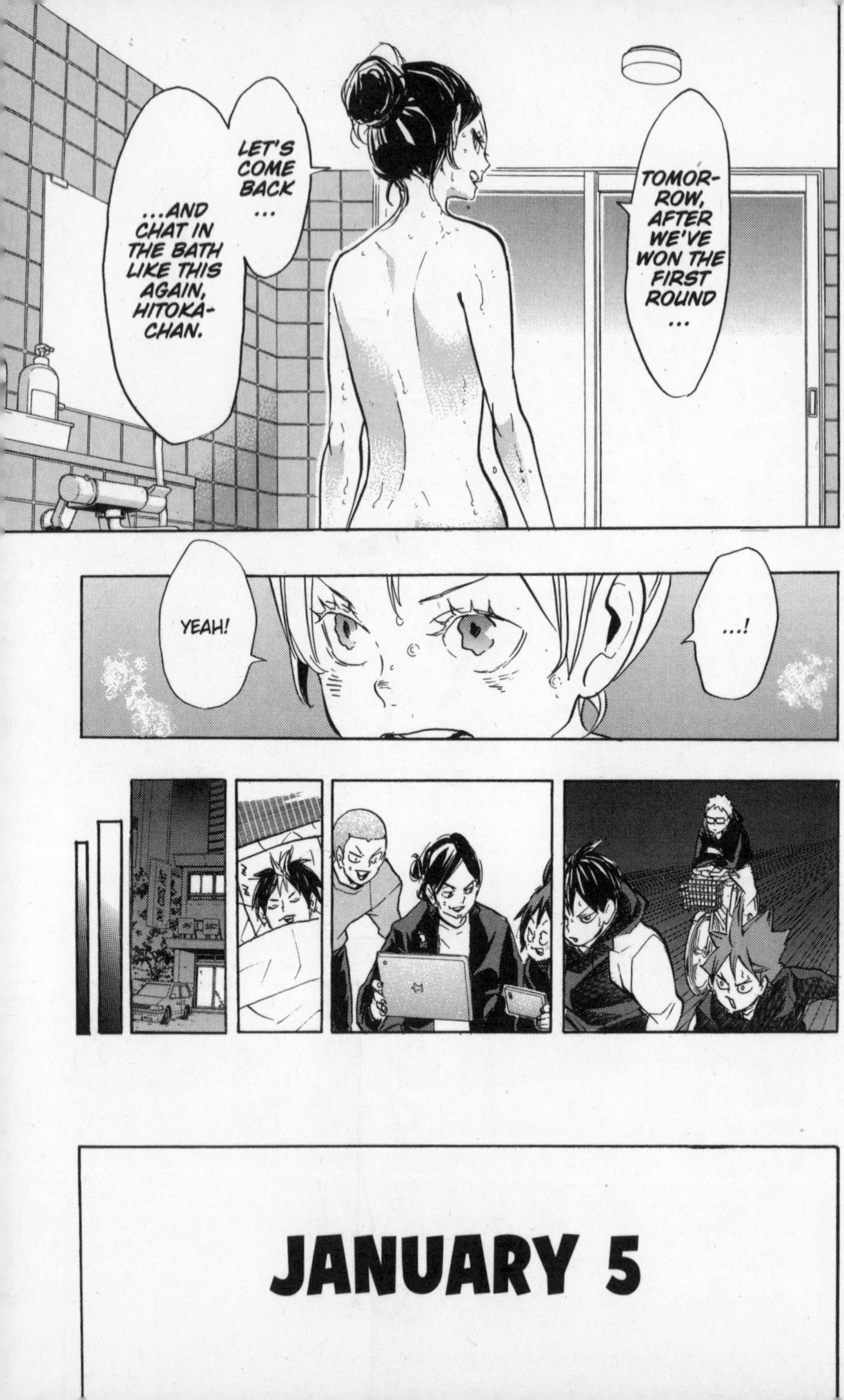
TOMORROW, AFTER WE'VE WON THE FIRST ROUND...
LET'S COME BACK...
...AND CHAT IN THE BATH LIKE THIS AGAIN, HITOKA-CHAN.
...!
YEAH!
JANUARY 5

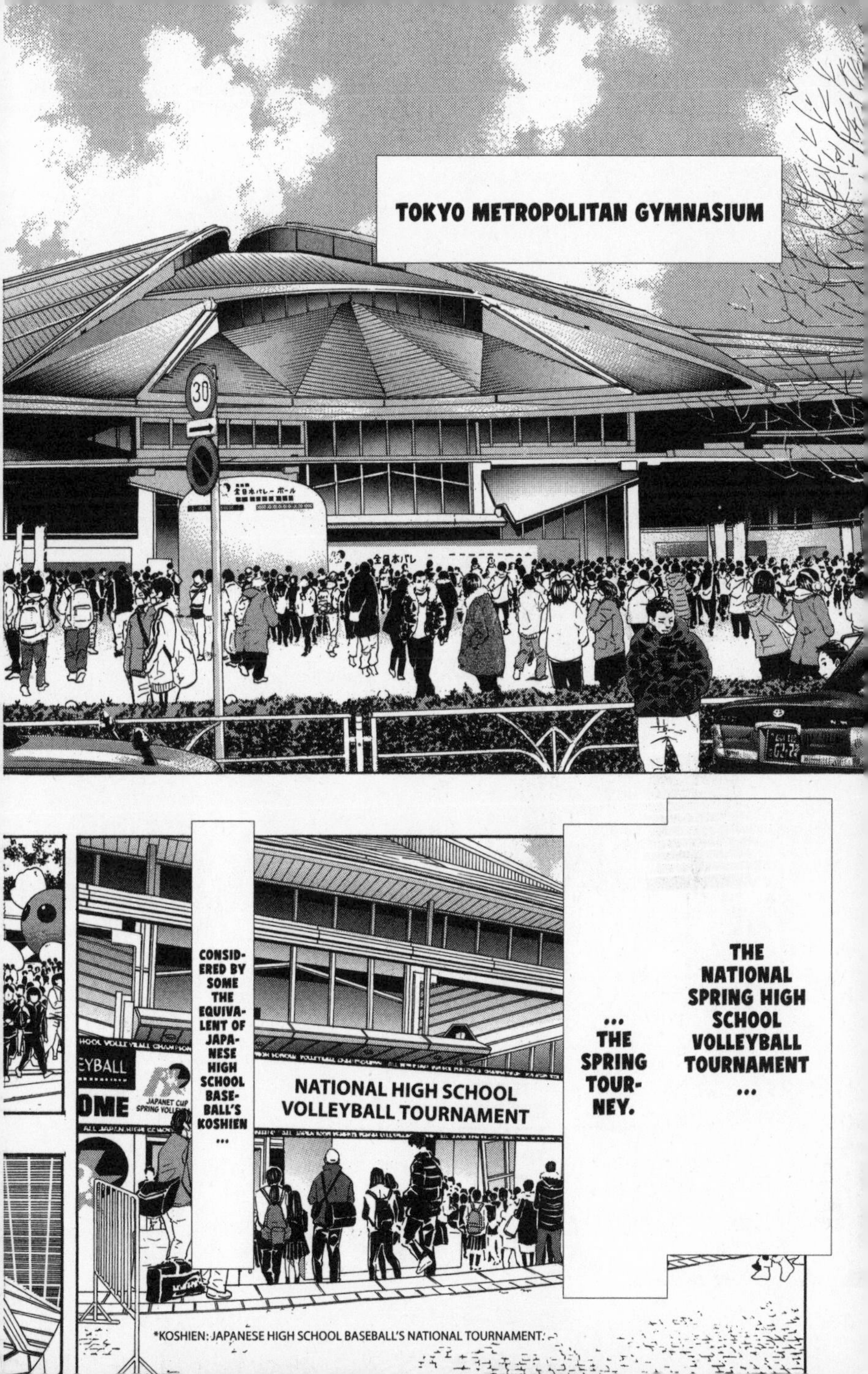
TOKYO METROPOLITAN GYMNASIUM
THE NATIONAL SPRING HIGH SCHOOL VOLLEYBALL TOURNAMENT ...
... THE SPRING TOURNEY.
CONSIDERED BY SOME THE EQUIVALENT OF JAPANESE HIGH SCHOOL BASEBALL'S KOSHIEN ...
NATIONAL HIGH SCHOOL VOLLEYBALL TOURNAMENT

*KOSHIEN: JAPANESE HIGH SCHOOL BASEBALL'S NATIONAL TOURNAMENT.

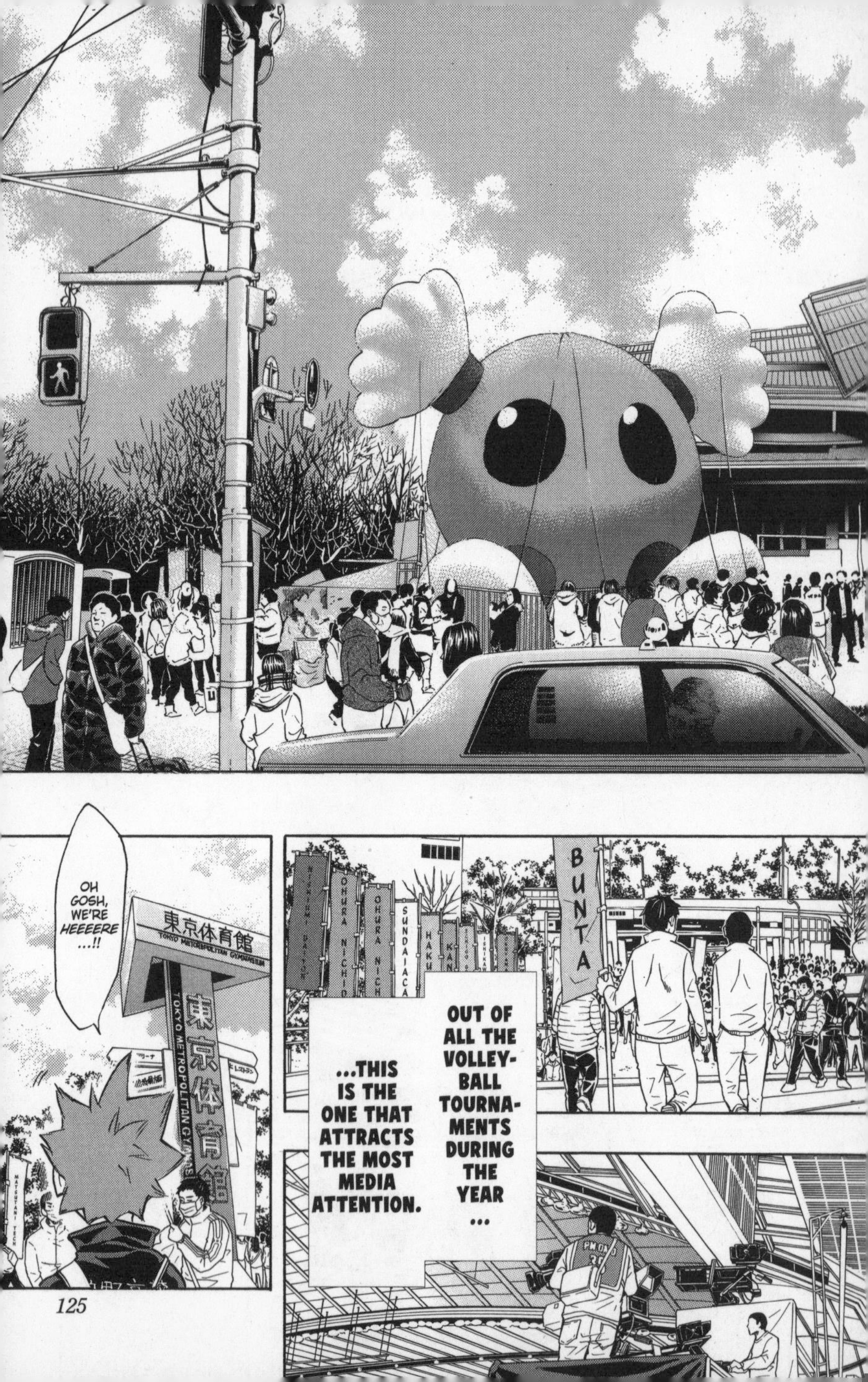
BUNTA
OUT OF ALL THE VOLLEY-BALL TOURNAMENTS DURING THE YEAR...
...THIS IS THE ONE THAT ATTRACTS THE MOST MEDIA ATTENTION.
OH GOSH, WE'RE HEEEERE...!!
東京体育館
TOKYO METROPOLITAN GYMNASIUM

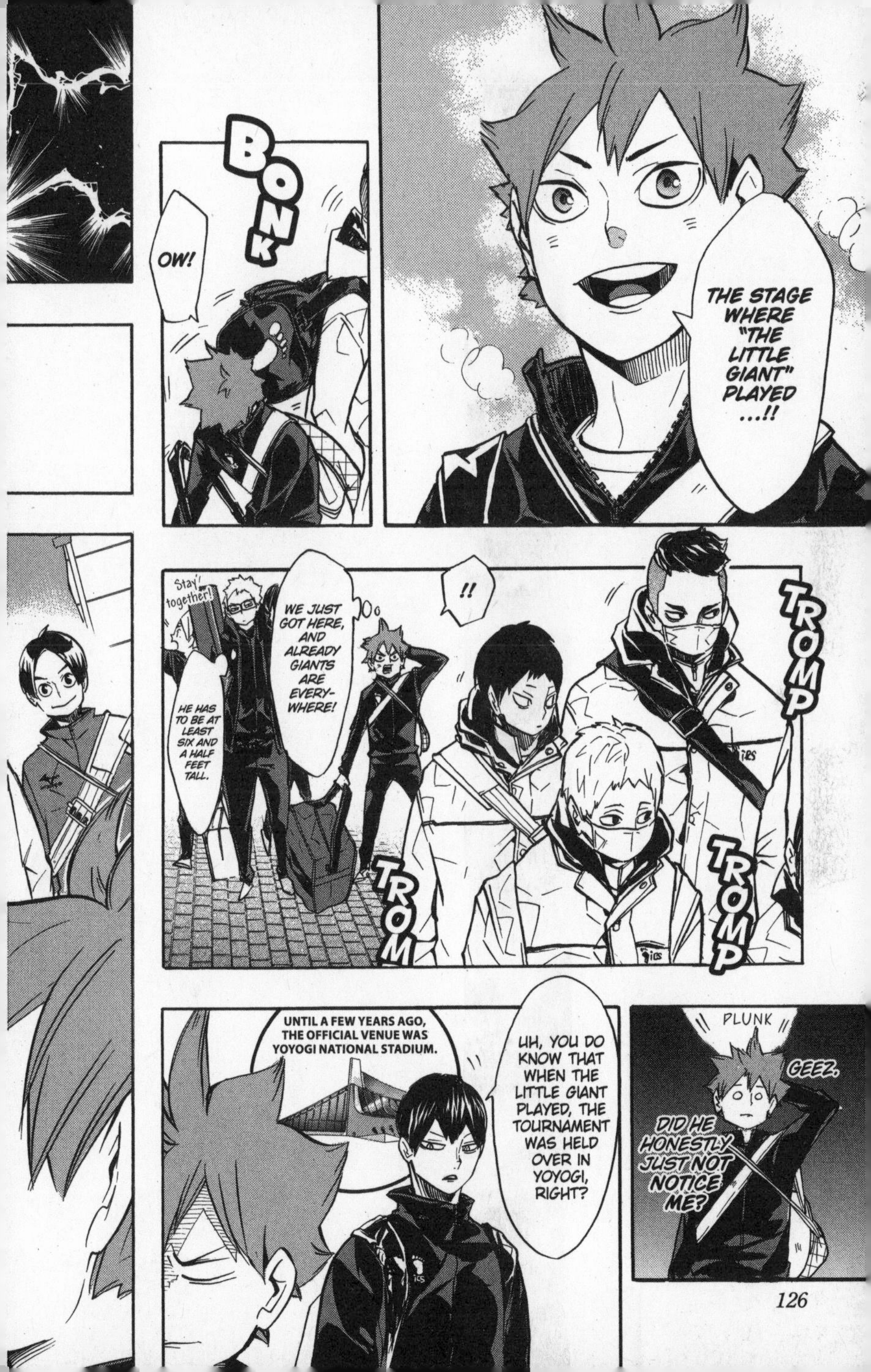
THE STAGE WHERE "THE LITTLE GIANT" PLAYED ...!!
BONK
OW!
TROMP
!!
WE JUST GOT HERE, AND ALREADY GIANTS ARE EVERYWHERE!
Stay together!
HE HAS TO BE AT LEAST SIX AND A HALF FEET TALL.
TROMP
TROM
PLUNK
GEEZ.
DID HE HONESTLY JUST NOT NOTICE ME?
UH, YOU DO KNOW THAT WHEN THE LITTLE GIANT PLAYED, THE TOURNAMENT WAS HELD OVER IN YOYOGI, RIGHT?
UNTIL A FEW YEARS AGO, THE OFFICIAL VENUE WAS YOYOGI NATIONAL STADIUM.

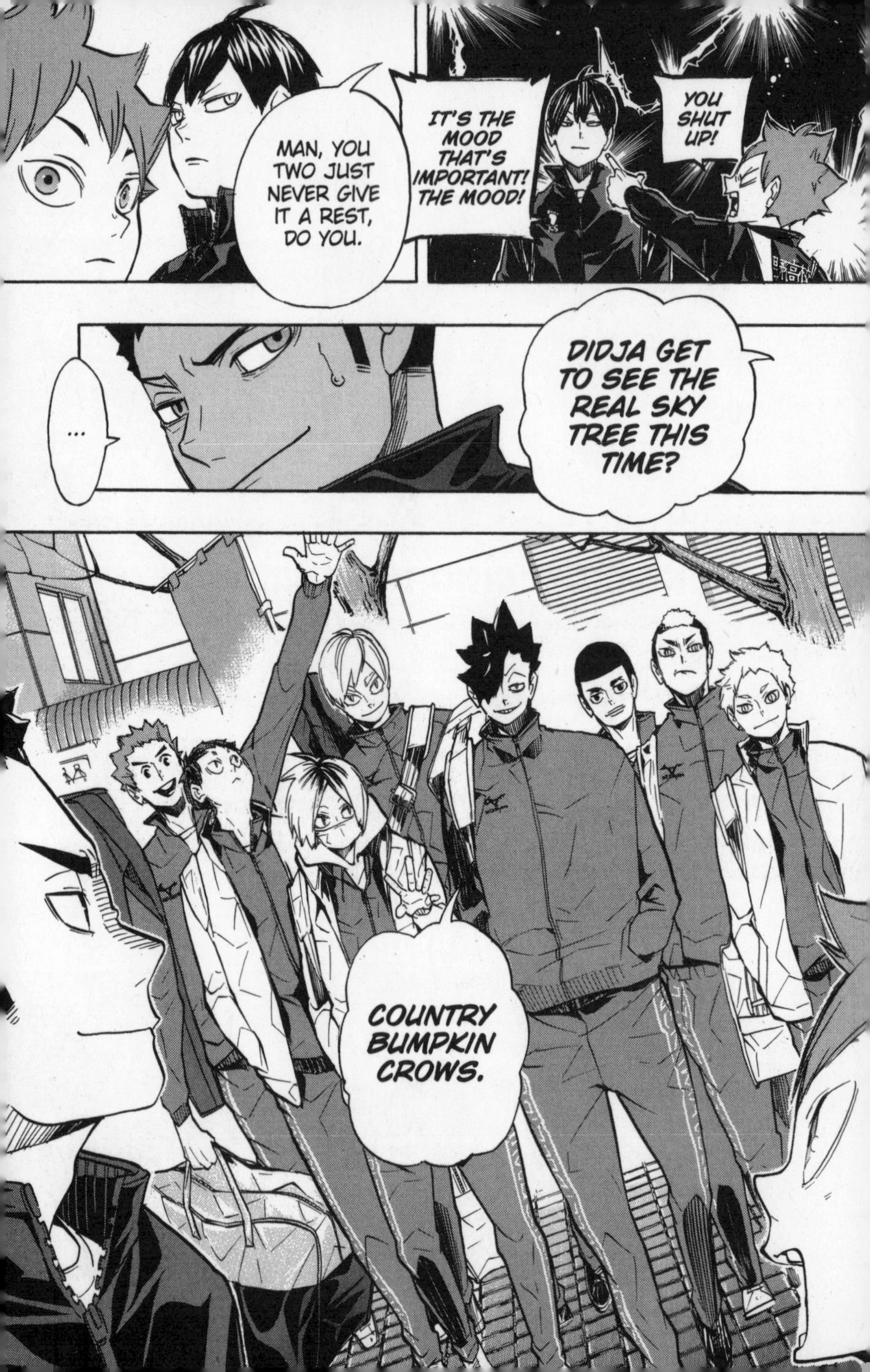
YOU SHUT UP!
IT'S THE MOOD THAT'S IMPORTANT! THE MOOD!
MAN, YOU TWO JUST NEVER GIVE IT A REST, DO YOU.
DIDJA GET TO SEE THE REAL SKY TREE THIS TIME?
...
COUNTRY BUMPKIN CROWS.

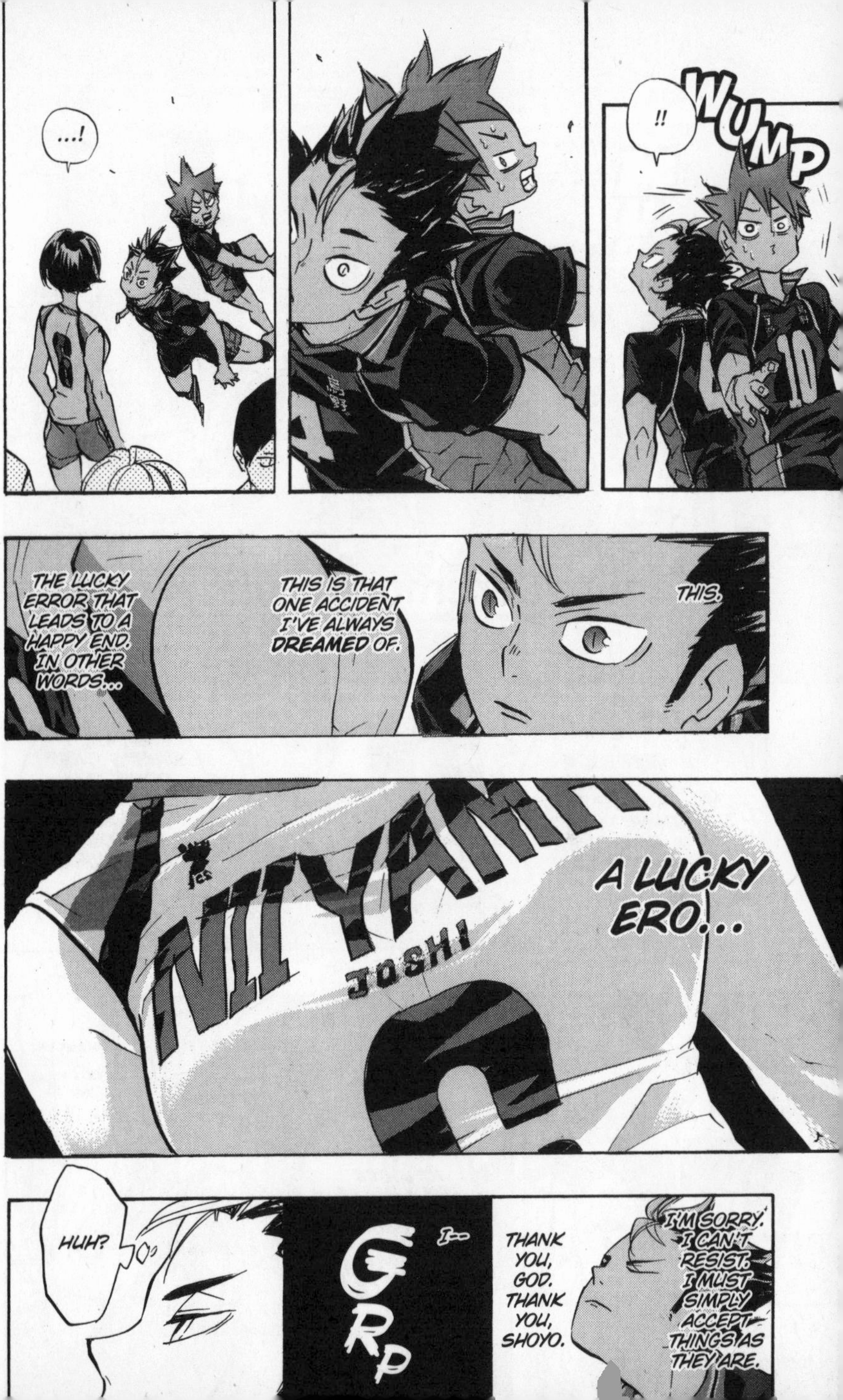
WUMP
!!
...!
THIS.
THIS IS THAT ONE ACCIDENT I'VE ALWAYS DREAMED OF.
THE LUCKY ERROR THAT LEADS TO A HAPPY END. IN OTHER WORDS...
A LUCKY ERO...
JOSHI
I'M SORRY. I CAN'T RESIST. I MUST SIMPLY ACCEPT THINGS AS THEY ARE.
THANK YOU, GOD. THANK YOU, SHOYO.
I--
GRP
HUH?

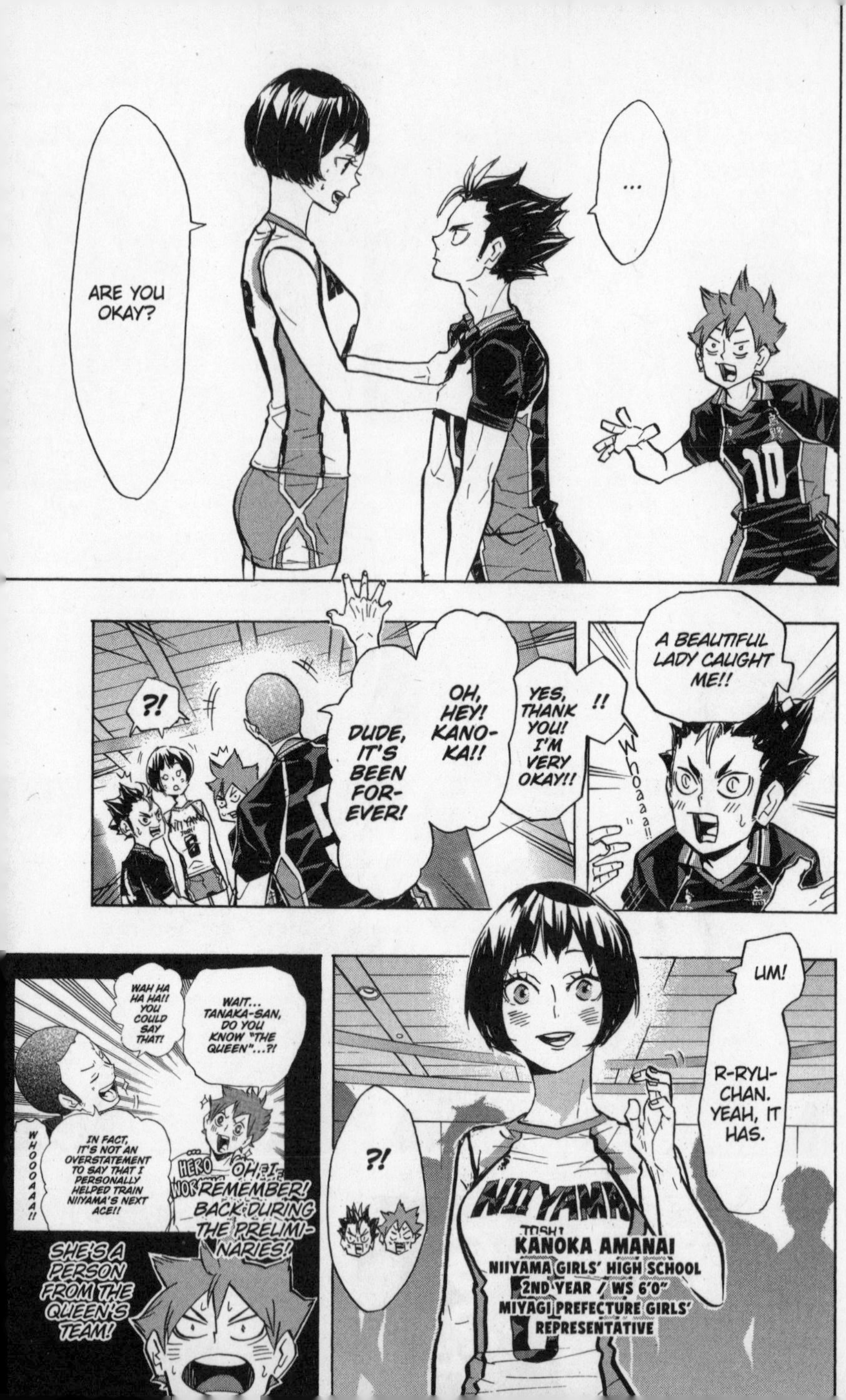
...
ARE YOU OKAY?
A BEAUTIFUL LADY CAUGHT ME!!
WHOAAAA!!
!!
YES, THANK YOU! I'M VERY OKAY!!
OH, HEY! KANOKA!!
DUDE, IT'S BEEN FOREVER!
?!
UM!
R-RYU-CHAN. YEAH, IT HAS.
?!
KANOKA AMANAI
NIIYAMA GIRLS' HIGH SCHOOL
2ND YEAR / WS 6'0"
MIYAGI PREFECTURE GIRLS' REPRESENTATIVE
WAIT... TANAKA-SAN, DO YOU KNOW "THE QUEEN"...?!
WAH HA HA!! YOU COULD SAY THAT!
IN FACT, IT'S NOT AN OVERSTATEMENT TO SAY THAT I PERSONALLY HELPED TRAIN NIIYAMA'S NEXT ACE!!
WHOOOAAAA!!
OH! I REMEMBER! BACK DURING THE PRELIMINARIES!
SHE'S A PERSON FROM THE QUEEN'S TEAM!

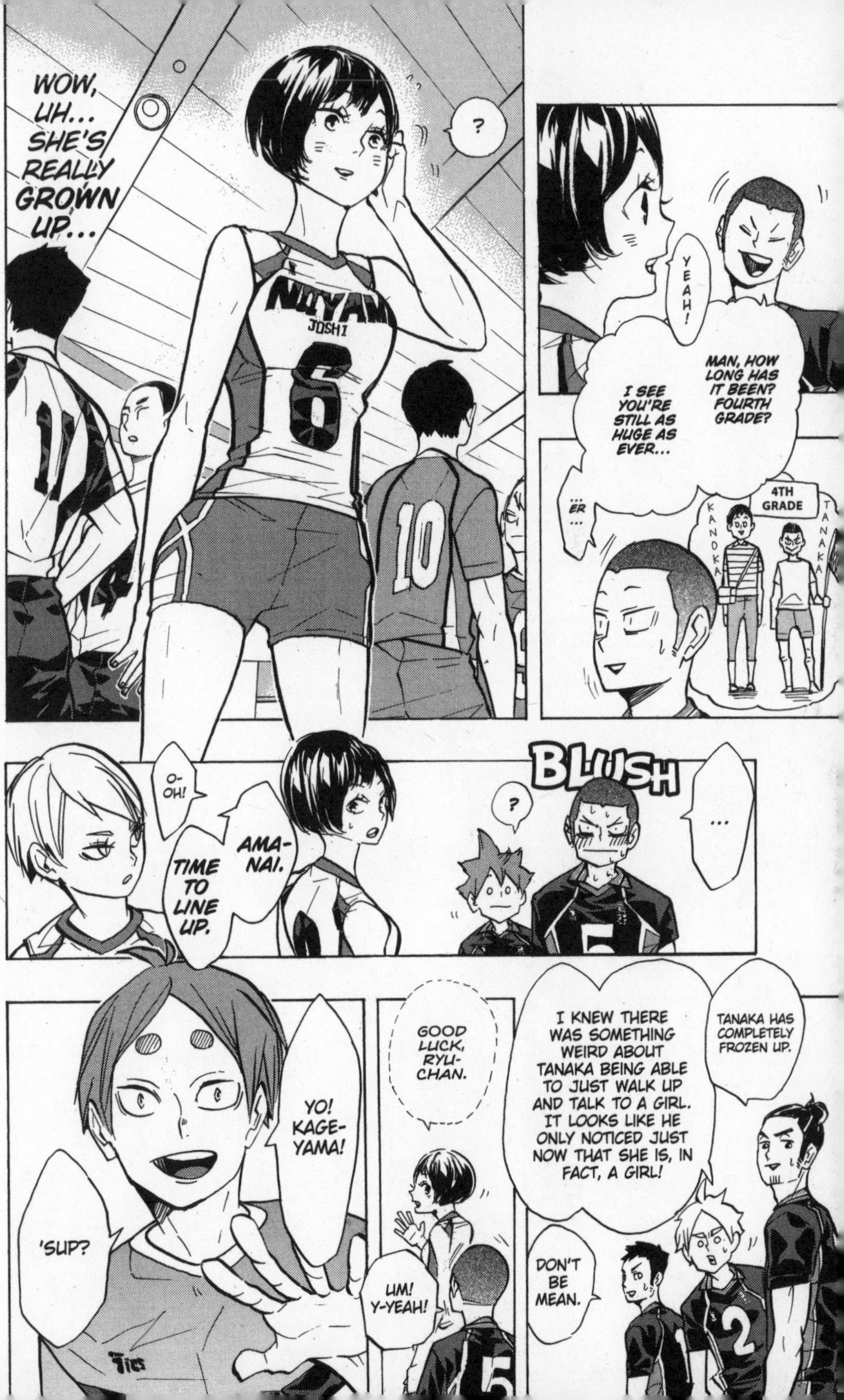
YEAH!
MAN, HOW LONG HAS IT BEEN? FOURTH GRADE?
I SEE YOU'RE STILL AS HUGE AS EVER...
...ER...
4TH GRADE
KANOKA
TANAKA
?
WOW, UH... SHE'S REALLY GROWN UP...
...
BLUSH
?
O-OH!
AMA-NAI.
TIME TO LINE UP.
TANAKA HAS COMPLETELY FROZEN UP.
I KNEW THERE WAS SOMETHING WEIRD ABOUT TANAKA BEING ABLE TO JUST WALK UP AND TALK TO A GIRL. IT LOOKS LIKE HE ONLY NOTICED JUST NOW THAT SHE IS, IN FACT, A GIRL!
DON'T BE MEAN.
GOOD LUCK, RYU-CHAN.
UM! Y-YEAH!
YO! KAGE-YAMA!
'SUP?

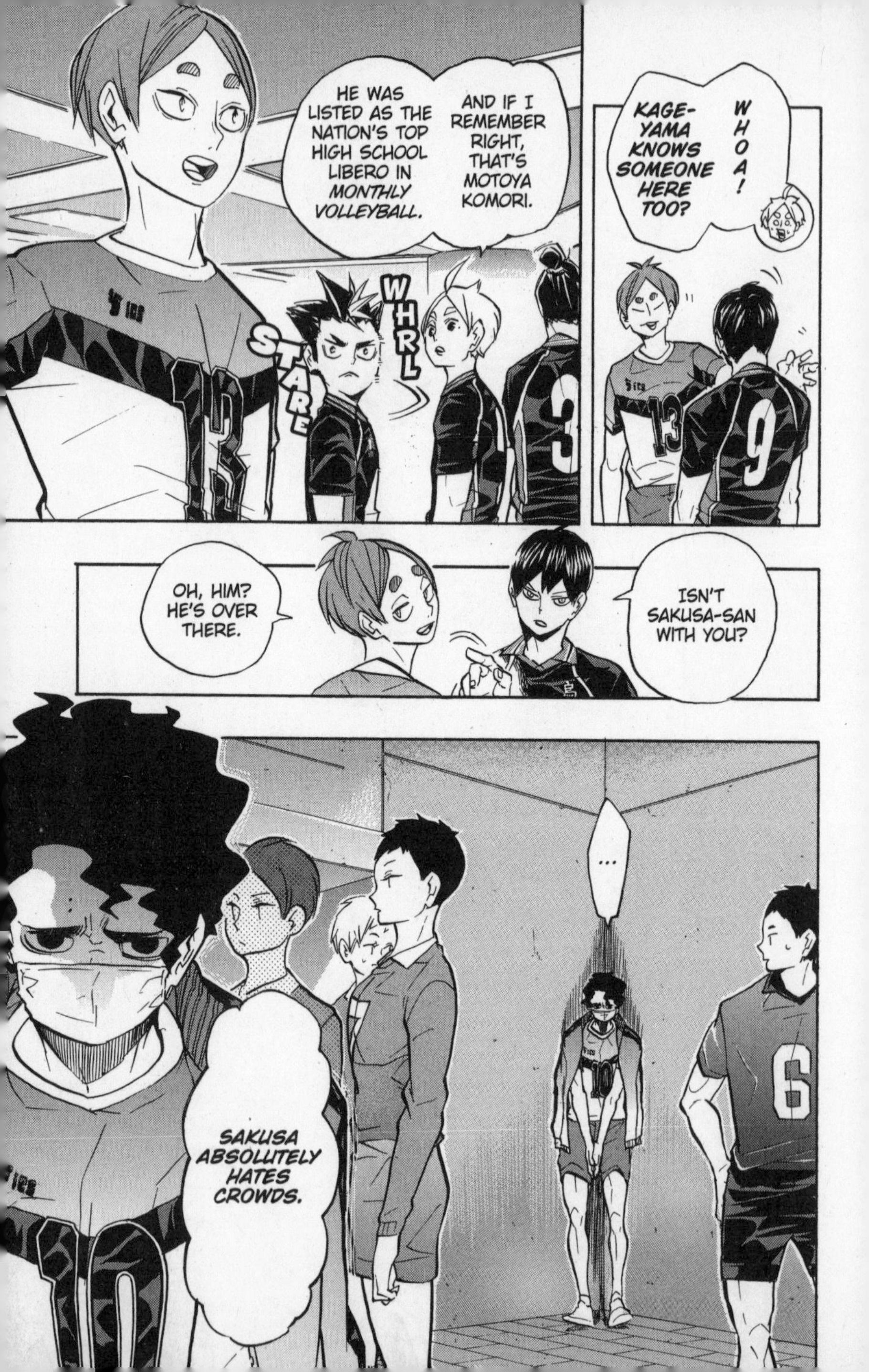
WHOA!
KAGE-YAMA KNOWS SOMEONE HERE TOO?
AND IF I REMEMBER RIGHT, THAT'S MOTOYA KOMORI.
HE WAS LISTED AS THE NATION'S TOP HIGH SCHOOL LIBERO IN *MONTHLY VOLLEYBALL.*
WHRL
STARE
ISN'T SAKUSA-SAN WITH YOU?
OH, HIM? HE'S OVER THERE.
...
SAKUSA ABSOLUTELY HATES CROWDS.

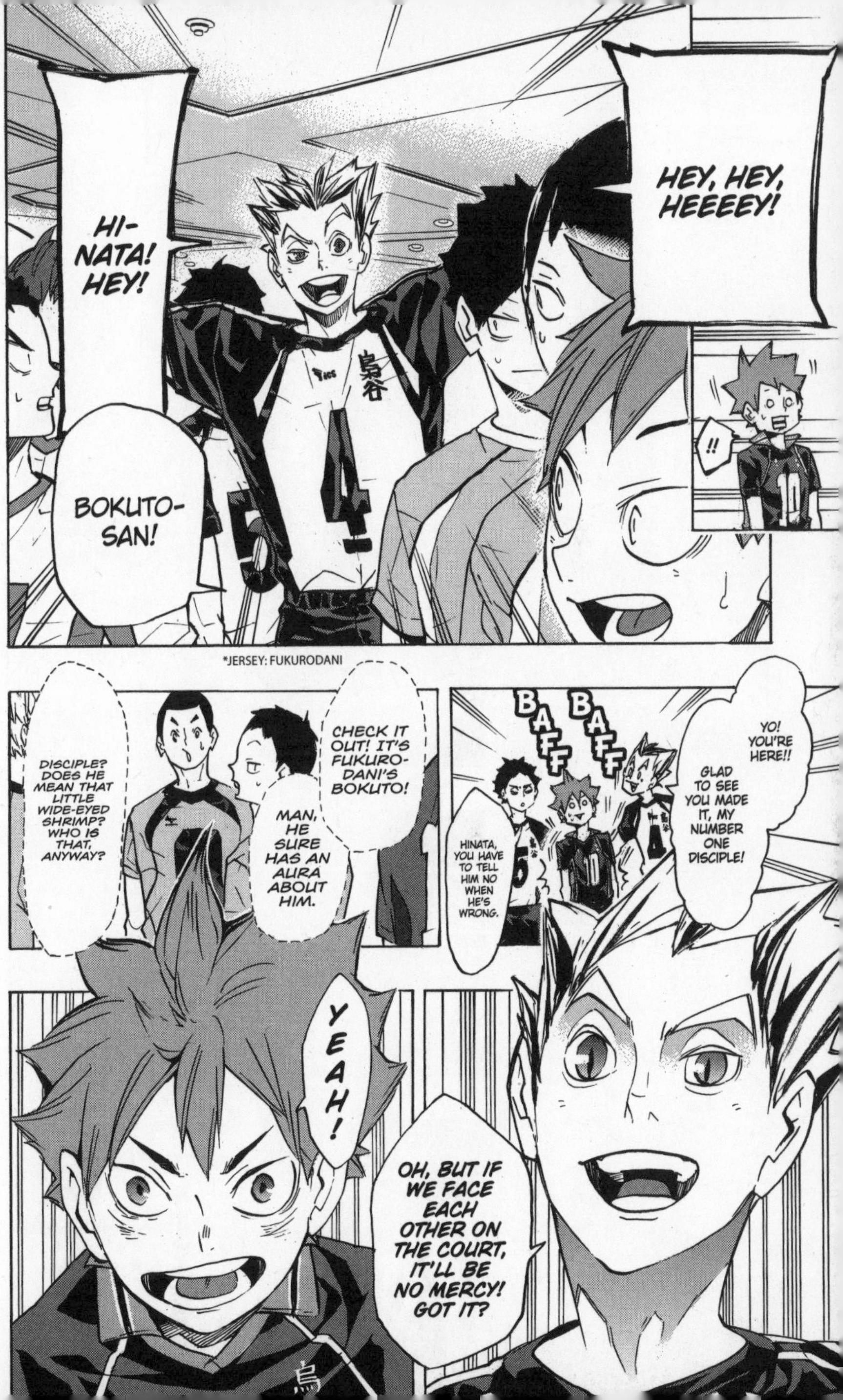
HEY, HEY, HEEEEY!
HI-NATA! HEY!
!!
BOKUTO-SAN!
*JERSEY: FUKURODANI
YO! YOU'RE HERE!!
GLAD TO SEE YOU MADE IT, MY NUMBER ONE DISCIPLE!
BAFF BAFF
HINATA, YOU HAVE TO TELL HIM NO WHEN HE'S WRONG.
CHECK IT OUT! IT'S FUKURODANI'S BOKUTO!
MAN, HE SURE HAS AN AURA ABOUT HIM.
DISCIPLE? DOES HE MEAN THAT LITTLE WIDE-EYED SHRIMP? WHO IS THAT, ANYWAY?
OH, BUT IF WE FACE EACH OTHER ON THE COURT, IT'LL BE NO MERCY! GOT IT?
YEAH!

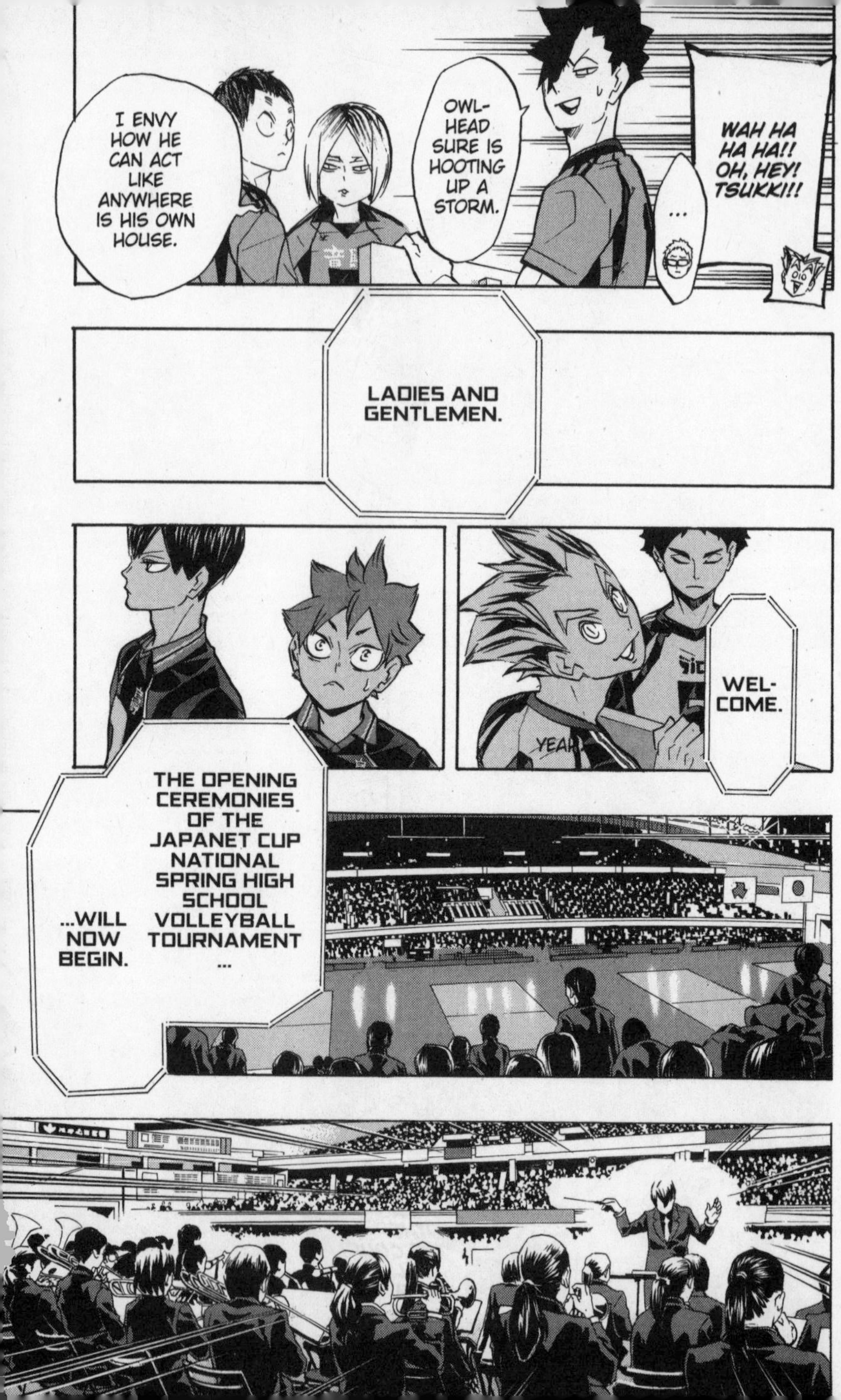
WAH HA HA HA!! OH, HEY! TSUKKI!!
...
OWL-HEAD SURE IS HOOTING UP A STORM.
I ENVY HOW HE CAN ACT LIKE ANYWHERE IS HIS OWN HOUSE.
LADIES AND GENTLEMEN.
WEL-COME.
YEAH
THE OPENING CEREMONIES OF THE JAPANET CUP NATIONAL SPRING HIGH SCHOOL VOLLEYBALL TOURNAMENT ...
...WILL NOW BEGIN.

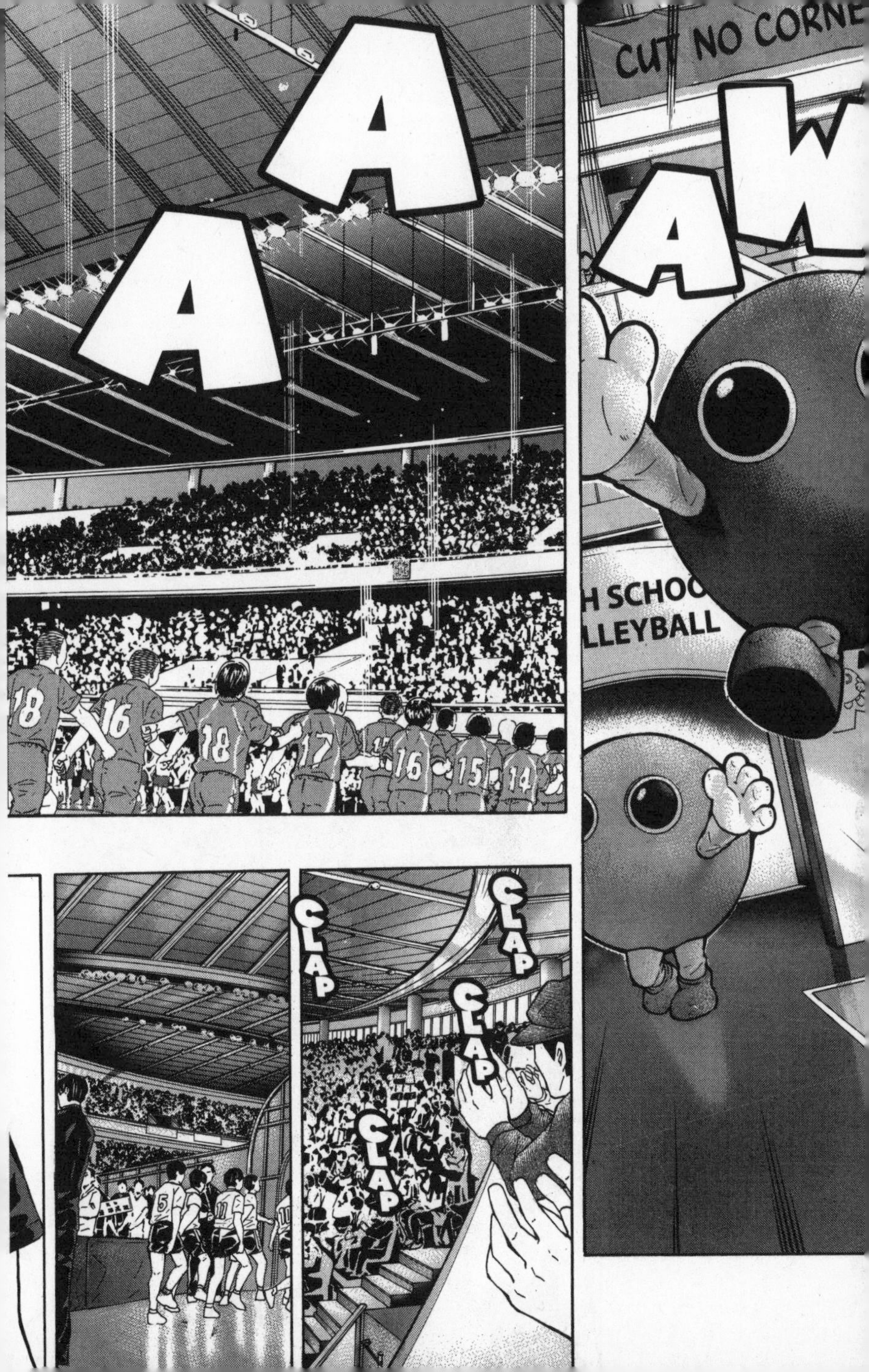
CUT NO CORNE
AW
A
H SCHOO
LLEYBALL
A
A
CLAP
CLAP
CLAP
CLAP
CLAP
CLAP

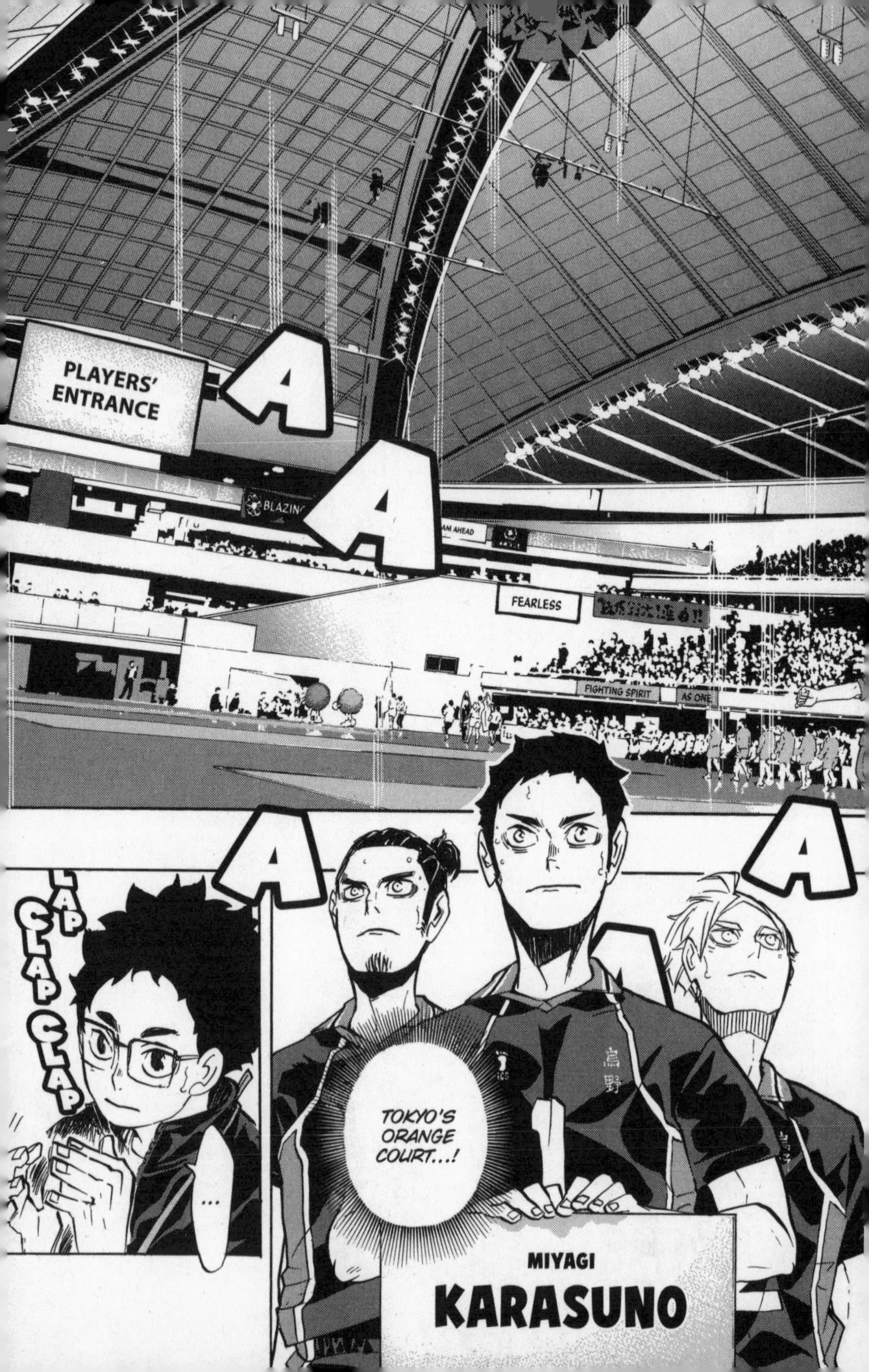
A
A
A
PLAYERS' ENTRANCE
FEARLESS
FIGHTING SPIRIT
AS ONE
A
A
TOKYO'S ORANGE COURT...!
MIYAGI
KARASUNO
CLAP CLAP CLAP
...

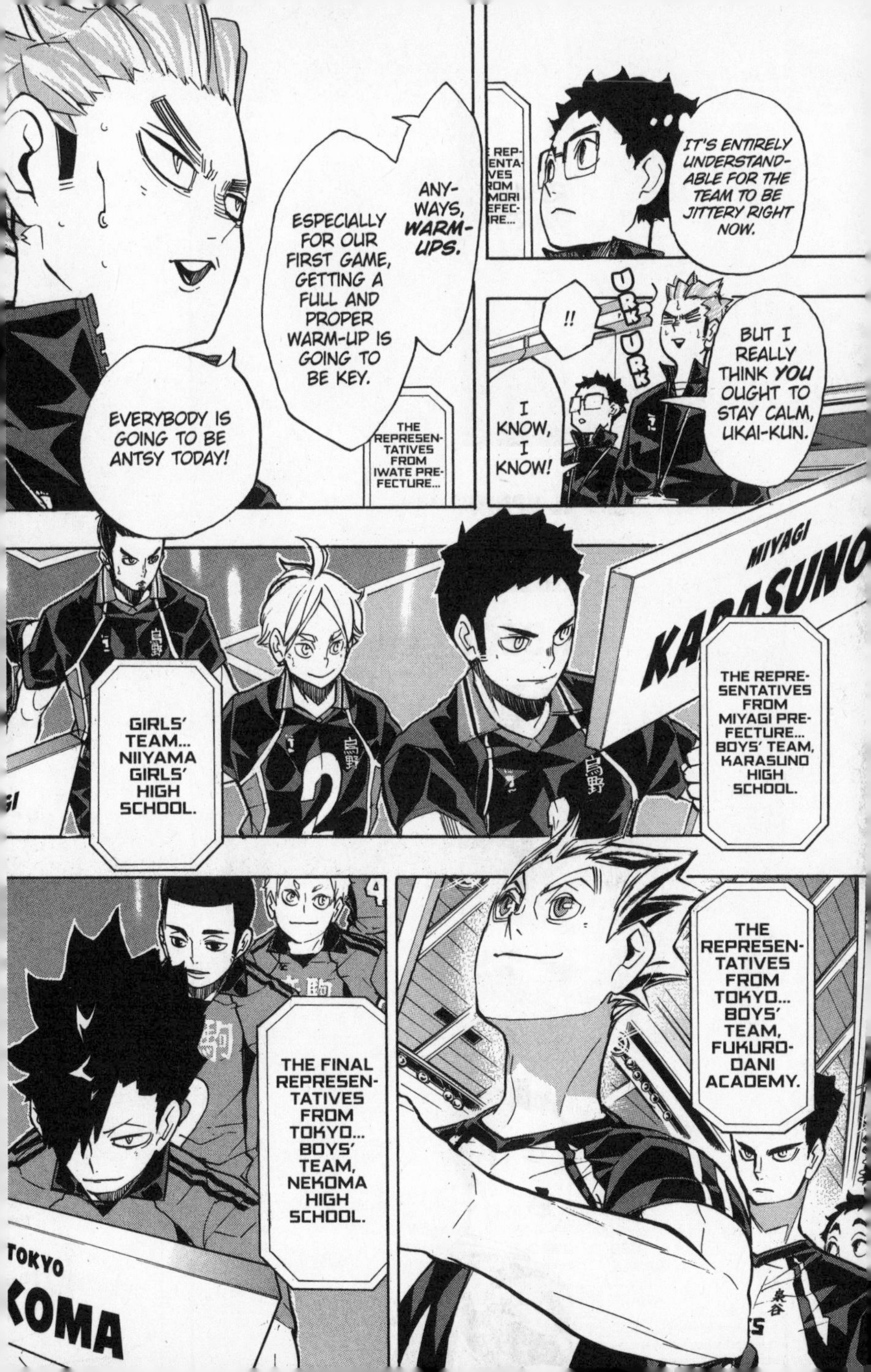
IT'S ENTIRELY UNDERSTANDABLE FOR THE TEAM TO BE JITTERY RIGHT NOW.
BUT I REALLY THINK *YOU* OUGHT TO STAY CALM, UKAI-KUN.
URK URK
!!
I KNOW, I KNOW!
EVERYBODY IS GOING TO BE ANTSY TODAY!
ESPECIALLY FOR OUR FIRST GAME, GETTING A FULL AND PROPER WARM-UP IS GOING TO BE KEY.
ANY-WAYS, *WARM-UPS.*
THE REPRESENTATIVES FROM IWATE PREFECTURE...
MIYAGI
THE REPRESENTATIVES FROM MIYAGI PREFECTURE... BOYS' TEAM, KARASUNO HIGH SCHOOL.
GIRLS' TEAM... NIIYAMA GIRLS' HIGH SCHOOL.
THE REPRESENTATIVES FROM TOKYO... BOYS' TEAM, FUKURODANI ACADEMY.
THE FINAL REPRESENTATIVES FROM TOKYO... BOYS' TEAM, NEKOMA HIGH SCHOOL.
TOKYO

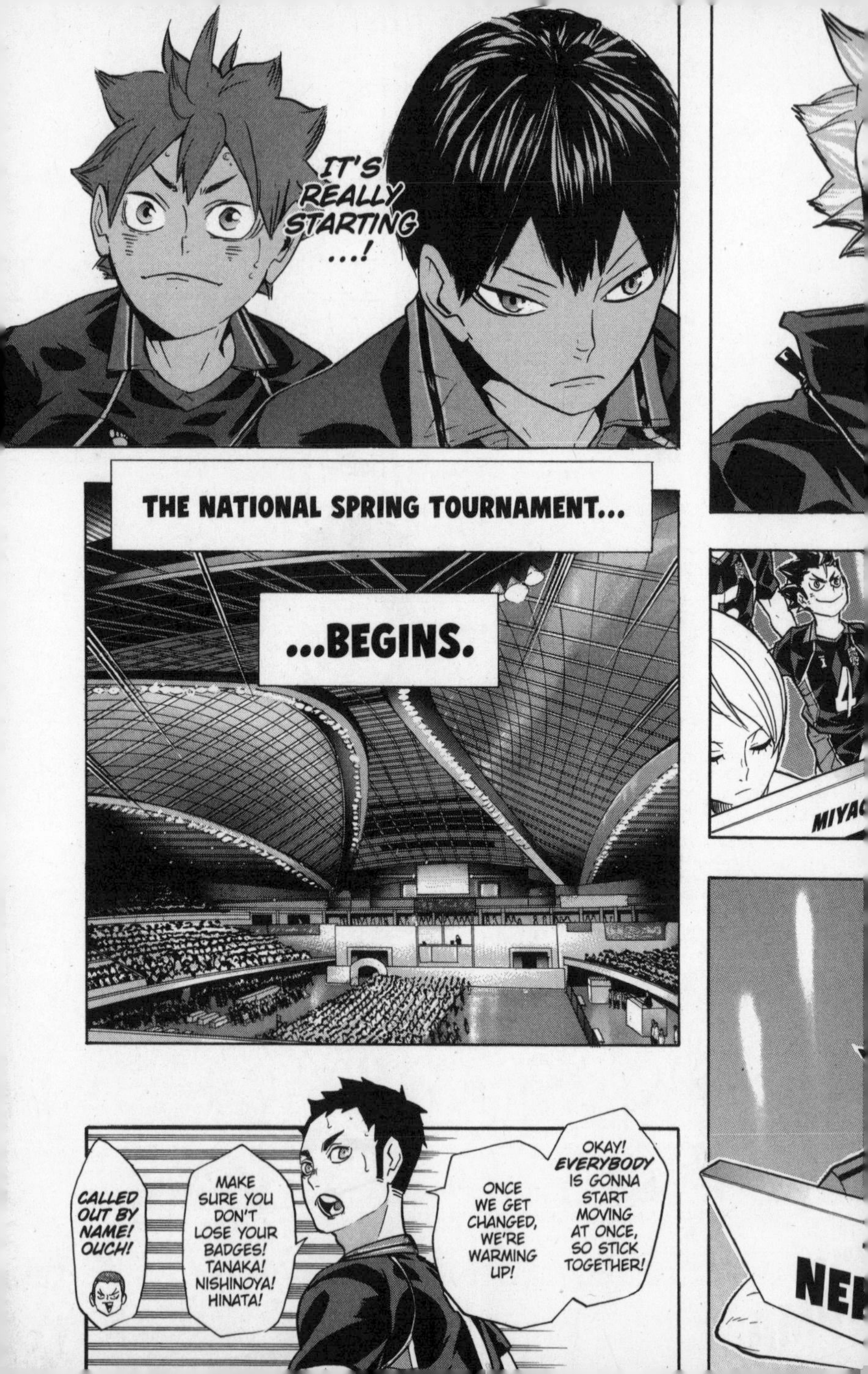
IT'S REALLY STARTING ...!
THE NATIONAL SPRING TOURNAMENT...
...BEGINS.
OKAY! EVERYBODY IS GONNA START MOVING AT ONCE, SO STICK TOGETHER!
ONCE WE GET CHANGED, WE'RE WARMING UP!
MAKE SURE YOU DON'T LOSE YOUR BADGES! TANAKA! NISHINOYA! HINATA!
CALLED OUT BY NAME! OUCH!

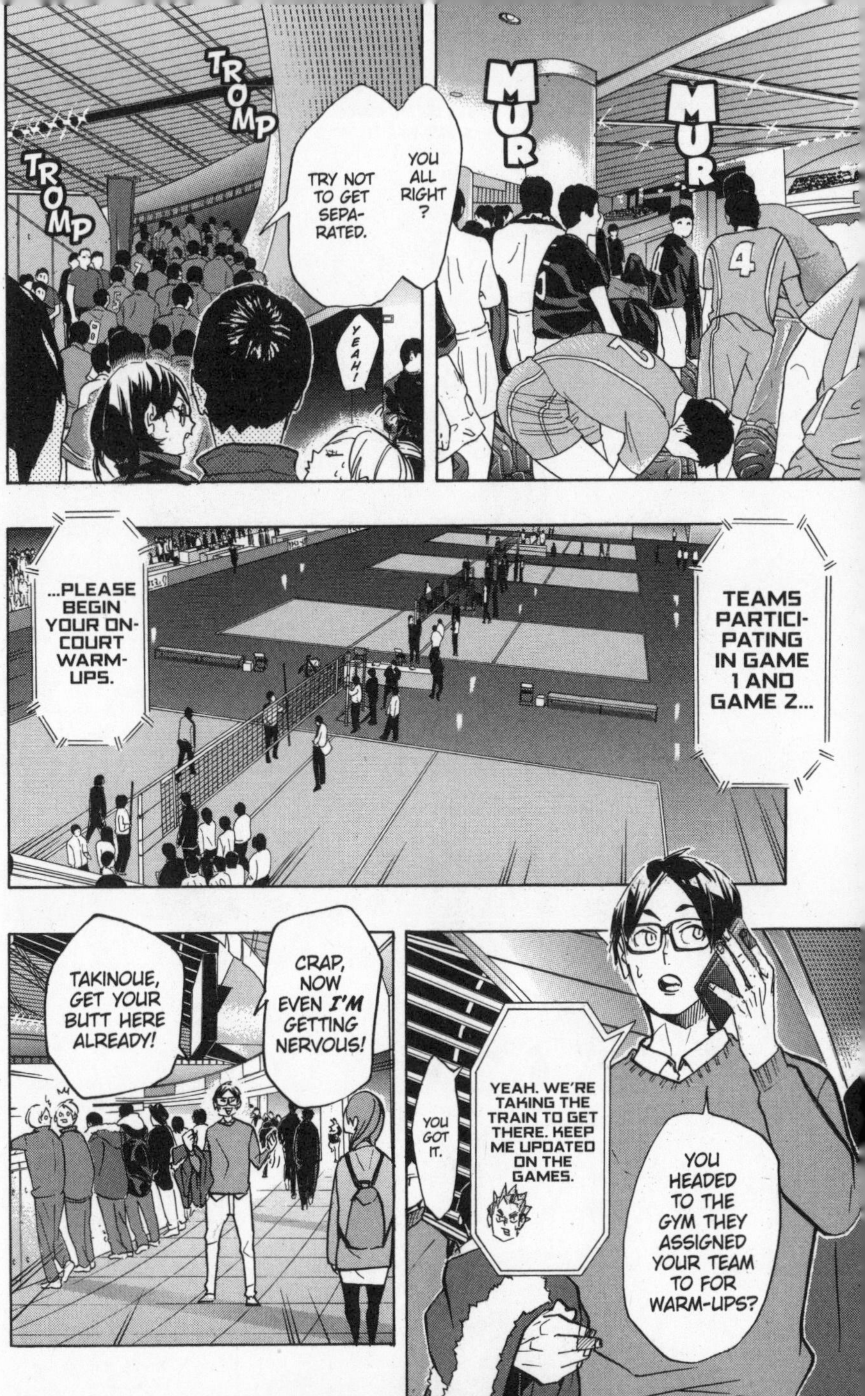
MUR
MUR
TROMP
TROMP
YOU ALL RIGHT?
TRY NOT TO GET SEPARATED.
YEAH!
TEAMS PARTICIPATING IN GAME 1 AND GAME 2...
...PLEASE BEGIN YOUR ON-COURT WARM-UPS.
YOU HEADED TO THE GYM THEY ASSIGNED YOUR TEAM TO FOR WARM-UPS?
YEAH. WE'RE TAKING THE TRAIN TO GET THERE. KEEP ME UPDATED ON THE GAMES.
YOU GOT IT.
CRAP, NOW EVEN *I'M* GETTING NERVOUS!
TAKINOUE, GET YOUR BUTT HERE ALREADY!

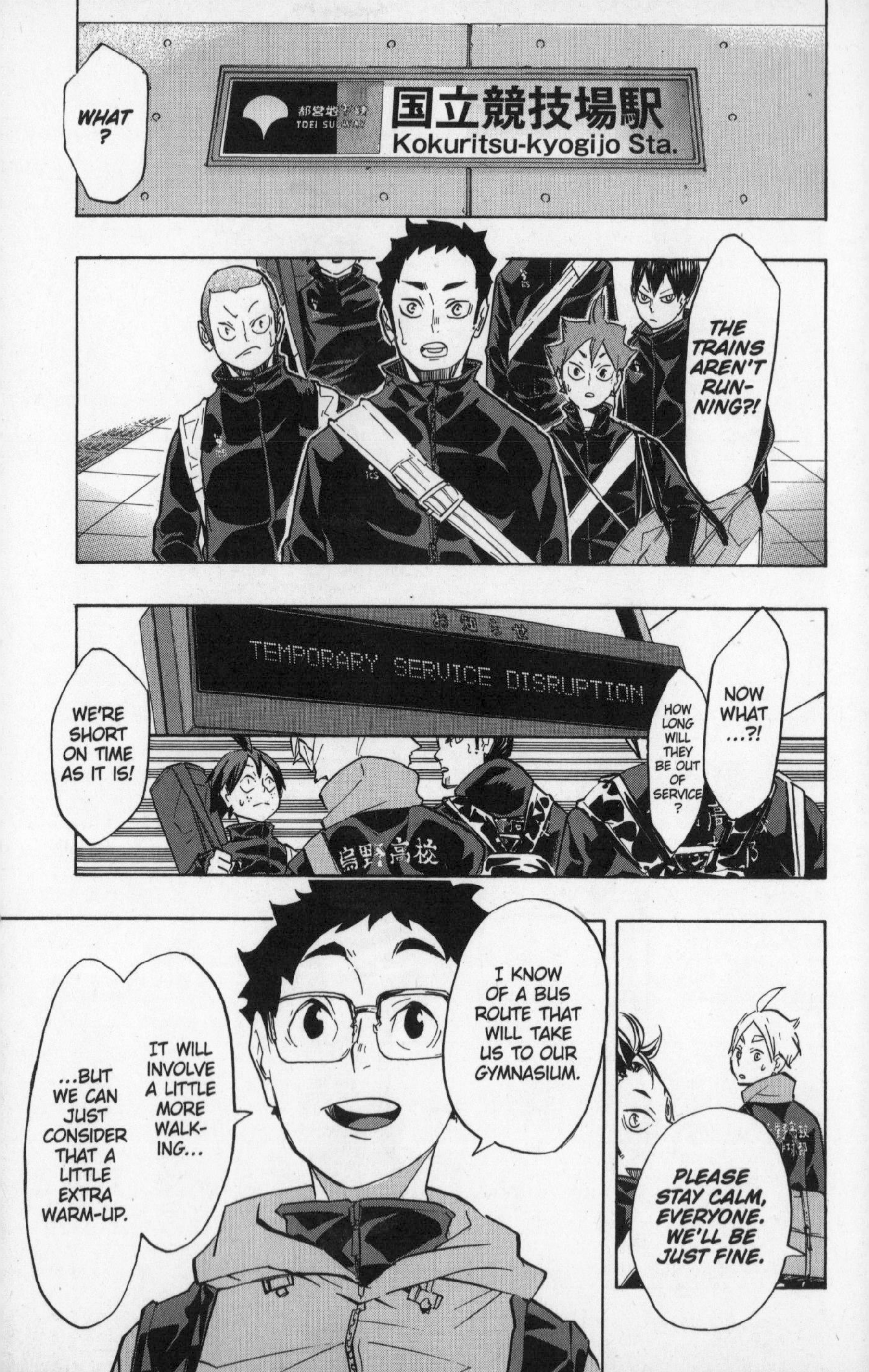
国立競技場駅
Kokuritsu-kyogijo Sta.
WHAT?
THE TRAINS AREN'T RUNNING?!
お知らせ
TEMPORARY SERVICE DISRUPTION
NOW WHAT...?!
HOW LONG WILL THEY BE OUT OF SERVICE?
WE'RE SHORT ON TIME AS IT IS!
烏野高校
PLEASE STAY CALM, EVERYONE. WE'LL BE JUST FINE.
I KNOW OF A BUS ROUTE THAT WILL TAKE US TO OUR GYMNASIUM.
IT WILL INVOLVE A LITTLE MORE WALKING...
...BUT WE CAN JUST CONSIDER THAT A LITTLE EXTRA WARM-UP.

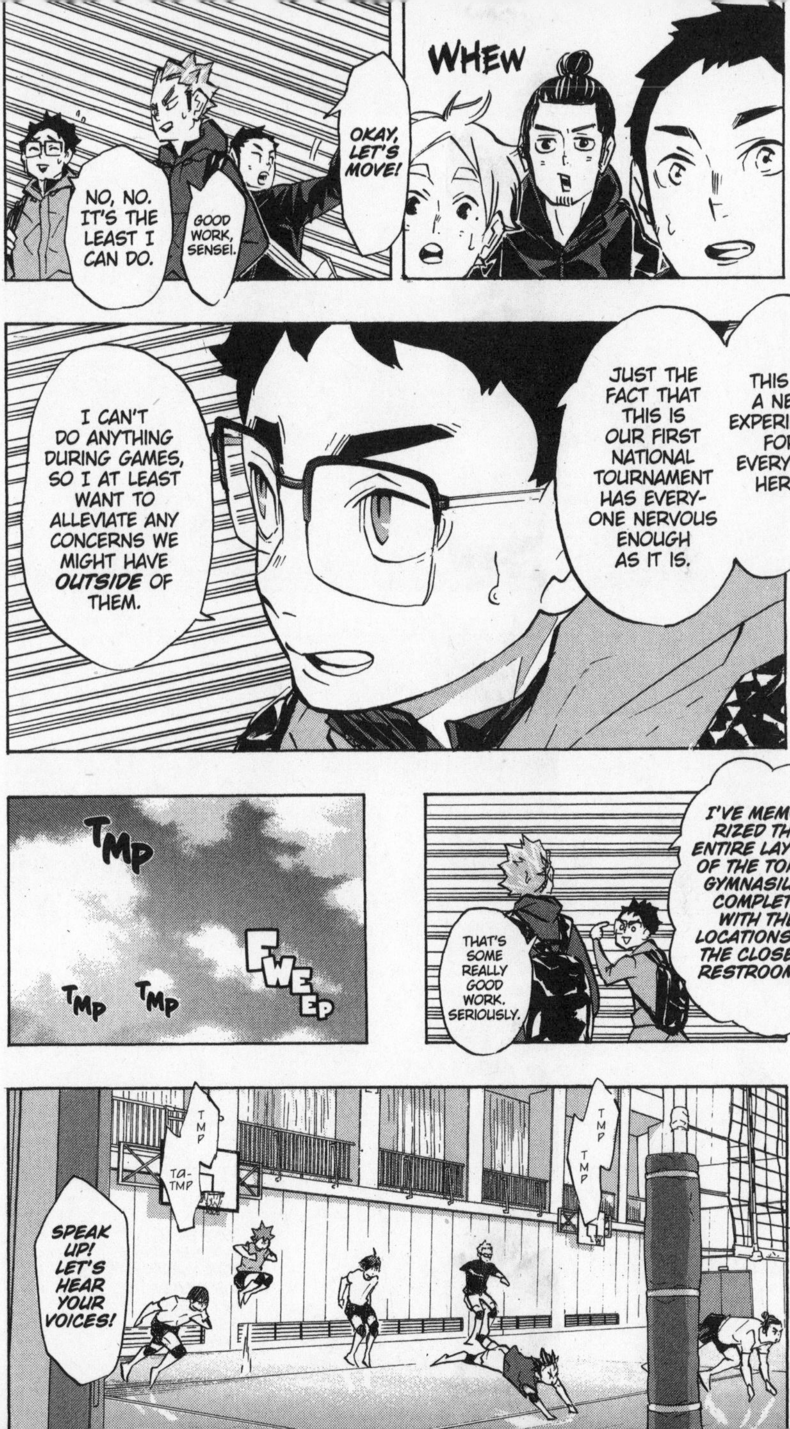
WHEW
OKAY, LET'S MOVE!
GOOD WORK, SENSEI.
NO, NO. IT'S THE LEAST I CAN DO.
THIS IS A NEW EXPERIENCE FOR EVERYONE HERE.
JUST THE FACT THAT THIS IS OUR FIRST NATIONAL TOURNAMENT HAS EVERY-ONE NERVOUS ENOUGH AS IT IS.
I CAN'T DO ANYTHING DURING GAMES, SO I AT LEAST WANT TO ALLEVIATE ANY CONCERNS WE MIGHT HAVE *OUTSIDE* OF THEM.
I'VE MEMO-RIZED THE ENTIRE LAYOUT OF THE TOKYO GYMNASIUM, COMPLETE WITH THE LOCATIONS OF THE CLOSEST RESTROOMS!
THAT'S SOME REALLY GOOD WORK. SERIOUSLY.
TMP
FWEEP
TMP
TMP
TMP TMP
TMP Ta-TMP
SPEAK UP! LET'S HEAR YOUR VOICES!

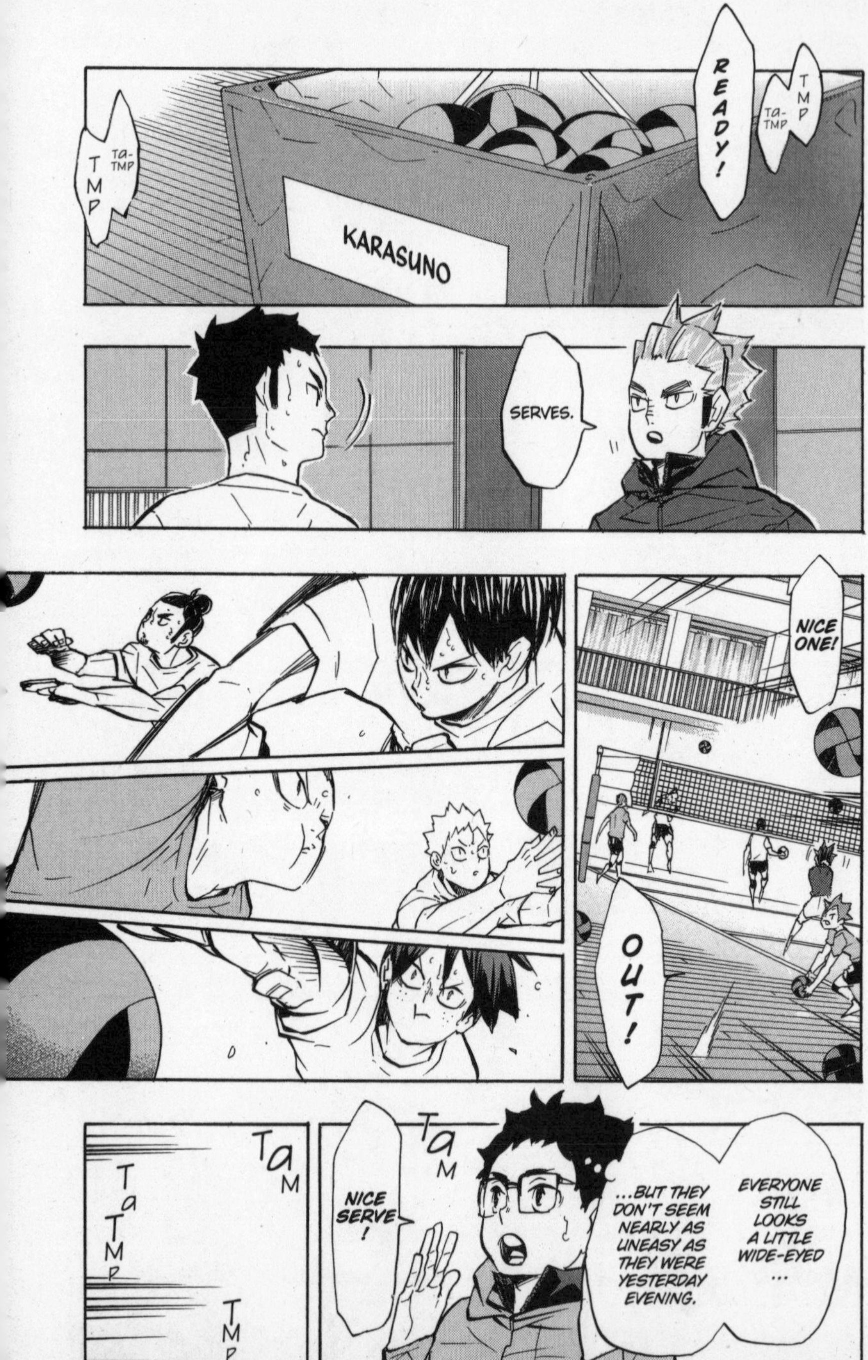
READY!
TMP Ta-TMP
Ta-TMP TMP
KARASUNO
SERVES.
NICE ONE!
OUT!
EVERYONE STILL LOOKS A LITTLE WIDE-EYED...
...BUT THEY DON'T SEEM NEARLY AS UNEASY AS THEY WERE YESTERDAY EVENING.
NICE SERVE!
TaM
TaM
TaTMP
TMP

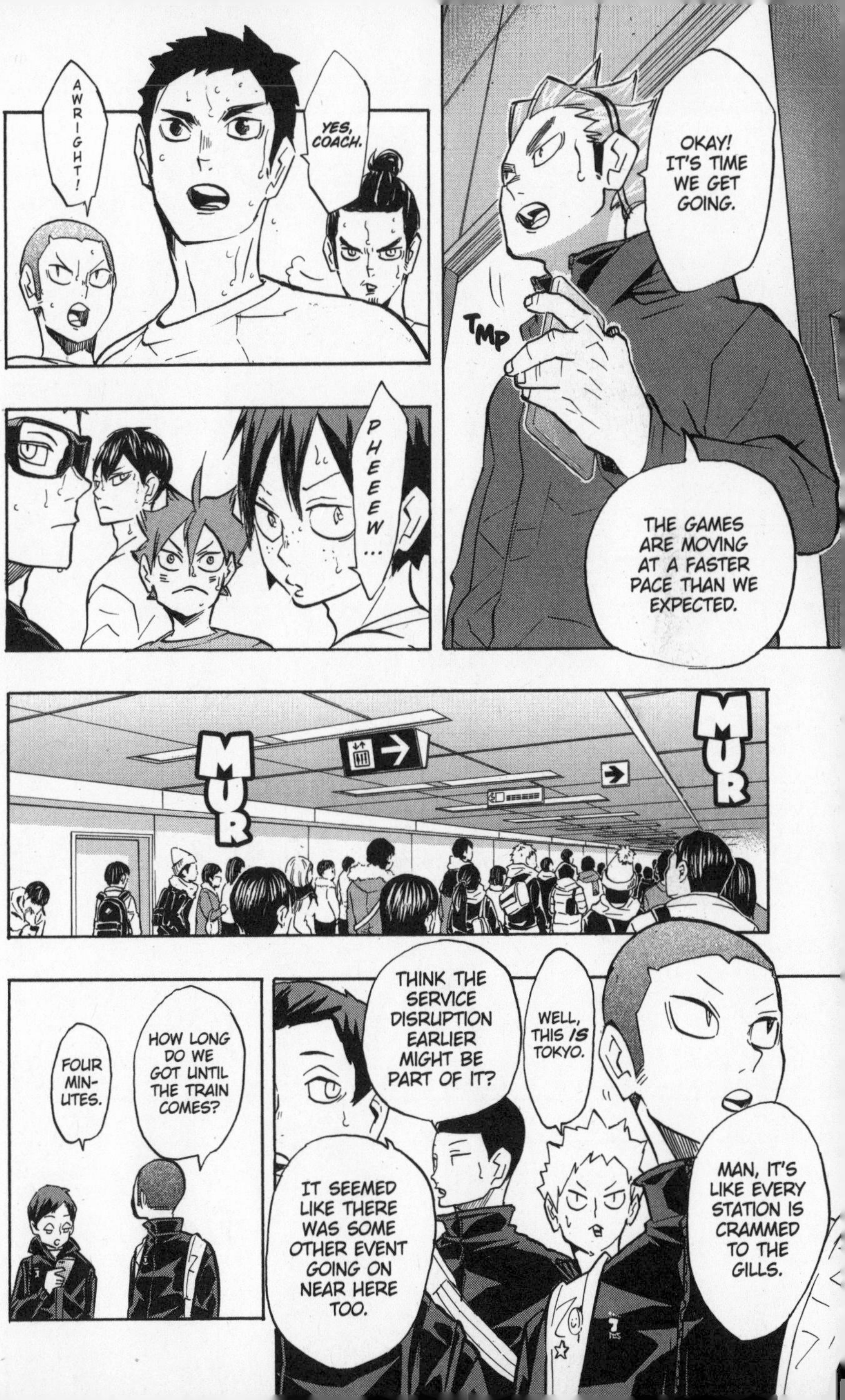
OKAY! IT'S TIME WE GET GOING.
TMP
THE GAMES ARE MOVING AT A FASTER PACE THAN WE EXPECTED.
YES, COACH.
AWRIGHT!
PHEEEEW...
MUR MUR
MUR MUR
MAN, IT'S LIKE EVERY STATION IS CRAMMED TO THE GILLS.
WELL, THIS *IS* TOKYO.
THINK THE SERVICE DISRUPTION EARLIER MIGHT BE PART OF IT?
IT SEEMED LIKE THERE WAS SOME OTHER EVENT GOING ON NEAR HERE TOO.
HOW LONG DO WE GOT UNTIL THE TRAIN COMES?
FOUR MIN-UTES.

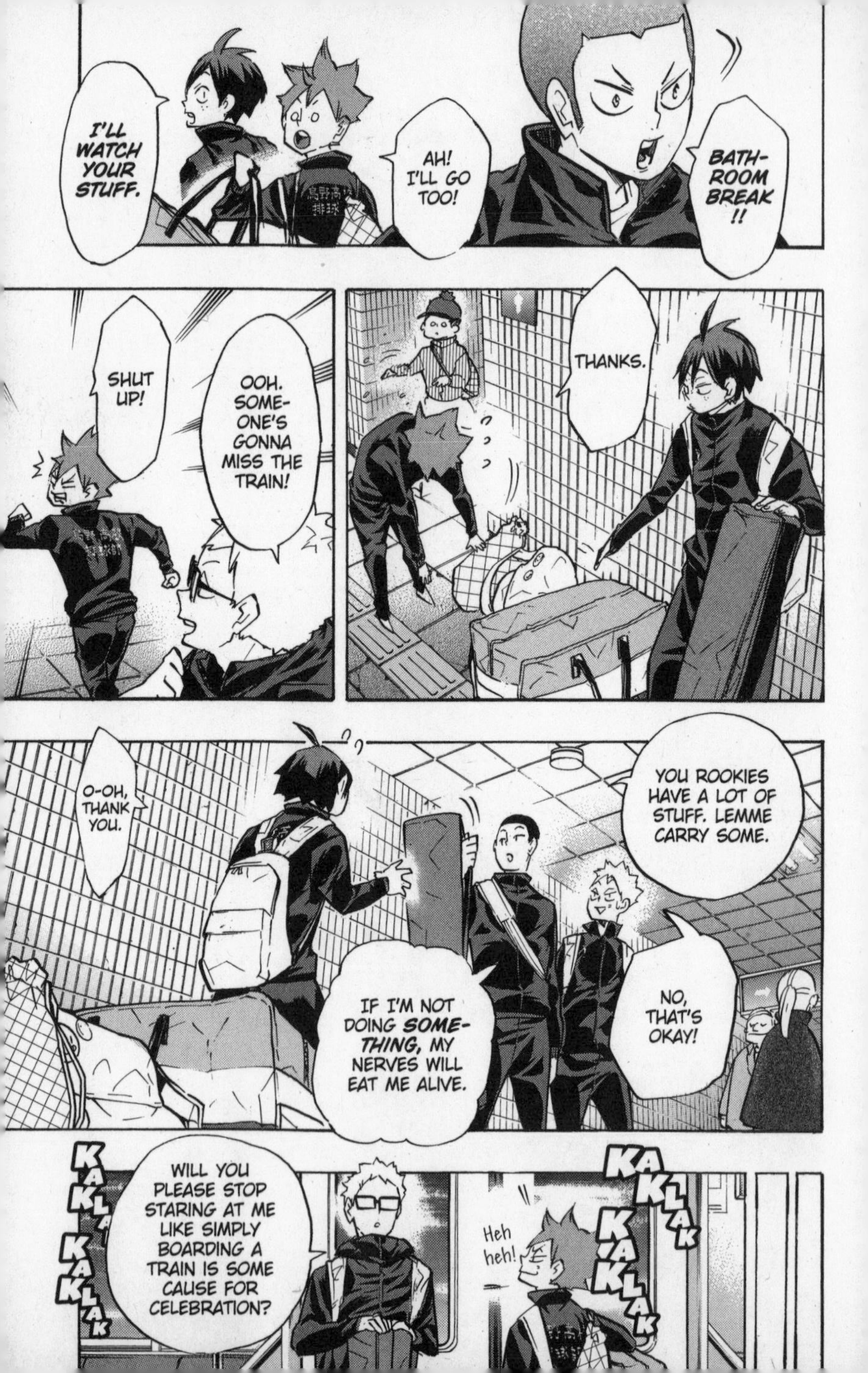
BATH-ROOM BREAK!!
AH! I'LL GO TOO!
I'LL WATCH YOUR STUFF.
THANKS.
OOH. SOME-ONE'S GONNA MISS THE TRAIN!
SHUT UP!
YOU ROOKIES HAVE A LOT OF STUFF. LEMME CARRY SOME.
NO, THAT'S OKAY!
IF I'M NOT DOING *SOME-THING,* MY NERVES WILL EAT ME ALIVE.
O-OH, THANK YOU.
KAKLAK KAKLAK
Heh heh!
WILL YOU PLEASE STOP STARING AT ME LIKE SIMPLY BOARDING A TRAIN IS SOME CAUSE FOR CELEBRATION?
KAKLAK KAKLAK

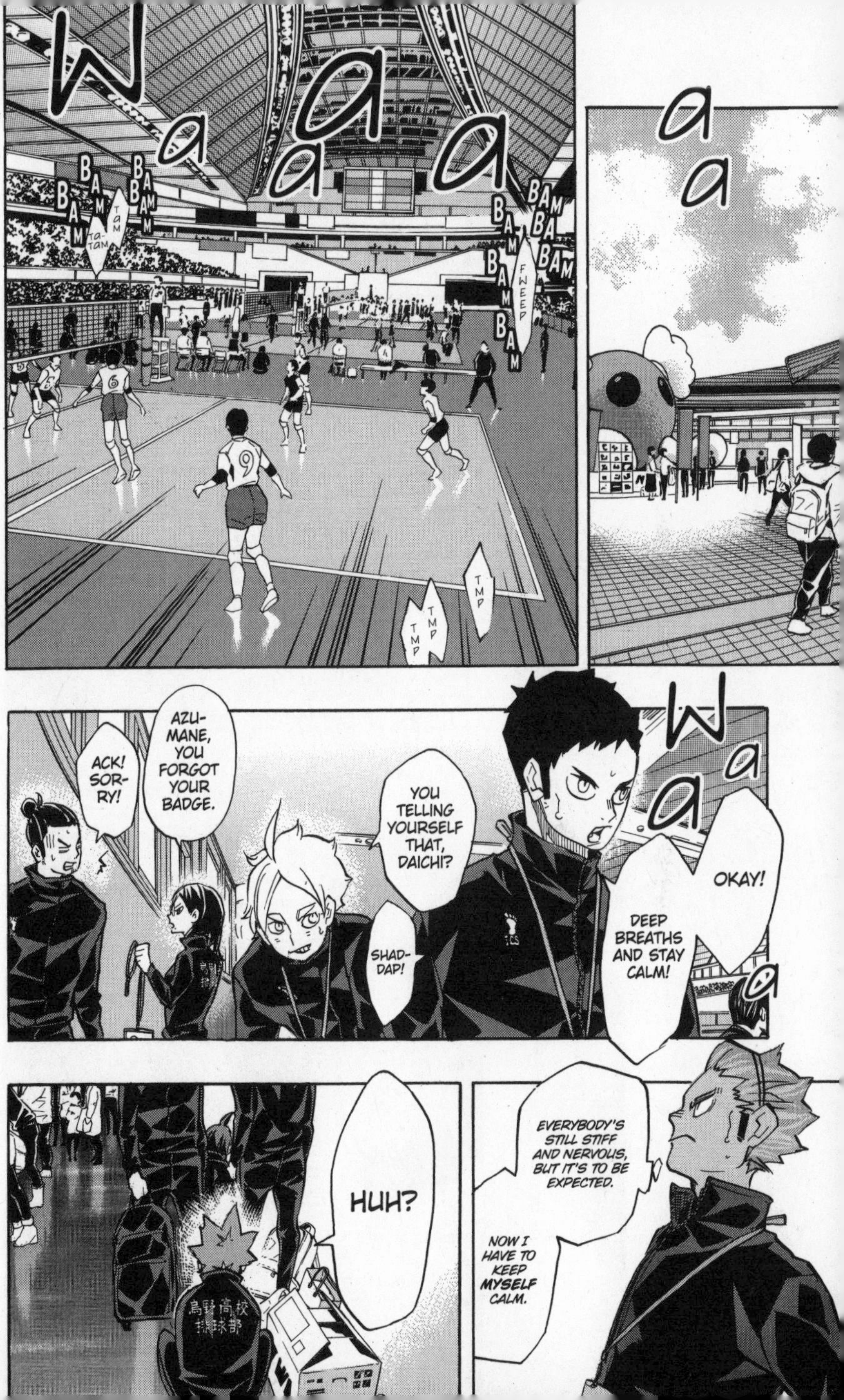
a
a
Wa
a
a
a
BAM
BAM
BAM
BAM
TAM
TA-TAM
BAM
BAM
BAM
BAM
BAM
BAM
BAM
FWEEP
TMP
TMP
TMP
Wa
a
a
OKAY!
DEEP BREATHS AND STAY CALM!
YOU TELLING YOURSELF THAT, DAICHI?
SHAD-DAP!
AZU-MANE, YOU FORGOT YOUR BADGE.
ACK! SOR-RY!
a
EVERYBODY'S STILL STIFF AND NERVOUS, BUT IT'S TO BE EXPECTED.
NOW I HAVE TO KEEP *MYSELF* CALM.
HUH?
烏野高校
排球部

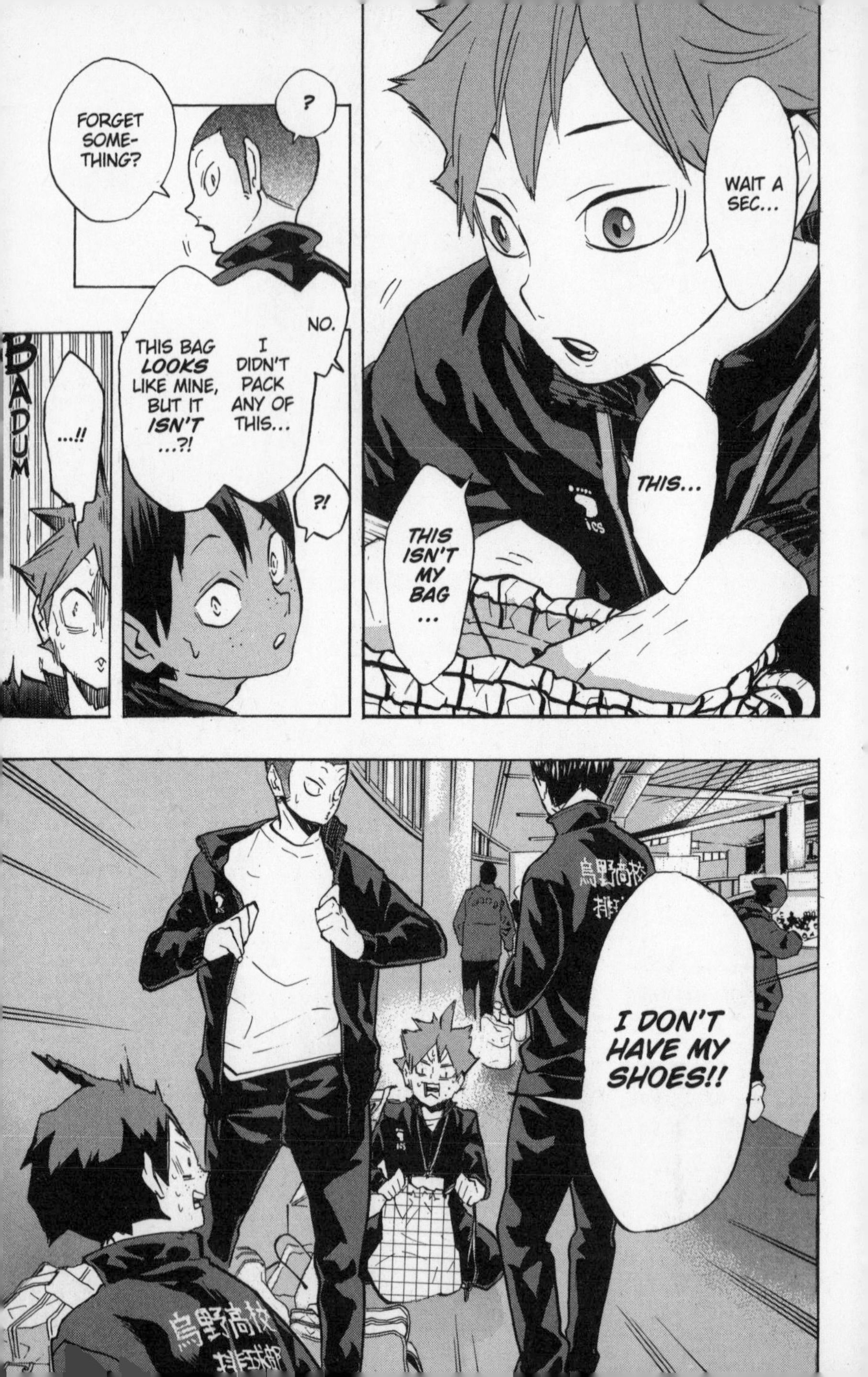
WAIT A SEC...
THIS...
THIS ISN'T MY BAG ...
?
FORGET SOME-THING?
NO.
I DIDN'T PACK ANY OF THIS...
THIS BAG **LOOKS** LIKE MINE, BUT IT ***ISN'T*** ...?!
?!
...!!
BADUM
I DON'T HAVE MY SHOES!!

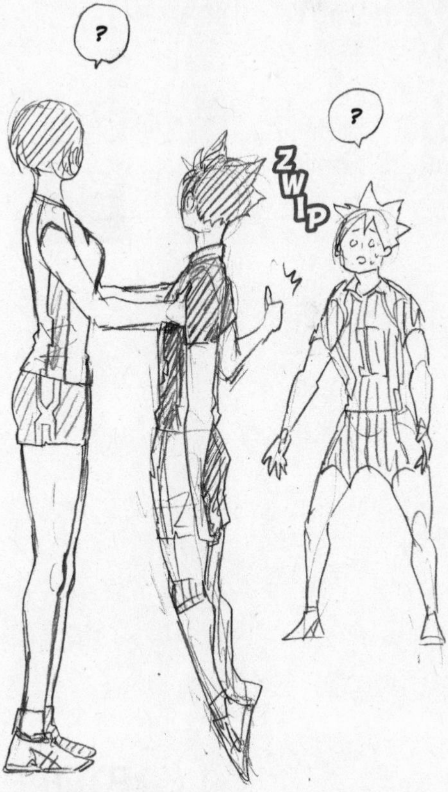
?
ZWIP
?

THE SMILE NOYA-SAN HAD ON HIS FACE RIGHT THEN WAS SO RADIANT AND CONTENT IT SOMEHOW GAVE ME A REALLY BAD FEELING.
(BY: SHOYO)

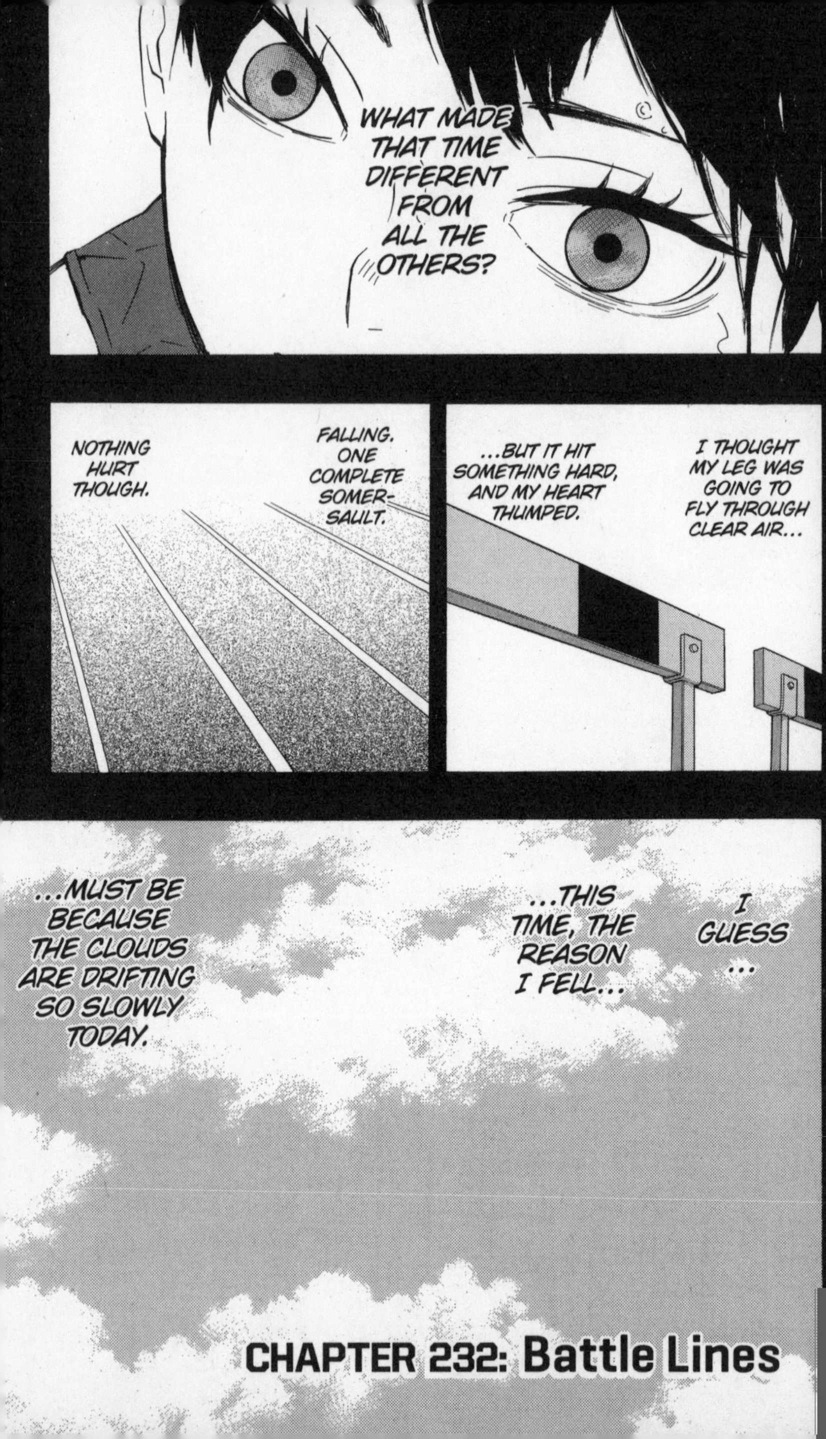
WHAT MADE THAT TIME DIFFERENT FROM ALL THE OTHERS?
I THOUGHT MY LEG WAS GOING TO FLY THROUGH CLEAR AIR...
...BUT IT HIT SOMETHING HARD, AND MY HEART THUMPED.
FALLING. ONE COMPLETE SOMER-SAULT.
NOTHING HURT THOUGH.
I GUESS...
...THIS TIME, THE REASON I FELL...
...MUST BE BECAUSE THE CLOUDS ARE DRIFTING SO SLOWLY TODAY.
CHAPTER 232: Battle Lines

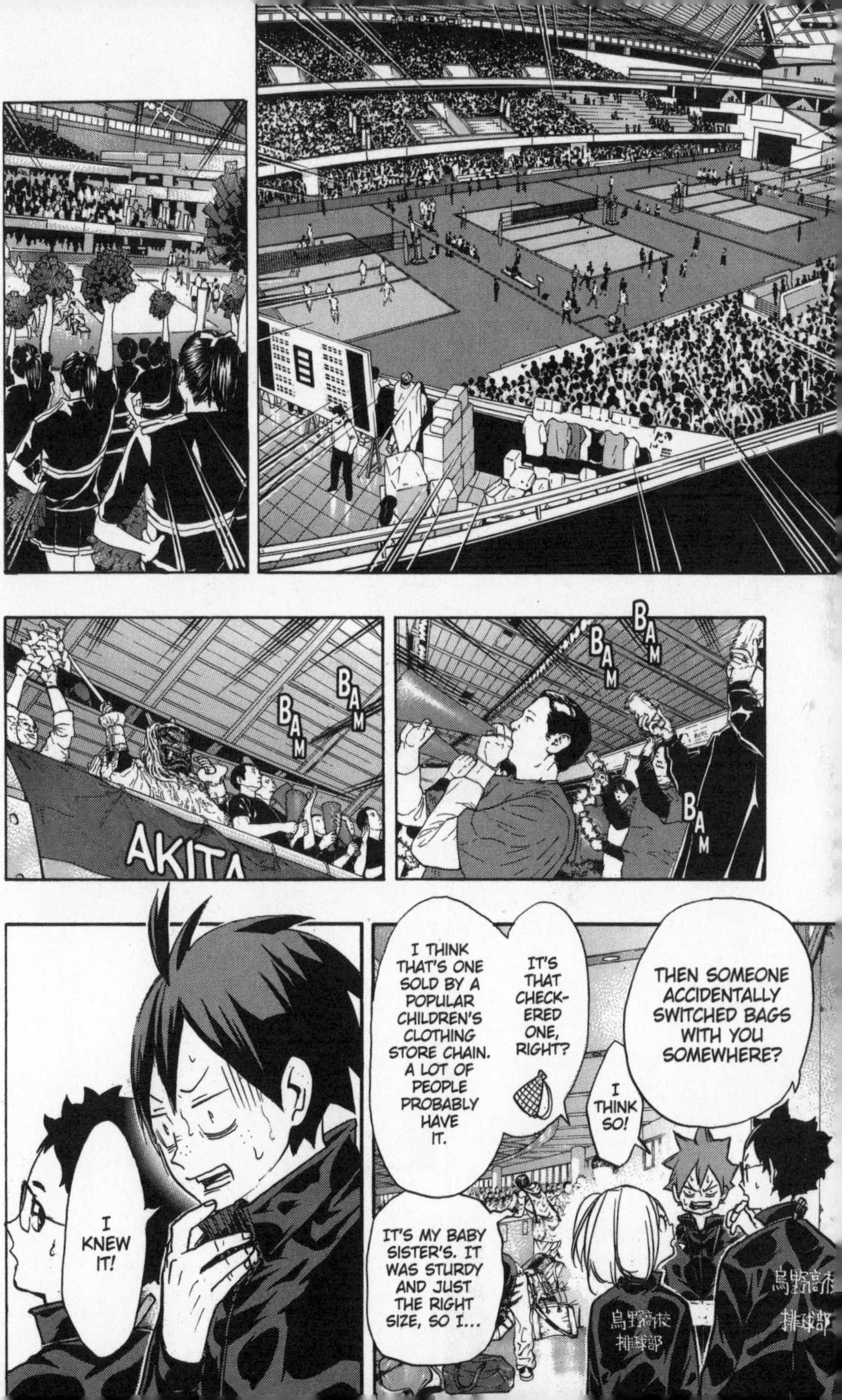
BAM
BAM
BAM
BAM
BAM
AKITA
THEN SOMEONE ACCIDENTALLY SWITCHED BAGS WITH YOU SOMEWHERE?
I THINK SO!
IT'S THAT CHECKERED ONE, RIGHT?
I THINK THAT'S ONE SOLD BY A POPULAR CHILDREN'S CLOTHING STORE CHAIN. A LOT OF PEOPLE PROBABLY HAVE IT.
IT'S MY BABY SISTER'S. IT WAS STURDY AND JUST THE RIGHT SIZE, SO I...
烏野高校
排球部
I KNEW IT!

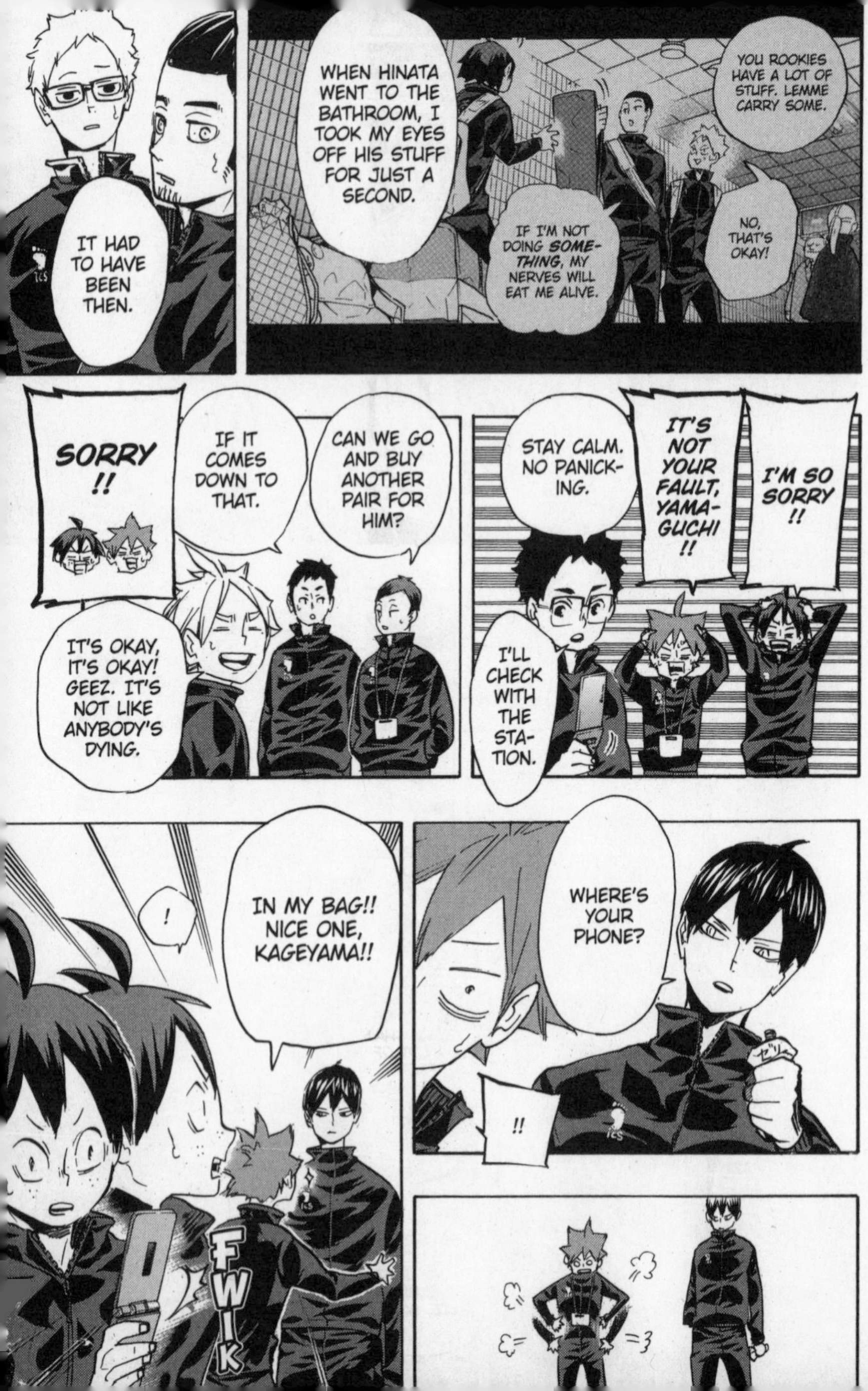
YOU ROOKIES HAVE A LOT OF STUFF. LEMME CARRY SOME.
NO, THAT'S OKAY!
IF I'M NOT DOING ***SOMETHING***, MY NERVES WILL EAT ME ALIVE.
WHEN HINATA WENT TO THE BATHROOM, I TOOK MY EYES OFF HIS STUFF FOR JUST A SECOND.
IT HAD TO HAVE BEEN THEN.
I'M SO SORRY !!
IT'S NOT YOUR FAULT, YAMAGUCHI !!
STAY CALM. NO PANICKING.
I'LL CHECK WITH THE STATION.
CAN WE GO AND BUY ANOTHER PAIR FOR HIM?
IF IT COMES DOWN TO THAT.
SORRY !!
IT'S OKAY, IT'S OKAY! GEEZ. IT'S NOT LIKE ANYBODY'S DYING.
WHERE'S YOUR PHONE?
!!
IN MY BAG!! NICE ONE, KAGEYAMA!!
!
FWIK

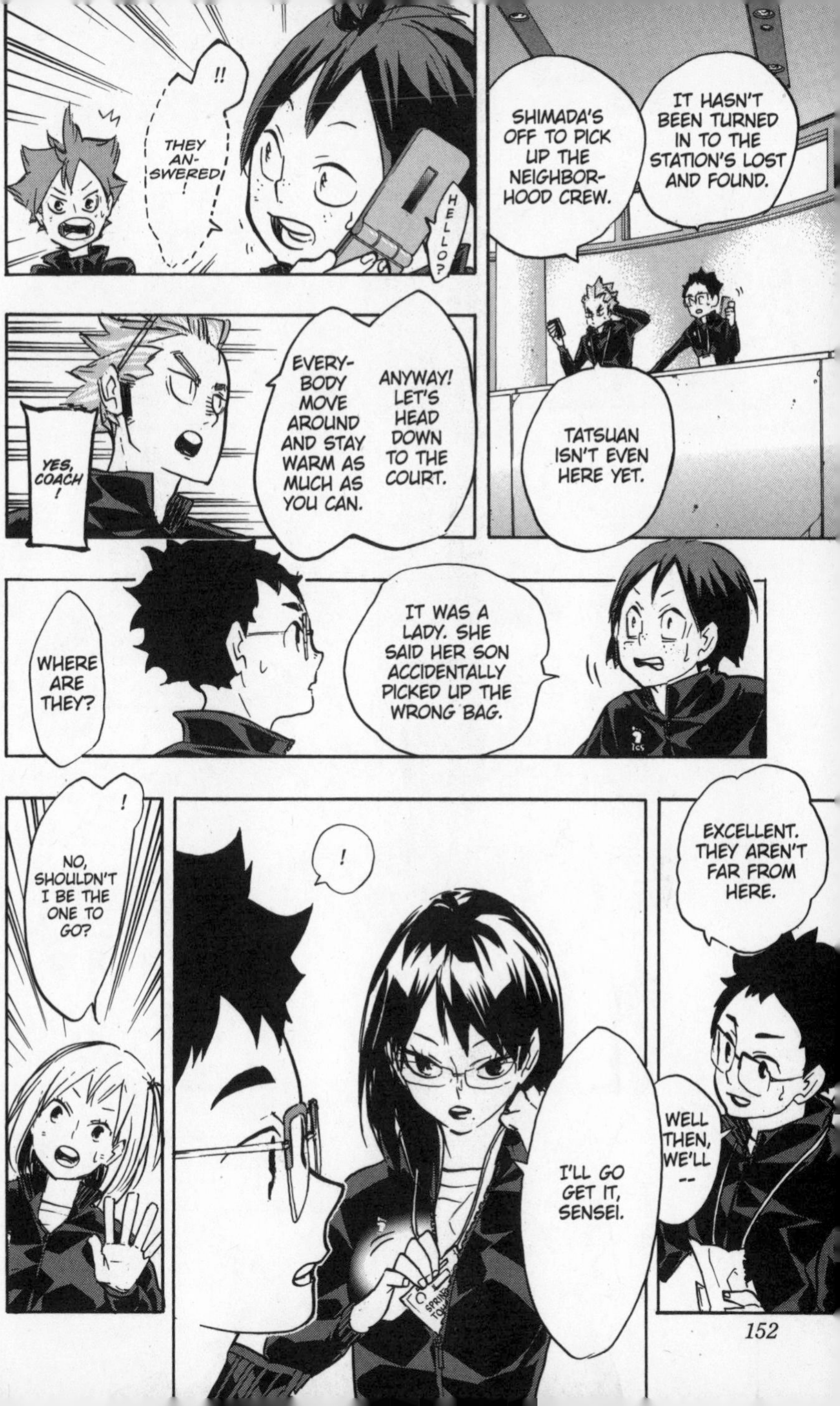
IT HASN'T BEEN TURNED IN TO THE STATION'S LOST AND FOUND.
SHIMADA'S OFF TO PICK UP THE NEIGHBOR-HOOD CREW.
TATSUAN ISN'T EVEN HERE YET.
HELLO?
!!
THEY AN-SWERED!
ANYWAY! LET'S HEAD DOWN TO THE COURT.
EVERY-BODY MOVE AROUND AND STAY WARM AS MUCH AS YOU CAN.
YES, COACH!
IT WAS A LADY. SHE SAID HER SON ACCIDENTALLY PICKED UP THE WRONG BAG.
WHERE ARE THEY?
EXCELLENT. THEY AREN'T FAR FROM HERE.
WELL THEN, WE'LL--
!
I'LL GO GET IT, SENSEI.
!
NO, SHOULDN'T I BE THE ONE TO GO?

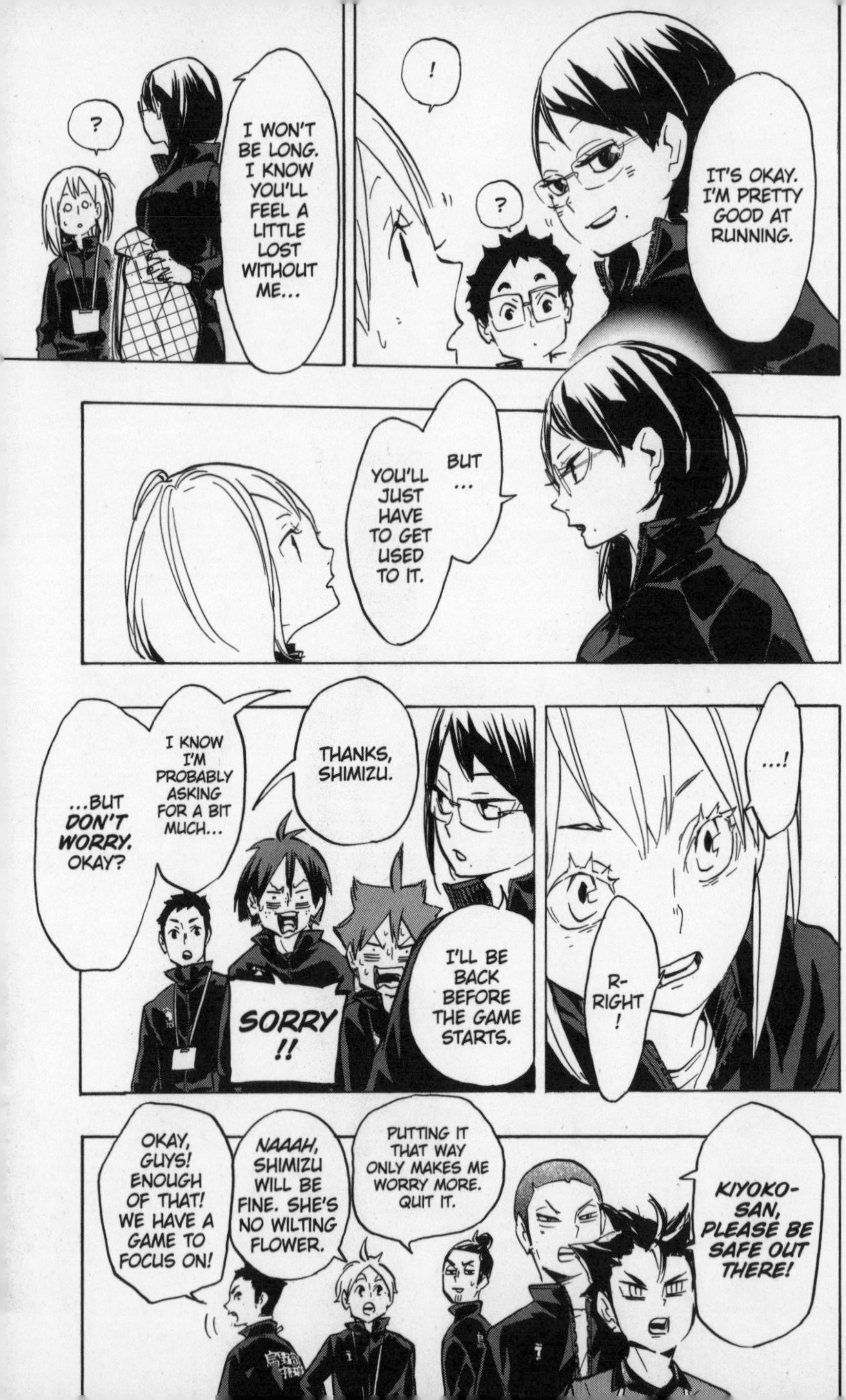

IT'S OKAY. I'M PRETTY GOOD AT RUNNING.
!
?
I WON'T BE LONG. I KNOW YOU'LL FEEL A LITTLE LOST WITHOUT ME...
?
BUT...
YOU'LL JUST HAVE TO GET USED TO IT.
...!
R-RIGHT!
THANKS, SHIMIZU.
I'LL BE BACK BEFORE THE GAME STARTS.
I KNOW I'M PROBABLY ASKING FOR A BIT MUCH...
...BUT *DON'T WORRY.* OKAY?
SORRY!!
KIYOKO-SAN, PLEASE BE SAFE OUT THERE!
PUTTING IT THAT WAY ONLY MAKES ME WORRY MORE. QUIT IT.
NAAAH, SHIMIZU WILL BE FINE. SHE'S NO WILTING FLOWER.
OKAY, GUYS! ENOUGH OF THAT! WE HAVE A GAME TO FOCUS ON!

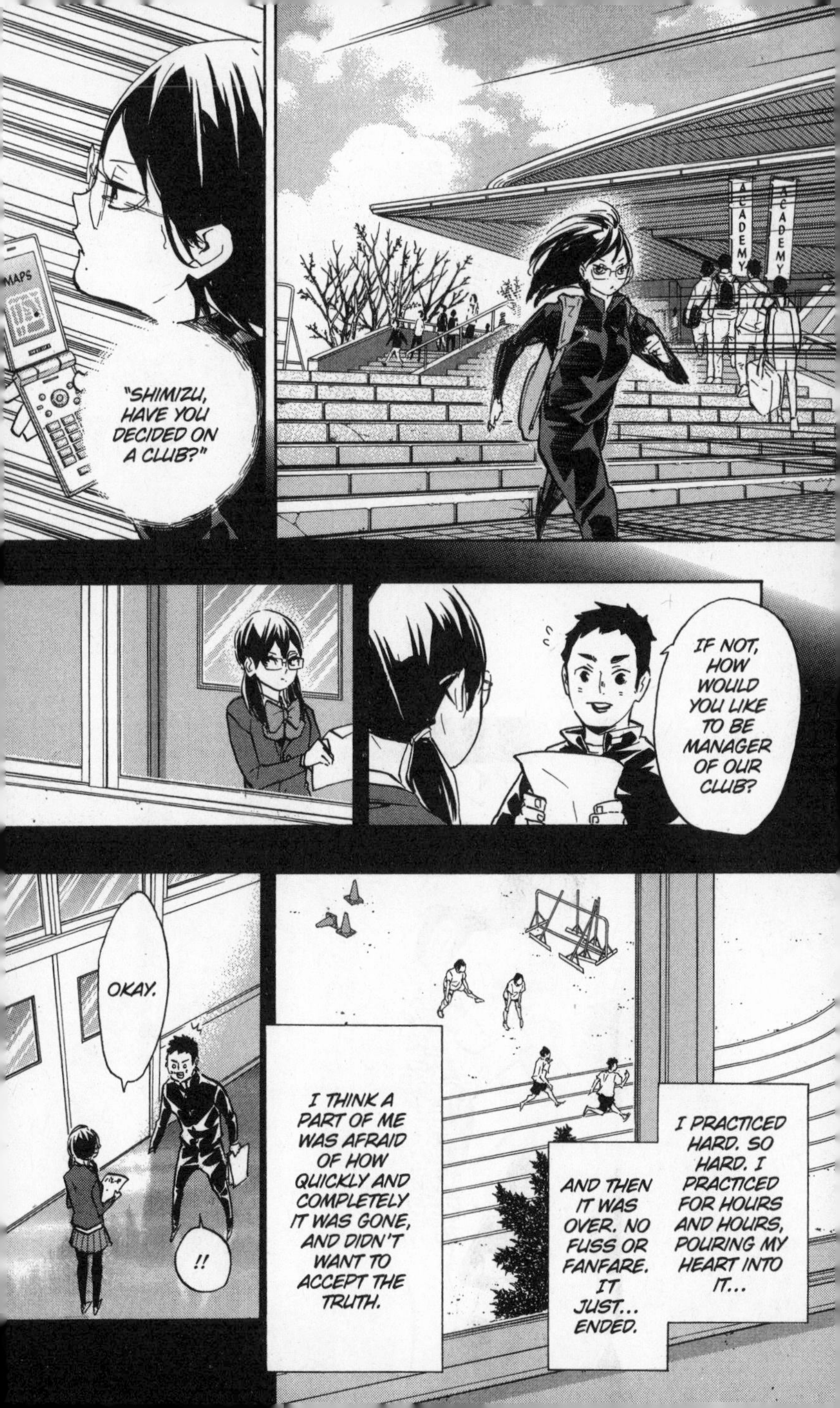
ACADEMY
ACADEMY
"SHIMIZU, HAVE YOU DECIDED ON A CLUB?"
IF NOT, HOW WOULD YOU LIKE TO BE MANAGER OF OUR CLUB?
I PRACTICED HARD. SO HARD. I PRACTICED FOR HOURS AND HOURS, POURING MY HEART INTO IT...
AND THEN IT WAS OVER. NO FUSS OR FANFARE. IT JUST... ENDED.
I THINK A PART OF ME WAS AFRAID OF HOW QUICKLY AND COMPLETELY IT WAS GONE, AND DIDN'T WANT TO ACCEPT THE TRUTH.
OKAY.
!!

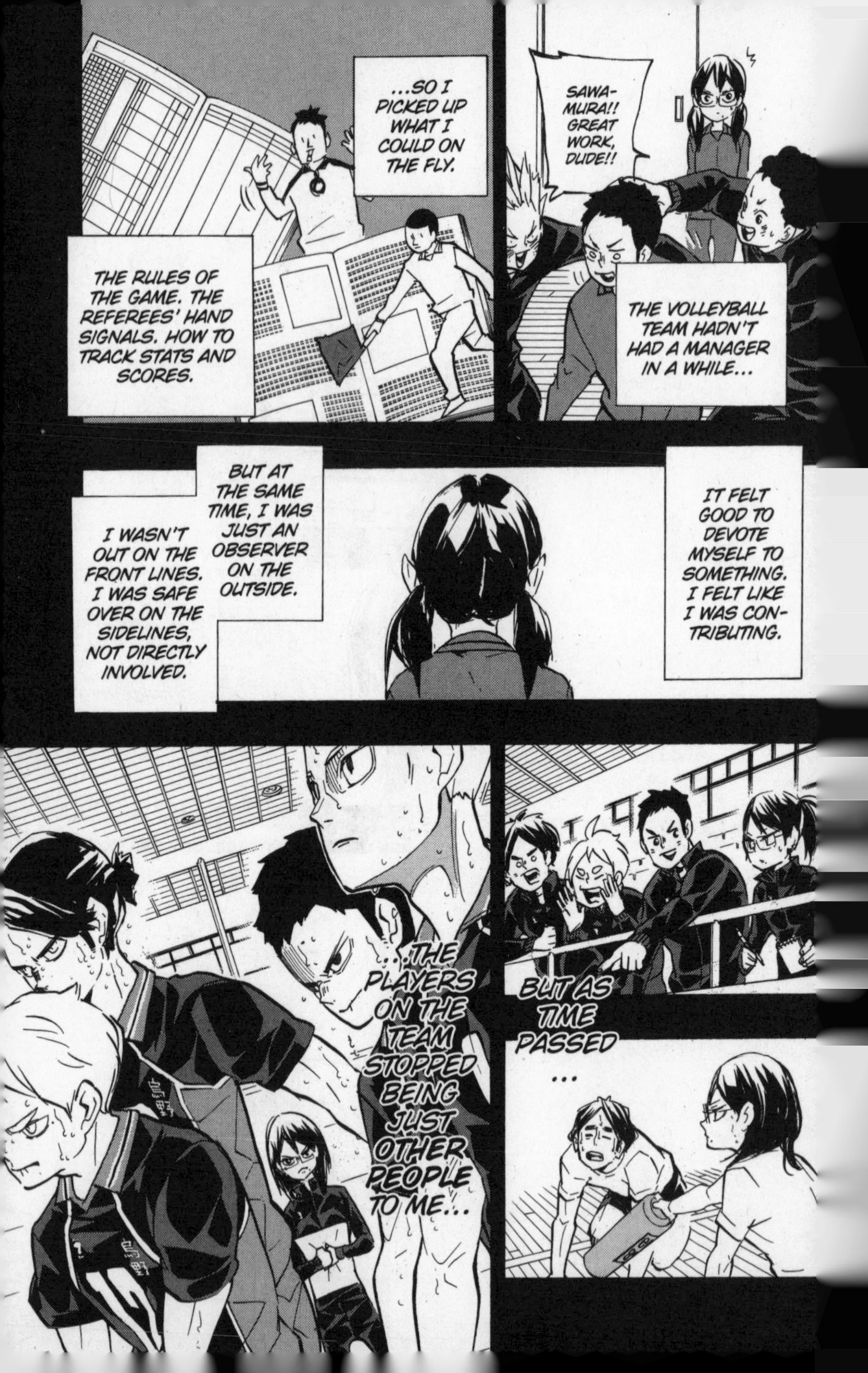
SAWAMURA!! GREAT WORK, DUDE!!
THE VOLLEYBALL TEAM HADN'T HAD A MANAGER IN A WHILE...
...SO I PICKED UP WHAT I COULD ON THE FLY.
THE RULES OF THE GAME. THE REFEREES' HAND SIGNALS. HOW TO TRACK STATS AND SCORES.
IT FELT GOOD TO DEVOTE MYSELF TO SOMETHING. I FELT LIKE I WAS CONTRIBUTING.
BUT AT THE SAME TIME, I WAS JUST AN OBSERVER ON THE OUTSIDE.
I WASN'T OUT ON THE FRONT LINES. I WAS SAFE OVER ON THE SIDELINES, NOT DIRECTLY INVOLVED.
BUT AS TIME PASSED...
...THE PLAYERS ON THE TEAM STOPPED BEING JUST OTHER PEOPLE TO ME...

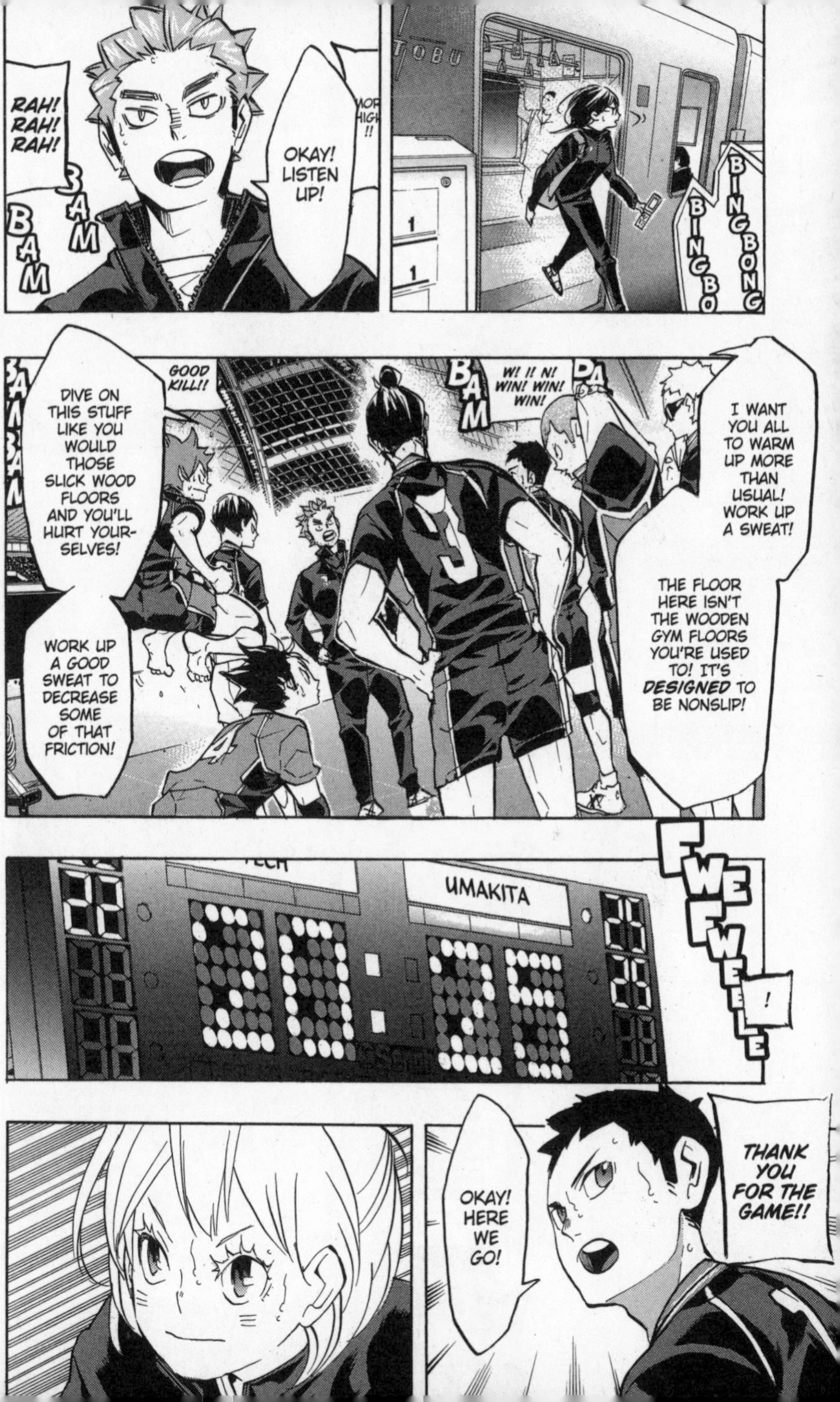
TOBU
BINGBONG
BINGBO
RAH! RAH! RAH!
BAM BAM
OKAY! LISTEN UP!
I WANT YOU ALL TO WARM UP MORE THAN USUAL! WORK UP A SWEAT!
THE FLOOR HERE ISN'T THE WOODEN GYM FLOORS YOU'RE USED TO! IT'S *DESIGNED* TO BE NONSLIP!
W! !! N! WIN! WIN! WIN!
BAM
GOOD KILL!!
DIVE ON THIS STUFF LIKE YOU WOULD THOSE SLICK WOOD FLOORS AND YOU'LL HURT YOURSELVES!
WORK UP A GOOD SWEAT TO DECREASE SOME OF THAT FRICTION!
FWEE FWEEE!
UMAKITA
THANK YOU FOR THE GAME!!
OKAY! HERE WE GO!

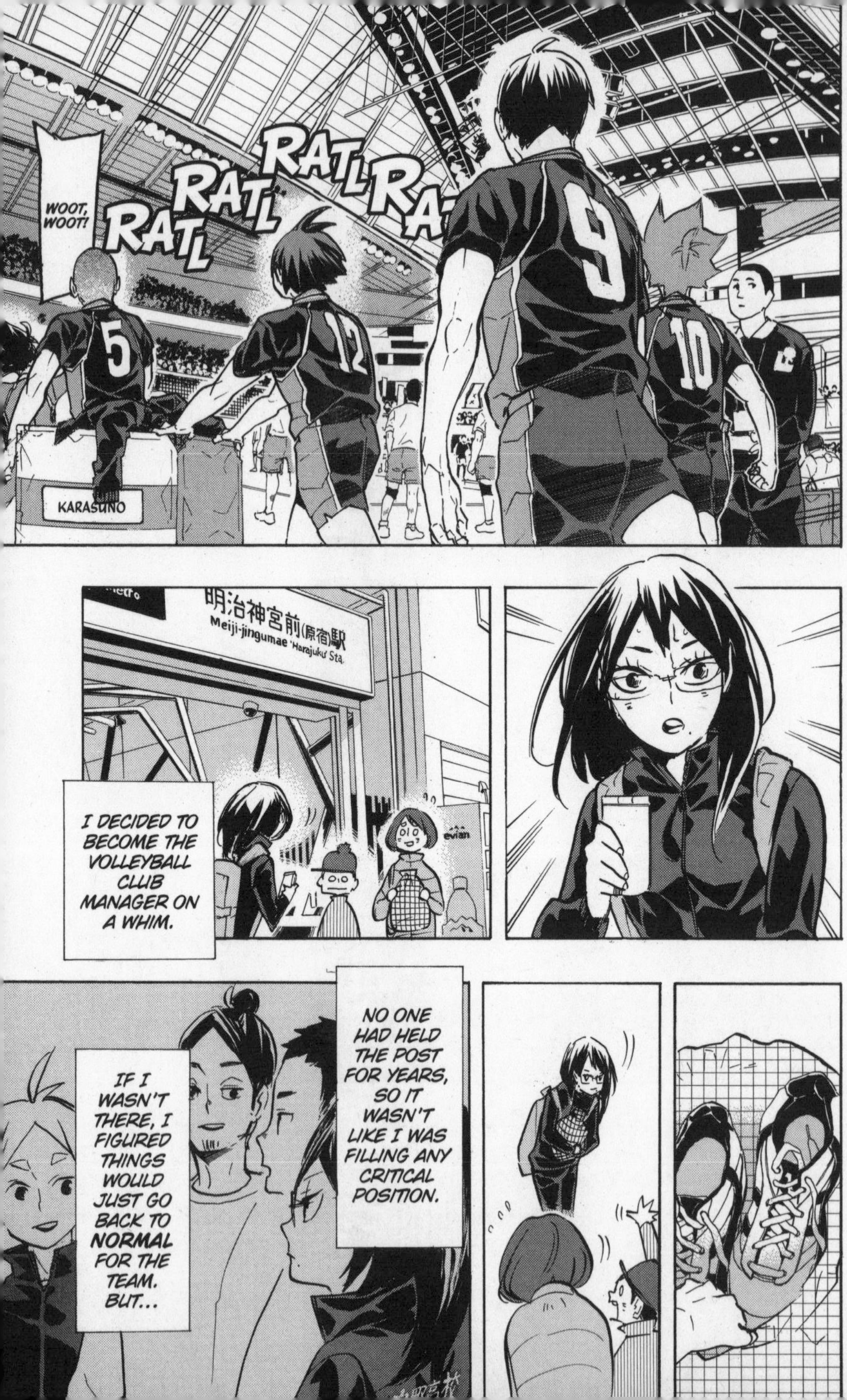
RATL RATL RATL RAT-
WOOT, WOOT!
KARASUNO
明治神宮前〈原宿〉駅
Meiji-jingumae 'Harajuku' Sta.
evian
I DECIDED TO BECOME THE VOLLEYBALL CLUB MANAGER ON A WHIM.
NO ONE HAD HELD THE POST FOR YEARS, SO IT WASN'T LIKE I WAS FILLING ANY CRITICAL POSITION.
IF I WASN'T THERE, I FIGURED THINGS WOULD JUST GO BACK TO NORMAL FOR THE TEAM. BUT...

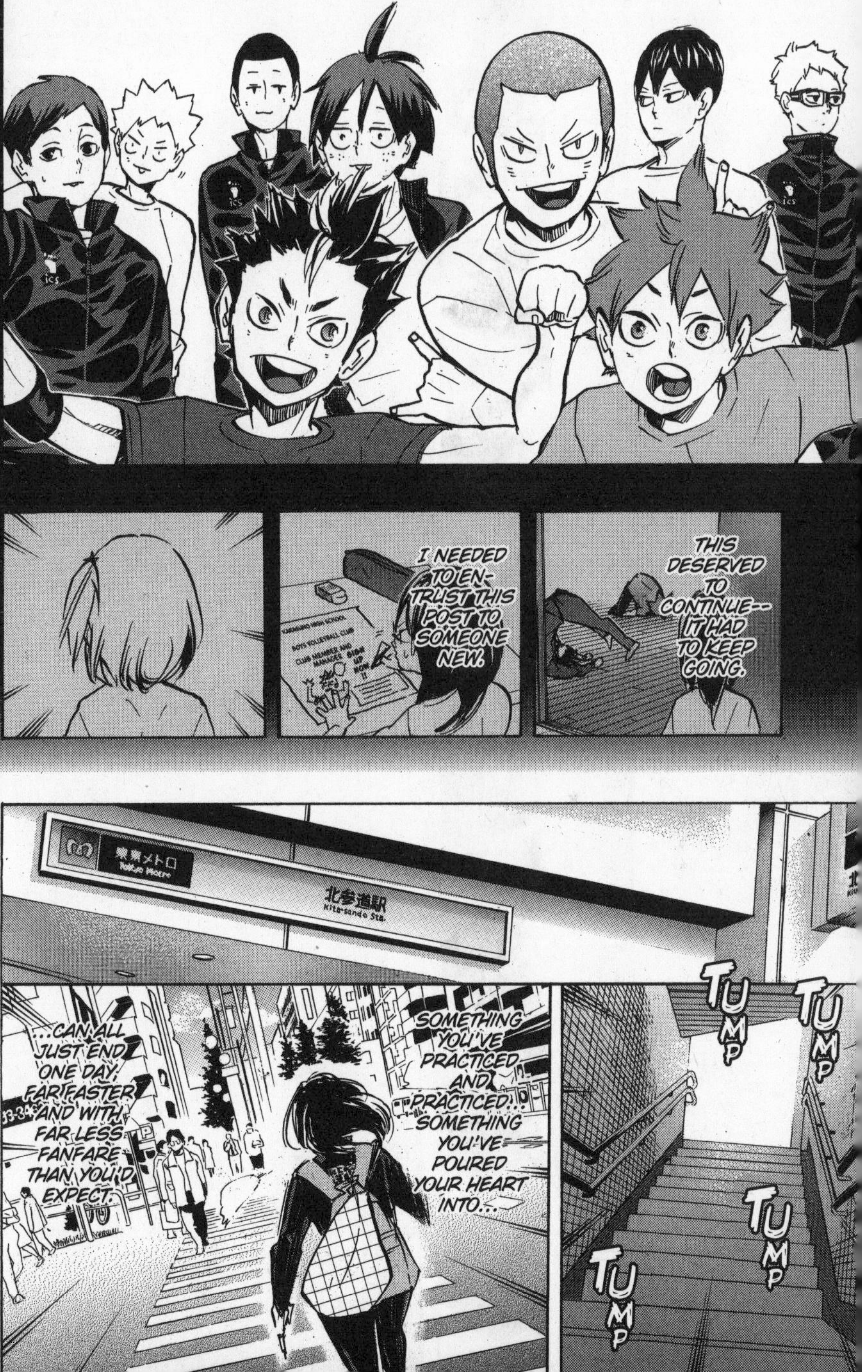
THIS DESERVED TO CONTINUE-- IT HAD TO KEEP GOING.
I NEEDED TO ENTRUST THIS POST TO SOMEONE NEW.
東京メトロ
Tokyo Metro
北参道駅
Kita-sando Sta.
TUMP
TUMP
TUMP
TUMP
SOMETHING YOU'VE PRACTICED AND PRACTICED... SOMETHING YOU'VE POURED YOUR HEART INTO...
...CAN ALL JUST END ONE DAY, FAR FASTER AND WITH FAR LESS FANFARE THAN YOU'D EXPECT.

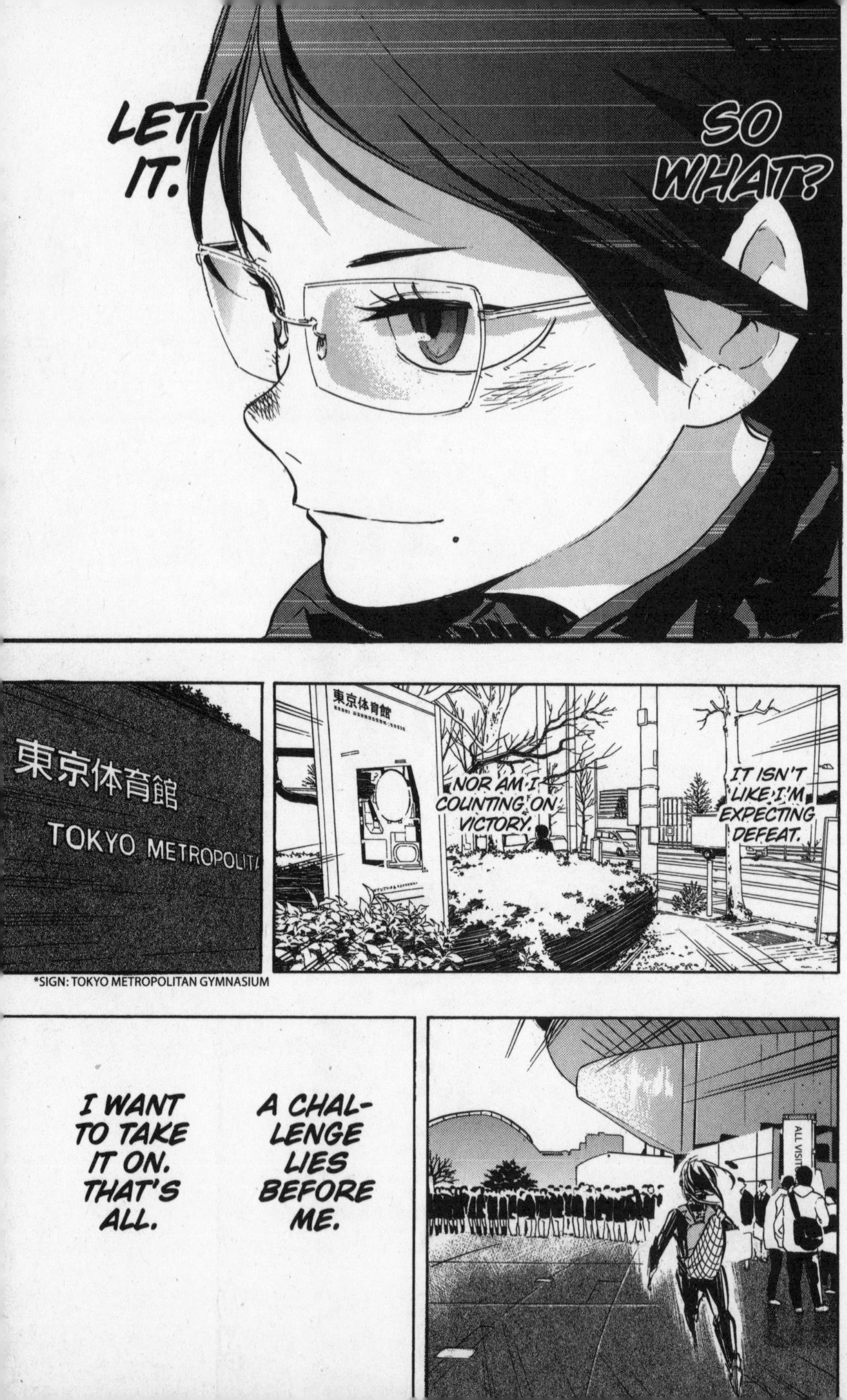
SO WHAT?
LET IT.
IT ISN'T LIKE I'M EXPECTING DEFEAT.
NOR AM I COUNTING ON VICTORY.
東京体育館
東京体育館
TOKYO METROPOLITA
*SIGN: TOKYO METROPOLITAN GYMNASIUM
A CHAL-LENGE LIES BEFORE ME.
I WANT TO TAKE IT ON. THAT'S ALL.

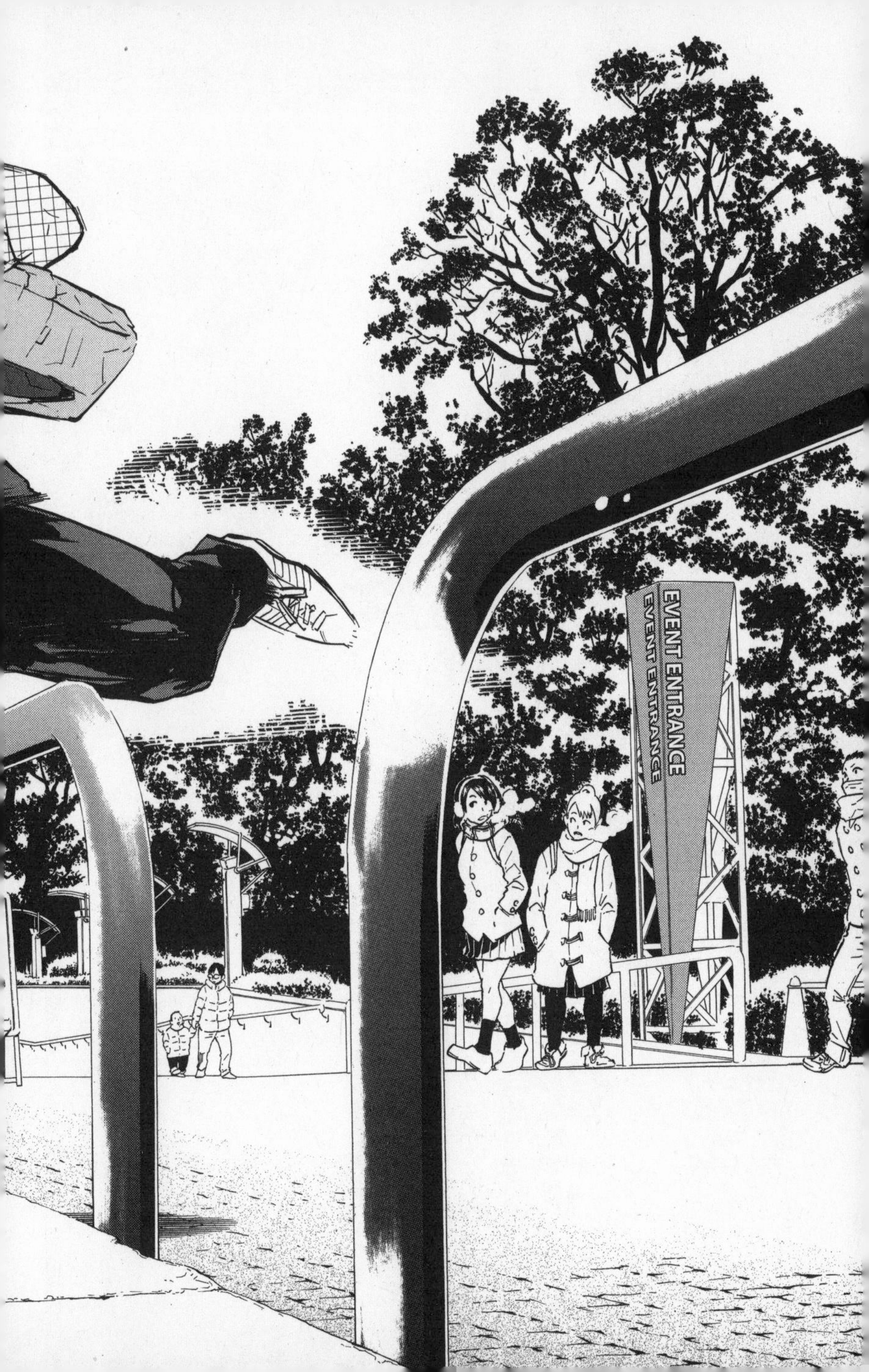
EVENT ENTRANCE
EVENT ENTRANCE

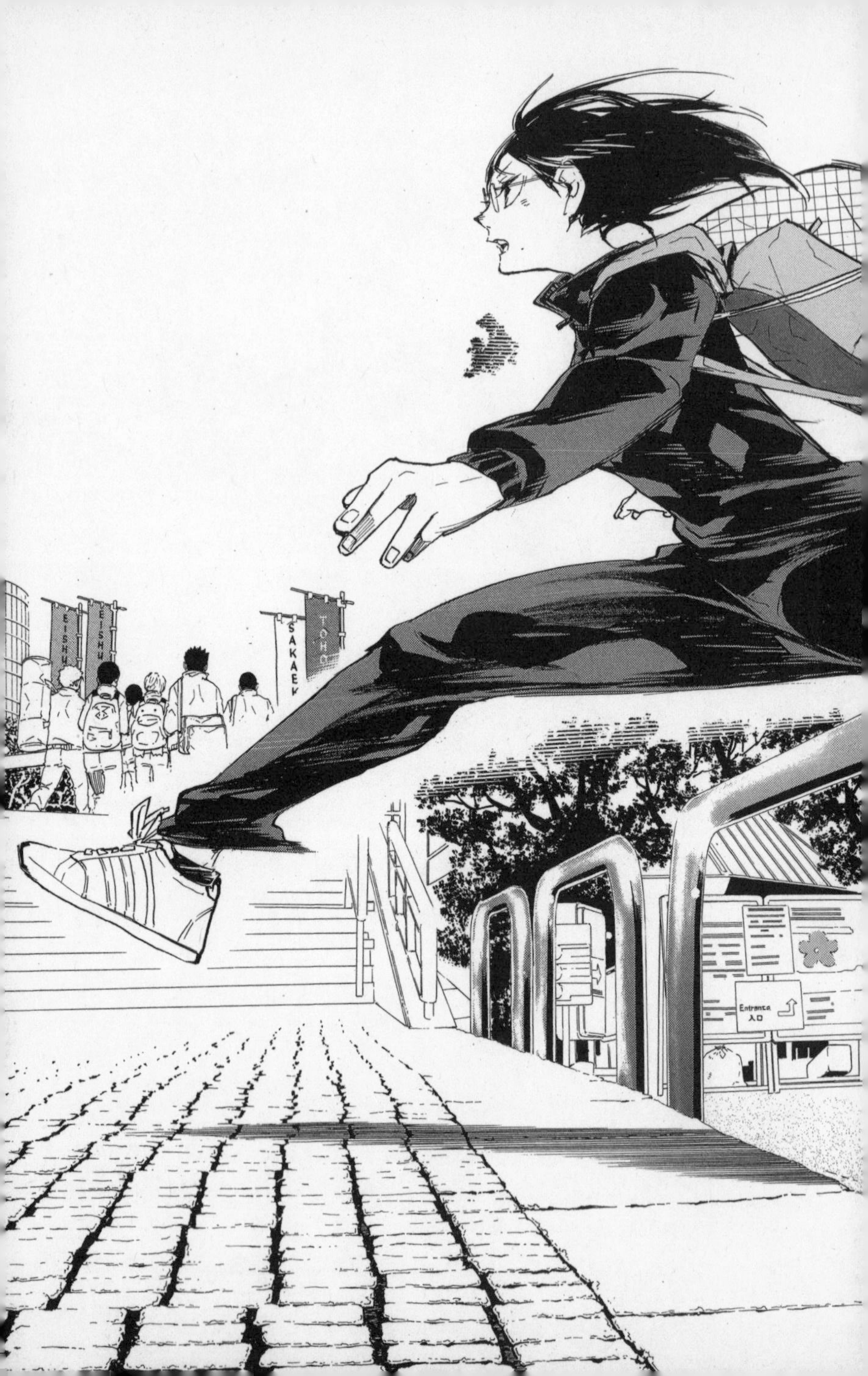
TOHO
SAKAEK
EISHU
EISHU
Entrance
入口

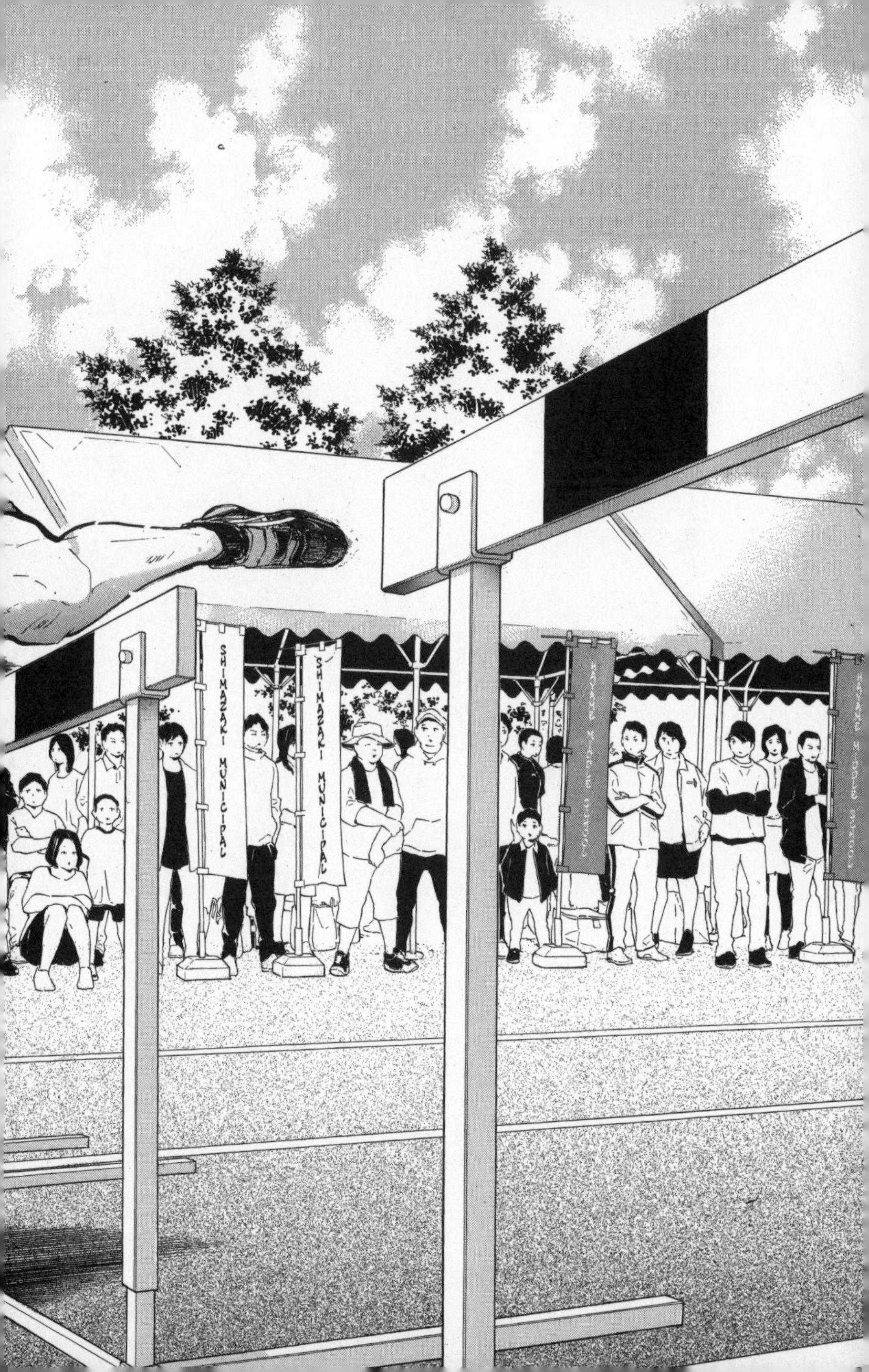
SHIMAZAKI MUNICIPAL
SHIMAZAKI MUNICIPAL

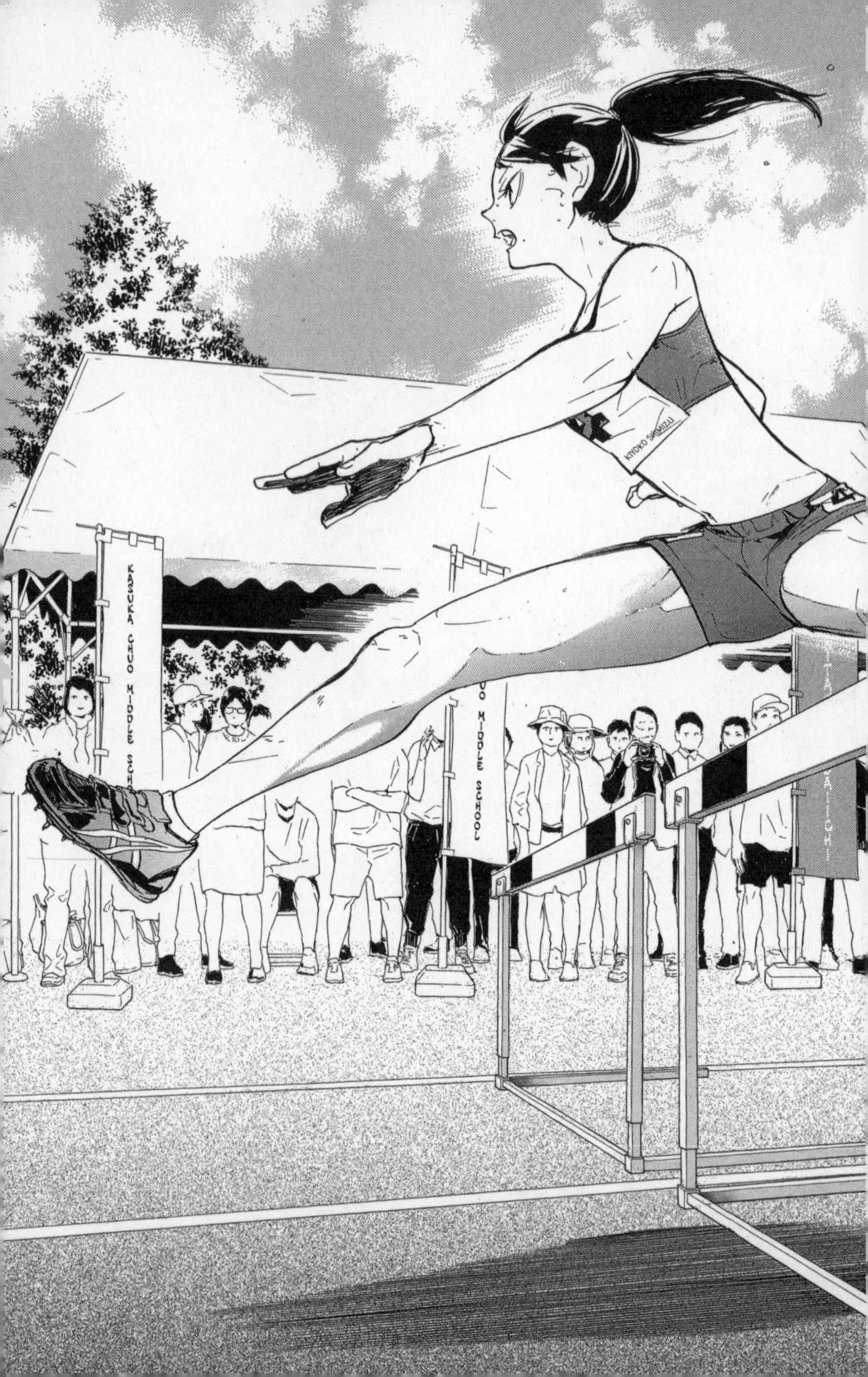
KIYOKO SHIMIZU
KASUKA CHUO MIDDLE
MIDDLE SCHOOL

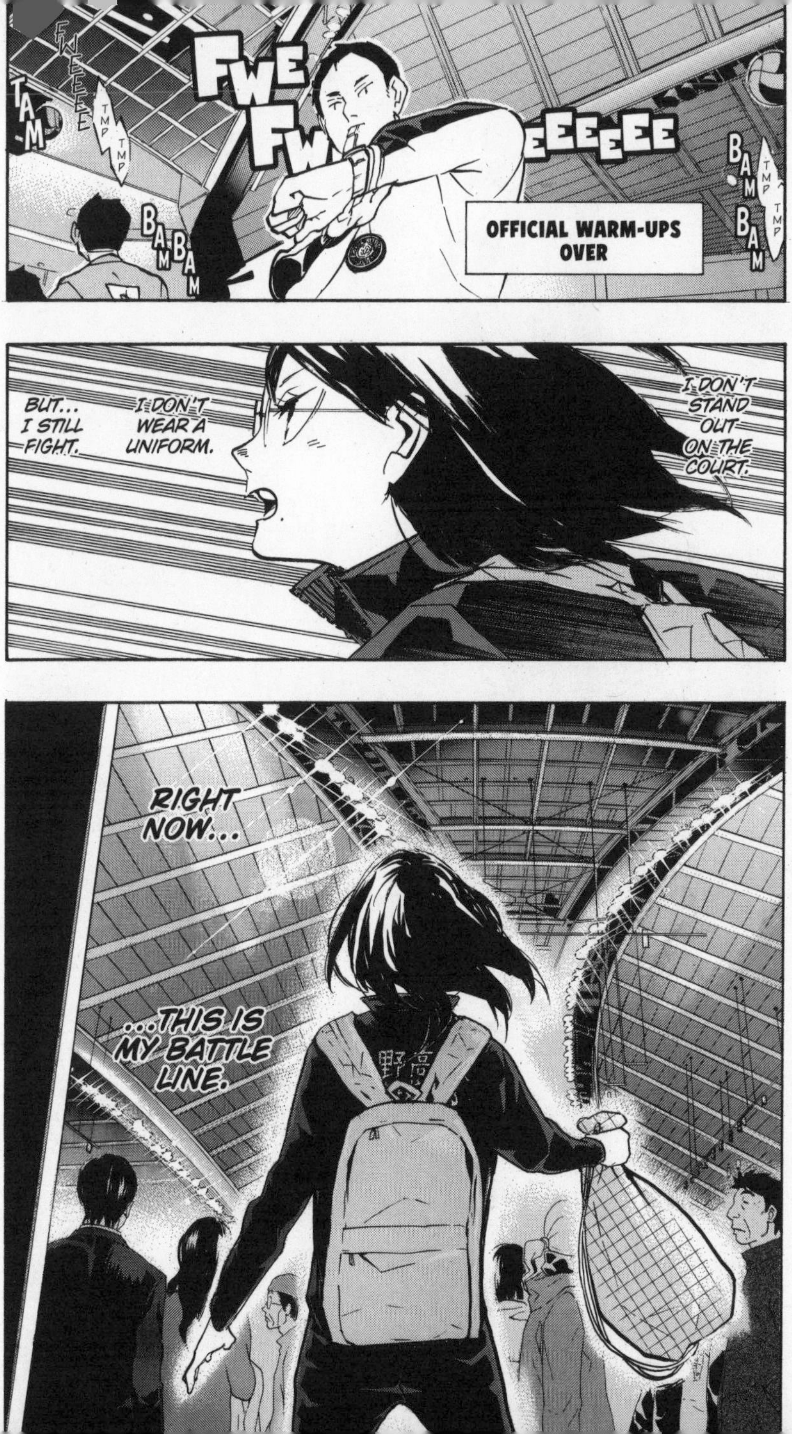
BAM TMP TMP BAM
FWE FWEEEEEEE
OFFICIAL WARM-UPS OVER
FWEEEE
TAM
TMP TMP
BAM BAM
I DON'T STAND OUT ON THE COURT.
I DON'T WEAR A UNIFORM.
BUT... I STILL FIGHT.
RIGHT NOW...
...THIS IS MY BATTLE LINE.

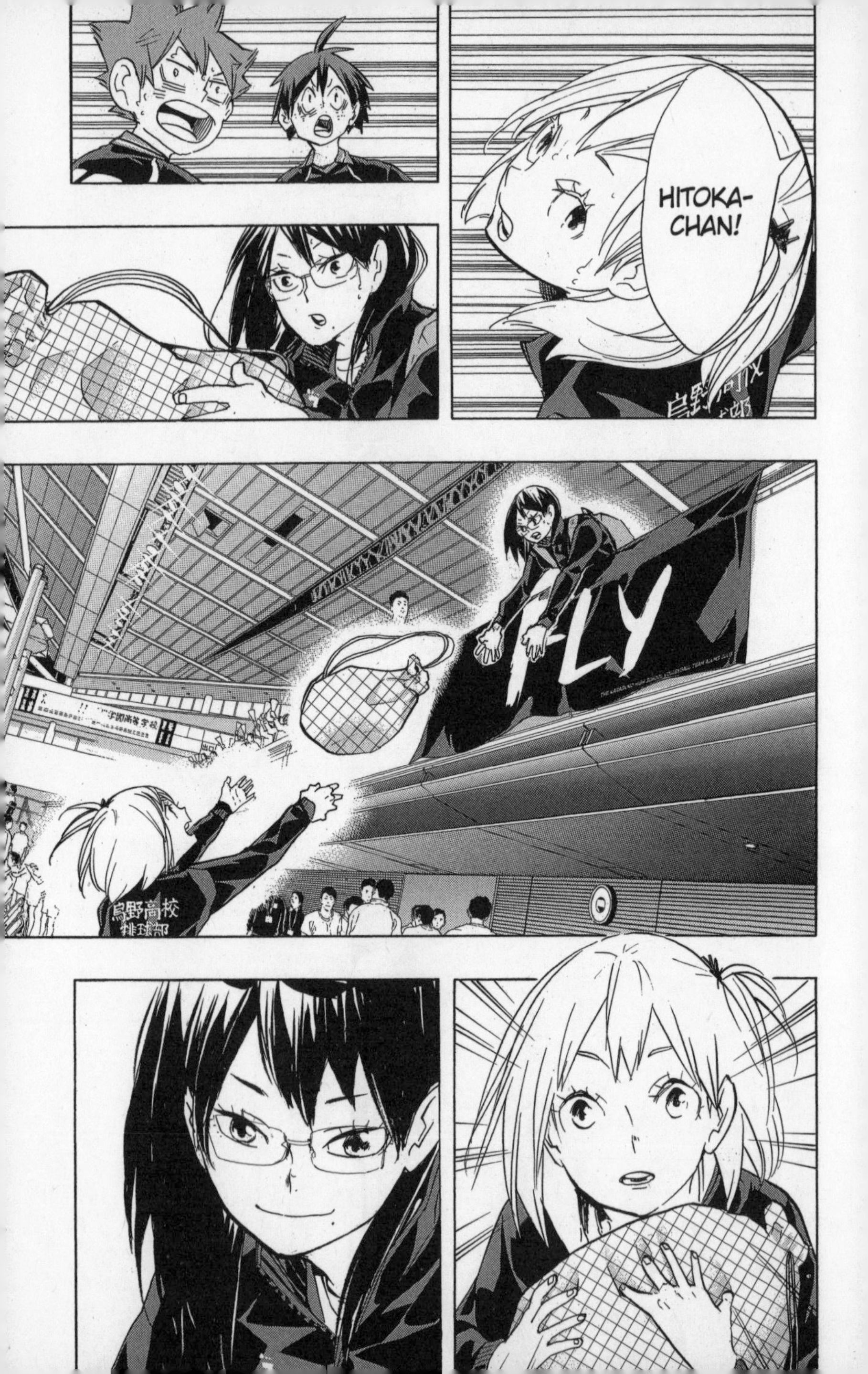
HITOKA-CHAN!

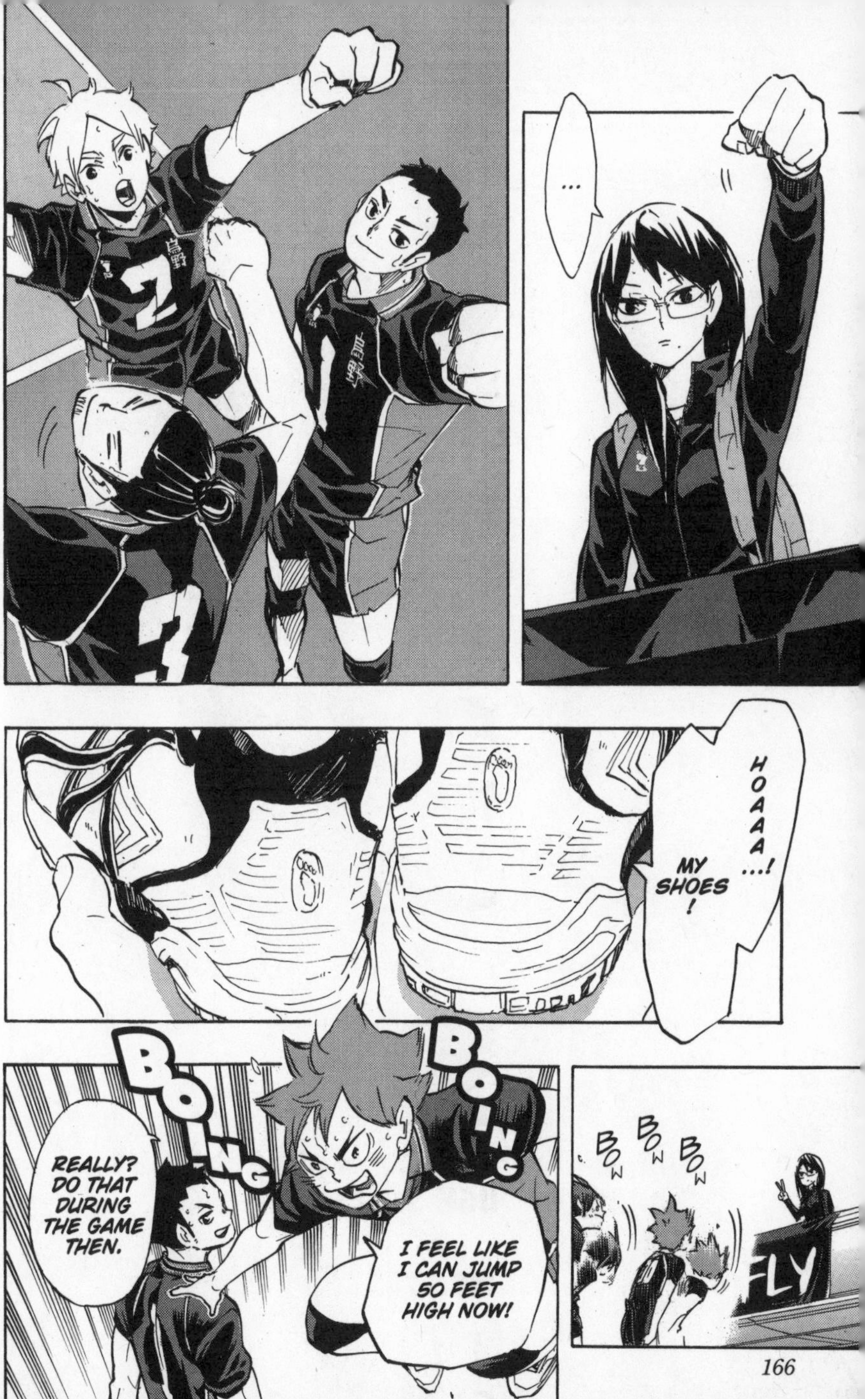
...
HOAAAA...!
MY SHOES!
BOW BOW BOW
FLY
BOING
BOING
I FEEL LIKE I CAN JUMP 50 FEET HIGH NOW!
REALLY? DO THAT DURING THE GAME THEN.

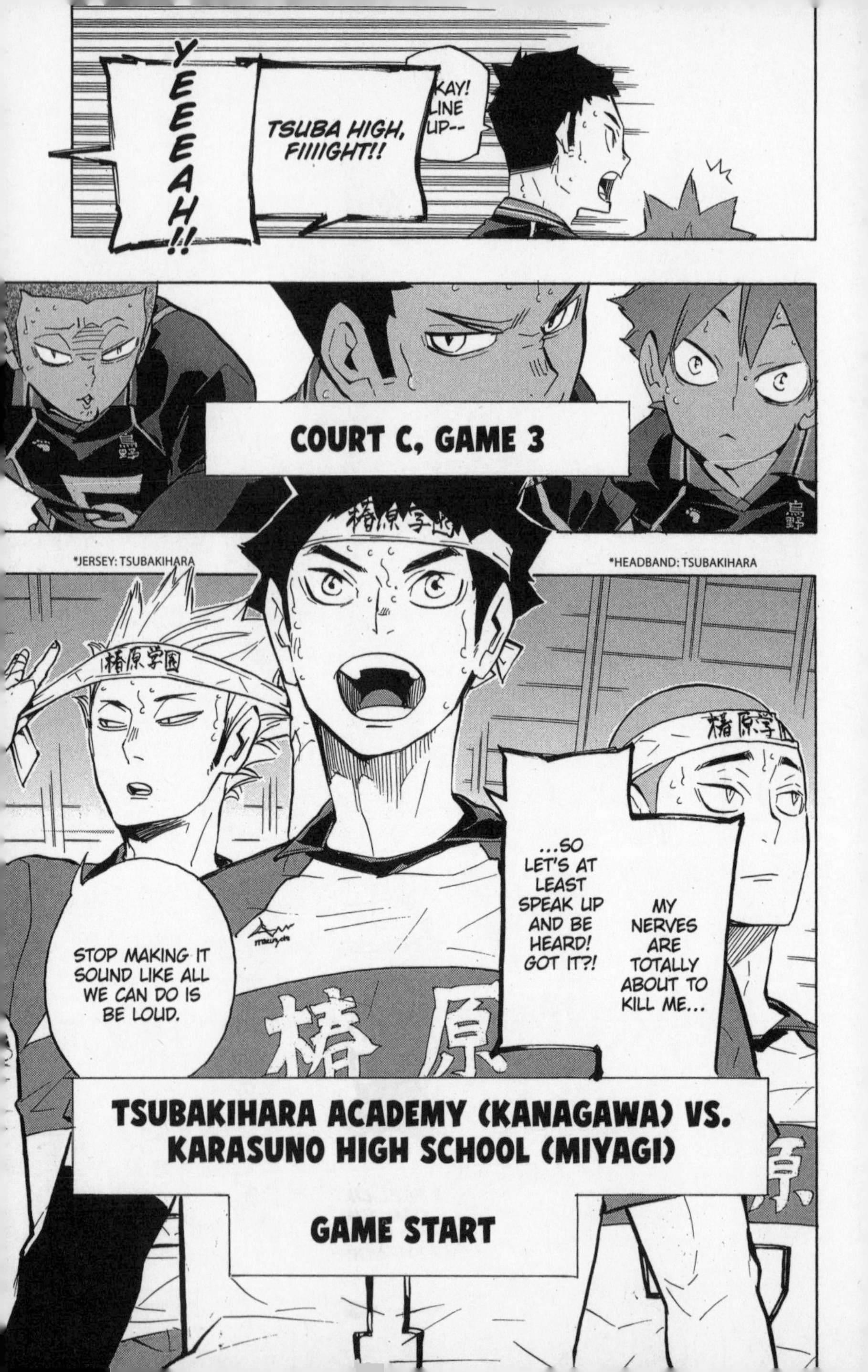
KAY! LINE UP--
TSUBA HIGH, FIIIIGHT!!
YEEEEAH!!
COURT C, GAME 3
*HEADBAND: TSUBAKIHARA
*JERSEY: TSUBAKIHARA
MY NERVES ARE TOTALLY ABOUT TO KILL ME...
...SO LET'S AT LEAST SPEAK UP AND BE HEARD! GOT IT?!
STOP MAKING IT SOUND LIKE ALL WE CAN DO IS BE LOUD.
TSUBAKIHARA ACADEMY (KANAGAWA) VS. KARASUNO HIGH SCHOOL (MIYAGI)
GAME START

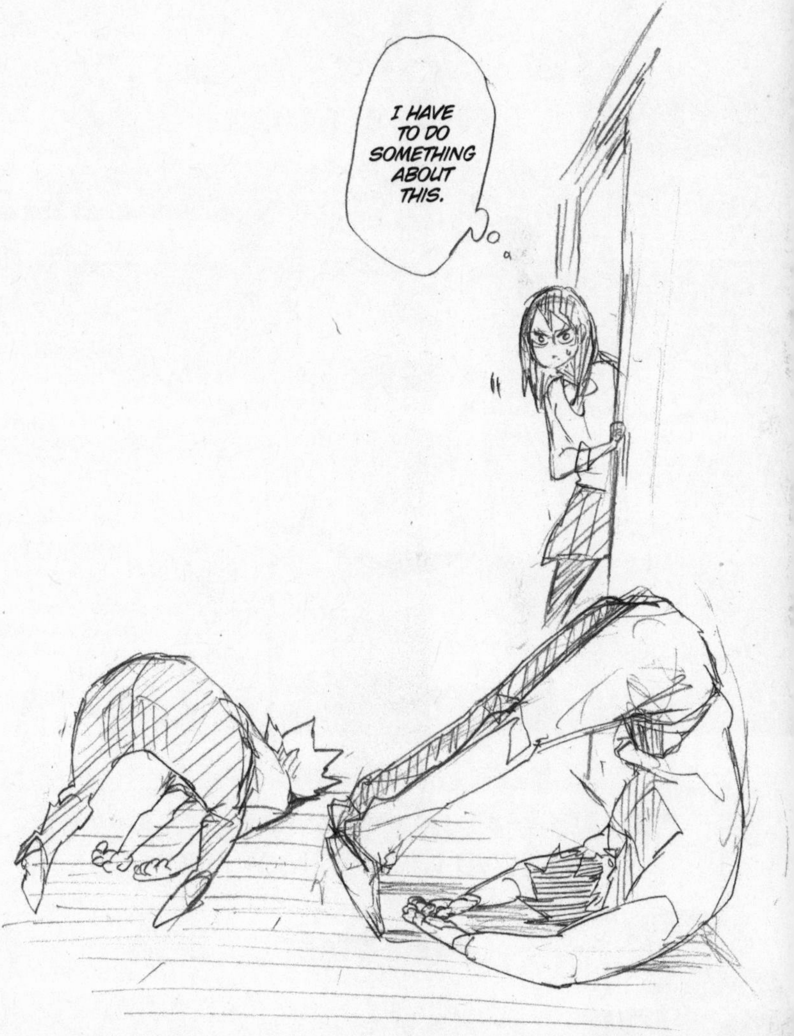
I HAVE TO DO SOMETHING ABOUT THIS.

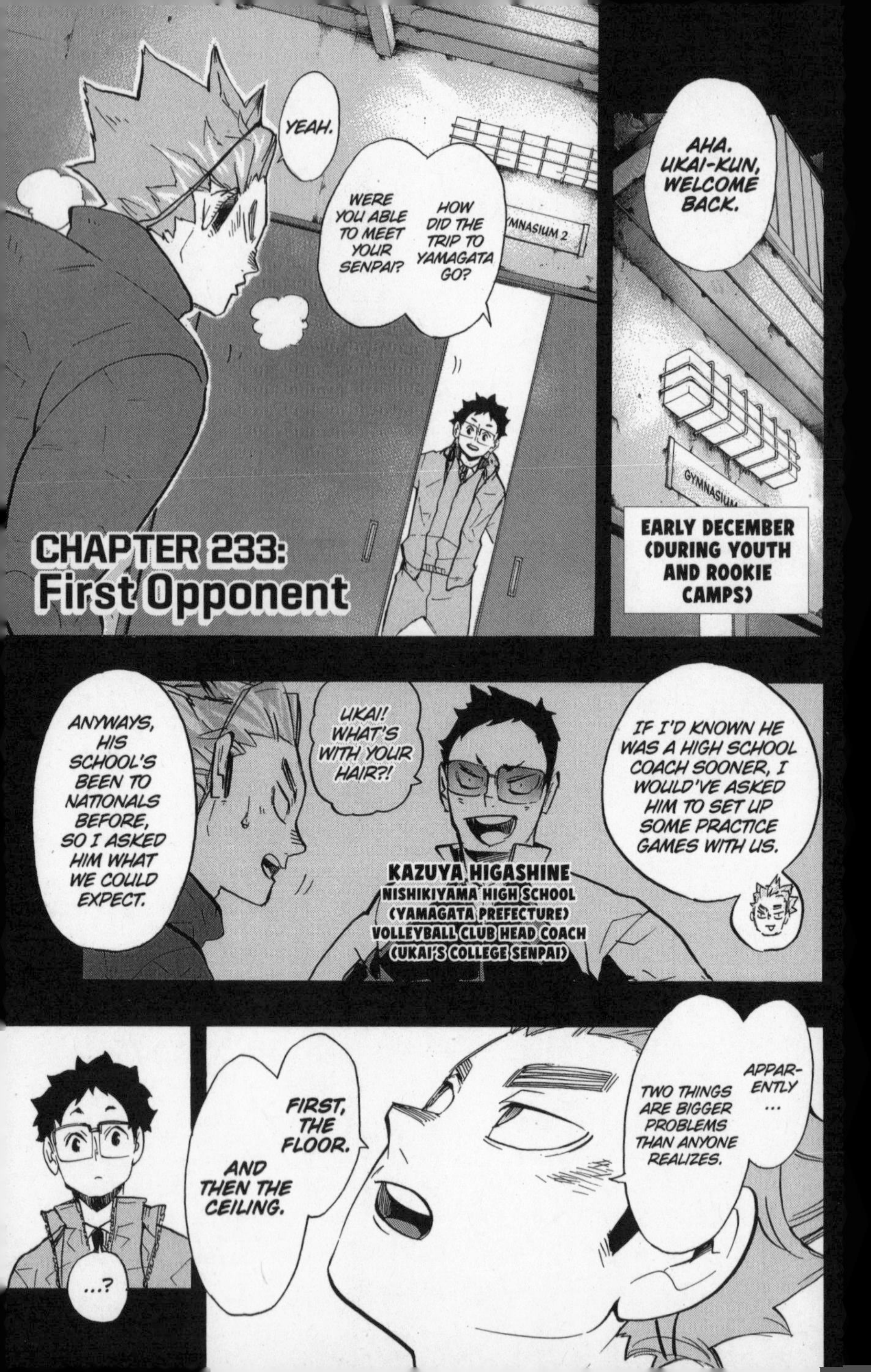
AHA. UKAI-KUN, WELCOME BACK.
GYMNASIUM
EARLY DECEMBER (DURING YOUTH AND ROOKIE CAMPS)
HOW DID THE TRIP TO YAMAGATA GO?
WERE YOU ABLE TO MEET YOUR SENPAI?
YEAH.
GYMNASIUM 2
CHAPTER 233:
First Opponent
IF I'D KNOWN HE WAS A HIGH SCHOOL COACH SOONER, I WOULD'VE ASKED HIM TO SET UP SOME PRACTICE GAMES WITH US.
KAZUYA HIGASHINE
NISHIKIYAMA HIGH SCHOOL (YAMAGATA PREFECTURE) VOLLEYBALL CLUB HEAD COACH (UKAI'S COLLEGE SENPAI)
UKAI! WHAT'S WITH YOUR HAIR?!
ANYWAYS, HIS SCHOOL'S BEEN TO NATIONALS BEFORE, SO I ASKED HIM WHAT WE COULD EXPECT.
APPARENTLY...
TWO THINGS ARE BIGGER PROBLEMS THAN ANYONE REALIZES.
FIRST, THE FLOOR.
AND THEN THE CEILING.
...?

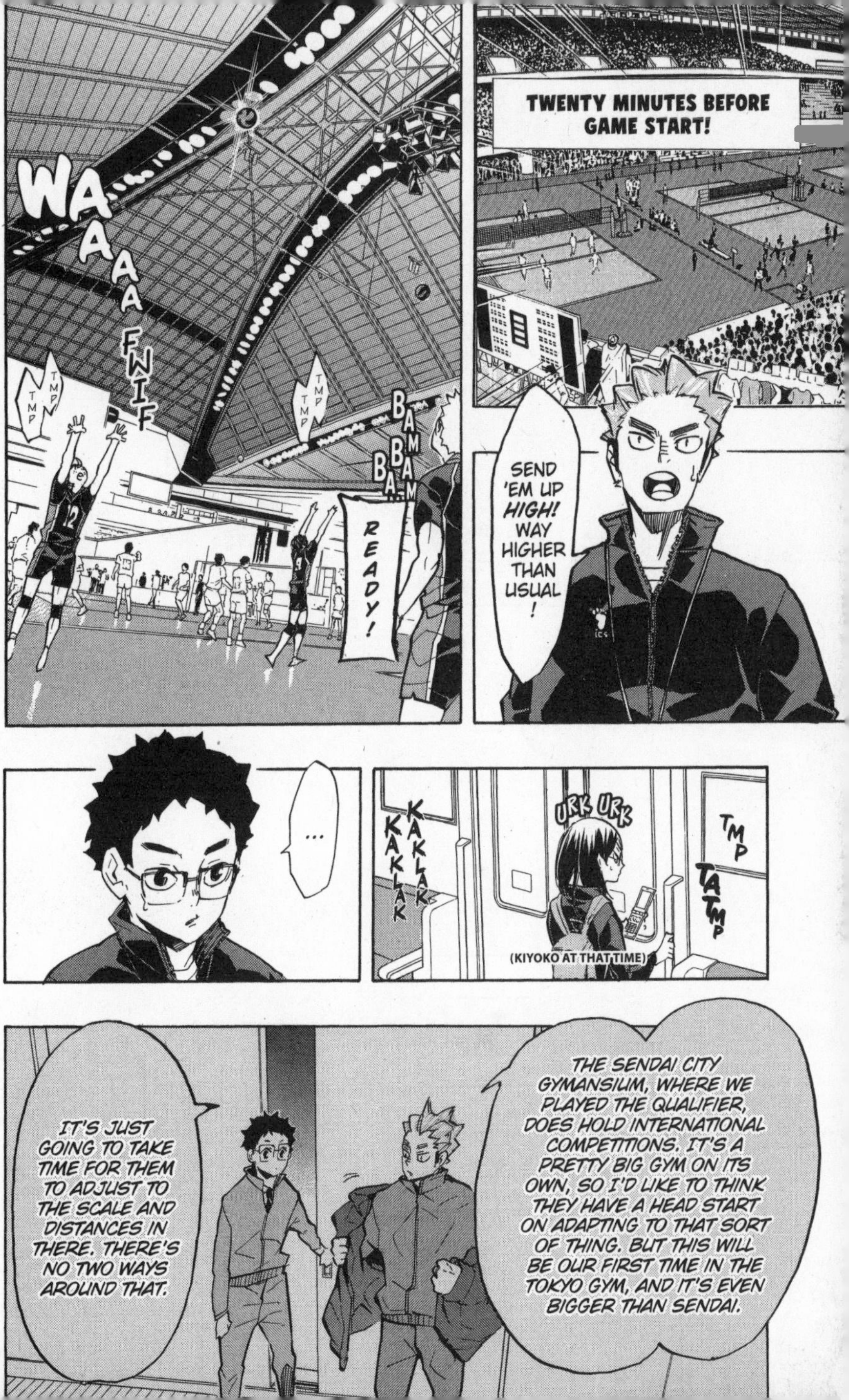
TWENTY MINUTES BEFORE GAME START!
SEND 'EM UP HIGH! WAY HIGHER THAN USUAL!
WAAAA
FWIF
TMP TMP
TMP TMP
BAM BAM BA
READY!
URK URK
TMP
TATMP
KAKLAK KAKLAK
(KIYOKO AT THAT TIME)
...
THE SENDAI CITY GYMANSIUM, WHERE WE PLAYED THE QUALIFIER, DOES HOLD INTERNATIONAL COMPETITIONS. IT'S A PRETTY BIG GYM ON ITS OWN, SO I'D LIKE TO THINK THEY HAVE A HEAD START ON ADAPTING TO THAT SORT OF THING. BUT THIS WILL BE OUR FIRST TIME IN THE TOKYO GYM, AND IT'S EVEN BIGGER THAN SENDAI.
IT'S JUST GOING TO TAKE TIME FOR THEM TO ADJUST TO THE SCALE AND DISTANCES IN THERE. THERE'S NO TWO WAYS AROUND THAT.

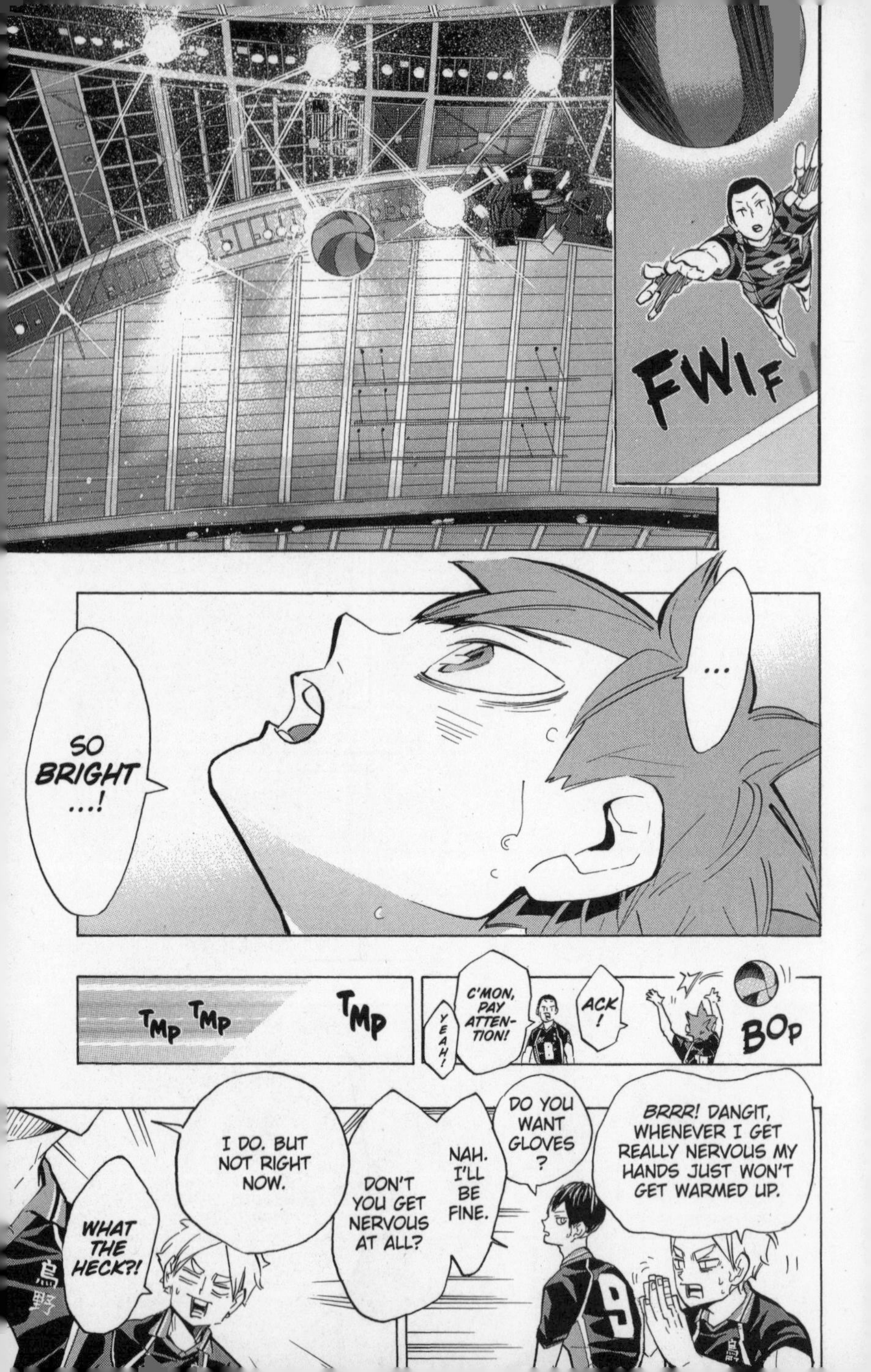
FWIF
...
SO BRIGHT ...!
BOP
ACK!
C'MON, PAY ATTENTION!
YEAH!
TMP TMP
TMP
BRRR! DANGIT, WHENEVER I GET REALLY NERVOUS MY HANDS JUST WON'T GET WARMED UP.
DO YOU WANT GLOVES?
NAH. I'LL BE FINE.
DON'T YOU GET NERVOUS AT ALL?
I DO. BUT NOT RIGHT NOW.
WHAT THE HECK?!

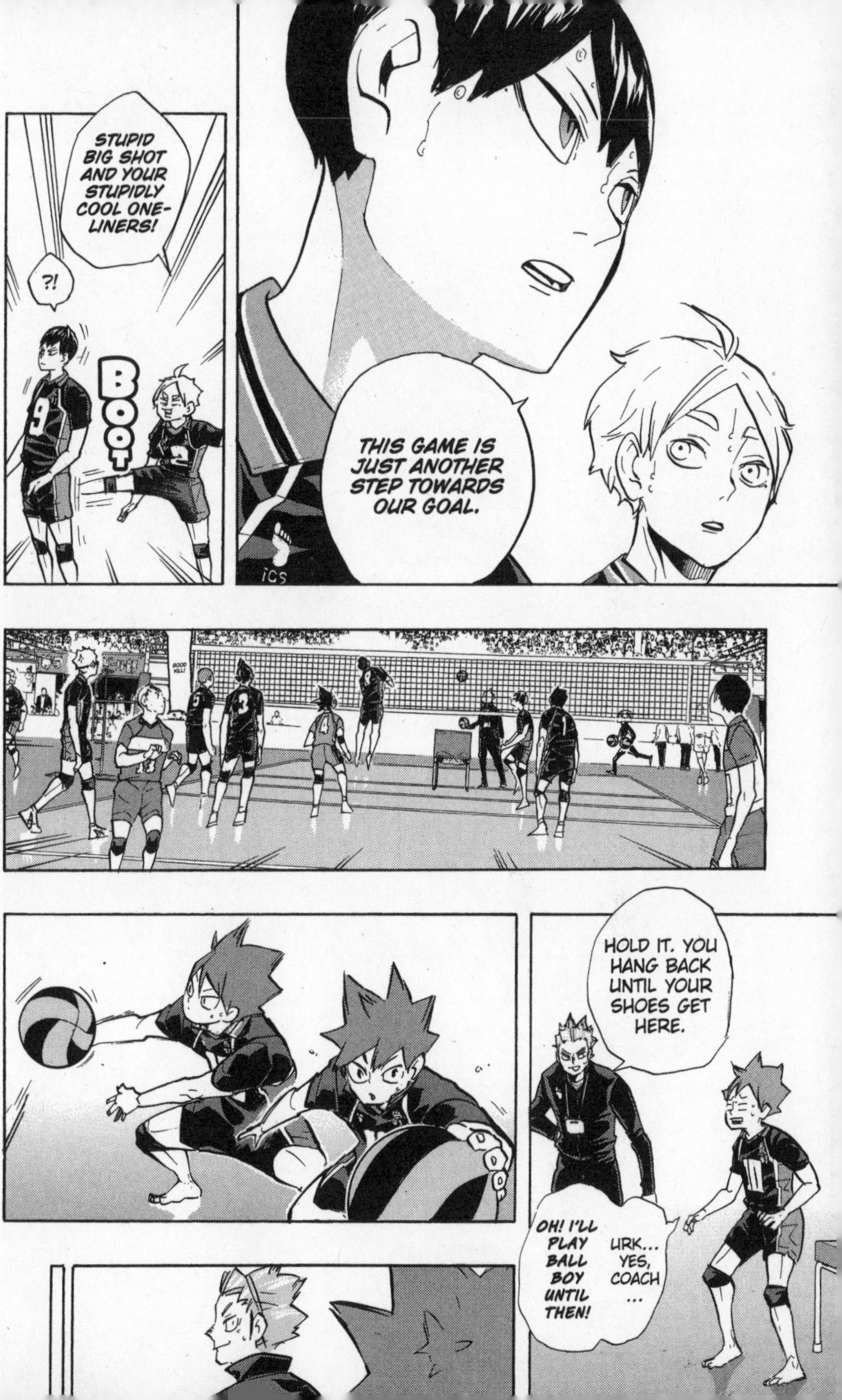
THIS GAME IS JUST ANOTHER STEP TOWARDS OUR GOAL.
STUPID BIG SHOT AND YOUR STUPIDLY COOL ONE-LINERS!
?!
BOOT
GOOD KILL!
HOLD IT. YOU HANG BACK UNTIL YOUR SHOES GET HERE.
URK... YES, COACH...
OH! I'LL PLAY BALL BOY UNTIL THEN!

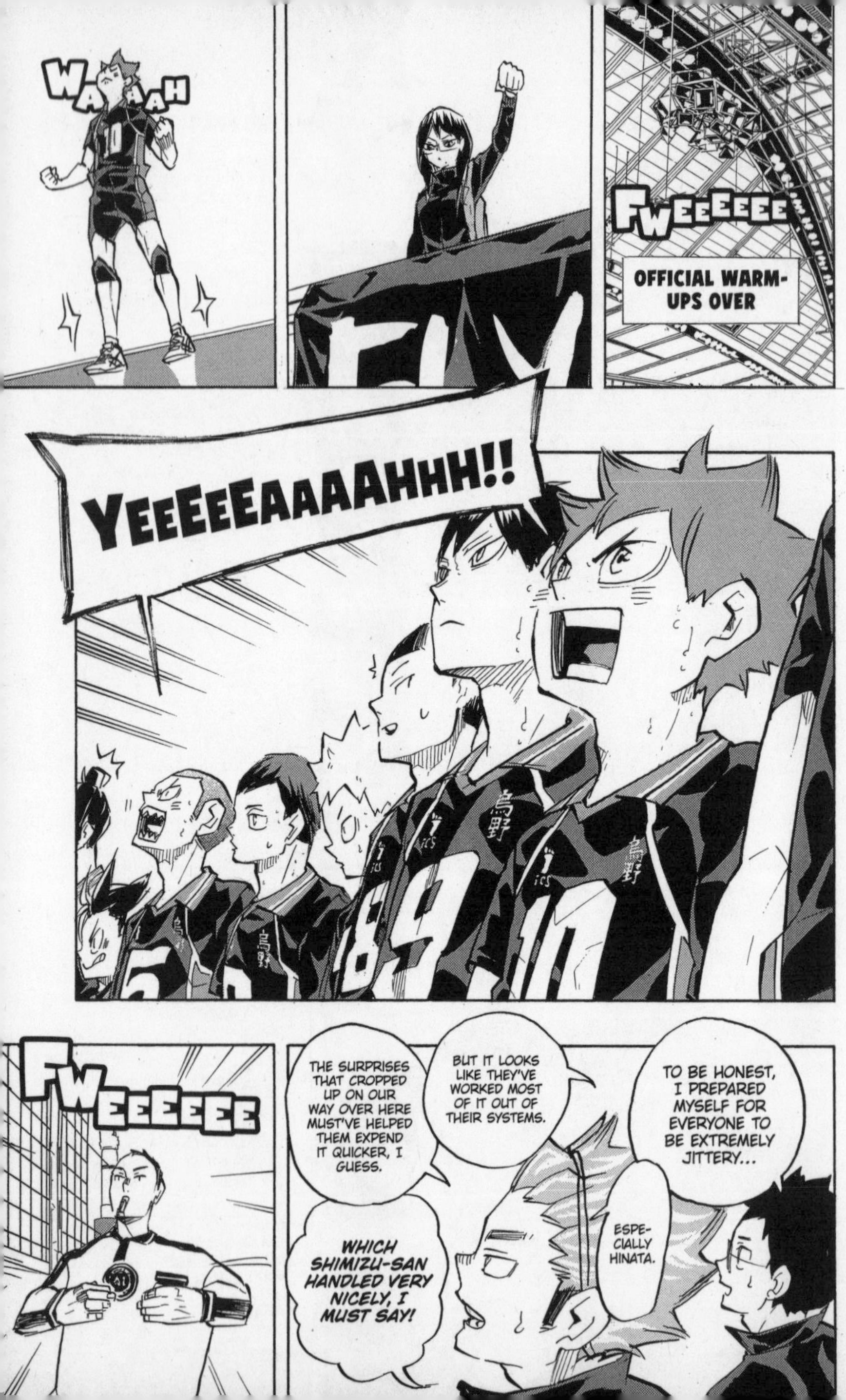
FWEEEEEE
OFFICIAL WARM-UPS OVER
WAAAH
YEEEEEAAAAAHHH!!
TO BE HONEST, I PREPARED MYSELF FOR EVERYONE TO BE EXTREMELY JITTERY...
ESPE-CIALLY HINATA.
BUT IT LOOKS LIKE THEY'VE WORKED MOST OF IT OUT OF THEIR SYSTEMS.
THE SURPRISES THAT CROPPED UP ON OUR WAY OVER HERE MUST'VE HELPED THEM EXPEND IT QUICKER, I GUESS.
WHICH SHIMIZU-SAN HANDLED VERY NICELY, I MUST SAY!
FWEEEEEE

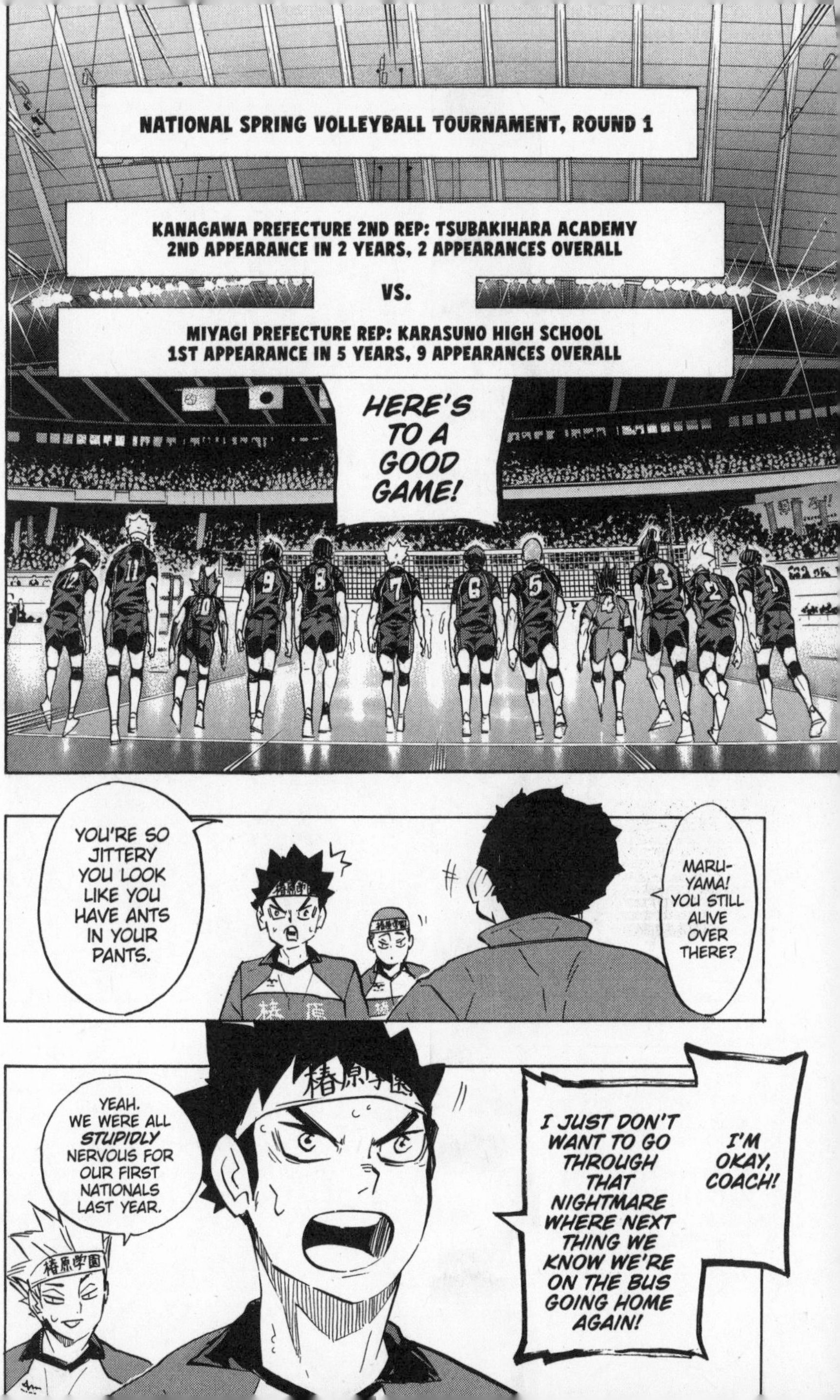
NATIONAL SPRING VOLLEYBALL TOURNAMENT, ROUND 1
KANAGAWA PREFECTURE 2ND REP: TSUBAKIHARA ACADEMY 2ND APPEARANCE IN 2 YEARS, 2 APPEARANCES OVERALL
VS.
MIYAGI PREFECTURE REP: KARASUNO HIGH SCHOOL 1ST APPEARANCE IN 5 YEARS, 9 APPEARANCES OVERALL
HERE'S TO A GOOD GAME!
MARU-YAMA! YOU STILL ALIVE OVER THERE?
YOU'RE SO JITTERY YOU LOOK LIKE YOU HAVE ANTS IN YOUR PANTS.
I'M OKAY, COACH!
I JUST DON'T WANT TO GO THROUGH THAT NIGHTMARE WHERE NEXT THING WE KNOW WE'RE ON THE BUS GOING HOME AGAIN!
YEAH. WE WERE ALL STUPIDLY NERVOUS FOR OUR FIRST NATIONALS LAST YEAR.

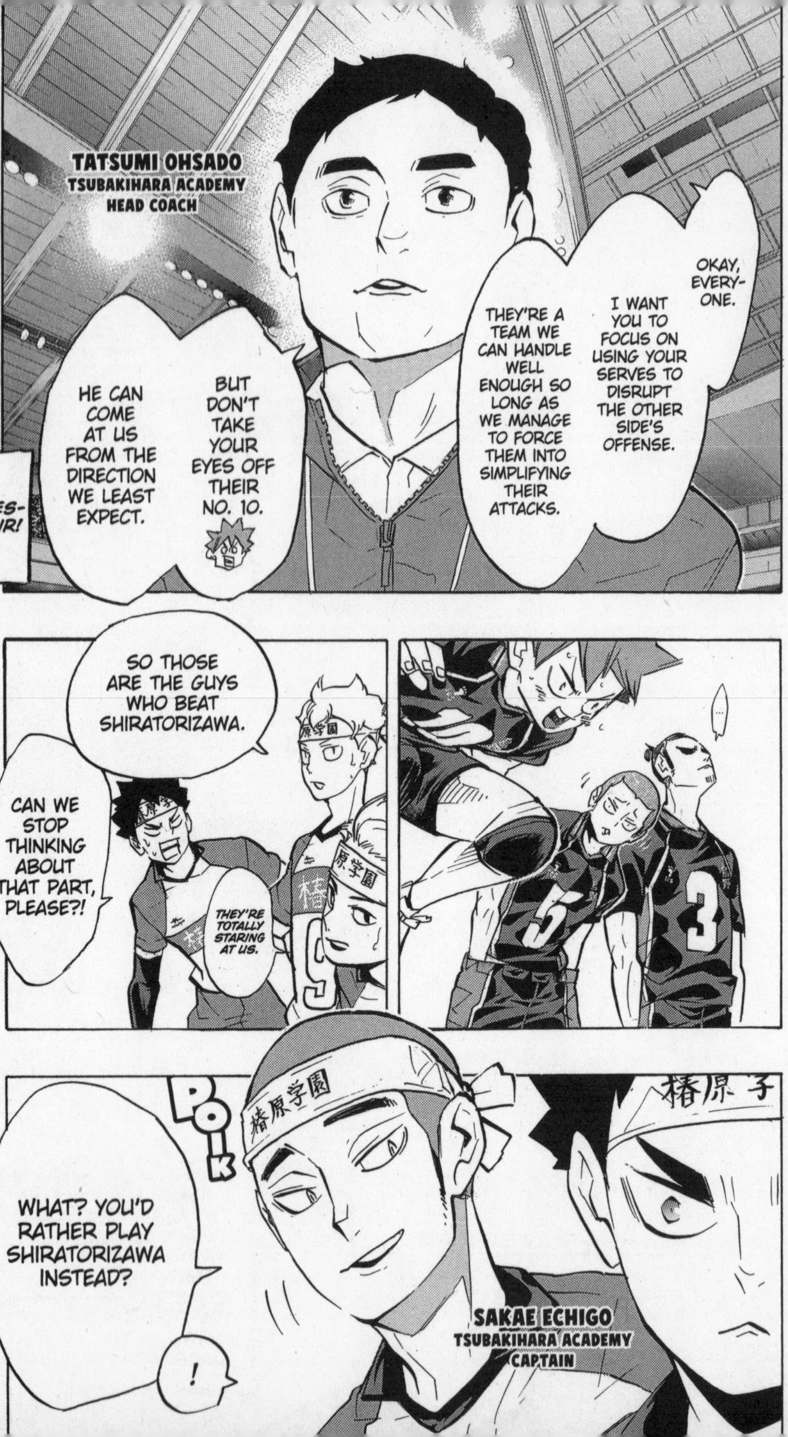
OKAY, EVERYONE.
I WANT YOU TO FOCUS ON USING YOUR SERVES TO DISRUPT THE OTHER SIDE'S OFFENSE.
THEY'RE A TEAM WE CAN HANDLE WELL ENOUGH SO LONG AS WE MANAGE TO FORCE THEM INTO SIMPLIFYING THEIR ATTACKS.
TATSUMI OHSADO
TSUBAKIHARA ACADEMY
HEAD COACH
BUT DON'T TAKE YOUR EYES OFF THEIR NO. 10.
HE CAN COME AT US FROM THE DIRECTION WE LEAST EXPECT.
YES-SIR!
...
SO THOSE ARE THE GUYS WHO BEAT SHIRATORIZAWA.
CAN WE STOP THINKING ABOUT THAT PART, PLEASE?!
THEY'RE TOTALLY STARING AT US.
POIK
WHAT? YOU'D RATHER PLAY SHIRATORIZAWA INSTEAD?
SAKAE ECHIGO
TSUBAKIHARA ACADEMY
CAPTAIN
!

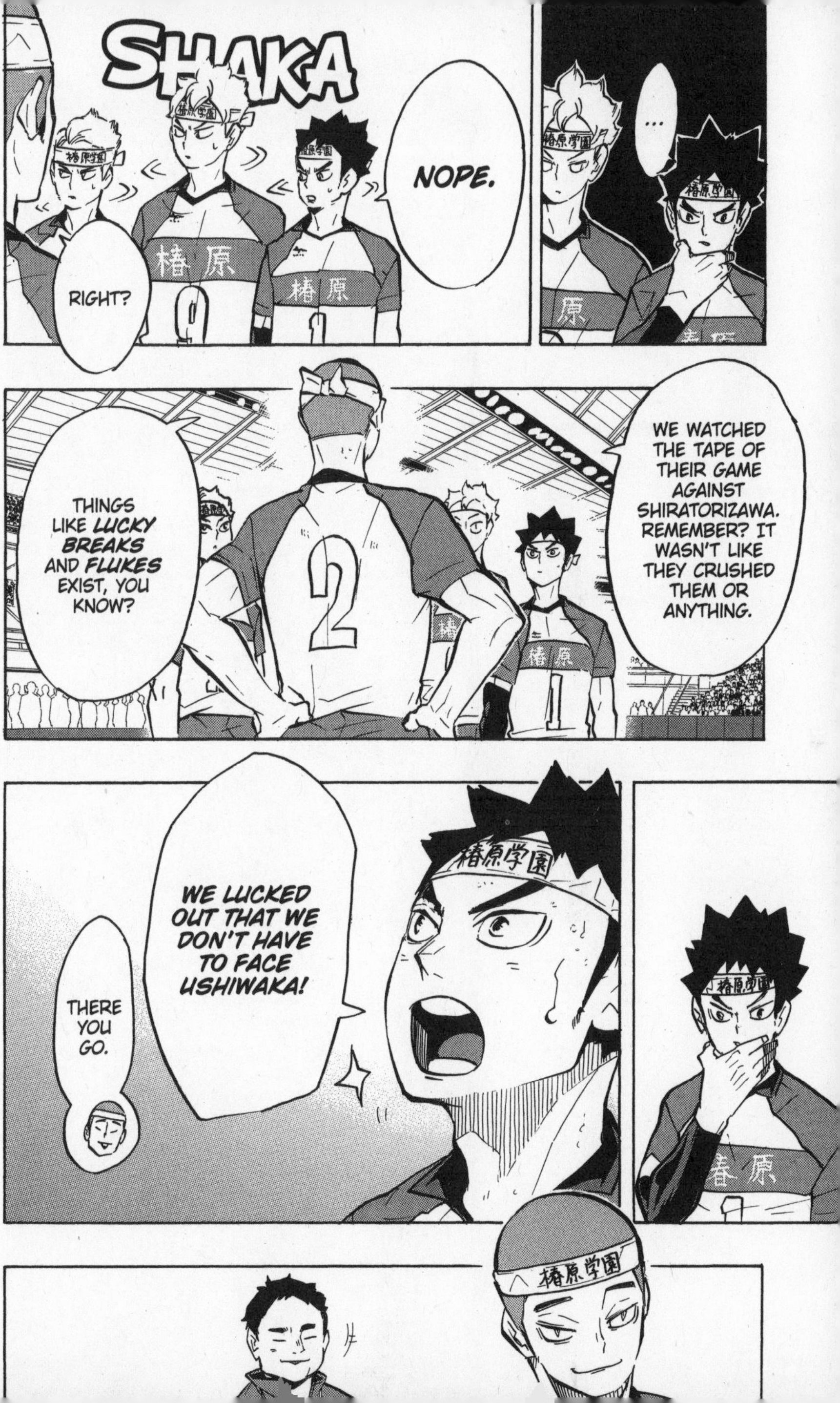
...
SHAKA
RIGHT?
NOPE.
WE WATCHED THE TAPE OF THEIR GAME AGAINST SHIRATORIZAWA. REMEMBER? IT WASN'T LIKE THEY CRUSHED THEM OR ANYTHING.
THINGS LIKE LUCKY BREAKS AND FLUKES EXIST, YOU KNOW?
WE LUCKED OUT THAT WE DON'T HAVE TO FACE USHIWAKA!
THERE YOU GO.

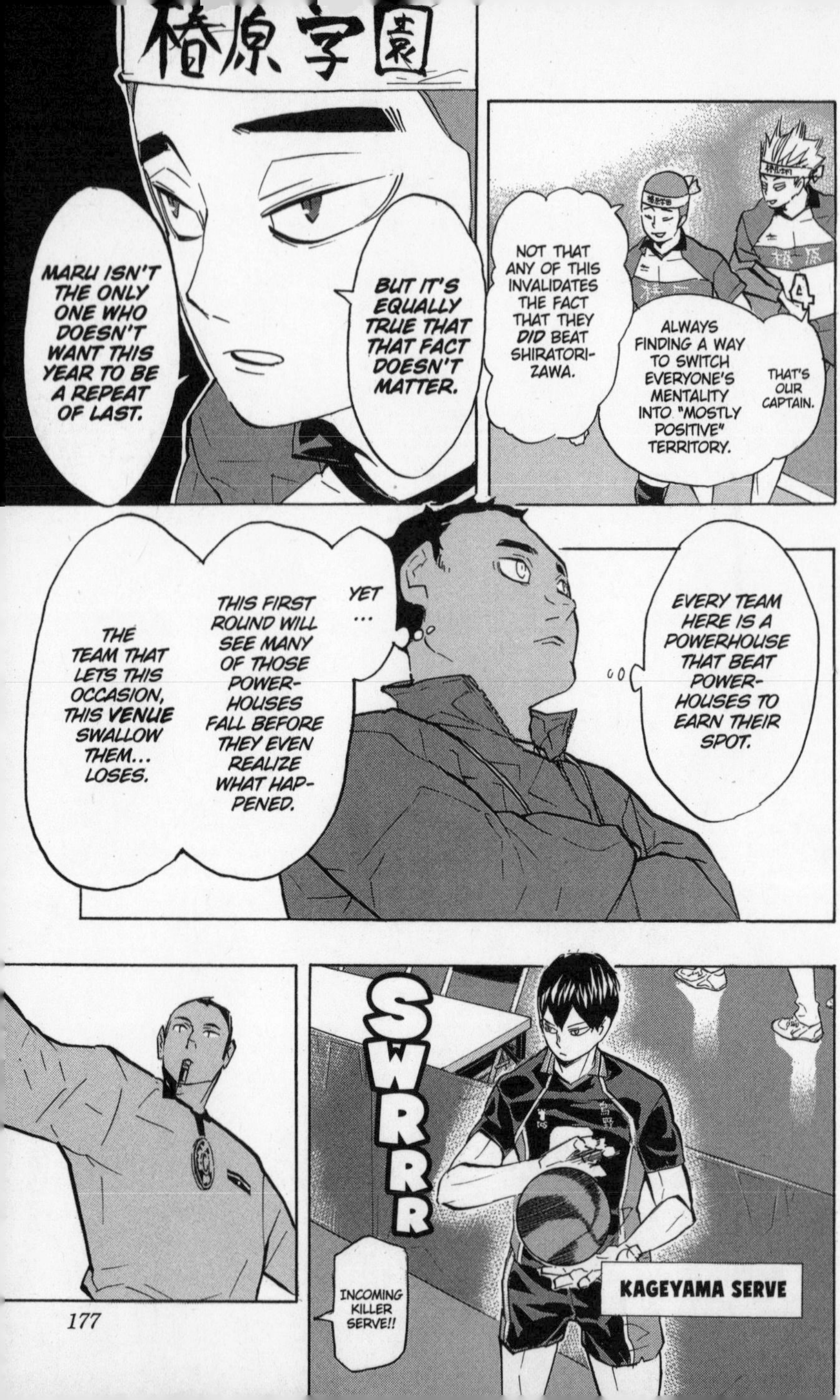
椿原学園
NOT THAT ANY OF THIS INVALIDATES THE FACT THAT THEY DID BEAT SHIRATORI-ZAWA.
ALWAYS FINDING A WAY TO SWITCH EVERYONE'S MENTALITY INTO "MOSTLY POSITIVE" TERRITORY.
THAT'S OUR CAPTAIN.
BUT IT'S EQUALLY TRUE THAT THAT FACT DOESN'T MATTER.
MARU ISN'T THE ONLY ONE WHO DOESN'T WANT THIS YEAR TO BE A REPEAT OF LAST.
EVERY TEAM HERE IS A POWERHOUSE THAT BEAT POWER-HOUSES TO EARN THEIR SPOT.
YET...
THIS FIRST ROUND WILL SEE MANY OF THOSE POWER-HOUSES FALL BEFORE THEY EVEN REALIZE WHAT HAP-PENED.
THE TEAM THAT LETS THIS OCCASION, THIS VENUE SWALLOW THEM... LOSES.
SWRRR
KAGEYAMA SERVE
INCOMING KILLER SERVE!!

○ TEAM CAPTAIN

IWAMURO
2ND YEAR / MB
6'1"

8

MAIKO
2ND YEAR / WS
5'9"

10

TERADOMARI
3RD YEAR / WS
6'3"

4

MARUYAMA
3RD YEAR / WS
5'10"

ECHIGO
3RD YEAR / S
6'0"

2

TSUBAKIHARA

● MARUYAMA	● ECHIGO	● ATEMA (KAIKAKE)
● IWAMURO	● MAIKO	● TERADOMARI
● SAWAMURA	● HINATA	● TANAKA
● AZUMANE	● TSUKKI (NOYA)	● KAGEYAMA

NG ORDER →

KARASUNO

○ TEAM CAPTAIN

HINATA
1ST YEAR / MB
5'5"

KAGEYAMA
1ST YEAR / S
6'0"

9

10

TANAKA
2ND YEAR / WS
5'10"

5

AZUMANE
3RD YEAR / WS
6'0"

SAWAMURA
3RD YEAR / WS
5'9"

1

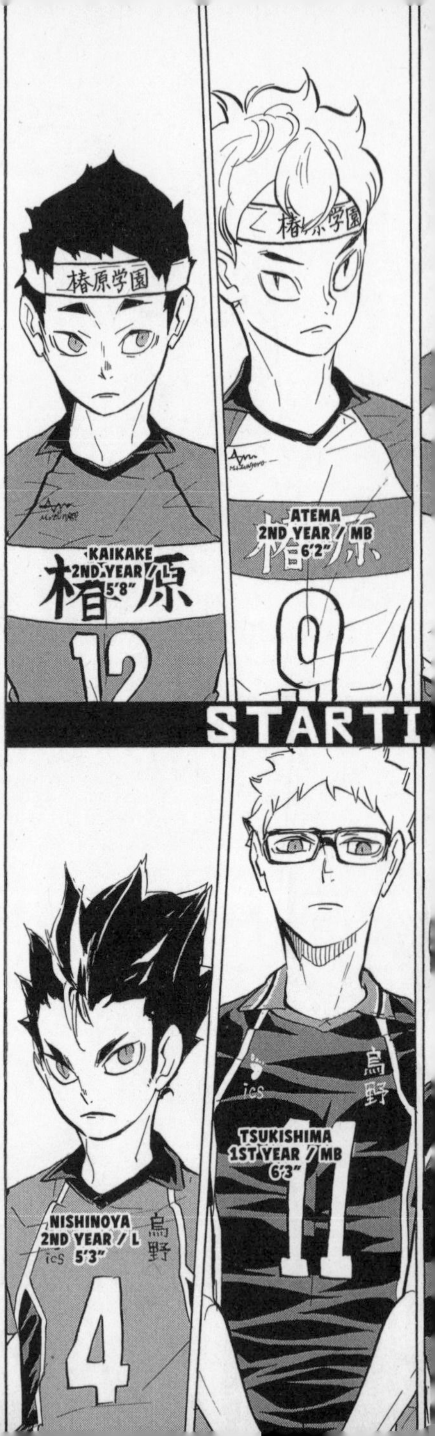
椿原学園
ATEMA
2ND YEAR / MB
6'2"
椿原学園
KAIKAKE
2ND YEAR
5'8"
STARTI
TSUKISHIMA
1ST YEAR / MB
6'3"
NISHINOYA
2ND YEAR / L
5'3"

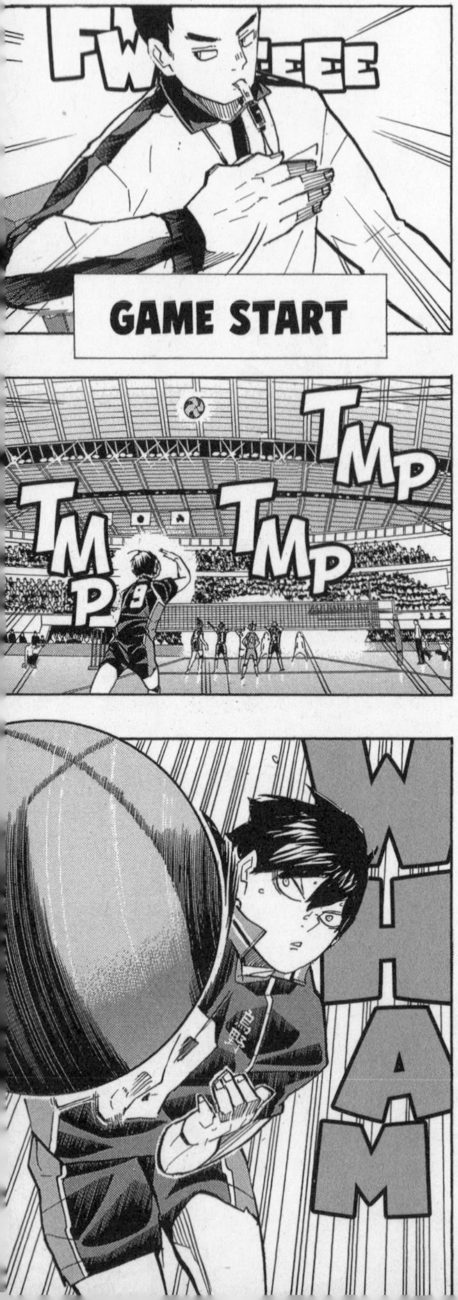
FWEEEE
GAME START
TMP
TMP
TMP
WHAM

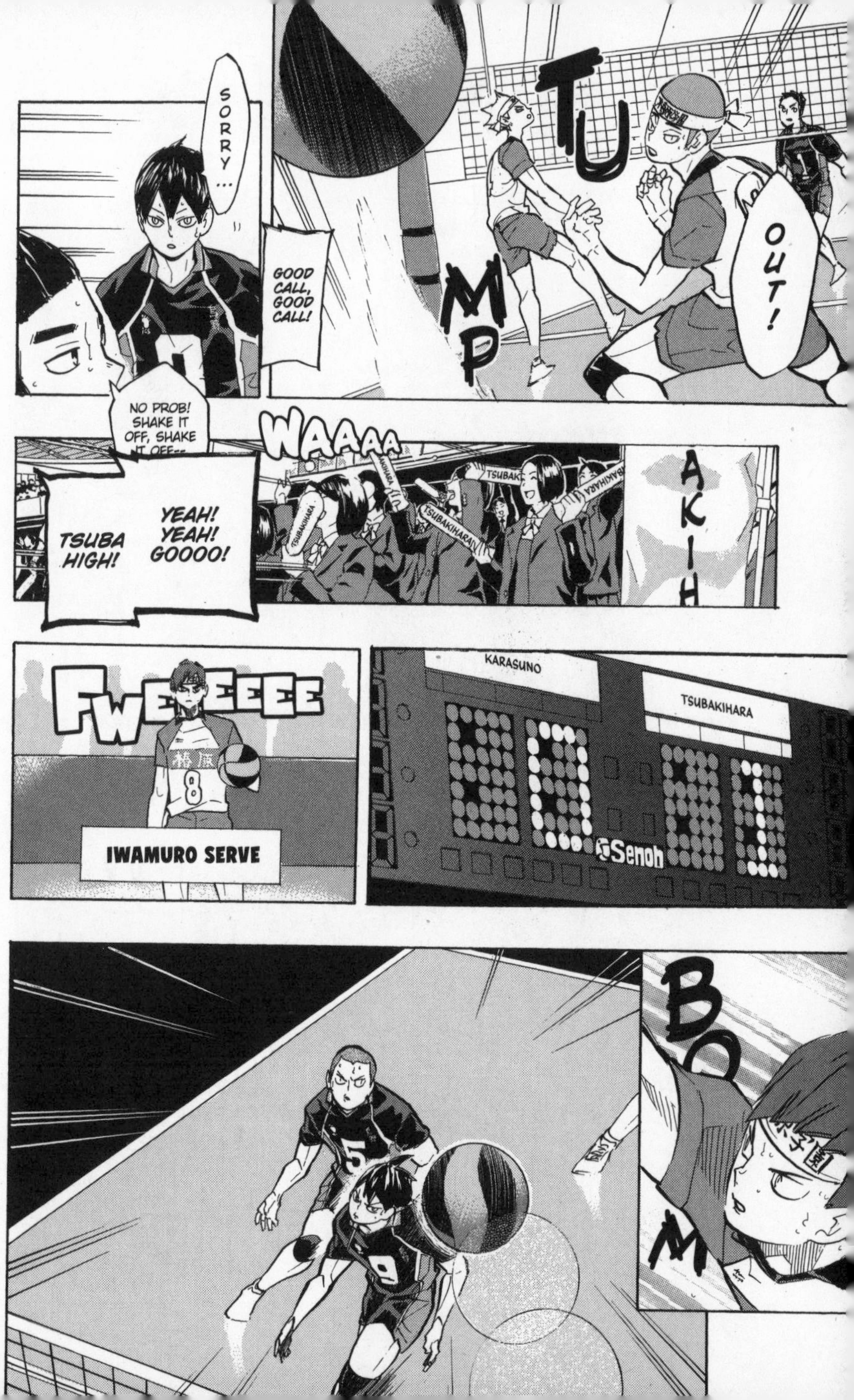
TUMP
OUT!
SORRY...
GOOD CALL, GOOD CALL!
NO PROB! SHAKE IT OFF, SHAKE IT OFF--
AKIH
WAAAA
TSUBAKIHARA
YEAH! YEAH! GOOOO!
TSUBA HIGH!
KARASUNO
TSUBAKIHARA
Senoh
FWEEEEE
IWAMURO SERVE
BOOM

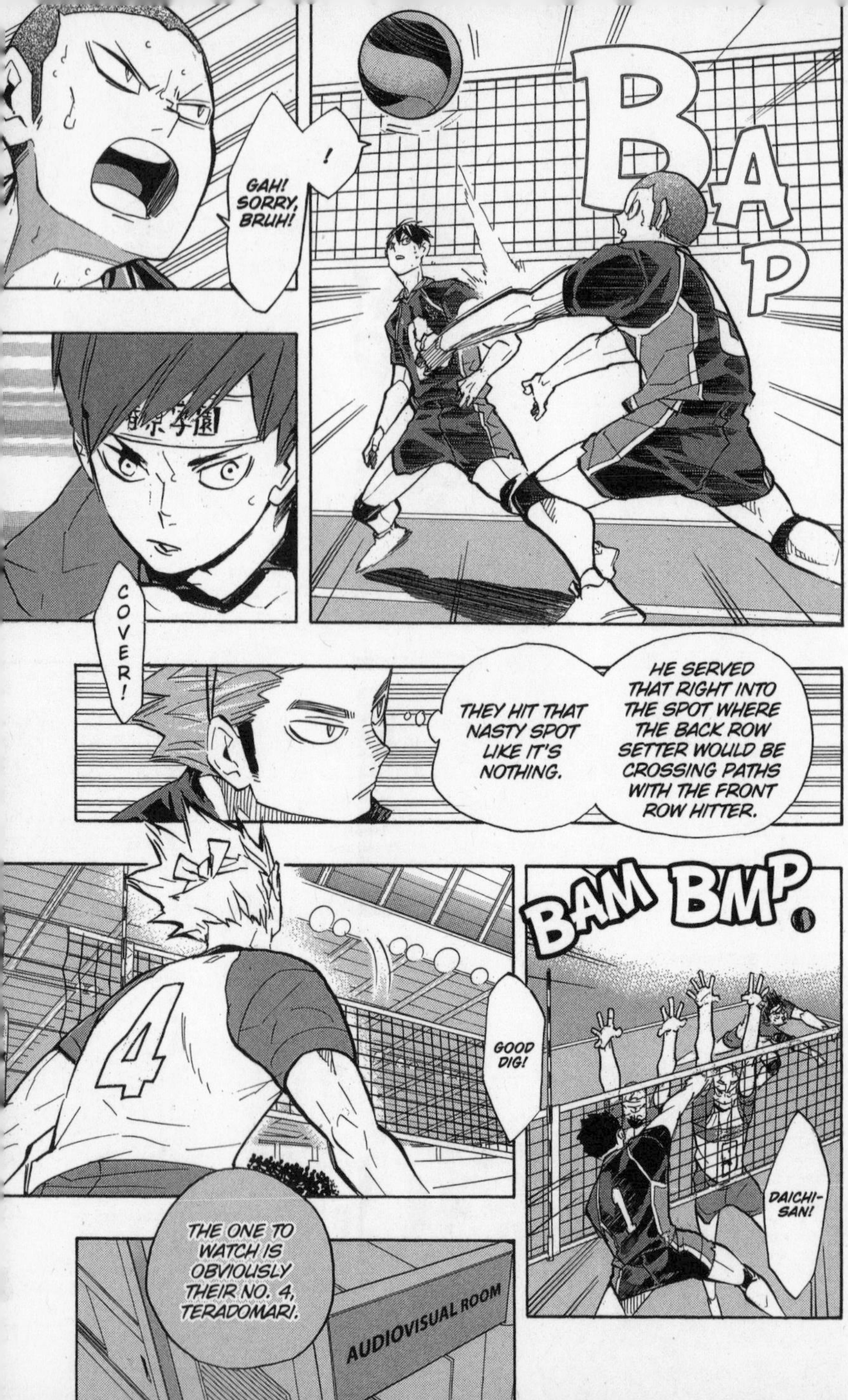
BAP
!
GAH! SORRY, BRUH!
COVER!
HE SERVED THAT RIGHT INTO THE SPOT WHERE THE BACK ROW SETTER WOULD BE CROSSING PATHS WITH THE FRONT ROW HITTER.
THEY HIT THAT NASTY SPOT LIKE IT'S NOTHING.
BAM BMP
GOOD DIG!
DAICHI-SAN!
THE ONE TO WATCH IS OBVIOUSLY THEIR NO. 4, TERADOMARI.
AUDIOVISUAL ROOM

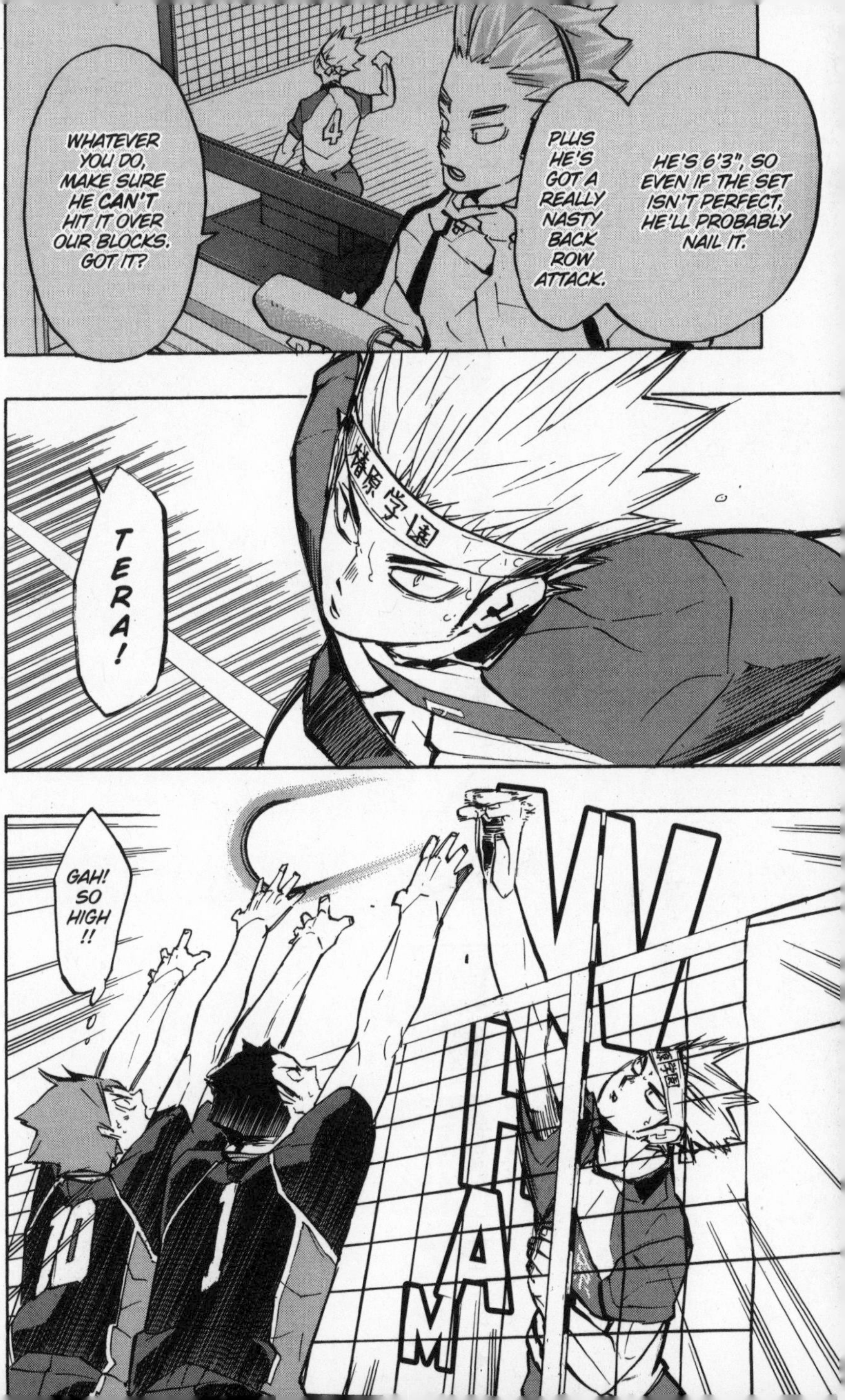
HE'S 6'3", SO EVEN IF THE SET ISN'T PERFECT, HE'LL PROBABLY NAIL IT.
PLUS HE'S GOT A REALLY NASTY BACK ROW ATTACK.
WHATEVER YOU DO, MAKE SURE HE CAN'T HIT IT OVER OUR BLOCKS. GOT IT?
椿原学園
TERA!
WHAM
GAH! SO HIGH!!

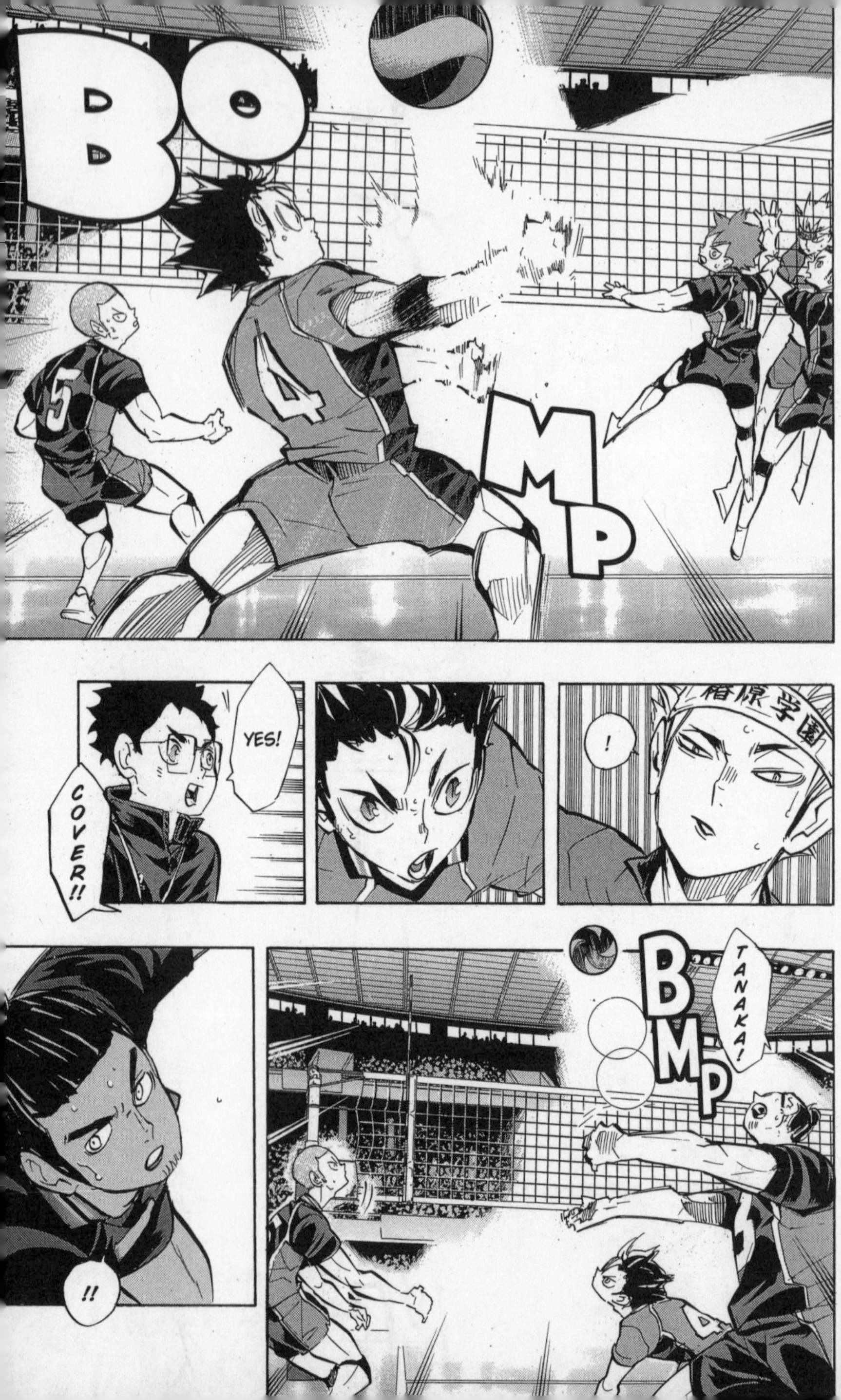
BOO
MP
椿原学園
!
YES!
COVER!!
TANAKA!
BMP
!!

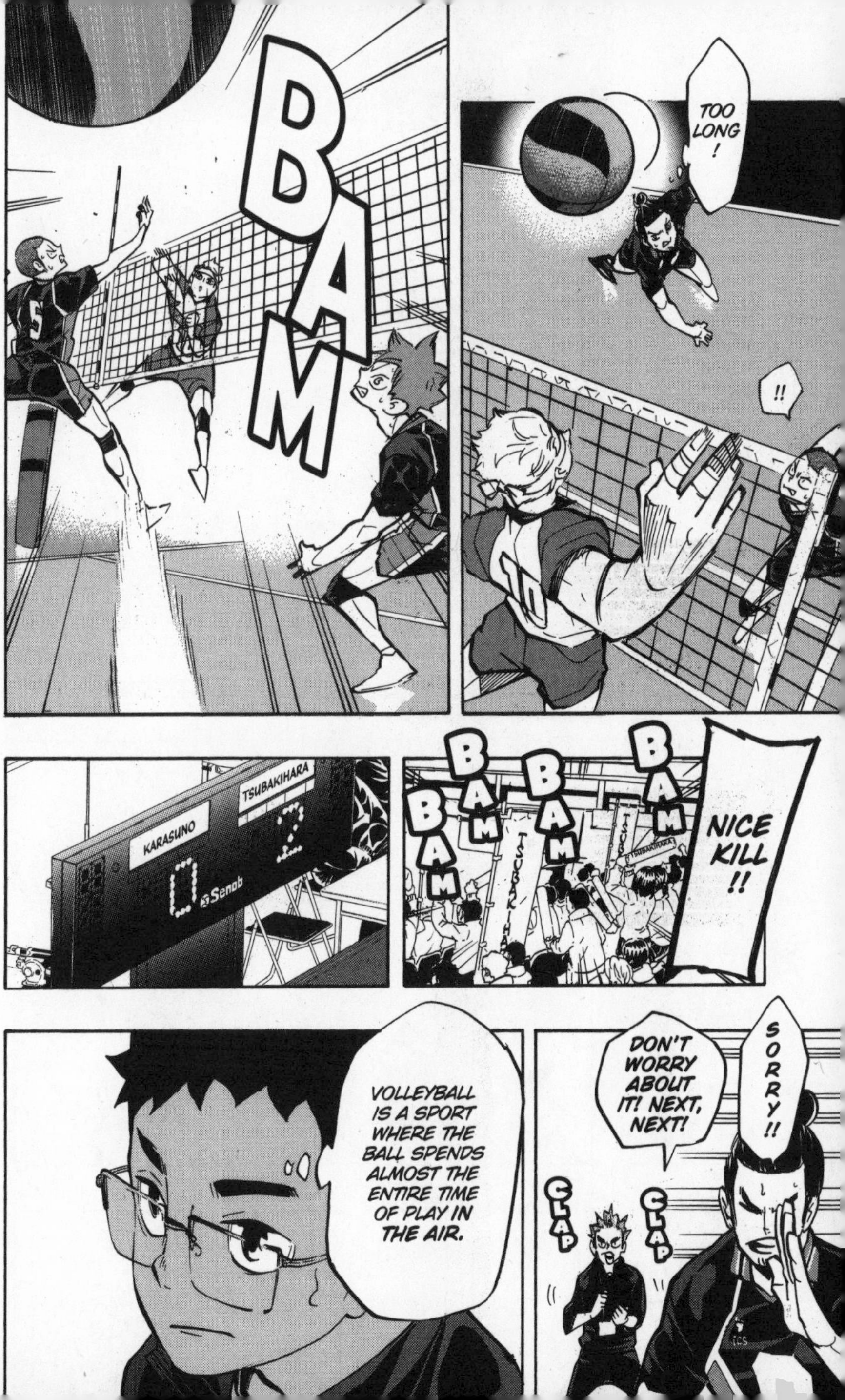

TOO LONG!
!!
BAM
NICE KILL!!
BAM
BAM
BAM
BAM
TSUBAKIHARA
TSUBAKIHARA
KARASUNO
TSUBAKIHARA
SORRY!!
DON'T WORRY ABOUT IT! NEXT, NEXT!
CLAP
CLAP
VOLLEYBALL IS A SPORT WHERE THE BALL SPENDS ALMOST THE ENTIRE TIME OF PLAY IN THE AIR.

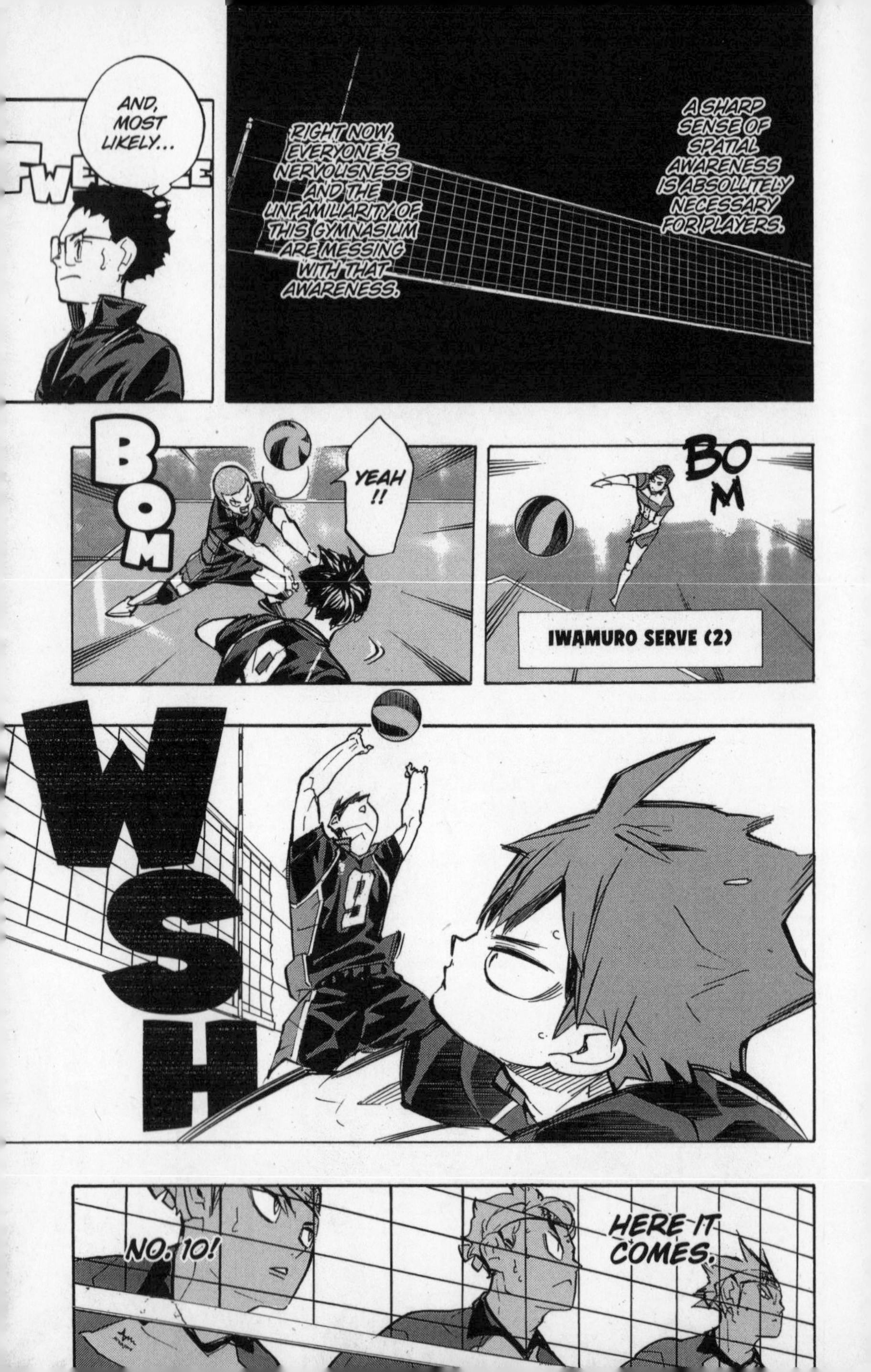
A SHARP SENSE OF SPATIAL AWARENESS IS ABSOLUTELY NECESSARY FOR PLAYERS.
RIGHT NOW, EVERYONE'S NERVOUSNESS AND THE UNFAMILIARITY OF THIS GYMNASIUM ARE MESSING WITH THAT AWARENESS.
AND, MOST LIKELY...
BOM
IWAMURO SERVE (2)
BOM
YEAH!!
WSH
HERE IT COMES.
NO. 10!

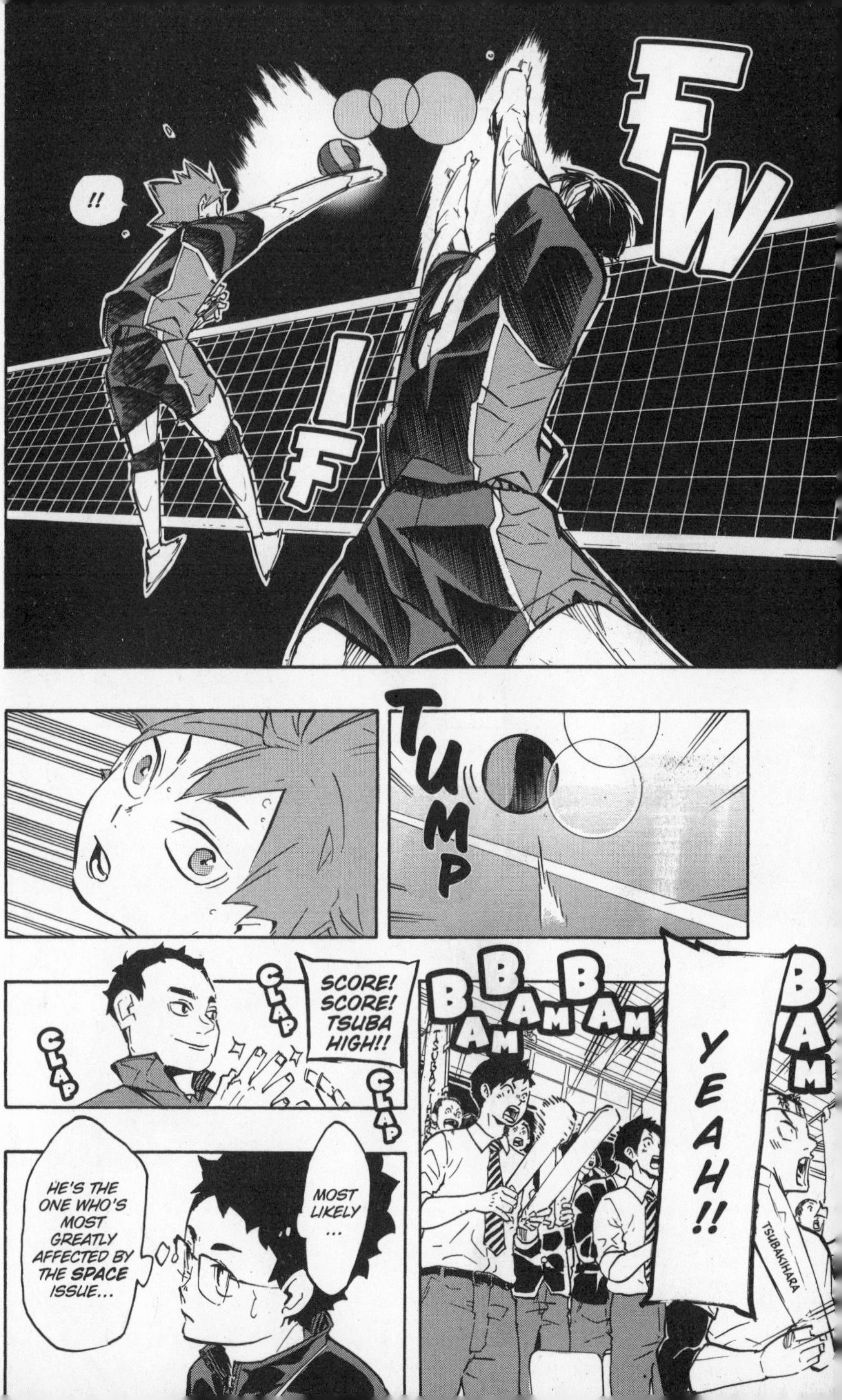

FWIF
!!
TUMP
BAM BAM BAM BAM
BAM
YEAH!!
TSUBAKIHARA
SCORE! SCORE! TSUBA HIGH!!
CLAP CLAP CLAP CLAP
MOST LIKELY...
HE'S THE ONE WHO'S MOST GREATLY AFFECTED BY THE SPACE ISSUE...

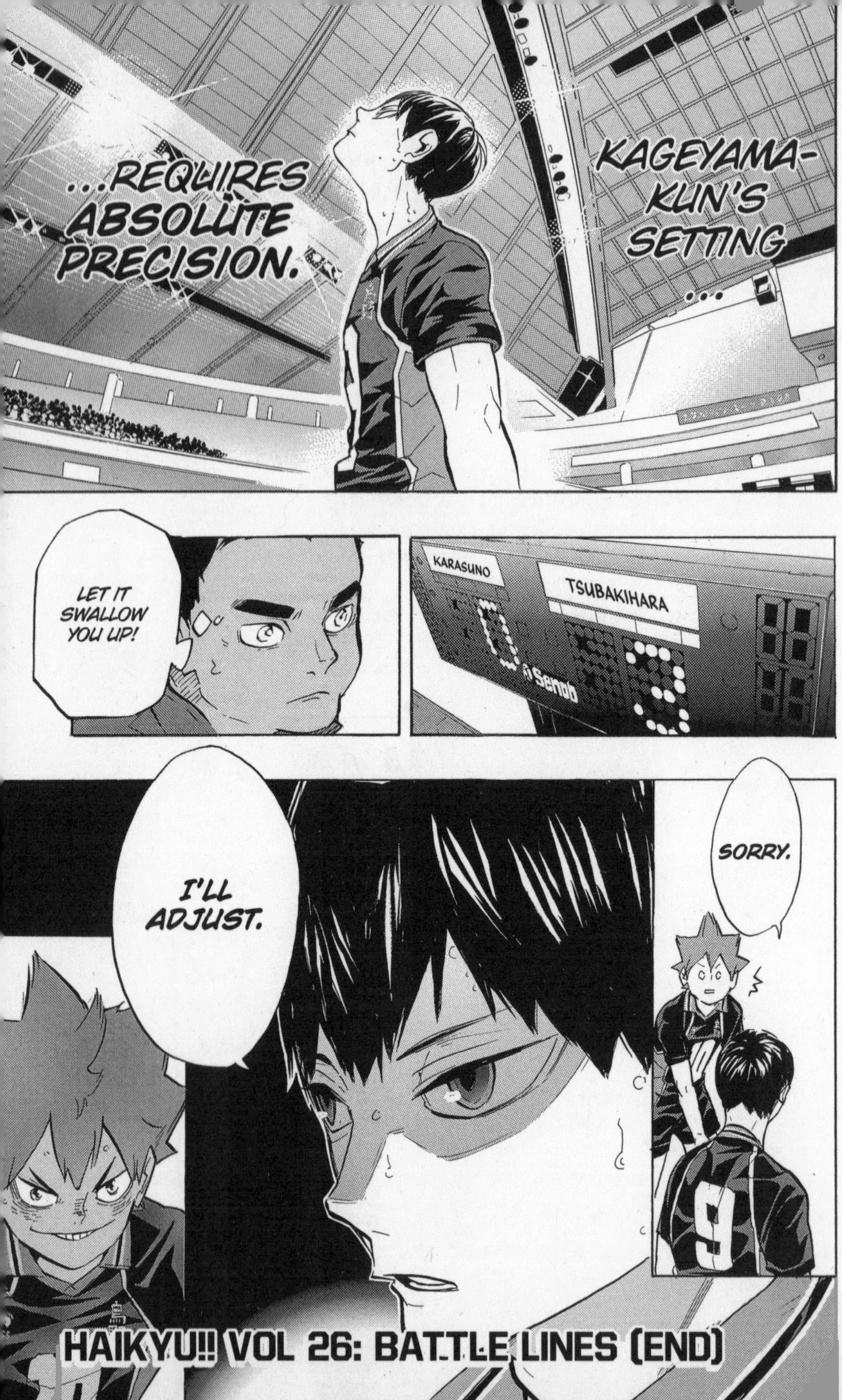
KAGEYAMA-KUN'S SETTING...
...REQUIRES ABSOLUTE PRECISION.
KARASUNO
TSUBAKIHARA
LET IT SWALLOW YOU UP!
SORRY.
I'LL ADJUST.
HAIKYU!! VOL 26: BATTLE LINES (END)

EDITOR'S NOTES

The English edition of Haikyu!! maintains the honorifics used in the original Japanese version. For those of you who are new to these terms, here's a brief explanation to help with your reading experience!

When saying someone's name in Japanese, a suffix is often attached to indicate how familiar the speaker is with the person. Some are more polite and respectful, while others are endearing.

1. **-kun** is often used for young men or boys, usually someone you are familiar with.

2. **-chan** is used for young children and can be used as a term of endearment.

3. **-san** is used for someone you respect or are not close to, or to be polite.

4. **Senpai** is used for someone who is older than you or in a higher position or grade in school.

5. **Kohai** is used for someone who is younger than you or in a lower position or grade in school.

6. **Sensei** means teacher.

BWOOOH...

MY HERO ACADEMIA

IZUKU MIDORIYA WANTS TO BE A HERO MORE THAN ANYTHING, BUT HE HASN'T GOT AN OUNCE OF POWER IN HIM. WITH NO CHANCE OF GETTING INTO THE U.A. HIGH SCHOOL FOR HEROES, HIS LIFE IS LOOKING LIKE A DEAD END. THEN AN ENCOUNTER WITH ALL MIGHT, THE GREATEST HERO OF ALL, GIVES HIM A CHANCE TO CHANGE HIS DESTINY...

BOKU NO HERO ACADEMIA © 2014 by Kohei Horikoshi/SHUEISHA Inc.

IN A SAVAGE WORLD RULED BY THE PURSUIT OF THE MOST DELICIOUS FOODS, IT'S EITHER EAT OR BE EATEN!

> "The most bizarrely entertaining manga out there on comic shelves. *Toriko* is a great series. If you're looking for an weirdly fun book or a fighting manga with a bizarre take, this is the story for you to read."
>
> —ComicAttack.com

TORIKO

Story and Art by **Mitsutoshi Shimabukuro**

In an era where the world's gone crazy for increasingly bizarre gourmet foods, only Gourmet Hunter Toriko can hunt down the ferocious ingredients that supply the world's best restaurants. Join Toriko as he tracks and defeats the tastiest and most dangerous animals with his bare hands.

RATED TEEN
ratings.viz.com

www.shonenjump.com

VIZ MEDIA
www.viz.com

You're Reading the
WRONG WAY!

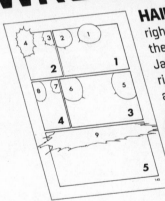

HAIKYU!! reads from right to left, starting in the upper-right corner. Japanese is read from right to left, meaning that action, sound effects and word-balloon order are completely reversed from English order.